Modern Economy

Volume IV

Modern Economy
Volume IV

Edited by **Derek Beaven**

CLANRYE
INTERNATIONAL

New Jersey

Published by Clanrye International,
55 Van Reypen Street,
Jersey City, NJ 07306, USA
www.clanryeinternational.com

Modern Economy: Volume IV
Edited by Derek Beaven

International Standard Book Number: 978-1-63240-365-0 (Hardback)

Printed in the United States of America.

Contents

Preface

Ever since there has been some level of demand, supply and exchange, economies have existed. The earliest system of economics, as we think of it today in terms of profit and loss was developed by the Babylonians. Sumer also developed a large-scale economy based on commodity money.

Essentially, any economy involves production, distribution and consumption of goods and services. However, other than these processes, it is a certain specific context and geographical location that an economy functions within. Technological evolutions, history, social organization, all play an integral part in the formation of an economy.

Over times, economies have developed and transformed. Ancient economy was based on subsistence farming. With the Industrial Revolution, farming took a backseat and commerce took over. In the modern economy, service sector has emerged as a frontrunner. Also, modern economy has been categorised into Primary, Secondary and Tertiary activities.

Economies have also been divided into market based and command based. A market-based economy is the one without obstruction or interference, commercial interaction takes place according to demand and supply between participants. A command-based economy is where a central authoritative power commands and determines the course of the supply and production environment.

I'd like to thank all the researchers who've shared their valuable work with us in this book, to make it an enlightening one.

Editor

Altruism and Exchange in Intergenerational Transfers: The Demand for Children Emergency Room

Ignacio Ortuño-Ortin[1], Andrés Romeu[2]
[1]Department of Economics, University Carlos III, Madrid, Spain
[2]Department of Economic Analysis, University of Murcia, Murcia, Spain

ABSTRACT

In this paper, we analyze the role of income as a determinant of parents' care for children. We show that the answer depends on whether Altruism or Exchange motives are the factors that explain intergenerational transfers. We then develop a test to discriminate between these alternatives. Unlike previous approaches, this test focuses on measures of parents' efforts on child care that are essentially non-monetary. Using data from the United States, we find a negative relationship between family income and the frequency of children's emergency room utilization which cannot be explained by several alternative controlling factors. In our framework, this is interpreted as evidence against the null of prominently altruistic behavior.

Keywords: Intergenerational Transfers; Altruism; Infant Health Demand

1. Introduction

Parents worldwide spend money, time and effort on the care and safety of their children. We investigate the nature of these transfers focusing on the two main competing paradigms prevailing in the literature. The altruistic behavior paradigm postulates that the welfare of children enters directly into the preferences of their parents. Altruism in this context was formalized early in the papers of [1,2]. From another perspective, parents may have an incentive to invest in their children if they expect some type of return in the future. This we will call the exchange hypothesis [3,4].

Although it is immediate that both factors may lie behind the observed parental behavior, it is also known that they generate different predictions on several topics of household economics or economic policy, such as the design and implementation of public retirement systems. Therefore, it is important to quantify the relevance of each of these two paradigms in explaining the observable parental behavior. Some papers analyze monetary transfers such as bequests [5] or gifts [6], investment in education or many other monetary transfers. Their results are inconclusive, however, because it is hard to disentangle the part of these transfers that arises as a reaction to market imperfections from that which is purely altruistically motivated. The main reason is that there exists an income effect distorting the results when we consider monetary transfers such as education expenditures or bequests.

Thus, this paper focuses on a class of parental actions that are mostly non-monetary: the demand for child emergency room services (ER, henceforth). When a sudden fever or other signals are observed in a child, parents need to decide whether the symptoms require immediate medical attention or not. Beyond the monetary cost implied by their insurance, parents incur the opportunity cost of leaving their current tasks. We show that if such a cost was similar for rich and poor families, there is a relationship between the frequency of ER utilization and family income. Under altruism, the relationship should be positive and rich families would take their children to the ER more often than would poor ones. Under exchange, the sign of the relationship is ambiguous and could be even the opposite.

We test this point empirically using the frequency of child ER visits in the United States. The main data source is the 1999 and 2000 National Health Interview Surveys (NHIS, henceforth). In addition to health-related variables and medical service expenditure, the surveys include information on the socioeconomic conditions and health insurance status of the families helping us to control those factors that may affect the frequency of visits.

The parameters estimated in an ordered-choice model for ER frequency utilization show that poor parents use ER services more frequently, beyond what can be explained by differences in health conditions, education, and ease of access due to type of insurance. Thus, the negative sign on family income leads us to reject the altruistic hypothesis as a main factor driving the use of ER services. Furthermore, the data do not reject and are consistent with a theoretical prediction of the exchange model, namely, that the differences in the use of ER services between rich and poor should be smaller in economies with a low level of social mobility. The interpretation of these results deserves a word of caution: although both hypotheses may actually lay behind child upbringing in most other cases, our general conclusion is that the exchange hypothesis provides a better explanation of the observed parental behavior in the case of ER use.

2. The Theoretical Model

In this section, we propose a simple theoretical framework for the relationship between family income and ER visits. We abstract from fertility considerations and assume families consisting of one mother and a single child. Individuals in each generation live for two periods. In the first period, the child is a minor and the mother is the only one who works and consumes. The mother consumes her whole current income, y_p in the first period so there are no savings or borrowings for the second period. During the first period the child might show symptoms potentially indicating a fatal illness that can have serious consequences but coursing with unspecific symptoms for instance, meningitis. Let us write $r = 1$ if the child gets the disease and $r = 0$ if she does not. The mother does not directly observe r but an informative signal s. We denote the conditional probability that the child has the disease as $p(s) \equiv p(r = 1|s)$. We assume that $p(s)$ increases with the signal. Having observed the signal s, the mother must decide whether or not to take the child to the ER. Taking the child to the ER requires a non-monetary effort of magnitude e. Effort e is assumed to be constant and independent of family income. It is reasonable to think that such an assumption is unrealistic, since rich and poor families might face a dissimilar value of e in response to differences in ease of access to the health system or differences in the shadow price or opportunity cost of time. We will return to this discussion when presenting the empirical implications of the model.

The consequences of the child's health are revealed in the second period. If she had the disease during childhood but she was not treated, it is assumed that she becomes disabled in economic terms and her utility is zero. If the child was treated or did not have the disease, she becomes a healthy adult, able to work and consume. Children's income is random and takes the value $\varepsilon_H y_c$ with probability $1 - \alpha$ and the value $\varepsilon_L y_c$ with probability α, where $\varepsilon_L < 1 < \varepsilon_H$. The y_c depends on the mother's first period income as $y_c = v(y_p)$ where the function $v(\cdot)$ is increasing and concave. Without loss

of generality, we further assume that the mother's income in the second period is deterministic and again equal to first period's y_p and that $\varepsilon_L \leq y_p/v(y_p) \leq \varepsilon_H$, i.e., a rich child is richer than her mother and a poor child is poorer than her mother.

2.1. The Altruistic Hypothesis

Back in the first period, the mother must decide whether to take her child to the ER when she observes s or not. An altruistic mother, as in [1] or [2], cares about the future welfare of her child by incorporating her child's utility in the second period. In other words, let $u_p(\cdot)$ be the utility function of the mother in the second period regarding their own consumption and $u_c(\cdot)$ the utility of her child. The mother's utility $U(c_p, c_c)$ is assumed to be quasi-linear in consumption, i.e.,

$$U(c_p, c_c) = u_p(c_p) + \beta u_c(c_c).$$

During this second period, monetary transfers are allowed between the mother and the child. Let $b \geq 0$ be the transfer to the child in the second period. The budget constraint imposes the condition that $b \leq y_p$. To simplify the analysis, we will assume that the mother gives transfer $b > 0$ to the child only when the child is poor and zero otherwise. If the degree of altruism towards the child is very high, parents may want to transfer even when the adult child is rich. However, the model is concerned with the decision of the parents regarding ER use in the first period. Decreasing marginal utility implies that the size of the bequest decreases with the child's income. Therefore, setting a bequest of zero for rich children does not alter the results on ER demand.

If the signal on child illness is very high, the mother will be impelled to take her child to the ER. If the illness does not reach a particular threshold, she will stay at home. Our primary interest is to characterize this threshold.

Proposition 1. *Under altruism, there exists a decreasing threshold signal function* $s_U(y_p)$ *that makes mother indifferent between taking her child to the ER and not doing so.*

Proof. *If the mother decides to take her child to the ER she must solve the maximization problem:*

$\max_b$:

$$\Pi^{ER} \equiv \alpha U(y_p - b, \varepsilon_L y_c + b) + (1 - \alpha)U(yp, \varepsilon_H y_c) - e$$

with first-order conditions of b^*, *interior solution of*

$$\beta = u_p'(y_p - b^*)/u_c'(\varepsilon_L y_c + b^*)$$

The solution b^* *depends on* y_p, *the mother's income. If the mother decides not to take her child to the ER, she must solve*

$$\max_b : \Pi^U \equiv \left(1 - p(s)\right)\left(\alpha U\left(y_p - b, \varepsilon_L y_c + b\right) + \cdots\right.$$
$$\left. + (1-\alpha) U\left(y_p, \varepsilon_H y_c\right)\right) + p(s) u_p\left(y_p\right)$$

with first-order conditions as above. Since b^* is the same in both cases, the threshold s that render the mother indifferent is given by the solution to $\Pi^{ER} = \Pi^U$. Differentiability and the implicit function theorem ensure the existence of a solution say $s(y_p)$. Now we want to show that $s(y_p)$ is decreasing in mother's income. Making $\Pi^{ER} = \Pi^U$ and simplifying terms we obtain:

$$\alpha\left(u_p\left(y_p - b^*\right) + \beta u_c\left(\varepsilon_L y_c + b^*\right)\right) + (1-\alpha)\beta u_c\left(\varepsilon_H y_c\right)$$
$$= e/p(s)$$

Since $p' > 0$ and $u_c\left(\varepsilon_H v\left(y_p\right)\right)$ is increasing in y_p, it is enough to show that

$$u_p\left(y_p - b^*\right) + \beta u_c\left(\varepsilon_L v\left(y_p\right) + b^*\right)$$

is increasing in y_p. Differentiating this expression, it suffices show that

$$\beta u_c\left(\varepsilon_L y_C + b^*\right)\left(\varepsilon_L y_C + b^*\right) \geq$$
$$u_p'\left(y_p\right) - u_p'\left(y_p - b^*\right)\left(1 - b'^*\right)$$

where b'^* is the slope of b^*, solution to $\max_b : \Pi^{ER}$. Substituting the solution and simplifying, the condition now reads

$$u_p'\left(y_p - b^*\right)\left(1 + \varepsilon_L v\left(y_p\right)\right) \geq u_p'\left(y_p\right)$$

Since $b^* \geq 0$ and $v'(\cdot) \geq 0$, concavity of u_p ensures that the above inequality holds.

Proposition 1 holds because the welfare of a child enters into the preferences of the mother as a normal good. A rich mother will value more the chance of giving bequests to her children so she will be more ready to pay cost e and the signal threshold that prompts her to act is lower.

Note that the cost e has been assumed to be the same for rich and poor families, and the risk of illness $p(s)$ is also the same. Therefore rich mothers, facing a lower hurdle, will use the ER more often.

Claim 1. *Ceteris paribus, if the altruistic hypothesis holds, rich families will make more intensive use of ER services.*

The *ceteris paribus* clause above is intended to mean similar health conditions and similar cost of effort for the rich and the poor. Therefore, to obtain an empirical test that is valid, controls for family health, insurance, and other socioeconomic conditions are needed. This is explained in Section 3.

2.2. The Exchange Hypohtesis

Altruism may not be the only motivation behind mother's

efforts. In many developing countries, the family is sometimes the only social institution for the care of the elderly. Although this is not the case in the developed world, there is some empirical evidence showing that children often make transfers to their parents when the latter are old [7,8]. Thus, if the mother expects some return from her child in the second period, she would have an incentive to raise a healthy child and to pay the cost e of taking her child to the ER after observing a signal. This we call the exchange hypothesis.

It is important to note that in this paper we do not model the decision of the child regarding transfers to the latter is old. There are three main approaches in the literature regarding this point: inverse altruism [9], social norms [10] and transfers in exchange for bequest [11], but the main results of our model are not affected by the specific channel and we just consider that the mother receives an amount $h > 0$ from her child in the second period. For simplicity we will assume that the mother expect to receive h only when her income is smaller than her child's and expects zero if the child is poor.[1] We make the magnitude of h depend on the mother's income, relative to her child's if the child is rich. Since y_c depends on y_p, we will simply write $h(y_p)$.

The mother's payoff depends exclusively on her total consumption and the possible effort of taking her child to the ER:

$$(1-\alpha)u_p\left(y_p + h\left(y_p\right)\right) + \alpha u_p\left(y_p\right) - e \qquad (1)$$

If the child is not taken to the ER, then the expected utility is

$$(1 - p(s))\left[(1-\alpha)u_p\left(y_p + h\left(y_p\right)\right) + \alpha u_p\left(y_p\right)\right]$$
$$+ p(s)u_p\left(y_p\right) \qquad (2)$$

The signal threshold s_E that makes (1) equal to (2) is characterized in the next proposition.

Proposition 2. *Under the exchange hypothesis, there exists a threshold signal function $s_E\left(y_p\right)$ such that:*
- *If $h'(\cdot) \leq 0$ then $s_E\left(y_p\right)$ is increasing.*
- *If $h'(\cdot) > 0$ then the sign of $s_E\left(y_p\right)$ is ambiguous.*

Proof. *Equating (1)-(2) and simplifying*

$$u_p\left(y_p + h\left(y_p\right)\right) - u_p\left(y_p\right) = e/(1-\alpha)p(s)$$

Let $s_E(y_p)$ be the solution. First, consider the case where h is constant, i.e., $h' = 0$. In this case, by concavity of the utility function, the expression

$$u_p\left(y_p + h\right) - u_p\left(y_p\right)$$

is decreasing in the mother's income. As $p(\cdot)$ is in-

---

[1]In the United States the average wealth at age 50 is higher than the average wealth for people over 65 [12].

creasing, $s'_E > 0$. *Following the same reasoning, the result also holds for* $h' < 0$. *In the case of* $h' > 0$ *though, we need a closed-form solution of* $s_E(y_p)$ *to determine the slope.* ■

The first case is perhaps the most realistic: it may happen if a rich mother has a rich child and child-to-mother transfers are increasing in child's income. In that case $s_E(y_p)$ may be increasing under some particular conditions.

Proposition 3. *Under the exchange hypothesis, if*

$$1 + h'(y_p) < u'_p(y_p)/u'_p(y_p + h(y_p))$$

holds and $h'(\cdot) > 0$ *then* $s'_E(\cdot) > 0$.

Proof. *To obtain* $s'_E > 0$, *the term*

$$u_p(y_p + h(y_p)) - u_p(y_p)$$

must be decreasing, i.e.,

$$u'_p(y_p + h(y_p))(1 + h'(y_p)) - u_p(y_p) < 0$$

Rearranging, we obtain the desired condition. ■

The condition in proposition 3 holds depending on the size of $h'(y_p)$. One case where it does is when children are altruistic towards parents and h is assumed to be endogenously determined as the solution to the maximization problem of the child,

$$\max_h : u_c(\varepsilon_H v(y_p) - h) + d u_p(y_p + h)$$

such that $h \geq 0$ where δ is the degree of altruism from the child to the parents.

Proposition 4. *Consider the class of utility functions* $u(x,t) = x^{1-t}/(1-t)$ *and say* $v(y_p) = ky_p^\gamma$ *concave function with* $k > 0$ *and* $0 < \gamma < 1$.
If

$$(1 + \delta - 1/t)\left(y_p/\left(\varepsilon_H ky_p^\gamma + y_p\right)\right) - k\gamma y_p^{\gamma-1} \geq 1$$

then $s'_E(\cdot) > 0$.

Proof. *The solution to the maximization problem of the child is given by*

$$h = \max\left[0, \varepsilon_H v(y_p)\delta^{1/t} y_p/\left(1 + \delta^{1/t}\right)\right]$$

For corner solutions with $h = 0$ *we would be in the case of the previous proposition. Otherwise, after substitution of* $v(y_p) = ky_p^\gamma$ *and h interior solution in the condition*

$$u'_p(y_p + h(y_p))(1 + h'(y_p)) - u_p(y_p) < 0$$

the second part of the proposition follows. ■

There exist reasonable values of the parameters that meet condition (4). In **Figure 1** we plot the shape of $s_E(\cdot)$ for different values of the parameters obtained from empirical sources. For instance, typical [13,14] estimates of γ range from 0.3 to 0.6 and we consider the cases of $\gamma = 0.4$, 0.5 and 0.6 cases. The remaining parameters are

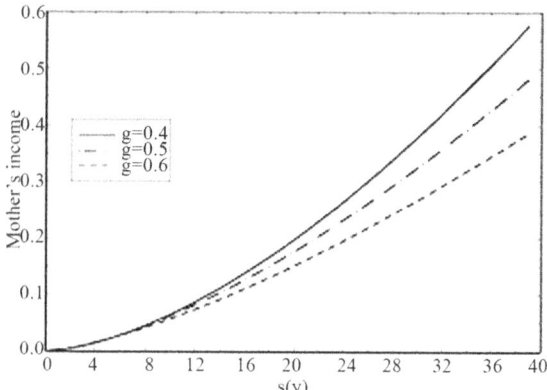

Figure 1. Signal threshold $s(\cdot)$ as a function of family income for different levels of the social mobility parameter γ.

taken as $\delta = 0.45$, $\tau = 2$, $k = 20$, $\varepsilon_H = 1.25$ and $\alpha = 0.5$. The conditional probability of illness is simply taken as $p(s) = s$. The mother's income y_p is in the range (0 - 40). In all three cases function s_E is increasing.

There is an interesting interpretation of the γ parameter in the context of our model. This parameter controls the concavity of the v function and is in fact an index of social mobility: a concave v implies that, in expected terms, the child in a rich family will become relatively less rich than the parent. Thus, investing in the child yields a higher return in poor families than in rich families, the effect being stronger the lower γ is. Moreover, in societies with a high level of social mobility (low values of γ) the gradient of the s_E function will be smaller. In the empirical section of the paper we will show that the evidence does not seem to contradict this result.

3. Data on the Demand for Child ER Services

We collected data from the NHIS of the National Center for Health Statistics[2] for the years 1999 and 2000. The basic purpose of the NHIS is to obtain information from US families on the amount and distribution of illness, the effects of the same in terms of disability and chronic impairments, and the kind of health services received in a sample of households across the 50 states. For each household with non-adult members a sample child is selected and the family respondent is prompted to answer questions regarding the child's health conditions. A total of 26,000 families with children were interviewed in 1999 and 2000. Our sample contains 3379 children of biparental families with at least one child between 0 and 5 years old, and covered by private insurance. We leave aside the uninsured or those covered by Medicaid since they have a reputation for abusing hospital emergency room services and not getting regular infant check-ups [15,16].

[2]Data are publicly available at the Center for Disease Control website http://www.cdc.gov/nchs

We use these data to build a test for the hypothesis that altruistic behavior is the main force driving ER demand. From the discussion in the previous section, this test should be based on the sign of the slope of the signal threshold function. Although the $s(\cdot)$ function is not observable, ER demand is. As explained in Claim 1, rich families should make more intensive use of child ER services, *ceteris paribus*.

Table 1 constitutes a first approach to this idea. We use the frequency of ER visits and family income to compute a cross-frequency table. Of the 5736 children who never went to the ER, 1702 live in families earning more than USD 75,000, 1134 in families earning between USD 55,000 and 75,000, 1334 in families earning between USD 35,000 and 55,000 and 1566 in the category of less than USD 35,000. Of the families in the top income category, 82.82% never visited the ER. This contrasts with the figure of 77.37% for the poorest. Moreover, if we consider those families that went at least once to the ER, the low-income families tend to show longer tails of frequency counts: for instance, of the 49 children who went four or five times to the ER, 18 lived in families earning less than USD 40,000 while only 11 fell in the category of more than USD 75,000.

The correlation in **Table 1** constitutes a preliminary approach. Recall that Claim 1 is done under the assumption of a *ceteris paribus*, but there may exist several factors that can be correlated with family income and ER demand simultaneously that should be included in the specification.

First, health and income are related both in adults and in infants [17] even in developed countries such as the United States. Controls for health include child's age, which is a key factor to determine poor health risk in children, and dummy variables for having suffered allergic (asthma or digestive allergies) or infectious conditions (otitis, urine infections). Finally, the parents' assessment of a child's general health condition is also included in the specification.

Second, the education of parents is related to family income and is a key factor for properly identifying the nature of the signal. The link between education and income is well documented [18]; thus, richer parents may use ER services less simply because the conditional distribution of the signal differs between rich and poor. It can also be the case that richer more educated mothers have healthier babies at birth because they followed healthier habits during pregnancy [19]. The educational level of parents is included as a regressor in the specification.

Third, it has been shown that the proximity of health facilities could be correlated with family income [20] and for this reason we include dummy variables for the region of the household (North, West, Midwest and South) and its location in a metropolitan area.

Fourth, insurance companies have been progressively introducing health management organizations (HMO) that lie between the patient and the medical system and that control the access of families to hospital services. We include a dummy for the presence of a HMO in the family insurance.

Fifth, individuals make long-term decisions on the basis of permanent income, not current income. Measuring permanent income is problematic because it cannot be observed. The gap between permanent and current income is expected to shrink as the individual approaches retirement age; therefore, the estimated ER/income gradient may also be expected to differ for those individuals whose permanent income is not actually far from their current income. To capture this effect, we include the cross-product of income with a dummy that indicates whether the head of the family is older than 40.

Sixth, the exchange model predicts that the slope becomes more negative the more concave $s(\cdot)$ is. To capture this effect, we include cross-products of income and the region of the United States.

The risk of accidents and the differences in the shadow price of time may also play a role. Regarding the first, the NHIS sample does not provide information on the accident history of the child. The literature[3] is also inconclusive regarding how the risk of injury and income are related. Regarding the second, it is a factor of unobserved variability in our model, and its relationship to family income is in principle ambiguous. It is sensible to hypothesize that time is more expensive for the rich, and so the effort e should be more costly for rich families. However, rich families also have access to better technology and services regarding child care, such as more flexible

Table 1. Cross-frequency table[a].

ER frequency of use	Family Income[b]				
	<35	35 - 55	55 - 75	>75	Total
0	77.37	79.40	82.77	82.82	80.46
1	13.83	13.99	12.41	12.94	13.34
2 - 3	7.31	5.71	3.94	3.70	5.25
4 - 5	0.89	0.60	0.73	0.54	0.69
6 - 7	0.25	0.06			0.08
8 - 9	0.25		0.15		0.10
10 - 12	0.05	0.18			0.06
13 - 15		0.01			0.06
16+	0.05				0.01

[a]Units are percentage points; [b]In thousands of USD.

[3]Reference [21] found that Mexican American infants have smaller odds of homicide or unintentional injury than Whites, but Native Americans (and Blacks to a minor degree) have higher ones. Reference [22] use data from an interview and find no relevant correlation between income and risk of injury in Canadian adolescents.

job schedules, own vehicle, baby-care or nursery services, etc., which could lower the cost of effort for the rich.

In addition to all the regressors above, dummies for sex, race, and Hispanic ethnicity of the children are also included.

The dependent variable is a categorical variable: ER demand expressed as intervals of the number of ER visits. For example, in the NHIS 2000, codes 1 to 7 are used for 0, 1, ···, 6 visits, code 8 for 13 to 15 visits, and code 9 for more than 16 visits[4]. Standard linear least squares methods are inappropriate in this context as the dependent variable and the factors of interest are not linearly related. Thus, we propose a modified version of the standard ordered-choice models [23] where the latent variable is a count process. Put formally, let $\{y_i, x_i\}$ for $i = 1, \cdots, N$ be a random sample of ER demand (y with support $\{1, \cdots, J\}$) and x a vector of covariates. Variable y is a transformation $y = T(y^*)$ from a latent count variable y^* with probability function $g(\cdot | x, \theta_0)$ where θ_0 is a vector of unknown parameters. The conditional probability of observing y_i is given by

$$\text{Prob}(y_i | x_i, \theta_0) = \sum_j \left[I_{(y=j)} \sum_i g(y^* | x_i, \theta_0) \right] \quad (7)$$

where $I_{(\cdot)}$ is the indicator function. A maximum likelihood estimator (MLE) of θ_0 solves the problem of maximizing the sum of (7) for the whole sample.

4. Main Results

Table 2 reports the MLE estimates of the model for three different choices of $g(\cdot)$. A first step is to consider that the latent y^* is a Poisson process with mean $\exp(x'\beta_0)$. If the income is measured in logs, the corresponding β parameters can be interpreted as the income elasticity of expected ER demand. The first column of **Table 2** reports this and the coefficients for some other variables of interest.

White children make less use of the ER than black or hispano and the frequency of use decreases with age, as expected. The regressors that control for poor health condition show a strong negative sign. Regarding family structure, the greater the number of siblings, having a step father and father education affects negatively the number of ER visits. The children of working mothers seem to use ER more frequently.

The income parameter is negative and significant at the 1% level. Roughly, each USD 10,000 increment in family income reduces the expected frequency of use of ER facilities by approximately 4%, thus pointing in the direction of rejecting the null of altruistic behavior.

Still, we were concerned about the possibility that an

---

[4]In the NHIS 1999 data set there were only 6 categories corresponding to 0, 1, 2 - 3, 4 - 9, 10 - 12 and more than 13 ER admissions.

Table 2. ER demand: income-related[a] coefficient estimates.

Parameters[b]	Ordered count model			
	Poisson	NegBin	Hurdle	
			Probit	Count
Constant	**−0.500**	**−0.426**	**−1.061**	**0.778**
Sex	0.007	0.024	0.126	**−0.237**
Age	**−0.069**	**−0.064**	−0.046	**−0.078**
White	**−0.287**	**−0.290**	−0.164	**−0.390**
Hispano	−0.067	−0.072	−0.205	0.320
Mother's education	0.003	−0.002	−0.111	0.029
Father's education	**−0.041**	**−0.042**	− 0.030	**− 0.490**
Step Mother	**−0.403**	−0.297	−0.488	0.071
Step Father	**0.812**	**0.714**	0.703	0.532
Mother works FT	**0.104**	0.096	0.060	0.137
No. sibling	**−0.109**	**−0.101**	−0.069	**−0.147**
Infection	**0.421**	**0.398**	0.383	**0.181**
Alergic	**0.408**	**0.425**	0.331	**0.282**
Perceived Health	**0.196**	**0.183**	0.134	**0.216**
Insurance HMO	**−0.096**	−0.068	−.0021	−0.143
Urban	**−0.332**	**−0.341**	−0.303	**−0.201**
Income	**−0.041**	**−0.039**	−0.008	**−0.115**
Income & Age > 40	−0.003	−0.003	−0.020	**0.051**
Midwest	0.122	0.009	−0.223	**0.569**
Northeast	0.039	−0.004	0.267	−0.549
South	−0.123	−0.163	0.113	−0.714*
Mid-W & Income	−0.017	−0.005	0.014	−0.052
North-E & Income	−0.036	−0.032	−0.070*	0.069
South & Income	0.029	0.032	−0.014	0.144*
Goodness of fit and specification tests				
Average Loglik	−0.401	0.231	0.564	
Sample Size1	3379	3379	3379	724
LK ratio p-value	0.000	0.0002	0.000	
Count	**Actual[4]**		**Fitted**	
0	78.57	73.56	78.87	78.55
1	15.12	21.68	14.15	14.08
2.3	5.38	4.64	5.81	6.55
4+	0.91	0.10	1.16	0.80
Pearson's test		**21.3**	0.44	0.77

[a]The table shows a summary of the estimated coefficients for the income-related covariates. Estimates for the remaining socio-economic and health related variables are not shown and are available from the authors upon request; [b]Bold means significant at 5%.

incorrect specification of the latent count process could bias the results. The bottom of **Table 2** reports some measures of fit and specification tests. We computed the frequencies of the observed data and the predictions using the model estimates. The Poisson model fails to fit the frequencies of the observed counts, and a chi-squared Pearson test statistic rejects the null of a correct specification.

The Poisson distribution is a one-parameter distribution with mean equal to variance: thus, it is not a good choice if the data show long tails and dispersion. In those cases, the negative binomial may help: if we denote as $\theta_0 \equiv (\beta_0, \alpha_0)$ the parameter vector with $\alpha_0 > 1$ and y^* is Negative Binomial with mean $\lambda_0 \equiv \exp(x'\beta_0)$, the variance of y^* equals $\alpha_0 \lambda_0$. Thus, the α_0 parameter may account for the over-dispersion of the data.

The second column shows the results for a negative binomial specification. The negative binomial model improves the fit significantly and the Pearson test on the expected versus observed frequencies does not reject the null of a correct specification.

Our sample is also characterized by the presence of a huge number of zero visits: as reported in **Table 1**, zeros represent about 80% of the ER observations. One could think that all those zeros may contain a mixture of two different sub-samples of children: those who did not have any health problem or symptom during the year of the interview and those who did but whose parents did not go to the ER. This interpretation of the zero counts is appealing and introduces a higher degree of flexibility to the model. Thus, we specify a third model where the counts are the result of the mixture of two different processes: one driving the zero/non-zero outcomes and another accounting for the frequency counts conditional on a non-zero outcome observed. In such a "hurdle" model, we assume that y_1^*, y_2^* are count latent variables for each process both negative binomial with probability functions $g_1\left(y_{1i}^* \middle| x_{1i}, \theta_0^1\right)$ and $g_2\left(y_{2i}^* \middle| x_{2i}, \theta_0^2\right)$. The conditioning variables in each of the processes may share some elements but all of them belong to the set of variables in x_i. The data-generating process is defined as $y_i = 0$ if $y_{i1}^* = 0$ and $y_i = y_{2i}^*$ if $y_{i1}^* > 0$, and the probability function of the latent count process is given by the following expression:

$$g\left(y_i \middle| x_i, \theta_0\right) = I_{(y_i=0)} g_1\left(0 \middle| x_{1i}, \theta_{01}\right) + \cdots$$
$$+ I_{(y_i>0)} \frac{g_2\left(y_i \middle| x_{2i}, \theta_{02}\right)}{1 g_2\left(0 \middle| x_{2i}, \theta_{02}\right)} \left(1 g_1\left(0 \middle| x_{1i}, \theta_{01}\right)\right)$$

Thus, under the hurdle model, the subpopulation of individuals who went at least once to the ER is allowed to differ in terms of its characteristics from the whole population [24]. Therefore, the income coefficient on the subpopulation of individuals who visited the ER at least once should include about only families who experienced at least one bad health episode and the income coefficient contains more information about the parents' decision which is what we are interested in. The last column of **Table 2** shows the coefficients of this sub-sample. We still find a significantly negative elasticity between income and ER utilization. Moreover, this elasticity is significantly greater for people under 40, precisely where

one would expect to find the greatest differences between current and permanent income. We also find that the elasticity differs significantly for different US regions and more specifically for the southern states.

Figure 2 plots the relationship between income and ER utilization in the four US regions. In the states of the South, where social mobility is lower [25], this relationship is much flatter. This result is in concordance with one the findings of the exchange model: a lower social mobility (greater γ parameter) implies a flatter relationship between income and ER demand.

5. Conclusions and Final Comments

We propose a two-period theoretical model where parents have to decide whether to take their children to the emergency room or not. Their decision is analyzed under two competing frameworks: either parents are motivated by altruism or their decisions are based on contemplating children as an investment. Under generic altruism, rich parents should ceteris paribus take their children more often to the emergency room when faced with a given sign of illness. We find that this testable prediction is not verified in an ordered latent count model where the frequency of emergency room utilization is regressed on a set of covariates that include family income. We also find that explanations other than those predicted by an exchange model do not affect this main result. First, although rich families could have better access to preventive care and hence replace the need for emergency room utilization by more continued well-baby check-ups, this substitution effect is not enough to explain the magnitude of the gradient observed. Second, a similar result follows when we include controls for the differences between permanent and current income. And third, we find that the predictions of the exchange model in terms of the relation between income gradient and social mobility are not rejected by the evidence at hand.

The evidence presented here suggests that children

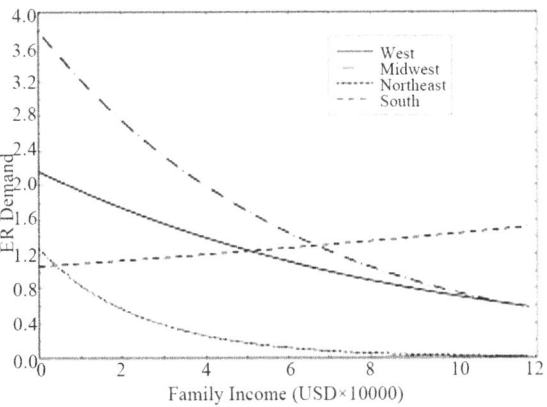

Figure 2. Child ER demand with respect to income in four US regions.

might still play an important role as assets for parents' old age in developed economies. Integrating parents' health investment in children with fertility decisions will be part of further research on this issue. There are economic measures other than the health investment decision analyzed here and those already considered in the relevant literature that should also be studied. For instance, if our analysis is correct and children can be seen as an investment, parents might invest less in pension funds than would adults with no children. This and other similar empirical questions will also be analyzed in future work.

6. Acknowledgements

We thank Manuela Lopez-Azorín for her assistance in technical questions on child health, and Klaus Desmet for helpful discussion. We acknowledge the financial support received from the Ministerio de Educación, SEJ-2007/67135ECON, ECO-2010-19830 and Fundación SENECA 11998-PHCS-09.

REFERENCES

[1] R. Barro, "Are Government Bonds Net Wealth?" *Journal of Political Economy*, Vol. 82, No. 6, 1974, pp. 1095-1117.

[2] G. Becker, "A Theory of Social Interactions." *Journal of Political Economy*, Vol. 82, No. 6, 1974, pp. 1063-1093.

[3] B. Bernheim, A. Shleifer and L. Summers, "The Strategic Bequest Motive," *Journal of Political Economy*, Vol. 93, No. 6, 1985, pp. 1045-1076.

[4] D. Cox, "Motives for Private Income Transfers," *Journal of Political Economy*, Vol. 95, No. 31, 1987, pp. 508-546.

[5] N. Tomes, "The Family, Inheritance, and the Intergenerational Transmission of Inequality," *Journal of Political Economy*, Vol. 89, No. 5, 1981, pp. 928-958.

[6] P. Menchik, "Primogeniture, Equal Sharing and the US Distribution of Wealth," *Quarterly Journal of Economics*, Vol. 94, No. 2, 1980, pp. 299-316.

[7] K. McGarry and R. F. Schoeni, "Transfer Behavior in the Health and Retirement Study: Measurement and the Redistribution of Resources within the Family," *The Journal of Human Resources*, Vol. 30, 1995, pp. 184-226.

[8] K. A. Couch, M. C. Daly and D. A. Wolf, "Time? Money? Both? The Allocation of Resources to Older Parents," *Demography*, Vol. 36, No. 2, 1999, pp. 219-232.

[9] M. Boldrin and L. E. Jones, "Mortality, Fertility and Saving Decisions in a Malthusian Economy," *Review of Economic Dynamics*, Vol. 5, No. 4, 2002, pp. 775-814.

[10] D. Cox and O. Stark, "Intergenerational Transfers and the Demonstration Effect," Boston College Working Papers in Economics No. 329, Boston College, Chestnut Hill, 1994. http://fmwww.bc.edu/EC-P/wp329.pdf

[11] L. Kotlikoff and A. Spivak, "The Family as Incomplete Annuities Market," *Journal of Political Economy*, Vol. 89, No. 2, 1981, pp. 372-391.

[12] S. Budriá-Rodríguez, J. Díaz-Gimenez and J. R. Rull, "Updated Facts on the US Distributions of Earnings, Income, and Wealth," *Quarterly Review*, Vol. 26, No. 3, 2002, pp. 1-35. www.minneapolisfed.org/research/QR/QR2631.pdf

[13] G. Solon, "Cross-Country Differences in Inter-Generational Earnings Mobility," *The Journal of Economic Perspectives*, Vol. 16, No. 3, 2002, pp. 59-66.

[14] M. Corak, "Do Poor Children Become Poor Adults? Lessons from a Cross Country Comparison of Generational Earnings Mobility," IZA Discussion Paper No. 1993, 2006. http://ftp.iza.org/dp1993.pdf

[15] V. Sharma, S. Simon, J. Bakewell, E. Ellerbeck, M. Fox and D. Wallace, "Factors Influencing Infant Visits to Emergency Departments," *Pedriatics*, Vol. 106, No. 5, 2000, pp. 1031-1039.

[16] J. Billings and T. Mijanovich, "Emergency Room Use: The New York Story," In: *Issue Brief*, The Commonwealth Fund, New York, 2000.

[17] A. Case, D. Lubotsky and C. Paxson, "Economics Status and Health in Childhood: The Origins of the Gradient," *American Economic Review*, Vol. 92, No. 5, 2002. pp. 1308-1334.

[18] O. Ashenfelter and C. Rouse, "Schooling, Intelligence and Income in America," Princeton University Press, Princeton, 2000.

[19] J. Currie and E. Moretti, "Mother's Education and the Intergenerational Transmission of Human Capital: Evidence from College Openings," *Quarterly Journal of Economics*, Vol. 118, No. 4, 2003, pp. 1495-523.

[20] J. Currie and P. Reagan, "Distance to Hospitals and Children's Access to Care: Is Being Closer Better, and for Whom?" *Economic Inquiry*, Vol. 41, No. 3, 2003, pp. 378-391.

[21] A. Jain, B. Khoshnood, K. Lee and J. Concato, "Injury Related Infant Death: The Impact of Race and Birth Weight," *Injury Prevention*, Vol. 7, No. 2, 2001, pp. 135-140.

[22] W. Pickett, M. Garner, W. Boyce and M. King, "Gradients in Risk for Youth Injury Associated with Multiple-Risk Behaviors: A Study of 11,239 Canadian Adolescents," *Social Science and Medicine*, Vol. 55, No. 6, 2002, pp. 1055-1068.

[23] D. A. Greene and W. H. Hensher, "Modelling Ordered Choices: A Primer," Cambridge University Press, Cambridge, 2008.

[24] P. Deb and P. Trivedi, "Demand for Medical Care by the Elderly: A Finite Mixture Approach," *Journal of Applied*

Econometrics, Vol. 12, No. 3, 1997, pp. 313-336.

[25] D. I. Levine and B. Mazumder, "Choosing the Right Parents: Changes in the Intergenerational Transmission of Inequality between the 1970s and the Early 1990s," Working Papers 2002-08, Federal Reserve Bank of Chicago, Chicago, 2002.
http://www.escholarship.org/uc/item/9r45b10r.pdf;origin=repeccitec

2

Econographication

Mario Arturo Ruiz Estrada

Faculty of Economics and Administration, University of Malaya, Kuala Lumpur, Malaysia

ABSTRACT

The rationale of Econographication revolves around the efficacy of multidimensional graphs as the most effective visual tool to understand any economic phenomenon from a multidimensional view. The main motivation behind the creation of Econographication is to evaluate multidimensional graphs evolved so far in economics and to develop new type of multidimensional graphs to facilitate the study of economics, as well as finance and business. Thereby, the mission of Econographication is to offer academics, researchers and policy maker's an alternative multidimensional graphical modeling approach to the research and teaching-learning process of economics, finance and business from a multidimensional perspective. Hence, this alternative multidimensional graphical modeling approach is offering a set of multidimensional coordinate spaces to build different types of multidimensional graphs to study any economic phenomenon. The following new types of multi-dimensional coordinate spaces are presented: the pyramid coordinate space (five axes and infinite axes); the diamond coordinate space(ten axes and infinite axes); the 4-dimensional coordinate space (vertical position and horizontal position); the 5-dimensional coordinate space (vertical position and horizontal position); the infinity-dimensional coordinate space (general approach and specific approach); the inter-linkage coordinate space; the cube-wrap coordinate space; the mega-surface coordinate space. All these multi-dimensional coordinate spaces mentioned previously, they are available to represent graphically 4-dimensions, 5-dimensions, 8-dimensions, 9-dimensions until infinity-dimensions.

Keywords: Graphs in Economics; Economics Teaching; Multidimensional Graphical Modeling

1. The Evolution of Graphical Methods in Economics

Research leading to this chapter shows a strong link between the introduction of graphical methods in economics and the development of theories, methods and techniques in statistics and mathematics. In the 18th century, for example, several new graphical methods were developed as a result of some mathematics and statistics research in the same century. These graphical methods include line graphs of time series data (since 1724), curve-fitting and interpolation (1760), measurement of error as a deviation from the graphed line (1765), graphical analysis of periodic variation (1779), a statistical mapping (1782), bar charts (1756) and printed coordinate chapter (1794) [1].

The application of graphical methods in the economic analysis, we have renowned economists like William Playfair [2], Francis Ysidro Edgeworth [3] and William Stanley Jevons [4]. According to Harro Maas [5], William Playfair constructed a wonderful collection of plates and graphs at the end of the eighteenth century. In his book entitled *Commercial and Political Atlas*, Playfair focused on the study of trade cycles. This placed him far ahead of other economists at the time in terms of visualizing socio-economic data. We would classify the development of the usage of graphical methods in economics into two phases. The first phase is the *descriptive graphical method*. It is supported by simple tables, histograms, line graphs and scatter-plots. All these types of graphs are based on the visualization of a single economic variable (vertical axis = Y) through a specific period of time (horizontal axis = X) in the first quadrant in the 2-dimensional Cartesian coordinate system is shown in **Figure 1**.

The main objective of the *descriptive graphical method* in economics is to study the behavior of a single economic variable (e.g. exports, imports, unemployment, GDP, inflation rate etc.) within a time frame (per decade, annually, monthly, weekly or daily) based on time-series. In fact, William Playfair may be considered the pioneer and promoter of the *descriptive graphical method*.

The second phase in the development of graphical methods for economics will be called the "*analytical*

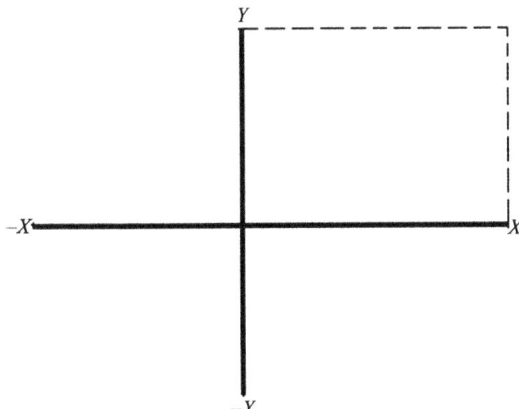

Figure 1. 2-Dimensional coordinate space.

graphical method". The *analytical graphical method* in economics features by 2-dimesnional and 3-dimensional coordinate systems. According to Harro Maas is William Stanley Jevons who first explored the merits of the graphical method for political economy. Jevons did this through the function called "King-Devenant Law of Demand" that he introduced. This is a case of the use of *analytical graphical method* in economics, where the form of the graph gives an idea of the possible class of the functions describing the relationship between X and Y variables respectively that suggest a causal interpretation of the relationship between X and Y.

Additionally, we like to mention also that the uses of the formal graphical method based on the 2-dimensional Cartesian plane was introduced in 1637 by René Descartes [6], whose contributions to different scientific disciplines, of which economics was one, were substantial. The 2-dimensional coordinate space opened a new era in economic analysis by providing for analysis of a single economic phenomenon based on the relationship between two variables.

However, it is necessary to mention the major contribution of Antoine Augustin Cournot [7]. Cournot derived the first formula for the rule of supply and demand as a function of price on 2-dimensional view. He was, in fact, also the first economist to draw the supply and demand curves on a graph. Cournot believed that economists must utilize graphs only to establish probable limits and express less stable facts in more absolute terms. He further held that the practical use of mathematics in economics involves not only strict numerical precision, but also graphical visualization. Besides Cournot and Jevons, other innovator economists that contributed to the analytical graph system in economics over time are Leon Walras (with general equilibrium), Alfred Marshall (with partial equilibrium) and Joseph Schumpeter (with business cycles) [8].

In the 20th century the use and application of *the analytical graphical method* among economists were often

based on sophisticated mathematical and graphical techniques introduced during the development of new economic models. In particular, calculus, trigonometry, geometry and statistical and forecasting methods started to be employed by economists in constructing their graphs during that time. In addition, 2-dimensional and 3-dimensional Cartesian coordinate systems were also a part of complex economics research Avondo-Bodino [9]. Consequently, the application of sophisticated mathematical and graphical techniques can be seen in the development of the following economic models and theories: welfare theory [10], IS-LM curve (Hansen, 1938) [11], development of static and dynamic analysis [12], econometrics [13], Phillips curve [14], Okun law [15], economic growth theory [16], game theory [17], introduction of dynamic models and econometrics [18], monetary theory [19], and rational expectations theory [20].

The rapid development of the *analytical graphical method* has been facilitated by high technology and sophisticated analysis instruments such as the electronic calculator and the computer. The development of analysis instruments in economics took place into two stages. The first stage involved the *"basic computational instruments"*, where electronic calculators were used to compute basic mathematical expressions (e.g. long arithmetic operations, logarithm, exponents and squares). This took place between the 1950's and 1960's. The second stage called *"advance computational instruments"* took place in the middle of the 1980's. This is when high speed and storage-capacity computers using sophisticated software were introduced for the first time. The use of sophisticated software enables easy information management, application of difficult simulations as well as the creation of high resolution graphs under 3-dimensional coordinate system. The analysis instruments undoubtedly contributed substantially to the development and research in economics.

Therefore, high computational instruments, backed by sophisticated hardware and software, are utilized to create graphical representations with high resolution and accuracy. In fact, the *descriptive graphical method* and *analytical graphical method* can be categorized according to functions or dimensional. In terms of function, these two graphical methods are either descriptive or analytical. In terms of dimension, these two graphical methods can be either 2-dimensional, 3-dimensional and multi-dimensional coordinates systems. The *descriptive graphical method* shows arbitrary information that is used to observe the historical data behavior from a simple perspective. On the other hand, the *analytical graphical method* is available to generate time-series graphs, cross-section graphs and scatter diagrams to show the trends and relationships between two or more variables from a multi-dimensional and dynamic perspective.

2. A Short Review about Dimension and Coordinate Systems (Cartesian Plane and Coordinate Space)

Initially, we like to review four basic definitions about dimension. According to the first definition about dimension by Poincarė [21], he defines dimension as a space that is divided by a large number of sub-spaces. It meant "however we please" and "partitioned". The second definition about dimension is given by Brouwer [22]. He defines dimension as "between any two disjoint compacta". Brouwer makes references about the existence of a group of sub-sets into different sets. It is based on the uses of the topological dimension of a compact metric space based on the concept of cuts [23]. The third definition about dimension is given by Urysohn and Menger [24], they defined dimension as "between any compactum and a point not belonging to it". These four authors are sharing common concepts into its definitions about dimension such as the uses of spaces, subspaces, sets, subsets, partitioned and cut concepts. This mean that any dimension needs to be studied by spaces/sets or subspaces/sub-sets or partitioned/cuts.

The idea about dimension is complex and deeper for the human mind. It is because we need to do often abstractions and parameterizations of time and space of any geometrical object that cannot be visualized in the real world [25]. Moreover, this part of our research is interested to propose an alternative definition about dimension. According to this book "dimension" can be defined "as the unique mega-space that is build by infinite general-spaces, sub-spaces and micro-spaces that are interconnected systematically." In the process to visualize different dimensions graphically, it is possible by the uses of coordinate systems. The coordinate systems are available to generate the graphical modeling frameworks to represent different dimension(s) in the same graphical space. The coordinate systems can be divided by two types: Cartesian plane and coordinate space.

The difference between the Cartesian plane and coordinate space is originated by the number of axes. In the case of the Cartesian plane is based on the uses of two axes and the coordinate space is based on the uses of three or more axes. Therefore, the Cartesian plane and coordinate space are available to generate an idea about dimension(s) graphically through the optical visualization of several lines in a logic order by length, width and height. The concept about dimension also can be explained by the Euclidian geometry under the uses of the Euclidian spaces. The Euclidian geometry can be divided by the 2-dimensional Euclidean geometry (plane geometry) and the 3-dimensional Euclidean geometry (solid geometry). Additionally, the study of the Euclidian geometry also involves the study of the n-dimensional space represented by R^n or E^n under the uses if the n-dimensional space and

n-vectors respectively.

3. How Multi-Dimensional Coordinate Spaces Work?

The main reason to apply multi-dimensional coordinate spaces is to study any economic phenomena from a multidimensional perspective. It is originated by the limitations that the 2-dimensional coordinate space shows in the moment to generate a multidimensional optical visual effect of any economic phenomena at the same graphical space. Hence, the multidimensional coordinate spaces leads an alternative graphical modeling more flexible and innovative than the 2-dimensional coordinate space in the moment to observe multi-variable data behavior.

The study of multi-dimensional coordinate spaces requests basic knowledge about the "n-dimensional space". The idea about the n-dimensional space was originated by many Greeks thinkers and philosophers such as Socrates, Plato, Aristotle, Heraclitus and Euclid (father of the geometry). The great contribution of Euclid in geometry was the design of the plane geometry under the 2-dimensional Euclidean geometry and the solid geometry under the 3-dimensional Euclidean geometry. However, the n-dimensional space can be defined as a mental refraction through the optical visualization and brain stimulation by several lines in a logic order by length, width, height and colors to represent the behavior of simple or complex phenomena in different periods of time in the same graphical space.

Usually, the study of n-dimensional space is based on the application of the "coordinate system". In fact, the coordinate spaces can be classified by 2-dimensional coordinate space, 3-dimensional coordinate space and multidimensional coordinate spaces. The main role of coordinate system is crucial in the analysis of the relationship between two or more variables such as exogenous variable(s) and endogenous variable(s) on the same graphical space. In fact, the Euclidean space is given only the mathematical theoretical framework, but not the graphical modeling to visualize the n-dimensions according to different mathematical theoretical research works. On the other hand, Minkowski's [26] introduce the idea about the 4-dimensional space or the "world". The world according to Minkowski's it is originated by the application of 3-dimensional continuum (or space). The difference between the 4-dimensional space and 3-dimensional space graphical model is that the first graphical model replace (X,Y,Z) by (X_1,X_2,X_3,X_4), thus $X_1 = X$; $X_2 = Y$; $X_3 = Z$ and $X_4 = \sqrt{-1}$. The X_4 is based on the application of the Lorenz transformation axiom. The 4-dimensional space by Minkowski's also never offer a specific graphical modeling or alternative Cartesian coordinate system to help visualize the 4-dimensional space, it is only offer a mathematical theoretical framework to describe the idea about 4-dimensional space. Moreover, the application of multi-dimensional coordinate spaces offer a large possibilities to adapt n-dimensions, sub-dimensions, micro-dimensions, nano-dimensions and ji-dimensions in the visualization of any economic phenomenon.

Basically, the uses of coordinate spaces by economists are based on plot different dots that represent the relationship between two or more variables (endogenous and exogenous) in the first and fourth quadrants in the 2-dimensional coordinate space. After, they proceed to join all these dots by straights lines until is possible to visualize histograms, line graphs and scatter-plots are shown in **Figures 1** and **2**. Hence, it is possible to observe the trend and behavior of different variables of any economic phenomenon. For example, the relationship between unemployment/inflation, interest-rate/investment, prices/quantity demand and supply, etc.

From our point of view, each dot is plotted on the 2-dimensional, 3-dimensional and multi-dimensional coordinate spaces represent a single rigid point. In fact, the plotting of a single rigid point in any coordinate space requests the application of two basic assumptions: first assumption is that two rigid points cannot occupy the same space at the same time. The second assumption is that different rigid point(s) deal in different n-dimensional spaces is moving under different speeds of time. The variable "time" in the case of multi-dimensional coordinate spaces needs to be classified by: the general time, partial time and constant time. The general time is running in the general-space but in the case of the sub-spaces, micro-spaces, nano-spaces are running under different partial times. In the case of JI-spaces always is fixed by the constant time. Recently, few economists start to use the 3-dimensional coordinate space in economics by the uses of three axes: "X-coordinate" (or exogenous variable), "Y-coordinate" (or exogenous variable) and the "Z-coordinate" (or endogenous variable). It is based on the construction of surfaces or 3-dimensional manifolds to visualize multi-variable economic data behavior are shown in **Figure 2**. According to our research the uses of the 3-dimensional coordinate space are not so popular among economists and policy makers.

Based on one thousand five hundred (1500) chapters published in twenty one (21) reputable economics journals[1] between the year 1939 and 2009 [27], it is possible

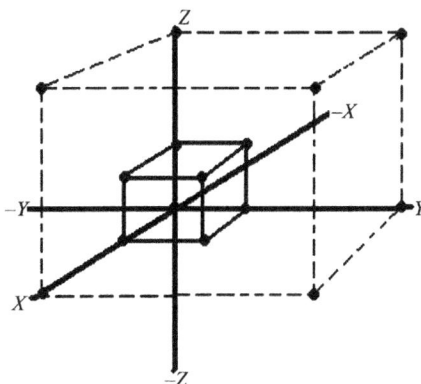

Figure 2. 3-Dimensional coordinate space.

to observe that the common types of graphical representations applied in the study of social sciences, especially in economics, were of the 2-dimensional coordinate spaces. It is according to 99.5% of these chapters applied 2-dimensional Cartesian coordinate system, and only 0.5% of them applied 3-dimensional coordinate spaces. Additionally, this research will find some reasons about **"why"** economists continue using 2-dimensional coordinate space or sometimes 3-dimensional coordinate space in the graphical representation of complex and dynamic economic phenomena, these reasons are following by:

- The 2-dimensional graphical models are established for long time, since the introduction of the 2-dimensional coordinate space by Descartes until today. The application of 2-dimensional coordinate space in the economic graphical analysis became by **"Tradition"**.

- The 2-dimensional space is **"easy to apply"** to visualize basic trends or values in the same graphical space. The logic explanation about the common uses of the 2-dimensional coordinate space, it can be originated by the easy way to plot, draw and visualize any economic phenomenon. Therefore, 2-dimensional coordinate space can generate a clear visual and mental refraction to understand complex and dynamic economic phenomena graphically in the same space and time.

Difficulty to find **"alternative and suitable multi-dimensional graphical models"** to generate the transition from 2-dimensional coordinate space graphical modeling to multi-dimensional spaces graphical modeling. This research found some difficulties to generate this crucial visual and mental transition from 2-dimensional coordinate space to multi-dimensional coordinate space. It can be originated by some difficulties in the process to plot, draw and visualization of multi-dimensional graphs.

Finally, a new set of multi-dimensional coordinate spaces is introduced in this document. The idea is to generate a new multidimensional optical visual effect to visualize complex economic phenomena. We can observe that into

---

[1]American Economic Review; Canadian Journal of Economics; Econometrica; Economica; Economic History Review; Economic Journal; International Economic Review; Journal of Economic History; Journal of Economic Literature; Journal of Political Economy; Oxford Economic Papers; Quarterly Journal of Economics; Review of Economic Studies; Review of Economics and Statistics; Canadian Journal of Economics and Political Science; Journal of Economic Abstracts; Contributions to Canadian Economics; Journal of Labor Economics; Journal of Applied Econometrics; Journal of Economic Perspectives; Publications of the American Economic Association; Brookings Papers on Economic Activity. Microeconomics and American Economic Association Quarterly (JSTOR, [14]).

the multidimensional coordinate spaces can keep a large number of exogenous variables that are changing constantly and affect directly on the endogenous variable(s) behavior in the same graphical space. These new type of multi-dimensional coordinate spaces are based on the pyramid coordinate space (five axes and infinite axes), the diamond coordinate space(ten axes and infinite axes), the 4-dimensional coordinate space (vertical position and horizontal position), the 5-dimensional coordinate space (vertical position and horizontal position), the infinite-dimensional coordinate space (general approach and specific approach), the inter-linkage coordinate space, the cube-wrap coordinate space, and the mega-surface coordinate space. Being multi-dimensional, it enables economists, academics and policy makers to analyze economic phenomena from multidimensional perspectives across time and space.

4. An Introduction to Omnia Mobilis Assumption

Basically, the idea to build an economic model is to simplify the real economic world. It is based on the uses of a large number of variables that interacting together into the same economic phenomenon. To analyze an economic phenomenon can be by induction (particular observations) or deduction (simple forecasting). According to our research, any economic model will try to show the interaction of different economic actors and different possible scenarios. The main problem is how to catch-up the dynamic changes across time (period of time in analysis) and space (geographical place in analysis) in any economic model as a whole.

For long time economists and academics are applied the Ceteris Paribus assumption to build economic models. Especially in old economic models such as demand and supply model that explain basically the relationship between two variables: endogenous variable (quantity) and exogenous variable (price) into a precise period of time and space. In other words, we leave the rest of variables out currently until we can get the final result from these two specific variables in analysis.

The Ceteris Paribus assumption also can be considered the most common assumption that is learned and applied by economists to understand different economic phenomena. This assumption translated from Latin that it means "all other things [being] the same". It facilitates the description of how a variable of interest changes in response to changes in other variables by examining the effect of one variable at a time. An extremely important contribution of Alfred Marshall, it supports the understanding of the application of Ceteris Paribus assumption in economic models. According to Marshall [28]:

"The element of time is a chief cause of those diffi-

culties in economic investigations which make it necessary for man with his limited powers to go step by step; breaking up a complex question, studying one bit at a time, and at last combining his partial solutions into a more or less complete solution of the whole riddle. In breaking it up, he segregates those disturbing causes, whose wanderings happen to be inconvenient, for the time in a pound called *Ceteris Paribus*. The study of some group of tendencies is isolated by the assumption *other things being equal:* the existence of other tendencies is not denied, but their disturbing effect is neglected for a time. The more the issue is thus narrowed, the more exactly can it be handled: but also the less closely does it correspond to real life. Each exact and firm handling of a narrow issue, however, helps towards treating broader issues, in which that narrow issue is contained, more exactly than would otherwise have been possible."

Marshall's approach thus allows the analyses of complex economic phenomena by parts where each part of the economic model can be joined to generate an approximation of the real world. This approach can be termed the Isolation Approach and according to Marshall [29] originates from two possible isolation clauses. First the Ceteris Paribus assumption allows some variables to be considered unimportant. This clause is called Substantive Isolation.

The Substantive Isolation considers that some unimportant variables cannot significantly affect the final result of the economic model. Second, the Ceteris Paribus assumption allows the influence of some important factors to be disregarded. The application of the Ceteris Paribus assumption in this case is purely hypothetical; therefore the second clause is called Hypothetical Isolation. It allows parts of the model to be managed more easily.

In other words, to explain a complex economic phenomenon, the Ceteris Paribus approach considers the effect partially of each variable in a set of m variables (termed usually independent variables, $X_j, j = 1, 2, ... , m$) upon a variable of interest (usually termed the dependent variable, Y). From a mathematical point of view, the Ceteris Paribus assumption in an economic model is equivalent to the partial derivative, which explains how one exogenous variable, say X_k, in a set of exogenous variables can affect directly on the endogenous variable Y while the other exogenous variables are being held constant. From a graphical point of view, the Ceteris Paribus assumption supports the elaboration of scenarios that can be visualized on 2-dimensional coordinate space.

More precisely, if "Y" is a function of, say, X_1 and X_2, the (partial) relationship between Y and X_1 can be visualized in the 2-dimensional space describing Y and X_1, assuming X_2 is held constant. In order to approximate real world, Marshall goes on to propose that "With each step more things can be let out of the pound; exact discussions can be made less abstract, realistic discussions can be made less inexact than was possible at an earlier stage." The real-world scenario is thus approximated by the cumulative effect of the partial effects of the X variables on Y. After our review about the Ceteris Paribus assumption, according to our research we find that part of the problem to suggest the application of Ceteris Paribus assumption can be originated by three basic reasons follow by:

- First reason is the historical momentum that this assumption was build to help explain a economic phenomenon, maybe the number of variables are accounted was less before than in our days.
- Second reason is that the Ceteris Paribus assumption can be considered the basic and classic tool for teaching-learning economics.
- Third reason is from the graphical modeling, it is based on the application of 2-dimensional coordinate space (X,Y) that is used for long time. According to our research the 2-dimensional coordinate space is not available to visualize multi-variable economic modeling into the same graphical space. Thereby, the 2-dimensional coordinate space is only available to visualize two variables: endogenous variable and exogenous variable simultaneously into the same graphical space.

The idea to introduce the Omnia Mobilis assumption—everything is moving—[30] is to reduce the dependency and less uses of Ceteris Paribus assumption in the economic modeling. We propose the openness of substantive isolation through the application of the Omnia Mobilis assumption. It is based on generate the relaxation of all variables without restrictions and limitation that the Ceteris Paribus assumption generates into the economic modeling. To generate this relaxation of a large number of variables in any economic modeling, we suggest the application of multi-dimensional coordinate spaces that is offer by Econographication [31]. The idea is to draw multidimensional graphs can help in the visualization all changes of several numbers of variables in the same graphical space. Additionally, the multidimensional graphs provide an alternative graphical approach to the Marshall view of step-by-step cumulative partial approach to the economic modeling. The main objective to apply multidimensional graphs is to visualize graphically all changes of the endogenous variable in response to the changes of several numbers of exogenous variables simultaneously. The multidimensional graphs can also be used to show the dynamic behavior of different variables in any economic model without any restriction. The ap-

plication if the Omnia Mobilis assumption is to capture all possible economic actors and different possible scenarios into the same picture. Therefore, this chapter proposes that Ceteris Paribus assumption is not necessary to be used when economists have opportunity to use the Omnia Mobilis assumption and multidimensional graphs.

The Omnia Mobilis assumption also suggests the application of economic modeling in real time to observe the changes of all variables in real time. It is to demonstrate that the economic modeling don't request the application of Ceteris Paribus assumption in the study of dynamic and complex economic phenomenon, because according to our research any economic phenomenon always still alive and never keep a constant behavior. The difference between Ceteris Paribus assumption and Omnia Mobilis assumption is that the Ceteris Paribus assumption only takes a photo just into a specific historical momentum of some economic phenomenon, but in the case of Omnia Mobilis assumption show a video that is running in real time. Moreover, the multidimensional graphs play a crucial role to understand the application of the Omnia Mobilis assumption in the economic modeling. In fact, the multidimensional graphs are available to visualize the changes of all exogenous variables simultaneously can affect on a single variable or endogenous variable in the same time and space. Finally, the Omnia Mobilis assumption opens a new era in the economic modeling under the application of multidimensional graphs and economic modeling in real time. We can say that the contribution of the Ceteris Paribus assumption in the economic modeling was great at the past, but in our days this assumption is not enough to explain the complexity and dynamicity of different economic phenomena as a whole.

5. The Classification of Multi-Dimensional Coordinate Space

The multi-dimensional coordinate spaces [32] can be classified by the pyramid coordinate space (five axes and infinite axes), the diamond coordinate space(ten axes and infinite axes), the 4-dimensional coordinate space (vertical position and horizontal position), the 5-dimensional coordinate space (vertical position and horizontal position), the infinity-dimensional coordinate space (general approach and specific approach), the inter-linkage coordinate space, the cube-wrap coordinate space, and the mega-surface coordinate space.

5.1. The Pyramidal Coordinate Space with Five Axes

The pyramidal coordinate space with five axes consist in four independent axes (X_1, X_2, X_3, X_4) and one dependent axis (Y^*). The Y^* axis is positioned in the center part of this coordinate space among of the other four axes: X_1, X_2, X_3, X_4. The function used by the pyramidal coordinate space with five axes is fixed by $Y^* = f(X_1, X_2, X_3, X_4)$, where X_1, X_2, X_3, X_4, Y^* axes are using only real positive numbers $\boldsymbol{R}_+$ under the condition $0 \geq \boldsymbol{R}_+ \leq +\infty$. The only uses of positive axes in the pyramidal coordinate space with five axes request the uses of absolute values. The uses of absolute values in each axis are based on the application of the non-negative property.

Hence, all axes $|X_1|$, $|X_2|$, $|X_3|$, $|X_4|$, $|Y^*|$ always use values large or equal than zero. The pyramidal coordinate space with five axes show clearly into the same graphical space any possible change(s) of any or all values plotted on each or all X_1, X_2, X_3, X_4 axes that can affect directly on the behavior of Y^* axis value. In order to plot different values in each axis into the pyramidal coordinate space with five axes, we need to plot each value directly on its axis line. At the same time, all values were plotted on each axis line need to be joined together by straight lines until we can visualize a pyramid-shaped figure with five faces are shown in **Figure 3**. Therefore, we have two possible graphical scenarios: first graphical scenario, if all or any X_1, X_2, X_3, X_4 axes values move from outside to inside, then Y^* axis value move down. Second graphical scenario, if all or any X_1, X_2, X_3, X_4 axes values move from inside to outside, then Y^* axis value move up. Basically, the pyramidal coordinate system with five axes is represented by:

$$([X_1, X_2, X_3, X_4], Y^*) \tag{1}$$

5.2. The Pyramidal Coordinate Space with Infinite Axes

The pyramidal coordinate space with infinite axes consist in infinite independent axes (X_1, X_2, X_3,…,X_∞) and one dependent axis (Y^*). The Y^* axis is positioned in the center part of this coordinate space among of the other infinite axes: X_1, X_2, X_3,…, X_∞. The function used by the pyramidal coordinate space with infinite axes is fixed by $Y^* = f(X_1, X_2, X_3,…, X_\infty)$, where X_1, X_2, X_3,…, X_∞, Y^* axes are using only real positive numbers $\boldsymbol{R}_+$ under the condition $0 \geq \boldsymbol{R}_+ \leq +\infty$.

The only uses of positive axes in the pyramidal coordinate space with infinite axes request the uses of abso-

lute values. The uses of absolute values in each axis are based on the application of the non-negative property. Hence, all axes $|X_1|$, $|X_2|$, $|X_3|$, $|X_4|$, $|Y^*|$ always use values large or equal than zero. The pyramidal coordinate space with infinite axes show clearly into the same graphical space any possible change(s) of any or all values plotted on each or all X_1, X_2, X_3,…, X_∞ axes that can affect directly on the behavior of Y^* axis value.

In order to plot different values in each axis into the pyramidal coordinate space with infinite axes, we need to plot each value directly on its axis line. At the same time, all values were plotted on each axis line need to be joined together by straight lines until we can build a pyramid-shaped figure with infinite faces are shown in **Figure 4**.

Therefore, we have two possible graphical scenarios: first graphical scenario, if all or any X_1, X_2, X_3,…, X_∞ axes values move from outside to inside, then Y^* axis value move down. Second graphical scenario, if all or any X_1, X_2, X_3,…, X_∞ axes values move from inside to outside, then Y^* axis value move up. The pyramidal coordinate system with infinite axes is represented by:

$$([X_1, X_2, X_3,…, X_\infty], Y^*) \tag{2}$$

5.3. The Diamond Coordinate Space with Ten Axes

The diamond coordinate space with ten axes has two levels of analysis and ten axes. Each level of analysis is represented by ($X_{L:i}$, $Y_{L:i}$), where "L" represents the level of analysis, in this case either level one (L_1) or level two (L_2); "i" represents the quadrant level of analysis (in this case, quadrant 1, 2, 3 or 4). In order to plot different values in each axis into the diamond coordinate space with ten axes, we need to plot each value directly on its axis line respectively. At the same time, all values were plotted on each axis line need to be joined together by straight lines until we can build a diamond-shaped figure with eight faces are shown in **Figure 5**. It is important to mention at this juncture that the first level (L_1) has five axes represented by $X_{1:1}$, $X_{1:2}$, $X_{1:3}$, $X_{1:4}$, Y_1. Four independent axes represented by $X_{1:1}$, $X_{1:2}$, $X_{1:3}$, $X_{1:4}$ and one dependent axis fixed by Y_1 respectively. The second level (L_2) has five axes represented by $X_{2:1}$, $X_{2:2}$, $X_{2:3}$, $X_{2:4}$, Y_2. We assume that does not exists any relationship between

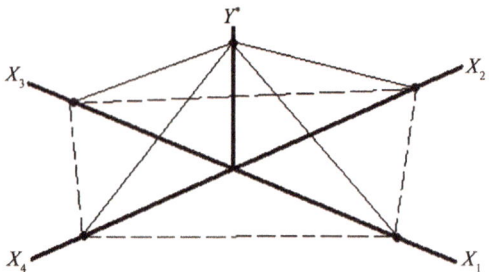

Figure 3. Pyramid coordinate space.

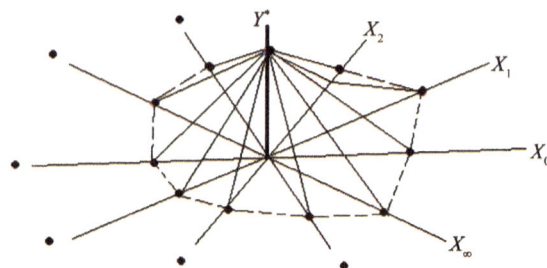

Figure 4. The pyramid coordinate space with infinite axes.

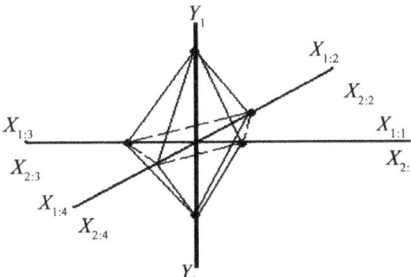

Figure 5. Diamond coordinate space.

level one (L_1) and level two (L_2) of analysis. The common issue between these two levels of analysis is that both levels use the same $X_{L:i}$ axes in the diamond coordinate space. However, level one (L_1) of the analysis cannot affect level two (L_2) of the analysis, and vice versa. If we draw different levels of analysis in the diamond coordinate space, we can visualize and compare two different scenarios in the same diamond coordinate space at the same time is shown in **Figure 5**. It is crucial to mention at this point that the fifth and tenth axes (Y_1 and Y_2) is positioned in the center part of the diamond coordinate space among the other eight axes: $X_{1:1}$, $X_{1:2}$, $X_{1:3}$, $X_{1:4}$, $X_{2:1}$, $X_{2:2}$, $X_{2:3}$, $X_{2:4}$.

We assume that both Y_L (Y_1, Y_2) use only real positive numbers $\boldsymbol{R}_+$. Therefore, the diamond coordinate space all $X_{1:1}$, $X_{1:2}$, $X_{1:3}$, $X_{1:4}$, Y_1, $X_{2:1}$, $X_{2:2}$, $X_{2:3}$, $X_{2:4}$, Y_2 axes are either on the positive side of respective axes together. The only uses of positive axes in the diamond coordinate space request the uses of absolute values. The uses of absolute values in each axis are based on the application of the non-negative properties. Hence, all axes $|X_{1:1}|$, $|X_{1:2}|$, $|X_{1:3}|$, $|X_{1:4}|$, $|Y_1|$, $|X_{2:1}|$, $|X_{2:2}|$, $|X_{2:3}|$, $|X_{2:4}|$, $|Y_2|$ always use values large or equal than zero. The final result, if the two levels of analysis are joined, is possible to visualize a diamond-shaped figure. The diamond coordinate system is represented by:

$$([X_{1:1},\ X_{1:2},\ X_{1:3},\ X_{1:4}],\ Y_1) \qquad (3.1)$$

$$([X_{2:1},\ X_{2:2},\ X_{2:3},\ X_{2:4}],\ Y_2) \qquad (3.2)$$

5.4. The Diamond Coordinate Space with Infinite Axes

The diamond coordinate space with infinite axes has two levels of analysis and infinite axes. Each level of analysis is represented by ($X_{L:i}$, $Y^{*}_{L:i}$), where "L" represents the level of analysis, in this case either level one (L_1) or level two (L_2); "i" represents the quadrant level of analysis (in this case, quadrant 1, 2, 3,..., ∞). In order to plot different values in each axis into the diamond coordinate space with infinite axes, we need to plot each value directly on its axis line respectively. At the same time, all values were plotted on each axis line need to be joined together by straight lines until we can build a diamond-shaped

figure with infinite faces are shown in **Figure 6**. It is important to mention at this juncture that the first level (L_1) has infinite axes represented by $X_{1:1}$, $X_{1:2}$, $X_{1:3}$,..., $X_{1:\infty}$, Y^{*}_1. Infinite independent axes represented by $X_{1:1}$, $X_{1:2}$, $X_{1:3}$,..., $X_{1:\infty}$ and one dependent axis fixed by Y^{*}_1 respectively. The second level (L_2) has infinite axes represented by $X_{2:1}$, $X_{2:2}$, $X_{2:3}$,..., $X_{2:\infty}$, Y^{*}_2. We assume that does not exists any relationship between level one (L_1) and level two (L_2) of analysis. The common issue between these two levels of analysis is that both levels use the same $X_{L:i}$ axes in the diamond coordinate space with infinite axes.

However, level one (L_1) of the analysis cannot affect level two (L_2) of the analysis, and vice versa. If we draw different levels of analysis in the diamond coordinate space with infinite axes, we can visualize and compare two different scenarios in the same diamond coordinate space at the same time. It is crucial to mention at this point that the Y^{*}_1-axis *and* Y^{*}_2-axis is positioned in the center part of the diamond coordinate space with infinite axes (among the other infinite axes $X_{L:i}$).

We assume that both Y^{*}_L (Y^{*}_1, Y^{*}_2) use only real positive numbers $\boldsymbol{R}_+$. Therefore, the diamond coordinate space all $X_{1:1}$, $X_{1:2}$, $X_{1:3}$,..., $X_{1:\infty}$, Y^{*}_1, $X_{2:1}$, $X_{2:2}$, $X_{2:3}$,..., $X_{2:\infty}$, Y^{*}_2 axes are either on the positive side of respective axes together. The only uses of positive axes in the diamond coordinate space with infinite axes request the uses of absolute values. The uses of absolute values in each axis are based on the application of the non-negative properties. Hence, all axes $|X_{1:1}|$, $|X_{1:2}|$, $|X_{1:3}|$,..., $|X_{1:\infty}|$, $|Y^{*}_1|$, $|X_{2:1}|$, $|X_{2:2}|$, $|X_{2:3}|$,..., $|X_{2:\infty}|$, $|Y^{*}_2|$ always use values large or equal than zero. The final result, if the two levels of analysis are joined, is possible to visualize a diamond-shaped figure. The diamond coordinate system is represented by:

$$([X_{1:1},\ X_{1:2},\ X_{1:3},...,\ X_{1:\infty}],\ Y^{*}_1) \qquad (4.1)$$

$$([X_{2:1},\ X_{2:2},\ X_{2:3},...,\ X_{2:\infty}],\ Y^{*}_2) \qquad (4.2)$$

5.5. The 4-Dimensional Coordinate Space: Vertical Position

The 4-dimensional coordinate space in vertical position

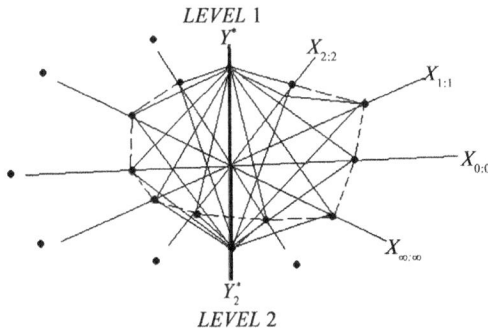

Figure 6. The diamond coordinate space with infinite axes.

offer four axes: Xv_1, Xv_2, Xv_3, Yv. All these four axes are distributed by three independent axes: Xv_1, Xv_2, Xv_3 and one dependent axis: Yv. The Xv_1, Xv_2, Xv_3, Yv axes are fixing positive and negative real numbers $R_{+/-}$.

In order to plot different values in each axis into the 4-dimensional coordinate space in vertical position, we need to plot each value directly on its axis line. All values were plotted on each axis line need to be joined together by straight lines until we can build pyramid-shaped figure with four faces in vertical position is shown in **Figure 7**.

Additionally, the Yv axis is positioned in the center part of the 4-dimensional coordinate space in vertical position (among the other three axes). It is the convergent point of all the other three axes: Xv_1, Xv_2, Xv_3. In other words, all Xv_1, Xv_2, Xv_3 axes converge always in the Yv axis. The 4-dimensional coordinate system in vertical position is represented by:

$$([Xv_1, \ Xv_2, \ Xv_3], \ Yv) \tag{5}$$

5.6. The 4-Dimensional Coordinate Space in Horizontal Position

The 4-dimensional coordinate space in horizontal position offer four axes: Xh_1, Xh_2, Xh_3, Yh. All these four axes are distributed by three independent axes: Xh_1, Xh_2, Xh_3 and one dependent axis: Yh. The Xh_1, Xh_2, Xh_3, Yh are fixing positive and negative real numbers $R_{+/-}$. In order to plot different values in each axis into the 4-dimensional coordinate space in horizontal position, we need to plot each value directly on its axis line. All values were plotted on each axis line need to be joined together by straight lines until we can build pyramid-shaped figure with four faces in horizontal position is shown in **Figure 8**.

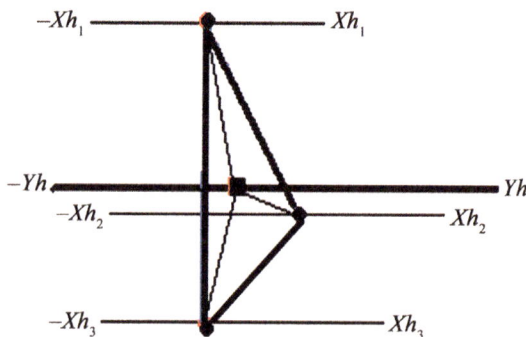

Figure 8. The 4-dimensional coordinate space in horizontal position.

Additionally, the Yh axis is positioned in the center part of the 4-dimensional coordinate space in horizontal position (among the other three axes). It is the convergent point of all the other three axes: Xh_1, Xh_2, Xh_3. In other words, all Xh_1, Xh_2, Xh_3 axes converge always in the Yh axis. The 4-dimensional coordinate system in horizontal position is represented by:

$$([Xh_1, \ Xh_2, \ Xh_3], \ Yh) \tag{6}$$

5.7. The 5-Dimensional Coordinate Space in Vertical Position

The 5-dimensional coordinate space in vertical position consists of five vertical axes: Xv_1, Xv_2, Xv_3, Xv_4, Yv. All these five axes are distributed by four independent axes: Xv_1, Xv_2, Xv_3, Xv_4 and one dependent axis Yv. The Xv_1, Xv_2, Xv_3, Xv_4, Yv are fixing positive and negative real numbers $R_{+/-}$. In order to plot different values in each axis into the 5-dimensional coordinate space in vertical position, we need to plot each value directly on its axis line. All values were plotted on each axis line need to be joined together by straight lines until we can build pyramid-shaped figure with five faces in vertical position is shown in **Figure 9**. Therefore, the Yv axis is positioned in the center of the 5-dimensional coordinate space in vertical position (among the other four vertical axes). The Yv axis is the convergent axis of all the other four vertical axes: Xv_1, Xv_2, Xv_3, Xv_4. The 5-dimensional coordinate system in horizontal position is represented by:

$$([Xv_1, \ Xv_2, \ Xv_3, \ Xv_4], \ Yv) \tag{7}$$

5.8. The 5-Dimensional Coordinate Space in Horizontal Position

The 5-dimensional coordinate space in horizontal position consists of five vertical axes: Xh_1, Xh_2, Xh_3, Xh_4, Yh. All these five axes are distributed by four independent axes: Xh_1, Xh_2, Xh_3, Xh_4 and one dependent axis Yh. The Xh_1, Xh_2, Xh_3, Xh_4, Yh are fixing positive and negative real numbers $R_{+/-}$.

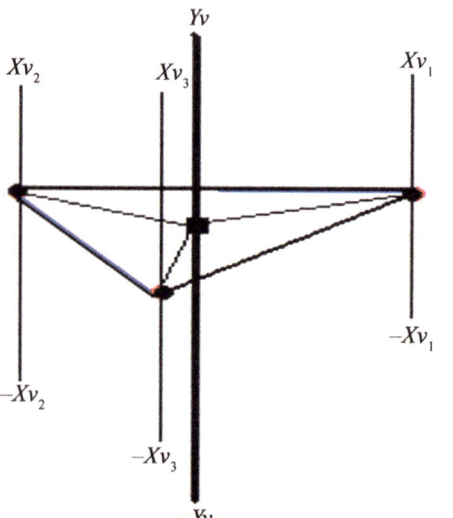

Figure 7. The 4-dimensional coordinate space in vertical position.

In order to plot different values in each axis into the 5-dimensional coordinate space in horizontal position, we need to plot each value directly on its axis line. All values were plotted on each axis line need to be joined together by straight lines until we can build pyramid-shaped figure with five faces in horizontal position is shown in **Figure 10**.

Therefore, the Yh axis is positioned in the center of the 5-dimensional coordinate space in horizontal position (among the other four horizontal axes). The Yh axis is the convergent axis of all the other four vertical axes: Xh_1, Xh_2, Xh_3, Xh_4. The 5-dimensional coordinate system in horizontal position is represented by:

$$([Xh_1,\ Xh_2,\ Xh_3,\ Xh_4],\ Yh) \qquad (8)$$

5.9. The Infinity Dimensional Coordinates Space under the General Approach

The infinity dimensional coordinates space under the general approach shows a series of n-number of sub-cylinders "C" located in the same general cylinder, each sub-cylinder in the same general cylinder is fixed by its Level "L" respectively. Where $L = \{1, 2, 3,...,k\}$, $k \rightarrow \infty$... To plot into the different sub-cylinders in the same general cylinder, it is based on the sub-cylinder location, axis position and ratio. Where $X_{C:L}$ is the independent variable in sub-cylinder "C" at level "L" lying in position

$P_{C:L}$ with value $R_{C:L}$. The position is based on $P_{C:L}$ by $0° \leq P_{C:L} \leq 360°$, is the position of $X_{C:L}$ in cylinder "C" at level "L". And finally the ratios location under the $R_{C:L}$ is the radius corresponding to the $X_{C:L}$ in cylinder "C" at level "L". Finally, the $Y_{C:L}$ is the dependent variable at level "L". The values of the independent axes $X_{C:L}$ affecting $Y_{C:L}$ simultaneously. The infinity dimensional coordinates space under the general approach, its function is given below by:

$$Y_{C:L} = f(X_{C:L},\ P_{C:L},\ R_{C:L}) \qquad (9)$$

For example, the value of a specific independent axis at time point 1, say $X_{1:1:1}$ is plotted as $R_{1:1:1}$ the radius pictured lying on a flat surface at angle $P_{1:1:1}$ is measured from $0°$ line used for its reference line. The points from the end of the radii are joined to meet in a single point on the top of each sub-cylinder at height $Y_{1:1}$, the level "L". The diameter of the sub-cylinder is twice the maximum radius. In order to plot different values in each axis into the infinity dimensional coordinates space under the general approach, we need to plot each value directly on its axis line. All values were plotted on each axis line need to be joined together by straight lines until we can build cone-shaped figure in vertical position is shown in **Figure 11**.

5.10. The Infinity Dimensional Coordinates Space under the Specific Approach

Basically, the infinity dimensional coordinates space under the specific approach offer a new coordinate system is shown in Expression 10. The basic coordinate space system is formed by three levels of analysis: general-space (i); sub-space (j); micro-space (k). In the case of plotting into this coordinate space start with define our specific general-space (i), sub-space (j), micro-space (k), alpha-space (α) and beta-space (β) respectively.

$$(\alpha_{<i:j:k>},\ \beta_{<i:j:k>}) \qquad (10)$$

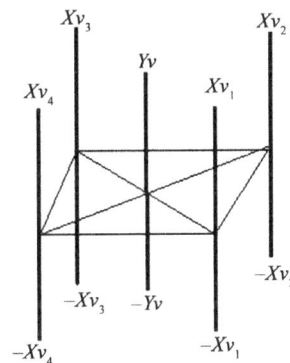

Figure 9. The 5-dimensional coordinate space in vertical position.

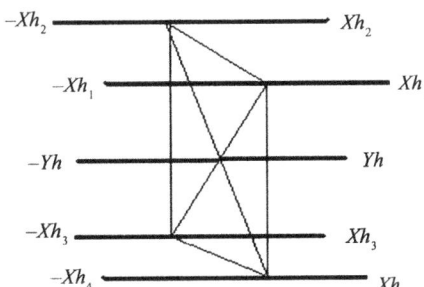

Figure 10. The 5-dimensional coordinate space in horizontal position.

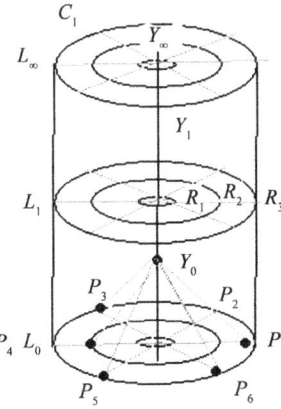

Figure 11. The infinity dimensional coordinates space (general approach).

The infinity dimensional coordinates space under the specific approach is available to show different dimensional that is not possible to be observed in the classic 2-dimensional Cartesian coordinate plane and 3-dimensional coordinate space. Hence, the 2-dimensional Cartesian coordinate plane and 3-dimensional coordinate space can be considered as sub-axes systems into the infinity dimensional coordinates space under specific approach. The structure of the infinity dimensional coordinates space under specific approach is formed by infinite general-spaces (i), sub-spaces (j) and micro-spaces (k). There are distributed into different places along the general cylinder is shown in **Figure 12**. Therefore, the infinity coordinate space under the specific approach starts from

the general space zero (i_0) until the general space infinity (i_∞). And each sub-space starts from sub-space zero (j_0) until the sub-space infinity (j_∞). Finally, the micro-space starts from micro-space zero (K_0) until the micro-space infinity (K_∞) is shown in Expression 11.

The infinity dimensional coordinates space under the specific approach is available to connect a large number of micro-spaces (k) distributed into the same sub-space (j) and general space (i) by the application of the inter-linkage connectivity of micro-spaces ($\overline{\overline{\pi}}$). At the same time, the infinity dimensional coordinates space under the specific approach is also available to connect a large number of general spaces in the same coordinate space. It is based on the application of the inter-linkage connectivity of general-spaces ($\frac{\text{JL}}{\text{TF}}$).

$$(\alpha_{<0:0:0>}, \beta_{<0:0:0>}) \, \overline{\overline{\pi}} \, (\alpha_{<0:0:1>}, \beta_{<0:0:1>}) \, \overline{\overline{\pi}} \cdots \overline{\overline{\pi}} \, (\alpha_{<0:0:\infty>}, \beta_{<0:0:\infty>})$$
$$\frac{\text{JL}}{\text{TF}}$$
$$(\alpha_{<0:1:0>}, \beta_{<0:1:0>}) \, \overline{\overline{\pi}} \, (\alpha_{<0:1:1>}, \beta_{<0:1:1>}) \, \overline{\overline{\pi}} \cdots \overline{\overline{\pi}} \, (\alpha_{<0:1:\infty>}, \beta_{<0:1:\infty>})$$
$$\frac{\text{JL}}{\text{TF}}$$
$$(\alpha_{<0:2:0>}, \beta_{<0:2:0>}) \, \overline{\overline{\pi}} \, (\alpha_{<0:2:1>}, \beta_{<0:2:1>}) \, \overline{\overline{\pi}} \cdots \overline{\overline{\pi}} \, (\alpha_{<0:2:\infty>}, \beta_{<0:2:\infty>})$$
$$\frac{\text{JL}}{\text{TF}}$$
$$\vdots$$
$$\frac{\text{JL}}{\text{TF}}$$
$$(\alpha_{<0:\infty:0>}, \beta_{<0:\infty:0>}) \, \overline{\overline{\pi}} \, (\alpha_{<0:\infty:1>}, \beta_{<0:\infty:1>}) \, \overline{\overline{\pi}} \cdots \overline{\overline{\pi}} \, (\alpha_{<0:\infty:\infty>}, \beta_{<0:\infty:\infty>})$$
$$\frac{\text{JL}}{\text{TF}}$$
$$(\alpha_{<\infty:0:0>}, \beta_{<\infty:0:0>}) \, \overline{\overline{\pi}} \, (\alpha_{<\infty:0:1>}, \beta_{<\infty:0:1>}) \, \overline{\overline{\pi}} \cdots \overline{\overline{\pi}} \, (\alpha_{<\infty:0:\infty>}, \beta_{<\infty:0:\infty>})$$
$$\frac{\text{JL}}{\text{TF}}$$
$$(\alpha_{<\infty:1:0>}, \beta_{<\infty:1:0>}) \, \overline{\overline{\pi}} \, (\alpha_{<\infty:1:1>}, \beta_{<\infty:1:1>}) \, \overline{\overline{\pi}} \cdots \overline{\overline{\pi}} \, (\alpha_{<\infty:1:\infty>}, \beta_{<\infty:1:\infty>})$$
$$\frac{\text{JL}}{\text{TF}}$$
$$(\alpha_{<\infty:2:0>}, \beta_{<\infty:2:0>}) \, \overline{\overline{\pi}} \, (\alpha_{<\infty:2:1>}, \beta_{<\infty:2:1>}) \, \overline{\overline{\pi}} \cdots \overline{\overline{\pi}} \, (\alpha_{<\infty:2:\infty>}, \beta_{<\infty:2:\infty>})$$
$$\frac{\text{JL}}{\text{TF}}$$
$$\vdots$$
$$\frac{\text{JL}}{\text{TF}}$$
$$(\alpha_{<\infty:\infty:0>}, \beta_{<\infty:\infty:0>}) \, \overline{\overline{\pi}} \, (\alpha_{<\infty:\infty:1>}, \beta_{<\infty:\infty:1>}) \, \overline{\overline{\pi}} \cdots \overline{\overline{\pi}} \, (\alpha_{<\infty:\infty:\infty>}, \beta_{<\infty:\infty:\infty>}) \tag{11}$$

5.11. The Inter-Linkage Coordinate Space

The inter-linkage coordinate space is formed by infinite number of general axes (A_0, A_1, ..., A_n ...), perimeter levels (L_0, L_1, ..., L_n ...) and windows refraction (W_0,

W_1, ..., W_n ...) are shown in **Figure 13**. Each window refraction is based on join its sub-x axis (X_{A-L}) with its sub-y axis (Y_{A-L}) respectively. Therefore, the window refraction (W_0, W_1, ..., W_n ...) is follow by the coordinate Space (X_{A-L}, Y_{A-L}). All windows refraction on the same

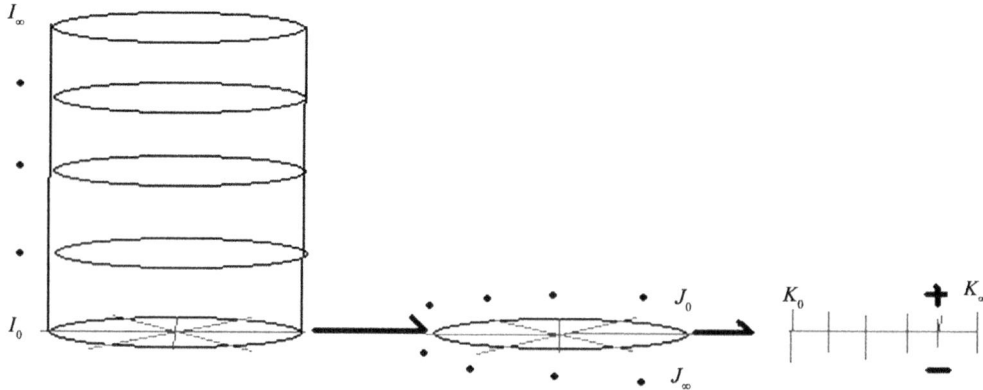

Figure 12. The infinity dimensional coordinates space under the specific approach.

general axis (A_0, A_1, ..., A_n ...) will be joined together under the application of the inter-linkage connectivity of windows refraction represented by "®". The inter-linkage connectivity of windows refraction is represented by the symbol "®". The inter-linkage connectivity of windows refraction "®" will inter-connect all windows refraction (W_0, W_1, ..., W_n ...) on the same general axis (A_0, A_1, ..., A_n ...) but in different perimeter levels (L_0, L_1,..., L_n ...). Moreover, the inter-linkage coordinate system is shown in Expression 12:

Perimeter level P_0 ® Perimeter level P_1 ® ... ® Perimeter level P_n

General Axis 0 (A_0): $\quad W_{0\text{-}0} = (x_{0\text{-}0}, y_{0\text{-}0})$ ® $W_{0\text{-}1} = (x_{0\text{-}1}, y_{0\text{-}1})$ ®...® $W_{0\text{-}\infty} = (x_{0\text{-}\infty}, y_{0\text{-}\infty})$

General Axis 1 (A_1): $\quad W_{1\text{-}0} = (x_{1\text{-}0}, y_{1\text{-}0})$ ® $W_{1\text{-}1} = (x_{1\text{-}1}, y_{1\text{-}1})$ ®...® $W_{1\text{-}\infty} = (x_{1\text{-}\infty}, y_{1\text{-}\infty})$

General Axis 2 *(A_2)*: $\quad W_{2\text{-}0} = (x_{2\text{-}0}, y_{2\text{-}0})$ ® $W_{2\text{-}1} = (x_{2\text{-}1}, y_{2\text{-}1})$ ®...® $W_{2\text{-}\infty} = (x_{2\text{-}\infty}, y_{2\text{-}\infty})$

General Axis 3 (A_3): $\quad W_{3\text{-}0} = (x_{3\text{-}0}, y_{3\text{-}0})$ ® $W_{3\text{-}1} = (x_{3\text{-}1}, y_{3\text{-}1})$ ®...® $W_{3\text{-}\infty} = (x_{3\text{-}\infty}, y_{3\text{-}\infty})$

General Axis 4 *(A_4)*: $\quad W_{4\text{-}0} = (x_{4\text{-}0}, y_{4\text{-}0})$ ® $W_{4\text{-}1} = (x_{4\text{-}1}, y_{4\text{-}1})$ ®...® $W_{4\text{-}\infty} = (x_{4\text{-}\infty}, y_{4\text{-}\infty})$

General Axis 5 (A_5): $\quad W_{5\text{-}0} = (x_{5\text{-}0}, y_{5\text{-}0})$ ® $W_{5\text{-}1} = (x_{5\text{-}1}, y_{5\text{-}1})$ ®...® $W_{5\text{-}\infty} = (x_{5\text{-}\infty}, y_{5\text{-}\infty})$

$$\cdots \qquad \cdots \qquad \cdots \qquad \cdots$$

General Axis n (A_∞): $W_{\infty\text{-}0} = (x_{\infty\text{-}0}, y_{\infty\text{-}0})$ ®.........................® $W_{\infty\text{-}\infty} = (x_{\infty\text{-}\infty}, y_{\infty\text{-}\infty})$ (12)

Finally, the inter-linkage coordinate space is available to fix a large number of different functions located in different windows refraction (W_0, W_1,..., W_n ...), pe- rimeter levels (L_1, L_2,..., L_n ...) and general axes (A_1, A_2, ..., A_n ...) are shown in Expression 13:

Perimeter level P_0 ® Perimeter level P_1 ® ... ® Perimeter level P_n

General Axis 0 (A_0): $\quad y_{0\text{-}0} = f(x_{0\text{-}0})$ ® $y_{0\text{-}1} = f(x_{0\text{-}1})$ ®......® $y_{0\text{-}\infty} = f(x_{0\text{-}\infty})$

General Axis 1 (A_1): $\quad y_{1\text{-}0} = f(x_{1\text{-}0})$ ® $y_{1\text{-}1} = f(x_{1\text{-}1})$ ®......® $y_{1\text{-}\infty} = f(x_{1\text{-}\infty})$

General Axis 2 (A_2): $\quad y_{2\text{-}0} = f(x_{2\text{-}0})$ ® $y_{2\text{-}1} = f(x_{2\text{-}1})$ ®......® $y_{2\text{-}\infty} = f(x_{2\text{-}\infty})$

General Axis 3 (A_3): $\quad y_{3\text{-}0} = f(x_{3\text{-}0})$ ® $y_{3\text{-}1} = f(x_{3\text{-}1})$ ®......® $y_{3\text{-}\infty} = f(x_{3\text{-}\infty})$

General Axis 4 (A_4): $\quad y_{4\text{-}0} = f(x_{4\text{-}0})$ ® $y_{4\text{-}1} = f(x_{4\text{-}1})$ ®......® $y_{4\text{-}\infty} = f(x_{4\text{-}\infty})$

General Axis 5 (A_5): $\quad y_{5\text{-}0} = f(x_{5\text{-}0})$ ® $y_{5\text{-}1} = f(x_{5\text{-}1})$ ®......® $y_{5\text{-}\infty} = f(x_{5\text{-}\infty})$

$$\cdots \qquad \cdots \qquad \cdots \qquad \cdots$$

$$\cdots \qquad \cdots \qquad \cdots \qquad \cdots$$

General Axis n (A_∞): $\quad y_{\infty\text{-}0} = f(x_{\infty\text{-}0})$ ®..........................® $y_{\infty\text{-}\infty} = f(x_{\infty\text{-}\infty})$ (13)

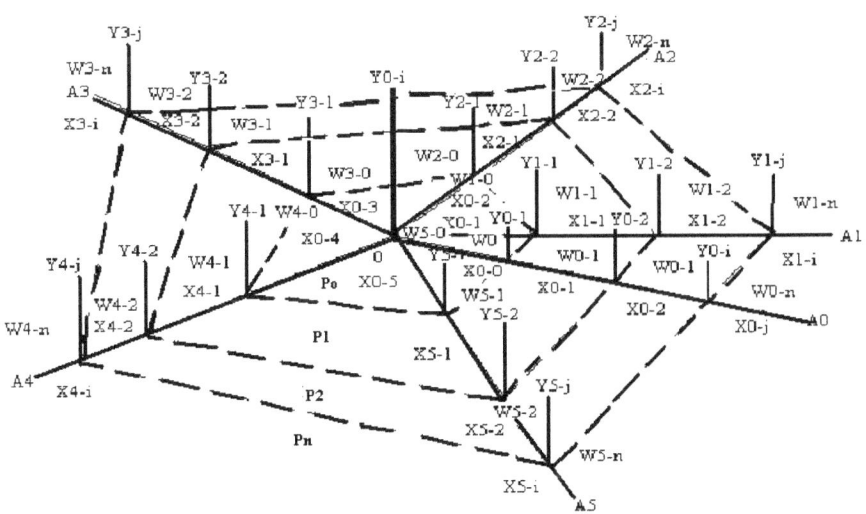

Figure 13. The inter-linkage coordinate space.

5.12. The Cube-Wrap Coordinate Space

The cube-wrap coordinate space is willing to offer an alternative coordinate space. The main objective of the cube-wrap coordinate space is to show unknown dimensions that cannot be visualized by the 2-dimensional Cartesian plane and 3-dimensional coordinate space.

Initially, the cube-wrap coordinate space is divided by two quadrants. The first quadrant is located on the top of the cube-wrap coordinate space that represents all $|X_i|$-axes. The second quadrant is located under the button of the cube-wrap coordinate space that represents all $|Y_j|$-axes are shown in **Figure 14**.

In the process to plot on this coordinate space start by plot each value on its axis line respectively. The space that exists between $|X_i|$-axes and $|Y_j|$-axes will be called "quadratic-space refraction" because each $|X_i|$-axis has its $|Y_j|$-axis respectively. The construction of the quadratic space refraction is based on two basic steps: the first step

is to plot each value on the $|X_i|$-axis line and $|Y_j|$-axis line, we suggest applying the inter-linkage connectivity of micro-spaces ($\mp$) are shown in Expression 14. Second step is to join the values located on $|X_i|$-axis and $|Y_j|$-axis by a single straight vertical line.

$$(|X_i| \mp |Y_j|) \tag{14}$$

We assume that between X_i–axes and Y_j–axes exists a common single straight vertical line that joint both set of axes. This common single straight line is called the zero space. Hence, the cube-wrap coordinate space starts from the quadratic space refraction zero (L_0) until the quadratic space refraction infinity (L_∞). According to the cube wrap coordinate space requests the application of absolute values $|R_{+/-}|$ because the cube wrap coordinate space works only with positive real numbers R_+. The final coordinate system to build the cube-wrap coordinate space is shown in Expression 15.

$$CW = [(S_0) = (|X_{00}| \mp |Y_{00}|) \; \underset{\mp}{\amalg} \; (S_1) = (|X_{01}| \mp |Y_{01}|) \; \underset{\mp}{\amalg} ... \underset{\mp}{\amalg} \; (S_\infty) = (|X_{\infty\infty}| \mp |Y_{\infty\infty}|)] \tag{15}$$

In the final stage of analysis in the cube-wrap space, it is based on its size. We can have three possible stages that the cube-wrap space can experience anytime:

If all values are growing constantly in $|X_i|$ and $|Y_j|$ then the cube-wrap experience an expansion-stage (16)

If all values are decreasing constantly in $|X_i|$ and $|Y_j|$ then the cube-wrap experience a contraction-stage (17)

If all values are keeping constant in $|X_i|$ and $|Y_j|$ then the cube-wrap experience a static-stage (18)

5.13. The Mega-Space Coordinate Space

The mega-space coordinate space is formed by infinite number of axes in vertical position. Each vertical axis (X_{ij}) show positive integer numbers on the top and negative integer numbers on the bottom in the same vertical axis. At the same time, all the vertical axes can be lo-

cated by its row number (i) and column number (j) in the mega-space coordinate space is shown in Expression 19.

The idea to apply the mega-surface coordinate space is to build the mega-surface. The mega-surface can show how a large number of variables behave together in the same graphical space. Initially, the construction of the mega-surface start by joins each vertical axis value by straight lines with its neighbor vertical axis: front side; left side; right side; back side is shown in **Figure 15**. To join all axes are necessary to apply the inter-linkage connectivity condition ($\underset{\mp}{\amalg}$) on all vertical axes simultaneously.

$$\underset{\mp}{\amalg} X_{ij} => \begin{bmatrix} \underset{\mp}{\amalg}X_{11} & \underset{\mp}{\amalg}X_{12}\underset{\mp}{\amalg} & ....\underset{\mp}{\amalg}X_{1\infty} \\ \underset{\mp}{\amalg}X_{21} & \underset{\mp}{\amalg}X_{22}\underset{\mp}{\amalg} & ....\underset{\mp}{\amalg}X_{2\infty} \\ \underset{\mp}{\amalg}X_{31} & \underset{\mp}{\amalg}X_{32}\underset{\mp}{\amalg} & ....\underset{\mp}{\amalg} X_{3\infty} \\ \underset{\mp}{\amalg}X_{\infty 1} & \underset{\mp}{\amalg}X_{\infty 2}\underset{\mp}{\amalg} & ....\underset{\mp}{\amalg} X_{\infty\infty} \end{bmatrix} \tag{19}$$

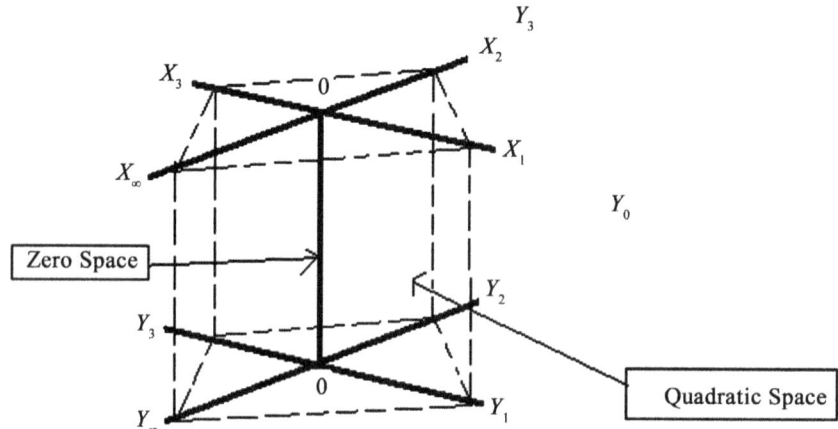

Figure 14. The cube-wrap coordinate space and the cube-wrap space.

The final analysis of the mega-surface is based on its location into the mega-space coordinate space. The possible stages that the mega-surface can experience:

> If all X_{ij} values > 0 then the mega-surface shows a expansion stage (20)

> If all X_{ij} values = 0 then the mega-surface shows a stagnation stage (21)

> If X_{ij} values < 0 then the mega-surface shows a contraction stage (22)

> If some X_{ij} is sharing positive, negative or zero values in different vertical axes then the mega-surface shows an unstable performance stage. (23)

5.14. The Cubes Coordinate Space

The cubes coordinate space is formed by infinity number of general axes (A_0, A_1,..., A_n). Where each axis shows different levels (L_0, L_1,..., L_n), perimeters (P_0, P_1, P_2...P_n), and Cubes with different sizes and colors ($C_{0/\beta}$, $C_{1/\beta}$... $C_{n/\beta}$). Therefore, the coordinate system of the cubes-coordinate space is represented by $S_{A:L:P:C} = (A_i, L_j, P_k, C_{s/\beta})$ respectively. Where i, j, k and s represents different values between 0 and ∞.... And β represent the different colors of each cube in different levels (L_0, L_1,..., L_n). All the cubes with different sizes and colors in the same axis under the same level (L_0, L_1,..., L_n) and different perimeters (P_0, P_1, P_2...P_n) will be joined together, it is based on the application of the concept is called "macroeconomics links structures" represented by the symbol "@". Moreover, the cubes-coordinate space coordinate system is shown in Expression 24 and **Figure 16**.

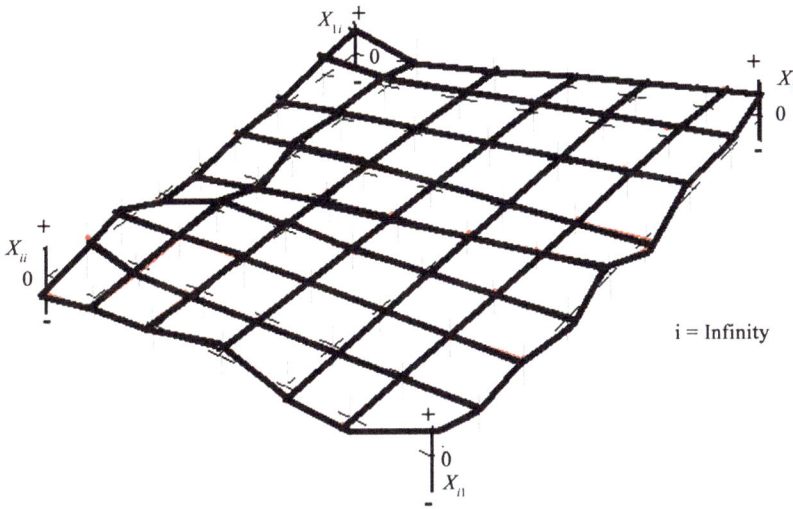

Figure 15. The mega-space coordinate space and the mega-surface.

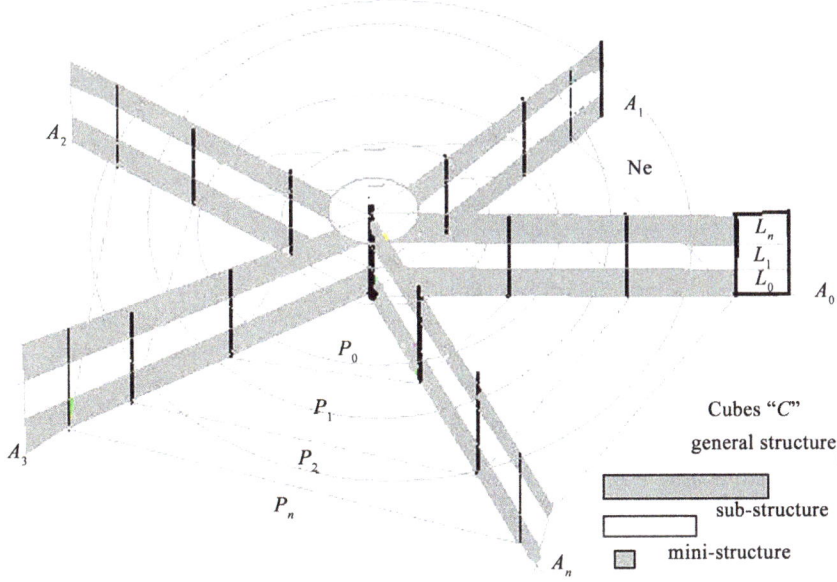

Figure 16. The cubes-coordinate coordinate space.

$$\text{Level } P_0 \ @ \dots\dots\dots @ \text{ Level } P_n \tag{24}$$

A_0: $S_{0:0:0:C(\alpha\beta)} = (A_0, L_0, P_0, C_{\alpha\beta}) @\dots\dots@ S_{0:0:\lambda:C(\alpha\beta)} = (A_0, L_0, P_\lambda, C_{\alpha\beta})$

$@$ $\qquad\qquad\qquad\qquad\qquad\qquad\qquad\qquad\qquad\qquad @$

$S_{0:1:0:C(\alpha\beta)} = (A_0, L_1, P_0, C_{\alpha\beta}) @\dots\dots@ S_{0:1:\lambda:C(\alpha\beta)} = (A_0, L_1, P_\lambda, C_{\alpha\beta})$

$@$ $\qquad\qquad\qquad\qquad\qquad\qquad\qquad\qquad\qquad\qquad @$

$\bullet$ $\qquad\qquad\qquad\qquad\qquad\qquad\qquad\qquad\qquad\qquad \bullet$

$@$ $\qquad\qquad\qquad\qquad\qquad\qquad\qquad\qquad\qquad\qquad @$

$S_{0:0:\lambda:C(\alpha\beta)} = (A_0, L_0, P_\lambda, C_{\alpha\beta}) @\dots\dots@ S_{0:1:\lambda:C(\alpha\beta)} = (A_0, L_1, P_\lambda, C_{\alpha\beta})$

$@$ $\qquad\qquad\qquad\qquad\qquad\qquad\qquad\qquad\qquad\qquad @$

A_1: $S_{1:0:0:C(\alpha\beta)} = (A_1, L_0, P_0, C_{\alpha\beta}) @\dots\dots@ S_{1:0:\lambda:C(\alpha\beta)} = (A_1, L_0, P_\lambda, C_{\alpha\beta})$

$@$ $\qquad\qquad\qquad\qquad\qquad\qquad\qquad\qquad\qquad\qquad @$

$S_{1:1:1:C(\alpha\beta)} = (A_1, L_1, P_0, C_{\alpha\beta}) @\dots\dots@ S_{1:0:\lambda:C(\alpha\beta)} = (A_1, L_1, P_\lambda, C_{\alpha\beta})$

$@$ $\qquad\qquad\qquad\qquad\qquad\qquad\qquad\qquad\qquad\qquad @$

$\bullet$ $\qquad\qquad\qquad\qquad\qquad\qquad\qquad\qquad\qquad\qquad \bullet$

$@$ $\qquad\qquad\qquad\qquad\qquad\qquad\qquad\qquad\qquad\qquad @$

$S_{1:0:\lambda:C(\alpha\beta)} = (A_1, L_\theta, P_\lambda, C_{\alpha\beta}) @\dots\dots@ S_{1:0:\lambda:C(\alpha\beta)} = (A_1, L_\theta, P_\lambda, C_{\alpha\beta})$

$@$ $\qquad\qquad\qquad\qquad\qquad\qquad\qquad\qquad\qquad\qquad @$

A_n: $S_{n:0:0:C(\alpha\beta)} = (A_n, L_0, P_0, C_{\alpha\beta}) @\dots\dots@ S_{n:0:\lambda:C(\alpha\beta)} = (A_n, L_0, P_\lambda, C_{\alpha\beta})$

$@$ $\qquad\qquad\qquad\qquad\qquad\qquad\qquad\qquad\qquad\qquad @$

$S_{n:1:1:C(\alpha\beta)} = (A_n, L_1, P_0, C_{\alpha\beta}) @\dots\dots@ S_{n:1:\lambda:C(\alpha\beta)} = (A_n, L_1, P_\lambda, C_{\alpha\beta})$

$@$ $\qquad\qquad\qquad\qquad\qquad\qquad\qquad\qquad\qquad\qquad @$

$\bullet$ $\qquad\qquad\qquad\qquad\qquad\qquad\qquad\qquad\qquad\qquad \bullet$

$@$ $\qquad\qquad\qquad\qquad\qquad\qquad\qquad\qquad\qquad\qquad @$

$S_{\theta:\lambda:C:\alpha\beta} = (A_n, L_\theta, P_\lambda, C_{\alpha\beta}) @\dots\dots@ S_{n+1:\theta+1:\lambda+1:C:\alpha+1\beta} = (A_{n+1}, L_{\theta+1}, P_{\lambda+1}, C_{\alpha+1\beta})$

Finally, the cubes-coordinate space shows a general function, where the dependent variable is identify by the national economy base "N_e". The N_e is the final result from ten macroeconomic structures. It is based on link of all macroeconomics structures ($S_0, S_1,\dots, S_n$) under different axes ($A_1, A_2,\dots, A_n$), levels ($L_1, L_2,\dots, L_n$), perimeters ($P_0, P_1, P_2\dots P_n$) and Cubes with different sizes and colors ($C_{0/\beta}, C_{1/\beta\dots} C_{n/\beta}$) in the same sub-coordinate space respectively, it is shown in Expression 25:

$$/\Delta N_e/ = [/\Delta A_o/ \ @ \ /\Delta A_1 / \ @ \ \dots@ \ /\Delta A_n/] \tag{25}$$

6. Introduction to Econographication

The Econographication is originated by the necessity to generate an alternative and specialized multidimensional graphical modeling for economics, business and finance. In fact, the Econographication main objective is focused on the research, develop and application of multidimensional coordinate spaces to generate different types of multidimensional graphs. Therefore, Econographication will maximize the uses of multi-dimensional graphs to minimize difficulties in the process of meta-database storage and multi-variable data behavior visualization. Hence, the Econographication is defined "*as a multi-dimensional graphical modeling theoretical framework can be applied on economics, as well as finance and business.*"

Additionally, the Econographication is divided into three large research areas are multidimensional graphs design, multidimensional graphs application and multidimensional graphs simulations. The multidimensional graphs design research area can be 2-dimensional, 3-dimensional and multi-dimensional coordinate spaces under linear and non-linear graph systems, the same section is divided into four sub-sections are coordinate spaces, graphs, charts and diagrams design. The multidimensional graphs application research area are used by two types of data, there are real and experimental data under micro and macro-level analysis in the short and long run is shown in **Diagram 1**.

The last section is the multidimensional graphs simulations research area, it is divided in two sections are electronic and prototypes. In the case of the electronic area is based on the application and uses of software and solutions. The idea to include prototypes in the multidimensional graphs simulations is to facilitate the easy understanding in the teaching- learning-research process of multi-variable data visualization.

7. Concluding Remarks

Firstly, this research concludes that the 2-dimensional space shows certain limitations to visualize complex economic phenomena simultaneously in the same graphical space and time. Therefore, the multi-dimensional coordinate spaces are available to expand a multidimensional optical effect to visualize different complex economic phenomena in the same graphical space and time according to this research.

Secondly, the Econographication attempts to be an alternative graphical method focus to support the metadatabase

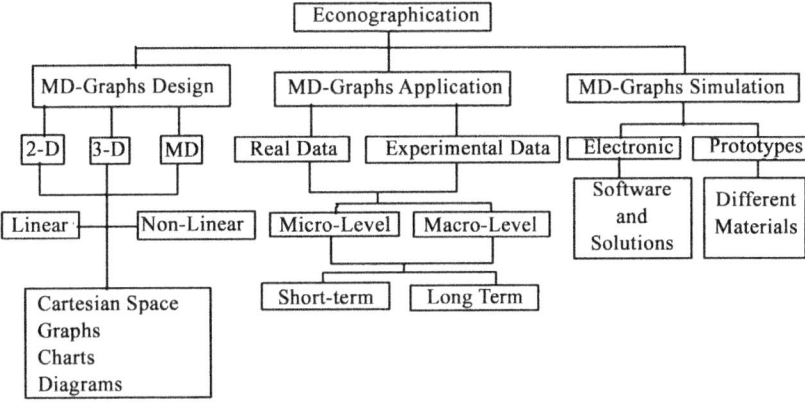

Source: Design by the author

Diagram 1. Econographication research areas.

storage and visualization of multi-variables data behavior, as well as finance and business. The main idea to build Econographication is to offer a new multi-dimensional graphs based on the application of alternative multi-dimensional coordinate spaces can facilitate the study of any economic, finance and business phenomena under macro-level and micro-level of analysis in the short and long run. In summation, the Econographication also will play important role in the research and teaching-learning process of economics through a series of new graphs methods and techniques that can be used by academics, researchers, economist and policy makers.

REFERENCES

[1]   J. Beniger and D. Robyn, "Quantitative Graphics in Statistics: A Brief History," *The American Statistician*, Vol. 32, No. 1, 1978, pp. 1-11.

[2]   W. Playfair, "Commercial and Political Atlas and Statistical Breviary (Original Version Was Published in 1786)," Cambridge University Press, Cambridge, 2005.

[3]   F. Edgeworth, "New Methods of Measuring Variation in General Prices," *Journals of the Royal Statistical Society*, Vol. 51, 1888, pp. 346-368.

[4]   W. Jevons, "On the Study of Periodic Commercial Fluctuations," Report of BAAS, Cambridge, 1862.

[5]   H. Maas, "William Stanley Jevons and the Making of Modern Economics," Cambridge University Press, Cambridge, 2005.

[6]   L. Lafleur, "Discourse on Method, Optics, Geometry, and Meteorology (Translation French to English from Rene Descartes-1637-)," The Liberal Arts Press, New York, 1960.

[7]   A. Cournot, "Mémoire sur les Applications du Calcul des Chances à la Statistique Judiciaire," *Journal des Mathématiques Pures et Appliquées*, Vol. 12, No. 3, 1838, pp. 257-334.

[8]   P. D. McClelland, "Causal Explanation and Model Building in History, Economics, and the New Economic History," Cornell University Press, New York, 1975.

[9]   G. Avondo-Bodino, "Economic Applications of the Theory of Graphs," Gordon & Breach Publishing Group, Newark, 1963.

[10] J. Hicks, "The Foundations of Welfare Economics," *Economic Journal*, Vol. 49, No. 196, 1939, pp. 696-712.

[11] A. Hansen, "Full Recovery or Stagnation?" W. W. Norton & Co., Inc., New York, 1938.

[12] P. Samuelson, "Foundations of Economic Analysis. US," Harvard University Press, Cambridge, 1947.

[13] L. Klein, "The Efficiency of Estimation in Econometric Models," Cowles Foundation, Yale University, Cowles Foundation Discussion Papers, No. 11, New Haven, 1956.

[14] A. W. Phillips, "The Relation between Unemployment and the Rate of Change of Money Wage Rates in the United Kingdom, 1861-1957," *Economica*, Vol. 25, No. 100, 1958, pp. 283-299.

[15] A. Okun, "Equality and Efficiency: The Big Tradeoff," *Journal of Economic Literature*, Vol. 13, No. 3, pp. 917-918.

[16] R. Solow, "A Contribution to the Theory of Economic Growth," *Quarterly Journal of Economics*," Vol. 70, No. 1, 1956, pp. 65-94.

[17] J. Nash, "The Bargaining Problem," *Econometrica*, Vol. 18, No. 2, 1950, pp. 155-162.

[18] J. Timbergen, "An Econometrics Approach to Business Cycle Problems, Impasses Economiques," Herman & C. Publisher, Paris, 1937.

[19] M. Friedman, "A Monetary and Fiscal Framework for Economic Stability," *American Economic Review*, Vol. 38, No. 3, 1948, pp. 245-264.

[20] R. Barro, "Rational Expectations and the Role of Monetary Policy," *Journal of Monetary Economy*, Vol. 2, No. 1, 1976, pp. 1-32.

[21] H. Poincarė, "The Foundations of Sciences: Sciences and Hypothesis, the Value of Sciences, Sciences and Method," The Sciences Press, New York, 1913.

[22] J. Brouwer,"Über den Natürlichen Dimensionsbegriff," *Journal für die Reine und Angewandte Mathematik*, Vol. 1913, No. 142, 1913, pp. 146-152.

[23] V. V. Fedorchuk, M. Levin and S. V. Shchepin, "On Brouwer's Definition of Dimension," *Russian Mathematic Survey*, Vol. 54, No. 2, 1999, pp. 432-433.

[24] E. V. Shchepin, "Topology of Limit Spaces with Uncountable Inverse Spectra," *Russian Mathematical Surveys*, Vol. 31, No. 5, pp. 191-226.

[25] A. Inselberg and B. Dimsdale, "Multidimensional Lines I: Representation," *SIAM Journal on Applied Mathematics*, Vol. 54, No. 2, 1994, pp. 559-577.

[26] A. Einstein, "Relativity: The Special and the General Theory," Three Rivers Press, New York, 1952.

[27] JSTOR: Journal of Economics Section. http://www.elsevier.com

[28] A. Marshall, "Principles of Economics," Macmillan and Co., Ltd., London, 1890.

[29] E. Schlicht, "Isolation and Aggregation in Economics," Springer-Verlag Publisher, Berlin, 1985.

[30] M. A. Ruiz Estrada, "Policy Modeling: Definition, Classification, and Evaluation," *Journal of Policy Modeling*, Vol. 33, No. 4, 2011, pp. 523-536.

[31] M. A. R. Estrada, "Econographicology," *International Journal of Economic Research*, Vol. 4, No. 1, 2007, pp. 75-86.

[32] M. A. R. Estrada, "Mulidimensional Coordinate Spaces," *International Journal of Physical Sciences*, Vol. 6, No. 3, 2011, pp. 340-357.

3

The Transmission Channels between Financial Sector and Real Economy in Light of the Current Financial Crisis a Critical Survey of the Literature

Georgios L. Vousinas
Department of Economics, Athens University, Athens, Greece

ABSTRACT

The present study undertakes a critical review of the research around the major issue of the transmission channels between financial sector and real economy. The aim of the study is to shed light on the interaction between the financial system and the economy, in the shadow of the current crisis. The literature documents the importance of these channels in the determination of economic activity and therefore, real economy as a whole. The study highlights the emergence of the liquidity channel as a key factor of the transmission of bank credit shocks to real economy and underlines the existing "regulation gaps". The paper concludes that the financial sector plays an even more crucial role these days and drastic measures along with intense supervision must be undertaken so as to work properly and serve the economic world.

Keywords: Transmission Channels; Bank Lending Channel; Financial Crisis; Regulation; Liquidity

1. Introduction

This literature review considers transmission channels between real and financial sector that potentially operate in both directions. Specifically, financial conditions are affected by the conditions in the real economy and in particular, households' and (financial and nonfinancial) firms' balance sheets and the conditions of households' and firms' balance sheets eventually affect real economic activity. The theoretical research on the linkages between the real and the financial sector is dominated by classic macroeconomic theory. Specifically, weaker macroeconomic conditions reduce the revenues and profits of businesses (including banks) and the incomes of households, which results in households' and businesses' net worth increasing more slowly or in some cases even decreasing. An additional implication of reduced business revenues and household profits is that it increases borrower default probabilities, which in turn affects bank losses and thereby bank balance sheets. The theoretical literature on the linkage that runs from the financial to the real sector represents the lion's share of the literature on real and financial sector transmission channels. At this point it must be highlighted that the interactions that exist between financial variables (such as interest rates) and real variables (such as consumption or investment), which arise purely from the intertemporal aspect of households' and firms' spending decisions—rather than as a result of any financial friction—do not constitute a financial and real sector transmission channel. For example, the permanent income model of consumption notes the relevance of the discounted value of a household's stream of future income in determining its current consumption. Because the appropriate discount factor for future income is the real interest rate, this results in the real interest rate, a nominally financial variable, influencing consumption. Similarly, in the neoclassical investment model, interest rates affect spending decisions because they represent the relevant variable for discounting future flows of capital rental income and/or depreciation allowances. It is important to note, however, that although these financial variables influence real activity in standard macro models of consumption and investment, there is no more than a trivial role for the financial sector. Indeed, the financial sector in these models serves only to transfer income across time; and it performs this role perfectly, without facing any of the financial frictions that in practice exist in the intermediation of credit. In studying the real and financial sector transmission channels, the major interests lie in understanding how informational asymmetries, incomplete markets, agency costs and costly contract enforcement, in conjunction with the financial sector's attempts to overcome these problems, influence the interactions between key financial and real sector decision variables that are absent from a standard, full-information, neoclassical model. This study reviews the existing literature that deals with these financial and real sector interactions. According to the theoretical literature, three channels have been identified to account for the transmission of shocks originating in the financial sector to the real economy and the amplification and retransmission, via the financial sector, of shocks originating in the real economy. The three channels, which broadly relate to the overall asset and liability position of either banks or their borrowers, are: 1) the borrower balance sheet channel; 2) the bank balance sheet channel; and 3) the liquidity channel. The following **Figure 1** summarizes the research findings through the identification of the aforementioned transmission channels.

The first two channels, which are often referred to as the financial accelerator [1], challenge the Modigliani-Miller view of the irrelevance of financing for a firm's (or for a bank's) investment decision. The borrower balance sheet channel and aspects of the bank balance sheet channel emphasise the influence of the net-worth or equity position of the borrower or bank on the credit conditions these agents face. Both balance sheet channels can arise as a result of capital-market frictions—such as information asymmetries, problems in contract enforcement and agency costs, while a specific bank balance sheet channel can also arise for banks as a result of regulatory requirements on bank capital. The third channel

emphasises the liquidity position of balance sheets and highlights the rigidities that can be present (either in all circumstances or at times of extreme stress) in altering balance sheet variables. These rigidities in turn then affect real economic variables. Interest in this channel has been fairly recent—in part, spurred on by the current crisis, and to date has been addressed for the most part in the context of banks.

2. The Borrower Balance Sheet Channel

The borrower balance sheet channel, which applies to both firms and households, stems from the inability of lenders
- to assess fully borrowers' risks and solvency
- to monitor fully their investments
- to enforce fully their repayment of debt

This leads lenders to require specific collateral for borrowing, which in fact means that the equity position of the borrower influences their access to credit funds. There are two broad classes of borrower balance sheet models in the literature. In the first class of models, which is associated with Bernanke and Gertler [2] and Carlstrom and Fuerst (1997), borrowers face an "external finance premium", which refers to a positive wedge between the costs of externally and internally raised funds. This wedge typically depends inversely on borrowers' creditworthiness. This means that the worst the solvency of the borrower the bigger the premium required and inversely, which in turn is tied to borrowers' net worth. The external finance premium arises from the fact that borrowers have an incentive to take on greater amounts of risk than are in lenders' interest, and lenders have limited means in order to restrict the amounts of risk that borrowers desire. Involving borrower net worth in the financing of a project is, however, one way to align more closely the risk-taking incentives of borrowers and lenders since doing so means that borrowers, along with lenders, will face similar losses in case of a project failure. Thus, the greater the net worth of the borrower, the lower is the premium required by the lender. This means that any kind of shock that affects net worth (such as a financial shock or a shock to aggregate demand that weakens firm profits and household income and in turn net worth) will affect the borrower's cost of financing, which (via standard user-cost or interest rate channels) will then affect the volume of expenditures that borrowers ultimately desire to undertake and thereby aggregate demand. Net worth is affected by shocks to aggregate demand and the real economy, which means that the presence and the properties of the external finance premium serve to propagate shocks to the real economy and amplify business-cycle fluctuations, hence the channel's name, the financial accelerator. In addition, financial shocks, such as fluctuations in asset prices also affect borrower

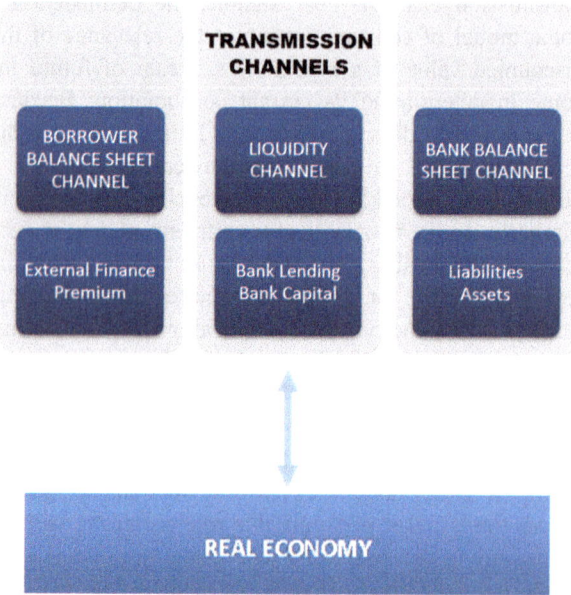

Figure 1. Table of research findings.

net worth, which means that the external financial premium also transmits financial shocks to the real economy. The second class of borrower balance sheet or financial accelerator model is associated with the work of Kiyotaki and Moore [3]. In this model, assets play a dual role in the economy, in that they are used to produce goods and services and to provide collateral for loans. The need for collateral in these models arises from the fact that lenders cannot force borrowers to repay their debts unless the latter are secured. These problems of debt-contract implementation create interactions between credit limits and asset prices through both a static, within-period multiplier and a dynamic, inter-temporal multiplier. Any financial shock leading to a fall in asset prices will tighten the collateral constraint, which in turn lowers production and spending and depresses asset prices farther. Note also that because reduced production and spending stemming from shocks to the real sector also depress asset prices, shocks to the real economy can also be propagated via this mechanism. Borrower collateral also plays a key role in Holmström and Tirole's [4] financial accelerator model, which allows for both intermediated credit (offered by banks) and non-intermediated credit (offered by investors). In this model, non-intermediated credit is less costly for borrowers, because it does not involve any monitoring, although it requires that greater collateral be offered by borrowers. If borrowers have insufficient collateral to obtain non-intermediated credit from investors, they must obtain credit from banks. This lending requires costly monitoring, which up to some point banks recoup by charging a higher cost of funds to borrowers. However, banks also have limited capital, which places a limit on their ability to monitor, so that borrowers with very low collateral are unable to obtain any type of credit. Adverse shocks to borrower collateral, which Holmström and Tirole call a "collateral squeeze", produce higher funding costs along with some borrowers failing to obtain credit, where the effects are most severe for poorly capitalised borrowers. Both of these effects restrain expenditure and result in lower aggregate demand.

3. The Bank Balance Sheet Channel

The bank balance sheet channel can be divided into two separate components: the traditional bank lending channel and the bank capital channel. Both channels recognise that adverse shocks to financial institutions' balance sheets, which may arise from changes in monetary and regulatory policy or bank capital losses, can entail sharp contractions in credit and result in such shocks having magnified effects on economic activity. One condition necessary for such amplified effects to occur is for some borrowers to be highly dependent on banks for credit. This dependence implies that if the supply of bank loans is severely disrupted, these borrowers, while not com-

pletely cut-off from credit, face indeed sizable difficulties and costs in finding and forming relationships with new lenders, and these results in these borrowers having to curtail their expenditures. Another condition that causes adverse bank balance sheet shocks to have amplified effects on economic activity is the inability of banks to fully insulate their supply of lending in response to such shocks. In the traditional bank-lending channel framework, monetary policy shocks have effects on the cost and availability of credit which go beyond the traditional effect through interest rates. In particular, when the latter of the two above conditions is met, both sides of banks' balance sheets contract in response to a negative monetary shock. On the liability side, a monetary policy tightening decreases money supply and money demand, which is the standard effect of monetary policy. On the asset side, it entails a change in the asset composition, leading to a stronger decline in credit supply, which is the lending channel [5]. Moreover, through the condition of high dependence on banks for credit, borrowers must reduce their real spending after a tightening in credit conditions by banks. This analysis can also be applied to other types of shocks such as bank capital losses. Recent developments in financial markets, most notably the emergence of private securitisation markets, have raised the question of whether the dramatic growth in securitisation has diminished the importance of the bank lending channel. For example, Nwogugu (2007) considers the interactions between capital reserve requirements and securitisation and shows that from a theoretical perspective the latter undermines the ability of the central bank's reserve requirements to limit the expansion of credit by commercial banks. The models discussed above assume that banks hold no capital and are entirely funded by external liabilities. Furthermore, there is no endogenous credit risk in these models (all loans are paid back), and so there is no room to analyse regulatory policy. Other models analyse why changes in banks' capital levels, which can arise for a number of reasons, influence the volume of loans that banks can extend, the bank capital channel. In Holmström and Tirole's [4] financial accelerator model, all bank lending is financed by capital, which provides the incentive for banks to monitor borrowers, and thereby overcome the moral-hazard problems present in borrowers' investment decisions. Consequently, a capital crunch will result in banks providing less credit to borrowers, where as was also the case with an adverse shock Another reason, noted by Stein [6], as to why bank capital can affect lending is directly analogous to the financial accelerator model discussed in the previous section, albeit for banks rather than households or firms. Specifically, the cost and availability of non-deposit funds for any given bank will depend on the perceived creditworthiness of the institution, which, like the borrower balance sheet model, is tied to bank capital. Intuitively, better capitalised banks are perceived to have stronger incentives to carefully underwrite and monitor loans and as a result are able to attract nondeposit funding at a lower cost. This implies that an external finance premium that depends negatively on bank capital is present for banks' non-insured financing. Since the external finance premium paid by banks is in turn reflected in the cost and availability of funds to bank-dependent borrowers a reduction in bank capital increases the cost of funds faced by banks and the cost of funds faced by borrowers and thereby constrains economic activity. As discussed by Van den Heuvel [7], a further reason why bank capital can affect lending stems from regulatory requirements. That is, due to regulatory capital requirements a bank's holding of capital places an upper bound on bank assets and thereby bank lending. Importantly, there are two conditions required for the bank capital channel to operate. First, banks should have no excess capital that can be used to buffer against shocks that deplete bank capital. And, second, the capital market is imperfect in that it is costly for a bank to raise capital. Any shock-financial or real that adversely affects bank capital will reduce banks' ability to extend credit, which in turn will restrain the volume of expenditures that the banks' borrowers can ultimately undertake. Shocks to aggregate demand, as well as conditions in real estate markets, may influence loan losses and, if not buffered by profits, can affect bank capital. In addition, changes in interest rates as well as changes to the slope of the yield curve, because they affect real activity and bank profits, can also affect bank capital. Van den Heuvel highlights the cushioning effect that above regulatory levels of bank capital have on this channel. In particular, he develops a dynamic model of bank asset and liability management in which interest rate shocks have a more delayed and amplified effect on lending by banks with depleted capital relative to banks that are well capitalised. That said bank capital is shown to affect lending even when the regulatory constraint is not momentarily binding, which implies that shocks to bank profits, such as loan defaults, can have a persistent impact on lending. Note also that financial sector shocks such as fluctuations in asset prices also affect banks' capital, which means that the bank capital channel also transmits financial shocks to the real economy. Basel II capital requirements have the potential to further exacerbate the effects of bank capital on lending and this has been a major source of concern in discussions on the impact of the revised regulatory framework for capital adequacy. As Lowe [8], Borio *et al.* [9], Altman and Saunders [10], and Goodhart *et al.* [11] all note, not only do worsening economic conditions deteriorate the actual bank capital ratio via the effect of loan losses on bank capital but in addition risk-weighted assets also rise. This

is because in downturns, credit risk, as measured by the borrower's probability of default (PD), loss-given-default (LGD) and exposure at default (EAD), typically increases thereby also increasing capital requirements, which under the Basel II framework are more closely tied to risk than under a "flat-rate" capital requirements framework, such as Basel I. Banks would therefore face much higher capital needs, while finding it more difficult to increase their capital because their profits and hence their capacity to build up reserves diminishes. Faced with these difficulties in raising new equity, banks would likely then de-lever their assets and reduce certain types of their assets—such as lending—which have higher risk weights. This would imply a reduction in the amount of credit extended to firms and households, which could in turn worsen the initial economic downturn. Conversely, during an economic upturn, banks holding excess capital would face much lower capital needs, expand credit further and fuel a credit-led boom. At present, this literature is largely empirical or simulation-based, although Jacques [12] presents a theoretical model that produces procyclical capital outcomes. The most common statistical model used by the literature for the examination of time series data, is the Vector Autoregressive (VAR) model. The VAR model has proven to be especially useful for describing the dynamic behavior of economic and financial time series and for forecasting.

4. The Liquidity Channel

The ongoing financial crisis has highlighted the importance of liquidity as an influence on banks' ability to extend credit and thereby on economic activity. In some cases, liquidity conditions merely influence the strength of existing real and financial sector transmission channels. In other cases, however, liquidity considerations create additional real and financial sector transmission channels. This point has long been established, although the recent crisis has led to an increased focus on these types of channels. High leverage ratios and large maturity mismatches in banks' balance sheets are a critical element in the propagation of funding liquidity shocks to bank lending and the real economy. Indeed these features of bank balance sheets and the adverse asset price spirals that they can engender were noted as early as Fisher [13], who described the strong links between distressed asset sales and banks' health. The basic mechanism is that given a liquidity or solvency shock, banks start to sell assets, which creates excess supply in asset markets and lowers asset prices. Falling asset prices in turn imply further asset sales (so as to meet resulting margin calls), which in turn means that a downward spiral in asset prices and balance sheet health sets in Diamond and Dybvig [14], in their seminal work on bank runs, also noted this mechanism while, more recently, Diamond and Rajan [15] stress the interaction and reinforcing effects of banks' liquidity shortages and solvency problems. Noting that because banks finance illiquid assets with short-term debt, Diamond and Rajan explain how aggregate liquidity shortages can emerge, such that if depositors (or liability holders more generally) unexpectedly demand payments (or are unwilling to roll over debt), banks can be forced to prematurely foreclose otherwise profitable loans. This can result in banks' facing sizable losses that will restrain future lending and at the extreme can drive contagious bank failures. In light of the current crisis, the literature has made the distinction between two types of liquidity: funding liquidity and market liquidity. Funding liquidity refers to the liability side of banks' balance sheets and can be defined as an institution's ability to get funding immediately, through asset sales or new borrowing, in order to meet payment obligations on debt at maturity. On the other hand, market liquidity refers to the asset side of banks' balance sheets and defines the ease with which an asset can be traded. In Diamond and Rajan, the presence of both funding and market liquidity can result in the anticipation of funding liquidity shortages inducing even healthy (*i.e.* liquidity ample) banks to refrain from lending. This occurs because the expectation of distressed banks being forced to sell (somewhat illiquid) assets in the future at fire-sale prices drives healthy banks to hoard liquid funds so as to allow them to take advantage of future investment opportunities. This mechanism appears to have been at work during the last financial market crisis. The presence of both funding and market illiquidity is an important feature of Brunnermeier and Pedersen [16]. These authors develop a formal model that links the market liquidity of a security and the funding liquidity of traders. The providers of market liquidity are traders—specifically, market makers, banks' proprietary traders and hedge funds—that act as intermediaries by buying and selling securities. In practice, the funding of traders impacts market liquidity and is itself also impacted by market liquidity, because traders are subject to funding constraints on their trading. In the model, funding liquidity risk is the risk of a binding funding constraint, which stems from the requirement that a trader must be able to finance all of his or her security positions at any point in time. While there are some differences in the definition of capital across the three major types of traders, the basic funding constraint is that total capital use must be smaller than the available net capital available plus available debt funding. When dealer capital is abundant, market liquidity is at its highest level and insensitive to marginal changes in capital and margins [7]. In contrast, when funding liquidity is scarce, traders become hesitant to acquire positions, especially capital-intensive positions that require high mar-

gins. As a result, market liquidity is lower. Moreover, low future market liquidity can increase the risk of financing trades, thus increasing margins. There are multiple competitive equilibriums in Brunnermeier and Pedersen's model under the (necessary and sufficient) condition that decreased market liquidity leads to either higher margin requirements or losses on dealers' existing positions. In the "liquid" equilibrium, markets are liquid, which leads to favourable margin requirements for dealers, which consequently helps dealers make markets liquid. In the "illiquid" equilibrium, markets are illiquid, resulting in larger margin requirements (or dealer losses), thereby restricting dealers from providing market liquidity. Once in this equilibrium, market liquidity becomes very sensitive to shocks due to two amplification mechanisms, so-called "liquidity spirals": the margin spiral and the loss spiral. During crises, decreases in market liquidity and funding liquidity are mutually reinforcing and produce either margin spirals or loss spirals. Margin spirals occur in the following way. A decrease in funding compels a dealer to provide less market liquidity. If margins increase as market liquidity decreases, the initial decline in funding tightens the dealers' funding constraint further, which in turn forces them to diminish their trading and so on, leading to a margin spiral. Loss spirals (asset price spillovers) occur along similar lines. The model explains the empirically documented features that market liquidity: 1) can suddenly dry up (*i.e.* is fragile); 2) has commonality (is correlated) across securities; 3) is related to volatility; 4) experiences flight to liquidity events; and 5) co-moves with the market. Cifuentes, Ferrucci and Shin (2005) show that mark to market accounting may turn out to be a channel for contagion and systemic risk. They analyse mark to market accounting in a model with regulatory solvency requirements and internal risk controls of banks. When a shock in the market reduces the market value of banks' assets, banks may be forced to sell parts of their assets in order to satisfy regulatory solvency requirements and/or internal risk limits. This causes market prices, and hence the market values of banks' assets, to decrease further when markets cannot perfectly absorb asset sales. The authors show that regulatory minimum liquidity requirements can mitigate this mechanism and hence also systemic risk. Wagner [17,18] explores the implication of a lack of market liquidity in times of stress. On the one hand, a lack of market liquidity implies that asset sales to meet liquidity demands lower asset prices even further, which can lead to the failure of other institutions. On the other hand, low market liquidity increases the cost of failure for individual firms, the more so, the larger the number of banks that fail. Hence, a bank's returns, as well as the negative externalities arising when it fails, will depend on the entire return distribution of the other banks' portfolios. An optimal regulatory regime has to take this into account and banks which are more correlated with each other should face higher capital and/or liquidity requirements. At the margin, commercial and universal banks expand and contract their balance sheets by borrowing in the repo market and in unsecured money markets. Such expansion and contraction of balance sheets is primarily constrained by regulation and credit-rating considerations. For example, when the haircut on AAA-rated mortgages is 5%, an intermediary can obtain a leverage of 20:1. When haircuts increase to 20%, the intermediary is forced to unwind as leverage has to drop to 5:1. Adrian and Shin [19] provide a micro foundation for the determination of total leverage. In a macro-setting, Kiyotaki and Moore provide a general equilibrium analysis of the value of assets as collateral. The interlinkages between funding liquidity and market liquidity can become a crisis-propagation channel in the presence of incomplete markets and asymmetric information. This is because in the face of such interlinkages, the absence of a complete set of contingent securities (which implies that it is not possible to hedge against future liquidity outcomes) combined with information asymmetries about the solvency of the banks (which implies that it is not possible to distinguish whether a bank is illiquid or insolvent), may stimulate fears of counterparty credit risk [20-22] belong to this literature. Another important topic concerning the liquidity channel is the relationship between the use of leverage by institutions and liquidity problems. Gromb and Vayanos [23] model financial market liquidity as provided by financially constrained arbitrageurs. They show that arbitrageurs, who depend on external capital (the so called "smart money") and undertake leveraged transactions, provide liquidity to the market and also cause liquidity dry-ups. Market liquidity increases with the level of arbitrage capital (that is, internal money), as well as external "smart money" that arbitrageurs can access frictionlessly. They show that liquidity dry-ups follow periods of low returns for arbitrageurs' risky investment opportunities and that liquidity is correlated across markets. Their welfare analysis shows that arbitrageurs may fail to take socially optimal positions (social welfare) in their investments, thereby adversely affecting their ability to provide market liquidity. This liquidity channel arises from their failing to internalise the price effects of their investment decisions. Acharya and Viswanathan [24] propose a model that explains the deleveraging phenomenon observed in the current crisis in terms of the agency problem confronted by leveraged institutions. They consider a moral hazard setup wherein leveraged institutions have incentives to take on excessive risks and are thus rationed when they attempt to roll over their debt. Institutions can sell assets to alleviate rationing. Liquidated assets are purchased by non-rationed institutions but their

borrowing capacity is also limited by the same principal-agent relationship. The market-clearing or liquidation price exhibits cash-in-the-market pricing. When a large number of firms are liquidating assets, the market price will be below the expected discounted cash flow and asset prices will thus depend on the entire distribution of leverage in the economy. The distribution of leverage and its form as rolled-over debt is derived endogenously, with each institution's choice of leverage affecting the difficulty of other institutions in rolling over their debt in the future. The model provides an agency-theoretic linkage between market liquidity and funding liquidity and formalises the deleveraging of financial institutions observed during crises. It also explains the role played by system-wide leverage in generating deep discounts in prices when adverse asset-quality shocks occur following a period of good times. Adrian and Shin point out another new feature of the current economic crisis, namely, that securitisation increased the importance of broker-dealers in the credit supply chain. They note that the growth of leveraged financial intermediaries that mark to market synchronises responses and increases feedback effects on the real economy. Financial stress may make it difficult to raise equity, in which case reducing leverage becomes synonymous with asset disposal. Increases in interest rate shocks or declines in asset prices can instigate the deleveraging cycle. Adrian and Shin also argue that because their liabilities are short-term, broker-dealers give a better signal of marginal funding conditions than commercial banks. Their findings also suggest that changes in the balance sheets of security broker-dealers help explain future real activity, especially for housing investment and durable goods consumption that are sensitive to credit supply. They find that the presence of broker-dealers leads to a faster and larger drop in housing investment in response to a Fed funds target increase, but also a quicker recovery. With their results in mind, one of the implications of the disappearance or conversion of all five major independent investment banks in the autumn of 2008 is that it signalled the severity of the approaching real sector storm, but also that their absence from the market could lengthen the time to recovery.

5. Conclusions

As perceived by the aforementioned, the meaningful issue of the transmission channels between financial sector and real economy stands in the foremost of the scientific attention over the last years and especially during the current financial crisis. The research literature has recognized three major channels concerning the transmission of shocks between financial sector and real economy, focusing on the two sides of balance sheets, assets and liabilities. These are the borrower balance sheet channel,

The Transmission Channels between Financial Sector and Real Economy in Light of the Current Financial Crisis a Critical Survey of the Literature

33

the bank balance sheet channel and the newly liquidity channel.

The emergence of the liquidity channel in times of economic recession as a key term in the equation of the transmission channels, has given food for extensive research and analysis in order to shed light on its shadow areas. The findings so far concentrate exclusively on banks but it is crucial for the research to deal with the non-bank systemic financial institutions whose failure have a large impact on the broad financial system and therefore on banks' ability to lend. This paper notes significant changes in the functioning of the bank lending channel due to financial innovation and changes in banks' business models. In comparison to earlier evidence, the paper documents that the standard bank-specific characteristics usually included in the literature (such as size, liquidity, capitalization) are not able to fully capture the functioning of the new dimensions of the bank lending channel. An important result is that the type of funding is a key element to assess banks' ability to withstand adverse shocks: short-term funding and securitisation activity seem to be particularly important in this respect. The amount of investment banking and other fee-based activities is also a relevant factor influencing the transmission mechanism. Banks with a high amount of more profitable but also more volatile non-interest income activities supplied more lending prior to the crisis but also limited credit to borrowers by more during the crisis. These results also hold when we account for weak supervision of financial activities by regulators. An important question in this respect is whether such changes in the transmission mechanism will remain in the near future or will tend to disappear as the crisis subsides. The functioning of the monetary transmission mechanism will be influenced by future developments in the securitization and regulation of financial intermediaries. For example, a dry-up in the securitization market will affect banks' possibilities to raise funds from the financial market and hamper their ability to respond to changes in loan demand in case of a monetary tightening. The bank lending channel will also be influenced by tighter regulation within the bounds of the new global regulatory standard by the Basel Committee on Banking Supervision (Basel III), that strengthen bank capital requirements and introduce new regulatory requirements on bank liquidity and bank leverage. A very important measure in this way is the introduction of Net Stable Funding Ratio, which is a global minimum liquidity standard for internationally active banks that includes a 30-day liquidity coverage ratio requirement underpinned by a longer-term structural liquidity ratio. Higher minimum capital and liquidity requirements, such as the above, will at least in the short-term, increase banks' funding costs thereby reducing their credit supply. By harnessing banks' capital and

liquidity positions, the new financial regulations are also likely to shore up banks' soundness lowering banks' risk premium as required by financial markets' investors on their long-term debt funding. While it is difficult to measure accurately the net benefit of new financial regulations, their impact on banks' profitability and cost of funding will have for sure an effect in the functioning of the bank lending channel in the years to come. Some very important conclusions can be derived from the paper. First of all, the stronger effectiveness of monetary policy detected during the crisis period has to be considered temporary against the backdrop of two concurrent factors: low interest rates and the use of unconventional monetary policy. Very low interest rates, close to the zero bound can be deemed a concern as they create distortions in the allocation of savings and investments. Under specific circumstances they can also raise the macroeconomic risks of approaching a deflationary trap [25,26]. The use of unconventional monetary policies aims at improving the impact of systemic risks in financial markets and provisional in nature. On the contrary, a prolonged period of excessive liquidity could distort manager decisions on long-term projects that are highly sensitive to interest rates. Indeed, the recent experience in Japan has illustrated how low policy rates contributed to "ever-greening" policies i.e. the roll over of non-viable loans [27]. Similarly, an asymmetric monetary policy response of cutting rates sharply when the economy is in trouble and not raising them quickly enough when it recovers gives the financial sector fewer incentives to worry about future credit or liquidity risks causing a classic moral hazard problem. Another policy implication is that monetary policy is not fully neutral from a financial stability perspective. Deregulation and financial innovation have made banks much more dynamic and probably more subject to market conditions and financial instability bouts. From a policy perspective, this is bringing financial stability and monetary policy considerations much closer to one another particularly when compared to the past decade. Finally, from an operative perspective, the undoubtedly strong impact of banks' conditions in determining their loan supply calls for extending the statistical coverage and analysis of the banking sector by central banks. This would include detailed standardised and comparable microeconomic balance-sheet information on individual banks matched with borrowers' conditions (i.e. including banks' lending terms and conditions to individual borrowers). A very useful initiative in this respect would be the creation of comprehensive and standardised credit registers available to central bankers on a confidential basis. It would also incorporate a comprehensive coverage of banks' off-balance-sheet activities, which could better capture changing business models and financial innovation developments [28,29]. Difference in data protection laws could be however a difficult obstacle to overcome [30]. Furthermore, the closer link between financial stability and monetary policy considerations would call for a better knowledge of banks' incentives towards risk-taking. The systemic dimension of risk-taking could have a macroeconomic impact on the aggregate loan supply. It would also call for a widening of the perimeter of statistical data collection to include the incentives of non-bank systemic financial institutions whose failure could potentially have a large impact on the broad financial system and therefore on banks' ability to lend. All in all this calls for a more forward-looking and dynamic approach towards data collection by central banks, supervisory authorities and statistical offices in a way that risk-taking incentives of large financial players are better understood. The recent crisis has prompted the creation of a number of institutions in charge of monitoring and containing the emergence of systemic risks in a number of countries. The coordination of the collection and analysing of the type of data mentioned earlier in close cooperation with central banks would be useful for a careful quantification of bank supply constraints. More broadly this cooperation might be paramount for ascertaining an optimal policy action to prevent or buffer future financial crisis. At this point and following the above, it's considered necessary to share some thoughts about certain aspects of the current financial crisis. Specifically, the interest lies in two major questions: Why is it so important for the central banks to intervene? And what is the extent to which deregulation caused the current credit crunch? In response, the following answers are provided: The principal reason the central banks needed to intervene was to minimize the damage caused by a credit crunch and prevent the expansion of the financial crisis. In the author's view, they failed in both ways coming to the conclusion that deregulation was a major factor for the credit crunch. The supervision was inadequate due to the fact that relied excessively on the rating agencies (Fitch, Moody's and S&P) as a benchmark and avoided systematically the intervention in markets in the name of consumer protection and the "free market". The authorities also failed to follow the financial innovations of the banking system with new entered products such as securitization, the evolution of CDS market and new lending technologies. In this direction, another important question arises on whether the regulatory structure should be extensively reorganized to meet with the new established standards. The current structure, which gives considerable authority to central banks, may still be the best model according to the author's opinion. Specifically, important synergies are developed in giving the authority for prudential supervision of banks, for consumer protection, for monetary policy and above all, for ensuring general financial stability. In this regard, it

might be better to focus on improving the central banks' future performance rather than restructuring the entire regulatory structure of our modern financial system, with attention to the analysis of systemic risks and the use of proper data. So it's in the authorities' hands to monitor the financial and banking conditions and intervene to the extent that every time is needed so as to ensure the proper functioning of the transmission channels and guarantee the systemic cash flows avoiding liquidity traps. Concluding, it is of major importance for the global financial system to confront to the same rules through common target policies of the central banks across the universe. The top economies of the world currently have different policies regarding the objectives of their regulation systems due to many reasons, but the financial crisis of our times has underlined the "chain effects" of shocks and proved that combined actions should be undertaken to prevent such situations. The authorities have to obey the same rules and that is a matter of strong political will and cooperation of the G-20 countries and the world organizations such as OECD and IIF, so as the economic system to work properly and in favor of the social welfare.

REFERENCES

[1]   B. S. Bernanke and M. Gertler, "Inside the Black Box: The Credit Channel of Monetary Policy Transmission," *Journal of Economic Perspectives*, Vol. 9, No. 4, 1995, pp. 27-48.

[2]   B. S. Bernanke and M. Gertler, "Agency Costs, Net Worth, and Business Fluctuations," *American Economic Review*, Vol. 79, No. 1, 1989, pp. 14-31.

[3]   N. Kiyotaki and J. Moore, "Credit Cycles," *Journal of Political Economy*, Vol. 105, No. 2, 1997, pp. 211-248.

[4]   B. Holmström and J. Tirole, "Financial Intermediation, Loanable Funds, and the Real Sector," *Quarterly Journal of Economics*, Vol. 112, No. 3, 1997, pp. 663-691.

[5]   B. S. Bernanke and A. S. Blinder, "Credit, Money, and Aggregate Demand," *American Economic Review*, Vol. 78, No. 2, 1988, pp. 435-439.

[6]   J. C. Stein, "An Adverse-Selection Model of Bank Asset and Liability Management with Implications for the Transmission of Monetary Policy," *RAND Journal of Economics*, Vol. 29, No. 3, 1998, pp. 466-486.

[7]   S. J. Van den Heuvel, "Does Bank Capital Matter for Monetary Transmission?" *Federal Reserve Bank of New York Economic Policy Review*, Vol. 8, No. 1, 2002, pp 259-265.

[8]   P. Lowe, "Credit Risk Measurement and Procyclicality," BIS Working Paper, No. 116, Basel, 2002.

[9]   C. E. V. Borio, C. Furfine and P. W. Lowe, "Procyclicality of the Financial System and Financial Stability: Issues and Policy Options," BIS Working Paper, No. 1, Basel,

The Transmission Channels between Financial Sector and Real Economy in Light of the Current Financial Crisis a Critical Survey of the Literature

35

2001.

[10] E. I. Altman and A. Saunders, "An Analysis and Critique of the BIS Proposal on Capital Adequacy and Ratings," *Journal of Banking and Finance*, Vol. 25, No. 1, 2001, pp. 25-46.

[11] C. A. E. Goodhart, B. Hofmann and M. Segoviano, "Bank Regulation and Macroeconomic Fluctuations," *Oxford Review of Economic Policy*, Vol. 20, No. 4, 2004, pp. 591-615.

[12] K. T. Jacques, "Capital Shocks, Bank Asset Allocation, and the Revised Basel Accord," *Review of Financial Economics*, Vol. 17, No. 2, 2008, pp. 79-91.

[13] I. Fisher, "The Debt-Deflation Theory of Great Depressions," *Econometrica*, Vol. 1, No. 4, 1933, pp. 337-357.

[14] D. W. Diamond and P. H. Dybvig, "Bank Runs, Deposit Insurance, and Liquidity," *Journal of Political Economy*, Vol. 91, No. 3, 1983, pp. 401-419.

[15] D. W. Diamond and R. G. Rajan, "The Credit Crisis: Conjectures about Causes and Remedies," *American Economic Review*, Vol. 99, No. 2, 2009, pp. 606-610.

[16] M. K. Brunnermeier and L. H. Pedersen, "Market Liquidity and Funding Liquidity," NBER Working Papers, No. 12939, 2007.

[17] W. Wagner, "Diversification at Financial Institutions and Systemic Crises," Tilburg University Center for Economic Research Discussion Paper, No. 71, 2006.

[18] W. Wagner, "The Homogenization of the Financial System and Financial Crises," *Journal of Financial Intermediation*, Vol. 17, No. 3, 2008, pp. 330-356.

[19] T. Adrian and H. S. Shin, "Liquidity and Financial Contagion," *Banque de France Financial Stability Review*, No. 11, 2008, pp. 1-8.

[20] F. Allen and D. Gale, "Financial Contagion," *Journal of Political Economy*, Vol. 108, No. 1, 2000, pp. 1-33.

[21] S. Brusco and F. Castiglionesi, "Liquidity Coinsurance, Moral Hazard, and Financial Contagion," *Journal of Finance*, Vol. 62, No. 5, 2007, pp. 2275-2302.

[22] P. Strahan, "Liquidity Production in 21st Century Banking", NBER Working Papers, No. 13798, 2008.

[23] D. Gromb and D. Vayanos, "Leverage and Liquidity Dry-Ups: A Framework and Policy Implications," 2008.

[24] V. V. Acharya and S. Viswanathan, "Moral Hazard, Collateral and Liquidity," Centre for Economic Policy Research, 2008.

[25] O. Jeanne and L. E. O. Svensson, "Credible Commitment to Optimal Escape from a Liquidity Trap: The Role of the Balance Sheet of an Independent Central Bank," *American Economic Review*, Vol. 97, No. 1, 2007, pp. 474-490.

[26] J. Bullard, "Seven Faces of the Peril," *Federal Reserve Bank of St. Louis Review*, Vol. 92, No. 5, 2010, pp. 339-352

[27] R. J. Caballero, T. Hoshi and A. K. Kashyap, "Zombie Lending and Depressed Restructuring in Japan," *American Economic Review*, Vol. 98, No. 5, 2008, pp. 1943-1977.

[28] T. Jappelli and M. Pagano, "Information Sharing in Credit Markets," *Journal of Finance*, Vol. 48, No. 5, 1993, pp. 1693-1718.

[29] T. Jappelli and M. Pagano, "Information Sharing, Lending and Defaults: Cross-Country Evidence," *Journal of Banking and Finance*, Vol. 26, No. 10, 2002, pp. 2017-2045.

[30] A. Matuszyk and L. Thomas, "The Evolution of Credit Bureaus in European Countries," *Journal of Financial Transformation*, Vol. 23, 2008, pp. 135-144.

4

Testing for Competition in the Nigerian Commercial Banking Sector

Rufus Adebayo Ajisafe[*]**, Anthony Enisan Akinlo**
Department of Economics, Obafemi Awolowo University, Ile-Ife, Nigeria

ABSTRACT

The study determined the degree of competition in the banking sector between 1990 and 2009 using Panzar and Rosse (PR) methodology. The data for the study were obtained from the annual reports and statement of accounts of fifteen commercial banks in Nigeria which were purposively selected for the study. The data collected were analysed using dynamic panel generalised method of moment estimation technique with fixed effect. The results of the analysis showed that the Nigerian commercial banks were characterised by monopolistic competition with H-statistic significantly different from zero for all sample periods and sub-sample periods. The value of H-statistic ranged between 0.0925 and 0.1168. The study concluded that the banking industry in Nigeria exhibited monopolistic competition which supports the results obtained from previous studies in the developed economies.

Keywords: Banking; Competition; PR Model; Dynamic Panel; H-Statistic

1. Introduction

The Nigerian banking system has experienced some fundamental changes since independence. At independence, the banking markets were dominated by a relatively small number of foreign banks. After about three and half decades, the number of banks expanded and the ownership structure diversified. Initially, it was dominated by the public sector banks, and later (1992 to be specific), the private sector banks became the dominant participants. As at this period, the government intervened in the banking markets to control resource allocation and promote the indigenization policy of the economy. The policies of financial repression pursued by the government directed at the Central Bank of Nigeria (CBN) during this period, was to control interest rates, volume and direction of credit in the economy [1].

Less attention has been paid to the issue of competition in the financial sector but such competition matters for a number of reasons. In the first place, the degree of competition in the financial sector can affect the efficiency of the production of services, the quality of products, and the degree of innovation in that sector. Secondly, it has been observed theoretically that the degree

of competition in the financial sector can affect the access of firms to external financing [2]. Also, less competitive banking can be more costly thereby lowering the quality of services which invariably reduces the effective demand for external financing and thus reduces growth. These effects may further vary by the degree of competition in the country over financial sector [3].

The impact of competitive and regulatory changes on banks can be judged by gross measures of performance (efficiency) such as profitability and failure rates, but how such changes can affect the efficiency with which banks transform resources into various financial services are of vital importance to the economists. The development in technology has shaped the way in which banks carry out their business. That is, a new and improved technology in the banking system is expected to reduce bank cost over time. This has facilitated development of new, more sophisticated financial products as well as the introduction of alternative delivery channels to the traditional branch network [3]. This in conjunction with deregulation has intensified the financial sector competition in the industrialized nation. The question that arises from the above is that: what is the degree of competition in the Nigerian banking sector? The study intends to know whether the recent legal and institutional reforms in the

---

[*]Corresponding author.

sector were sufficient to transform the market structure into a more competitive mode or whether there are still some serious obstacles inherited from the earlier system that prevent the realization of competition. Thus, the objective of this study is to determine the degree of competition in the Nigerian banking sector.

In the remaining part of this paper, Section 2 focuses on the literature review, Section 3 discusses the model used in the study; while Section 4 gives the result of the analysis and Section 5 concludes the study.

2. Literature Review

Replete of literature abound on the degree of competition in the banking sector among which are Prasad and Ghosh (2005), Panzar and Rosse (PR) (1987), Bikker and Haaf (2001) and Claessens and Laeven (2004) among others.

[4] analysed whether competition has yielded significant benefits in terms of greater product sophistication and cost reduction. This was done by examining the degree of competition in the Indian banking system for the period 1996-2004 and the two-sub periods, 1996-1999 and 2000-2004. The study was carried out with the perception that competition in Indian banking sector has increased since the introduction of the financial sector reforms in 1992. The estimated model used interest revenue and total revenue as dependent variables and employed PR methodology in its estimation due to its advantage of using bank specific data and hence captures the unique characteristics of different banks. The results point to monopolistic behaviour of banks across time periods and across bank groups, with a more robust H-statistic for the second sub-period and for private and foreign banks.

[5] argued that a higher degree of banking competition is a major issue for economic development and it is expected to provide welfare gains by reducing monopoly power of banks and cost inefficiencies, favoring the reduction of loan rates and then investment. The study used quarterly data for Czech banks, in order to provide evidence on the effects of banking competition in the Czech Republic. In the first place, the study measured the level and the evolution of banking competition between 1994 and 2005, using both the traditional IO approach and the new empirical IO approach. The traditional approach proposed structural test while the new empirical approach proposed the non-structural test. According to the traditional approach, competition was measured by concentration indices such as the market share of the five largest banks or the Herfindahl index calculated for total bank assets and loans. This approach suffers from the fact that they infer the degree of competition from indirect proxies such as market shares. The new empirical IO approach infers banks' conduct directly. The new ap-

proach also takes into consideration the measure of contestability. The approach therefore uses the Rosse-Panzar model which is a non-structural test to measure the degree of competition using the H-statistic which is the sum of the elasticities of total revenues to input prices. The authors find no improvement in banking competition during the transition period.

[6] examined competitive conditions and market structure in the banking industry, and investigate their interrelationship. That is, the study tested empirically the relationship between concentration and competition. Also, the study seeks to measure the degree of competition in the European banking markets. As a result of the deficiencies of the structural models, the study developed the non-structural models of competitive behaviour and applied the Panzar and Rosse (PR) model to measure the degree of competition without using explicit information about the structure of the market. The PR model assessed the elasticities of interest revenues with respect to changes in banks' input prices. In order to distinguish competitive behaviour on local, national and international markets, for each country, three sub samples were taken: small or local banks, medium-sized banks and large or international banks. For all the 23 countries considered in the estimation, the result showed the existence of monopolistic competition in the banking industry.

[7] examined what drives bank competition and was of the opinion that competition in the financial sectors matters for a number of reasons. They observed that the degree of competition in the financial sector can matter for the efficiency of the production of financial services, the quality of financial products and the degree of innovation in the sector. They used bank- level data, and applied the PR methodology of competitiveness to estimate the extent to which changes in input prices are reflected in revenues earned by specific banks in 50 countries' banking systems. The competitiveness measure was then related to indicators of countries' banking system structures and regulatory regimes. The study found out that systems with greater foreign bank presence and fewer activity restrictions in the banking sector were more competitive and that entry restriction on commercial banks could reduce competition. The study equally found out that more concentrated banks are more competitive. The above findings confirmed that contestability determines effective competition especially by allowing (foreign) bank entry and reducing activity restrictions on banks. While the result suggested that structure is less important for the competitive behaviour of the banking sector, it shows that competition policy in the financial sector is more complicated than perhaps previously thought. In part, this might be as a result of the financial service industries undergoing rapid changes, triggered by deregulation and technological advances. These changes have

made the definition of a financial market and any particular financial service more complex, and may have made market structure indicators less valuable measures of the competitive nature of financial systems. Developing proper competitiveness test and methodologies will remain an important area of research and policy focus.

[8] examined the effect of the changes in the structure of the Jamaican economy on the banking industry. This study is relevant as a result of the consolidation trend in the industry following the financial crisis during this period. It was observed that increase in market concentration has significant implications for the level of competition as well as the welfare of the customers in the banking sector. In analysing the changes in the level of concentration and competition in the banking industry over the period, the study used the Herfindahl-Hirschman Index. The results from the analysis revealed that there was a slight increase in competition following financial liberalisation. It is to be noted that after the financial crisis in the mid 1990s, the industry became more concentrated which might suggest that there was a decline in competition among the banks. However, as a result of the ambiguity in the result obtained from the structural model, the study used a more robust PR methodology to measure the market power of the industry. The result from this alternative methodology revealed that competition fell slightly immediately following the liberalisation period. Furthermore it was revealed that the hypothesis of monopoly and perfect competition were both rejected in favour of monopolistic competition for the entire sample period. The interaction term used in capturing the changes in market power over time indicated that there was a steady decline in competition throughout the specified sample period.

[9] assessed the degree of bank competition and discussed efficiency with regard to banks' financial intermediation in Ghana. In the study they applied panel data to variables derived from a theoretical model and find support for the presence of a noncompetitive market structure in the Ghanaian banking system, possibly hampering financial intermediation. The economic costs of the noncompetitive behaviour might have been exacerbated by the persisting domestic financing needs of the government, making it captive to the banks' behaviour and fostering inefficiency in the banking system. Also, large deficit financing through the issuance of treasury bills has not only crowded out the private sector in capturing banks investments, but has also put pressure on interest rates, thereby making access to bank lending even more difficult for the private sector thus hampering private sector development. Therefore, further private sector development appears to be very much dependent upon sound fiscal adjustment, and the possible link between fiscal policy and the efficiency of the banking sys-

tem should deserve further attention. The result of the study further indicated that consolidation of the Ghanaian banking sector is expected due to scale matters. Furthermore, barrier to competition on interest revenue is an indication that competition is stifled in the Ghanaian banking system. This could be as a result of the non transparent fee structure of the banks which help to shield the bank market structure from competition. Following from here, there is the need for further study in the area of competition and efficiency in the banking industry.

[10] analysed the competitive nature of the Tanzanian banking industry from 2004 to 2008. Utilizing a rich bank level data set, the study employed the PR methodology to compute the competitive index, taking into account risk, efficiency, regulatory and macroeconomic factors. The result showed that banks in Tanzania earned their income under conditions of oligopolistic conduct. Moreover, the competitive index derived from an interest revenue equation was not significantly different from that obtained using an aggregate revenue measure. This suggests that the degree of contestability from traditional intermediation activities approximates overall bank behaviour. The overall message is that greater market contestability can be achieved by adopting measures aimed at stimulating competitiveness in the banking sector, including consolidating gains on the macroeconomic front and allowing more foreign bank entry so as to increase the spread of banking services.

[11] investigated the degree of bank competition in the euro area, the US and UK before and after the recent financial crisis, and revisits the issue whether the introduction of EMU and the euro have had any impact on bank competition. The results suggested that the level of bank competition converged across euro area countries in the wake of the EMU. The recent global financial crisis led to a fall in competition in several countries and especially where large credit and housing booms had preceded the crisis. The result obtained showed that the degree of competition in the US and UK banking sector support monopolistic competition. This corroborate the work of [7,12] which applied this method to a large sample of countries, finding evidence of monopolistic bank competition with varying degree across .countries.

[13] assessed the degree of competition and relative efficiency of the FYR Macedonia's banking system—a sector which has undergone a substantial amount of change since the mid-1990s. In their analysis, PR methodology was adopted to test for the degree of competition using quarterly data for the period 2002-2005 for 20 commercial institutions in Macedonia. In general, the results obtained show that competition in the banking sector remains relatively weak.

From the literature review, it was observed that majority of the banks in various countries exhibited monopolistic competition. To buttress the above literature, [14] found monopolistic competition for New York banks, [15] in his study of European banking using data for 1986-1989 found monopolistic competition for Spain, UK, France, Germany and monopoly for Italy. Also, [16] using 1992-1996 data obtained monopolistic competition for France, Germany, Italy and the US. The degree of competition has been tested in the European area, US and to some extent in Africa but to the best of our knowledge, it has not been tested in the Nigerian banking sector. Thus, there is the need for the study.

3. The Empirical Model and Technique of Analysis

3.1. Empirical Model

To measure the degree of competition, the study adopted the methodology of Panzar and Rosse (1987). The PR methodology developed from a general equilibrium market model relied heavily on the premise that competition is measured by the extent to which changes in factor input prices are reflected in firms' equilibrium revenues [17]. Let us consider the revenue and cost relationship facing a particular bank:

Thus,

$$R_i = R_i\left(y_i, n_i, z_i^R\right) \tag{1}$$

$$C_i = C_i\left(y_i, w_i, Z^c\right) \tag{2}$$

Where:
R_i = Total revenue of bank i;
C_i = Total costs of banks i;
y_i = Output of the bank i;
n = Number of banks;
w_i = Vector of factor input prices of bank i;
z_i^R = is the vector of J exogenous variables affecting the revenue function;
z_i^e = is the vector of L exogenous variables affecting the cost function.

From Equations (1) and (2), profit is defined as:

$$\Pi_i = R_i\left(y_i, n_i, Z^R\right) - C_i\left(y_i, w_i, Z^c\right) \tag{3}$$

For profit to be maximized, marginal revenue must equal marginal cost [18]. Thus we differentiate Equation (3) with respect to the revenue and cost function and equate to zero as shown:

$$\Pi_i(.) = \frac{dR_i}{dR_i\left(y_i, n, Z^R\right)} - \frac{dC_i}{dC_i\left(y_i, w_i, Z^c\right)} = 0$$

$$R_i^1\left(y_i, n_i, Z^R\right) = C_i^1\left(y_i w_i Z^c\right) \tag{4}$$

From Equation (4), the profit maximization condition holds at the market equilibrium level.

Given that the profit maximizing output level representing the equilibrium value is defined as:

$$y_i^* = y^*\left(Z_i^R, w_i, Z_i^c\right) \tag{5}$$

Substituting Equation (5) into Equation (1) and assume that n is endogenously determined in the model, then Equation (1) becomes:

$$R_i^* = R^*\left(y_i^*, w_i, Z_i^R\right) \tag{6}$$

Equation (6) is the reduced form for revenues of the representative bank which is the product of the equilibrium output of bank i and the common price level.

It is important to note that market power is measured by the extent to which a change in factor input prices (∂w) is reflected in the equilibrium revenue (∂R^*) earned by the bank and the measure of competition defined as H-statistic formulated by PR evaluates the elasticity of total revenue with respect to changes in factor input prices [4,9,17].

$$H = \sum_{k=1}^{K}\left(\frac{dR_i^*}{dW_{ki}} \cdot \frac{W_{ki}}{R_i^*}\right) \tag{7}$$

where k is the number of factor input prices used, representing the price of capital, price of labour and price of fund respectively.

Empirically, if we write Equation (4) in mathematical form, and follow the work of [9] we have,

$$\text{Ln}\left(R_i^1\right) = \alpha_0 + \alpha_1 \text{Ln}\left(y_i\right) + \sum_{J=1}^{J} d_j \text{Ln}\left(Z_{ji}^R\right)$$

and

$$\text{Ln}\left(C_i^1\right) = \beta_0 + \beta_1 \text{Ln}\left(y_i\right) + \sum_{K=1}^{K} b_k \text{Ln}\left(W_{ki}\right) + \sum_{l=1}^{L} V_l \text{Ln}\left(Z_{li}^c\right) \tag{8}$$

The natural logarithms of the variables used in Equation (8) are taken, because it is assumed that, time series data have overall trends of exponential growth.

For profit maximizing bank, MR = MC, therefore Equation (8) becomes

$$\alpha_0 + \alpha_1 \text{Ln}\left(y_i^* + \sum_{j=1}^{J} dj \text{Ln}\left(Z_{ji}^R\right)\right)$$

$$= \beta_0 + \beta_1 \text{Ln}\left(y_i^*\right) + \cdots + \sum_{K=1}^{K} b_k \text{Ln}\left(W_{Ki}\right) + \sum_{l=1}^{L} V_l \text{Ln}\left(Z_{li}^c\right) \tag{9}$$

Rearranging Equation (9) and collecting the like terms gives

$$\left(\alpha_1 - \beta_1\right) \text{Ln}\left(y_i^*\right) + \sum_{j=1}^{J} dj \text{Ln}\left(Z_{ji}^R\right)$$

$$= \left(\beta_0 - \alpha_0\right) + \sum_{k=1}^{k} b_k \text{Ln}\left(W_{ki}\right) + \sum_{l=1}^{L} V_l \text{Ln}\left(Z_{li}^c\right) \tag{10}$$

$$Ln\left(y_i^*\right) = \left(\frac{1}{\alpha_1 - \beta_1}\right)\left(\beta_0 - \alpha_0\right) + \sum_{k=1}^{k} b_k Ln\left(W_{ki}\right)$$
$$+ \sum_{l=1}^{L} V_l Ln\left(Z_{li}^c\right) - \sum_{j=1}^{J} dj Ln\left(Z_{ji}^R\right) \tag{11}$$

Equation (11) is a mathematical representation of Equation (4) written in log linear form.

It could be observed from Equation (6) that the reduced form equation for the revenue function is the product of the equilibrium output of the bank and its common prices [9,18] written in logarithm form as shown in Equation (12).

$$Ln\left(R^*\right) = Ln\left(y_i^* w^*\right). \tag{12}$$

Operationalising Equation (12) gives:

$$Ln\left(R_{it}^*\right) = \alpha + \sum_{K=1}^{K} \beta_k Ln\left(W_{ki}\right) + \mu Ln\left(Y_i^*\right)$$
$$+ \sum_{q=1}^{Q} \rho Ln\left(Z_{qi}\right) + \varepsilon_i \tag{13}$$

where z is a vector of exogenous and Q bank specific characteristics without reference to their origin, either from cost or revenue functions. Y^* is a scale variable which represents the output of the bank i (Bank size), W_{ki} is a vector of factor input prices, representing the price of labour, price of capital and price of fund respectively and R^* is the equilibrium revenue scaled by the total asset of the bank. From Equation (13), we now evaluate our H-statistic, which is now defined as:

$$H = \sum_{K=1}^{K} B_k \tag{14}$$

where B_k represents the coefficients of the three dimensional factor input prices defined earlier on. The sign and magnitude of H-statistic matters in its interpretation. In a monopoly market structure, an increase in factor input prices (W_i) will increase marginal cost thereby reducing equilibrium output (Y^*) and invariably reduce the total revenue generated in that market. This implies that the value of H-statistic is less than or equal to Zero ($H \le O$). For a perfectly competitive market, an increase in factor input prices will increase marginal costs as well as average costs by the same proportion. This may not have any effect on the equilibrium output of banks. As a result, inefficient banks are forced out of the market. This made the remaining firms to face increased demand which eventually leads to an increase in output prices and revenue in the same proportion as costs. The value of H-statistic is then equal to unity ($H = 1$). In the case of monopolistic competition, an increase in input prices will lead to a less than proportional increase in revenue, as the demand for banking facing individual banks is inelastic. The value of H-statistic lies between 0 and 1 [8,9,17,19].

It has been observed that one of the assumptions of the methodology of Panzar and Rosse that makes it valid for further analysis is that, the banking sector is assumed to be in equilibrium. In line with this assumption, an equilibrium test will be performed using Equation (15) (see [3,7-9].

$$Ln\left(1 + ROA_{it}\right) = \alpha + \sum_{K=1}^{K} \beta k Ln\left(W_{ki}\right) + \mu Ln\left(Y_i\right)$$
$$+ \sum_{q=1}^{Q} \rho Ln\left(Z_{qi}\right) + \Sigma i \tag{15}$$

ROA is the unadjusted return on assets. $(1 + ROA)$ is used as the dependent variable instead of ROA for the sake of convenience, since it is believed that ROA can take on small or negative values. The result of the equilibrium test obtained from equation 15 is then tested using F-statistic that the sum of $E = \beta_1 + \beta_2 + \beta_3 = 0$.[1] The main reason for this test is to be sure that, in equilibrium, returns on bank assets should not be statistically correlated with input prices.

3.2. Techniques of Analysis

In order to estimate our models in Equations (13) and (15), each of the variables used in the model are tested for stationarity using panel unit root test [20-23]. This is necessary because of the nature of our time series data. It has been observed that most of our time series data are not stationary at levels and that the series are adequately represented by first difference [24].

[25] developed a procedure utilizing pooled cross section time series data to test the null hypothesis that each individual time series contains a unit root against the alternative hypothesis that each time series is stationary. As both the cross section and time series dimensions of the panel grow large, the panel unit root test statistic has a limiting normal distribution. They concluded that the use of panel unit root tests may prove to be particularly useful in analyzing industry—level and cross country data. It was also observed that the pooling approach or panel based unit root tests yields higher test power than performing a separate unit root test for each individual.

Various approaches have been used in performing panel unit root tests. This include: [23,25,26], Fisher-type tests using ADF and PP test, see [27-29].

In the process of estimating the models, we first employ the panel pooled least square estimate and then used the panel GMM to test for the robustness of the model. From Equation (13), we determine the degree of competition using the value of H-statistic, while Equation (15) is an equilibrium test used for the validity of H-statistic.

---

[1]β_1, β_2, and β_3 are the coefficients of the factor input prices w_1, w_2, and w_3.

3.3. Measurement of Variables

In this section, the variables used in the estimation of our models are given appropriate definition. They are defined as used in Equations (13) and (15): R^* is the equilibrium total revenue of the bank. It is proxied by the gross earnings scaled by the total assets of the bank. It is denoted by Geta in the model which represents the dependent variable. The total revenue of the banks is considered because the value of non-interest income has increased over the years. This view is supported among others by [4,9, 14]. In other to account for size differences, the total revenue is divided by total assets.

w_{ki} is a vector of factor input prices, representing the price of labour, price of capital and price of fund respectively. In the estimated model, w_1 represents the price of labour which is measured as a ratio of personnel expenses to total asset or personnel expenses as a ratio of number of employee. In this study, the ratio of personnel expenses to total assets is considered as our indicator because there are missing data for the number of staffs for many banks. w_2 represents the price of capital which is the ratio of capital expenses to fixed asset, while w_3 represents the price of fund which is the ratio of interest expenses to total deposits [2,8,17].

The output of the firm is measured by the amount of loans. The intermediation approach considers banks as financial intermediaries that convert deposits and borrowed funds into loans and investment. In this study, we consider only loan as our output variable which is measured in value terms. Other variables included in the study are bank specific factors which reflect differences in costs, size, risk, structure and product mix. The bank specific variables include: ratio of equity to total assets represented by r_1, ratio of loans to total assets represented by r_2, ratio of non-performing loans to total loans represented by r_3, the ratio of total deposit to total assets represented by TDTA, and total assets which is the scale variable represented by TA, controls for size of the bank and proxy for scale economies.

4. Empirical Results

4.1. Result of Panel Unit Root Test

The result of the Panel unit root tests are presented in **Tables 1** and **2** respectively. **Table 1** presents the result of the panel unit root test with individual effects while **Table 2** presents the unit root test with individual effects and linear trends. All the variables used in the estimation of our model are in their log form. The two results are reported for comparison purposes. It could be observed from the tables that all the variables are stationary at levels. That is, they are integrated of order zero $I(0)$. Given the unit root property of the variables, we then proceed to the estimation of our model across full sample and

Table 1. Panel unit root test with individual effects.

Variables	LLC	Im, PS	ADF	PP
Geta	−5.1866 (0.0000)*	−4.1368 (0.0000)*	70.2001 (0.0000)*	70.9097 (0.0000)*
w_1	−4.7746 (0.0000)*	−4.3085 (0.0000)*	69.9997 (0.0000)*	66.8623 (0.0001)*
w_2	−3.6826 (0.0000)*	−3.5804 (0.0002)*	65.2885 (0.0002)*	78.9850 (0.0000)*
w_3	−7.0522 (0.0000)*	−4.9593 (0.0000)*	79.8558 (0.0000)*	78.3564 (0.0000)*
r_1	−4.3766 (0.0000)*	−3.7849 (0.0001)*	74.8309 (0.0000)*	88.3325 (0.0000)*
r_2	−5.5761 (0.0000)*	−3.8708 (0.0000)*	68.7083 (0.0001)*	52.9294 (0.0060)*
r_3	−11.7358 (0.0000)*	−6.2662 (0.0000)*	141.079 (0.0000)*	53.0870 (0.0058)*
TDTA	−4.0040 (0.0000)*	−4.2909 (0.0000)*	74.6859 (0.0000)*	82.2604 (0.0000)*
TC	−4.5110 (0.0000)*	0.7085 (0.7607)	35.7271 (0.2171)	72.3450 (0.0000)*
TA	−2,7858 (0.0000)*	2.4463 (0.9928)	28.0932 (0.5655)***	35.1073 (0.2388)**
ROA	−5.3909 (0.0000)*	−4.4541 (0.0000)*	71.1317 (0.0000)*	71.3469 (0.0000)*

*1%; **5%; ***10%. This indicates rejection of null hypothesis of unit root. Probabilities for Fisher tests are computed using an asymptotic Chi-square distribution. All other tests assume asymptotic normality. LLC—Levin, Lin and Chu, Im, Ps—Im, Pesaran and Shin, ADF—Augmented Dickey Fuller, PP—Phillip Peron. The probability values are shown in parenthesis.

Table 2. Panel unit root test with individual effects and individual linear trends.

Variables	LLC	Im, PS	ADF	PP
Geta	−6.6115 (0.0000)*	−4.8454 (0.0000)*	75.7351 (0.0000)*	75.2799 (0.0000)*
w_1	−4.3564 (0.0000)*	−3.0586 (0.0011)*	58.0802 (0.0016)**	69.3816 (0.0001)*
w_2	−3.8412 (0.0000)*	−2.0077 (0.0223)**	45.7881 (0.0326)**	52.9538 (0.0060)**
w_3	−5.3098 (0.0000)*	−4.9991 (0.0000)*	79.0128 (0.0000)*	74.4125 (0.0000)*
r_1	−4.1658 (0.0000)*	−4.6474 (0.0000)*	71.8909 (0.0000)*	121.795 (0.0000)*
r_2	−5.5629 (0.0000)*	−3.9652 (0.0000)*	65.8378 (0.0002)*	42.1233 (0.0699)***
r_3	−2.3228 (0.0101)*	−3.3521 (0.0004)*	55.4353 (0.0032)**	95.3294 (0.0000)*
TDTA	−5.3857 (0.0000)*	−4.9420 (0.0000)*	75.8075 (0.0000)*	103.296 (0.0000)*
TC	−3.16775 (0.0008)*	−1.6474 (0.0497)**	41.8319 (0.0740)***	28.8452 (0.5257)
TA	−5.3588 (0.0000)*	−3.9667 (0.0000)*	67.6595 (0.0001)*	59.1609 (0.0012)*
ROA	−6.3775 (0.0000)*	−4.5513 (0.0000)*	69.6873 (0.0001)*	76.2273 (0.0000)*

*1%; **5%; ***10%. This indicates rejection of null hypothesis of unit root. Probabilities for Fisher tests are computed using an asymptotic Chi-square distribution. All other tests assume asymptotic normality. LLC—Levin, Lin and Chu, Im, Ps—Im, Pesaran and Shin, ADF—Augmented Dickey Fuller, PP—Phillip Peron. The probability values are shown in parenthesis.

sub-sample periods using both the pooled least square estimate and the GMM techniques.

4.2. Results of Competition in the Banking Industry

After the unit root test has been performed, and found out that our variables are stationary at levels, the model in equation 13 which is linear in its unknown parameters are then subjected to empirical investigation using panel data with fixed effects to account for any heterogeneity among the industry (banks) as well as to avoid specification problems. The common effect specification has been chosen for our model because the firms operating in the industry are country specific and they are likely to share the same characteristics. The model in Equation (13) is estimated using the Pooled Least Square and the result is presented in **Tables 3-5**.

It could be observed from the result presented that the banking sector in Nigeria exhibited a monopolistic competition over the entire sample period based on the value of H-statistic which lies between zero (0) and one (1). This is sufficed to say that the null hypothesis of perfect competition and monopoly is rejected at one percent level of significance, in favour of the alternative hypothesis, that the banking sector in the country is characterized by monopolistic competitive market. The Wald test performed on the significance of H-statistic showed that, it is statistically significant and different from zero and one with F-statistic of 29.5034 and 1688.343 at one percent (1%) respectively (see **Table 3**).

The results as presented in **Table 3** show that the price of loanable fund (w_3) is positively related to the gross earnings and contributed the highest portion of the H-statistic for the entire period (1990-2009). This was

Table 3. Pooled least square estimate with fixed effects (1990-2009).

Variables	Geta	
	Coefficient	t-statistic
C	0.651686	6.893248[*]
Log (w_1)	0.037949	2.664913[*]
Log (w_2)	0.018881	1.398503
Log (w_3)	0.059928	4.049425[*]
Log (TA)	−0.005801	−1.249893
Log (r_1)	0.018498	1.349923
Log (r_2)	0.005493	0.329003
Log (r_3)	−0.007859	−0.275876
Log (TDTA)	0.067172	2.212112[**]

([*]) Statistically significant at 1percent level. ([**]) Statistically significant at 5 percent level. Summary statistics: R^2 = 0.2671; F-statistics = 3.909 (0.000); DW = 2.1770; Schwarz criterion = −1.7768; H-statistics = 0.1168; F-statistic on Wald test for $H = 0$:29.5034, p value = 0.0000; F-statistic on Wald test for $H = 1$: 1688.343, p value = 0.0000; Ho: $H = 0$ (Monopoly); Ho: $H = 1$ (Perfect Competition); Ho: $0 < H < 1$ (Monopolistic Competition).

Table 4. Pooled least square estimate with fixed effects (1990-2004).

Variables	Geta	
	Coefficient	t-statistic
C	0.6236	4.1872[*]
Log (w_1)	0.0345	1.8181[***]
Log (w_2)	0.0156	0.9061
Log (w_3)	0.0584	2.8543[*]
Log (TA)	−0.0032	−0.46006
Log (r_1)	0.0325	1.5692
Log (r_2)	0.0011	0.0423
(r_3)	−0.0112	−0.2922
Log (TDTA)	0.0631	1.6388[***]

([*]) Statistically significant at 1percent level. ([**]) Statistically significant at 5percent level. ([***]) Statistically significant at 10 percent level. Summary statistics: R^2 = 0.1930; F-statistics = 4.1093 (0.0100); DW = 2.2673; Schwarz criterion = −1.4376; H-statistics = 0.1085; F-statistic on Wald test for $H = 0$:13.3222, p value = 0.0003; F-statistic on Wald test for $H = 1$:897.9538, p value = 0.0000; Ho: $H = 0$ (Monopoly); Ho: $H = 1$ (Perfect Competition); Ho: $0 < H < 1$ (Monopolistic Competition).

Table 5. Pooled least square estimate with fixed effect (2005-2009).

Variables	GETA	
	Coefficient	t-statistic
C	0.50201	6.1423[*]
Log (w_1)	0.0085	0.7188
Log (w_2)	0.0089	0.6715
Log (w_3)	0.0751	8.8101[*]
Log (TA)	−0.0036	−0.7155
Log (r_1)	−0.0064	−0.8355
Log (r_2)	0.0059	0.7473
(r_3)	0.0117	0.4226
Log (TDTA)	0.1029	4.88803[*]

([*]) Statistically significant at 1percent level. ([**]) Statistically significant at 5percent level. ([***]) Statistically significant at 10 percent level. Summary statistics: R^2 = 0.90; F-statistics = 14.3500 (0.0000); DW = 2.0176; Schwarz criterion = −4.516; H-statistics = 0.0925; F-statistic on Wald test for $H = 0$:31.7597, p value = 0.0000; F-statistic on Wald test for $H = 1$:3053.759, p value = 0.0000; Ho: $H = 0$ (Monopoly); Ho: $H = 1$(Perfect Competition); Ho: $0 < H < 1$ (Monopolistic Competition).

followed by the price of labour (w_1) which is positively significant with a value of 0.037949. This equally shows that labour is an important factor that influence the revenue earned by each bank. The coefficient of the price of capital (w_2) was positive but not significant and consistently lower than the coefficient of the price of labour and price of fund. The non-significance of the price of capital could be as a result of high operating expenses and heavy fixed cost incurred during the sample period. In respect of the other explanatory variables in the model, the ratio of equity to total asset (r_1) is positively related to the gross earnings (Geta). This implies that the banking industry in Nigeria supports risk taking in their portfolios in order to increase their earning capacity. It can be deduced that a higher level of risk capital leads to an increase in the gross earnings of the banking industry. The ratio of loans to total asset (r_2) is positively related to the gross earnings (Geta). The positive sign on the r_2 coefficient is expected because accumulation of more loans reflects more potential income through interest revenue. The ratio of non-performing loan to total loans (r_3) revealed a negative sign and is not significant. This shows that as the non-performing loan increases in value, the amount of income generated by the bank decreased. Total asset (TA) which is expected to have a positive relationship does not conform to a priori expectation. The result showed that total asset is negatively related to gross earnings. Total deposit as a ratio of total assets (TDTA) reported the right sign in its coefficient and statistically significant. This shows the importance of deposit in the balance sheet. As more deposits are received in the industry, the asset base of the industry expands, which eventually increase the income generated in the industry.

For robustness check, the time dimension of the sample period was divided into two, 1990-2004 and 2005-2009. The reason for the subdivision is to check whether there could be an improvement on the result, due to the reform introduced in the sector in 2004. **Tables 4** and **5** depict the result of the subsample periods for 1990-2004 and 2005-2009. The two periods represents the pre and post reform era in the Nigerian banking industry. The period 1990-2004 marked the period of bank liquidation while the 2005-2009 coincided with the period when Nigerian bank recapitalized which marked a serious reformation in the sector.

In the pre-consolidation era, the result obtained for the period is not encouraging. The result showed that the price of loanable fund is statistically significant and possessed the appropriate sign with t-statistic of 2.854. Also, it contributed the highest coefficient of the H-statistic with 0.0584. The value of the H-statistic as obtained from the table is 0.1085 which is statistically different from zero (0) and one (1). It shows that the banking industry in Nigeria for that period exhibits monopolistic competition which supports the result obtained from other studies (see [8,30,31]). To corroborate the significance of the H-statistic, the F-statistic obtained from the Wald test is highly significant at one percent with a value of 13.222 and 897.9538 for $H = 0$ and $H = 1$ respectively (see **Table 4**). Total deposit as a ratio of total asset (TDTA) is statistically significant at 10% level of significance with a value of 1.6387 and conforms to a priori expectation. Other factor prices (prices of capital and price of labour) also conform to a priori expectation but their contributions to gross earnings are very low, though not significantly different from the entire sample period. The price of labour is significant at 10 percent and increases the revenue earnings of the bank by about 0.04 percent. The low contribution of the factor inputs is due to the fact that most of the banks as at this period are weak in terms of capital inadequacy, violation of banking law, rules and regulations, and lack of proper management among others.

The result of the second sub-sample period (2005-2009) is presented in **Table 5**. The result shows that price of fund is statistically significant and conform to a priori expectation. The variable is significant because of the increase in the level of deposit in the banking industry as a result of the introduction of the reforms in the sector. The reform in the sector possibly led to the effective mobilization of saving for investment purposes, which ultimately boosted increased in the deposits of the banking sector. The price of capital and price of labour conform to a priori, but not significant. The value of the H-statistic is 0.09254 which is slightly lower than the pre consolidation period (1990-2004). It was observed from the result that all the variables follow the same trend as in the first sub sample period and the entire sample period (1990-2009). The ratio of deposit to total asset is highly significant in all the period which shows the importance of deposit in the banking industry.

4.3. Generalized Least Squares Estimation

One of the assumptions underlying Ordinary Least Squares Estimation (OLSE) is that the mean and variance are constant and that errors are uncorrelated with one another [23,27]. But when using cross section data, this assumption may not be true since it is possible for the variances of the observations to differ from each other. When this happens, we say that the random variable and the random error are heteroskedastic. The cross section heteroskedasticity allows for a different residual variance for different cross section (Eviews 7, pg. 304). To allow for a different variance for each bank, we estimate equation 13 using cross section weights. The result of the estimation is as shown in **Table 6**. The results in **Table 6** showed that all the independent variables are statistically significant and positively related to gross earnings (total revenue) of the banks with the exception of the scale variable (TA) which is negatively significant. The R^2 is very high with a value of 0.7278, meaning that the variation of the explanatory variable with respect to the dependent variable is about 73%. The F-statistic is also highly significant at 1% level. The Durbin Watson statistic is also close to 2, which show that there is no serial correlation among the variables. The result showed that bank specific characteristics or weights is very important in determining the relationship between the factor prices (price of labour, price of capital and price of fund) and the total revenue of the banks. Furthermore, the H-statistic value ranges between zero and one which supports the

Table 6. Pooled generalised least square estimate with cross section weight (1990-2009).

Variables	GETA	
	Coefficients	t-statistic
C	0.5955	16.5828[*]
Log (w_1)	0.0220	3.7758[*]
Log (w_2)	0.0159	3.1350[*]
Log (w_3)	0.0546	10.1115[*]
Log (TA)	−0.0067	−3.9357[*]
Log (r_1)	0.0182	3.7937[*]
Log (r_2)	0.0109	1.8186[***]
(r_3)	0.0010	0.1105
Log (TDTA)	0.0647	6.0822[*]

([*]) Statistically significant at 1percent level. ([**]) Statistically significant at 5percent level. ([***]) Statistically significant at 10 percent level. Summary weighted statistics: R^2 = 0.7279; F-statistics = 28.6965 (0.0000); DW = 1.8093; H-statistics = 0.0925; F-statistic on Wald test for $H = 1$:1329.01, p value = 0.0000; *Ho*: $H = 0$ (Monopoly); *Ho*: $H = 1$(Perfect Competition); *Ho*: $0 < H < 1$ (Monopolistic Competition).

Table 7. Panel generalised method of moments with fixed effects.

VARIABLES	GETA	
	Coefficients	t-statistic
GETA (−1)	0.0790	1.2562
Log (w_1)	0.0181	2.1300[**]
Log (w_2)	0.0128	1.7237
Log (w_3)	0.0599	8.0387[*]
Log (TA)	−0.0090	−3.2110[*]
Log (r_1)	0.0097	1.2018
Log (r_2)	0.0145	1.4259
(r_3)	−0.0021	−0.0856
Log (TDTA)	0.0828	4.3367[*]

([*]) Statistically significant at 1percent level. ([**]) Statistically significant at 5percent level. ([***]) Statistically significant at 10 percent level. J-statistic = 115.8269; Instrument rank = 148; H-statistics = 0.0908; F-statistic on Wald test for $H = 0$:33.9453, p value = 0.0000; F-statistic on Wald test for $H = 1$: 4706.536, p value = 0.0000; *Ho*: $H = 0$ (Monopoly); *Ho*: $H = 1$ (Perfect Competition); *Ho*: $0 < H < 1$ (Monopolistic Competition).

previous results of monopolistic competition with a value of 0.092592. The F-statistic obtained from the Wald test showed that the null hypothesis of $H = 0$ and $H = 1$ are rejected at one percent level of significance with a value of 138.3748 and 13290.01 respectively.

4.4. Generalized Method of Moment Estimates (GMM)

As a robustness check, we estimate Equation (13) using the Generalised Method of Moment (GMM) estimation technique. A fundamental assumption of regression analysis is that the right hand side of a model is uncorrelated with the disturbance term. If this assumption is violated, both ordinary least square and weighted least square are biased and inconsistent. Where the right hand side is correlated with the residual, instrumental variable regression can be estimated. One of the approaches adopted is the use of Generalized Method of Moments (GMM). GMM generally account for heteroskedasticity and serial correlation between exogenous variables and the disturbance term. The GMM specification used in this study is based on orthogonally condition between a function and instruments. The study employed the Arellano-Bond estimation with lagged endogenous variable and cross section fixed effect. In the study, period specific predetermined instruments were used to indicate that the number of instruments expand dynamically over time. Aside, the technique allows us to relax the assumption of strict exogeneity of pooled least square estimation technique.

The results of the Generalised Method of Moment (GMM) estimate is reported in **Table 7** for the full sample period (1990-2009) which confirmed the result of the generalized least square estimate in **Table 6**. The factor prices: price of labour (w_1), price of capital (w_2) and price

of fund (w_3) are all significant and conform to a priori expectation. The price of fund is positive and significant with a t-value of 8.0387 and coefficient value of 0.059930. The price of capital is also significant at 10% with a t-value of 1.7237 and coefficient value of 0.012838 while the price of labour is also positive and significant with a t-value of 2.1300 and coefficient value of 0.018054. The lagged endogenous variable (Geta) is positively related not significant. It shows that the revenue earned by the bank in the previous period is positively related to the revenue earned in the current period, but with little impact on the total revenue. All other variables follow the trends observed in **Table 3**. Moreover, from the result in **Table 7**, the value of our H-statistic is 0.0908, which is the sum of elasticities of banks equilibrium revenue with respect to the factor input prices, that is, the sum of the coefficients of price of labour, price of capital and price of funds as shown in Equation (14). This value confirmed the result of the other H-statistic obtained in this study. This means that commercial banks in Nigeria is characterised by monopolistic competition but the level of competition is too low as observed by [30] which reports a low H-statistic for Austria (0.154) and Denmark (0.050). The price of fund (w_3) contributed the highest value of the H-statistics which support the Pooled OLS and generalized least square estimate.

From the result of our H-statistic, it could be observed that the result is consistent with previous studies which support monopolistic competition. Furthermore, our results also support the fact that, price of capital contributes minimally to total revenue when compared to other input prices. This is the least important component of H-statistics see [8,15]. The values of the J-statistic and instrument rank showed that the instrument used is valid since the value of the instrument rank (148) is greater than the number of estimated coefficient (9). The J-statistic calculated is 0.924355. When compared with the values of the following information criteria (BIC = 0.982, HQIC = 0.966, RNIC = 0.986) in order to determine the validity of the instrument, it was then concluded that the instrument used is valid. The model selection criteria perform reasonably well for sample sizes above 250.

4.5. Market Equilibrium Test for H-Statistic

An important feature of the H-statistic is that equilibrium tests must be performed on observations that are in long-run. The equilibrium test is suggested based on the fact that, in equilibrium, rates of return across banks should not be correlated statistically with input prices [30]. To test whether this assumption holds in the case of Nigeria, we remodeled the PR methodology by using the return on asset as proposed in the literature [3,9,30].

It should be noted that, the measure of ROA can take on negative values on some occasion due to banks' losses in any year, thus, the variable is adjusted simply for the small negative values and computed as (1 + ROA) for convenience. Equation (15) is then estimated for the market equilibrium test. The results obtained from the pooled data revealed that the market is in equilibrium based on the value of H-statistic of 0.043055 with F-statistic of 43.3222 and p value of 0.0000 obtained from the Wald test. This is statistically significant and different from zero and one at 1% level (see **Table 8**). The results from the equilibrium test also show that all the factor input prices are positively related to return on asset and statistically significant with the exception of the price of capital. The price of labour (w_1) contributes mostly to the value of H in contrast to our previous results in which the

price of fund contributes the highest coefficient to H-statistic. This implies that as a result of an increase in the price of labour, they are encouraged to improve on their capacity, which invariably increases their contribution to the total revenue of the industry (banks net income). Based on our calculation of H-statistic, the result obtained from our estimation of equilibrium test shows that our observations are in equilibrium. This is premised on the value of H-statistic reported earlier ($H = 0.04305$). This value is closer to zero than one (1). This implies the rejection of the null hypothesis of $H = 0$ and $H = 1$ at 1 percent level of significance.

Other variables in the model are statistically significant with the exception of non-performing loans (r_3). This is because some of the loans granted by the banks to individuals or firms were diverted to other uses rather than what they were meant for which made the repayment difficult.

5. Conclusion

Competition in the banking sector has received greater attention of the economists in recent years but the degree of competition has generated a serious debate both in the developed and developing economies. It has been observed in the literature that a higher degree of competition in banking industry is expected to provide welfare gains through reduction in the prices of factor input and thereby accelerating growth. From the empirical analysis of the study, it was observed that commercial banks in Nigeria showed evidence of monopolistic competition which corroborate the result obtained in the previous studies.[2] The result obtained is in contrast to the theory which emphasizes oligopolistic nature of the industry because of the dominance of some banks in the industry.

Table 8. Pooled generalised least square estimate with cross section weights (Equilibrium Test).

Variables	1 + ROA	
	Coefficients	t-statistic
C	0.3780	12.1189*
Log (w_1)	0.0253	5.1205*
Log (w_2)	0.0067	1.5287
Log (w_3)	0.0110	2.3391**
Log (TA)	−0.0054	−3.6304*
Log (r_1)	0.0118	2.8802*
Log (r_2)	0.0077	1.4301
(r_3)	−0.0011	−0.1336
Log (TDTA)	0.0218	2.3481**

(*) Statistically significant at 1percent level. (**) Statistically significant at 5percent level. (***) Statistically significant at 10 percent level. Summary weighted statistics: R^2 = 0.4519; F-statistics = 8.8475 (0.0000); DW = 1.2960; H-statistics = 0.04305; F-statistic on Wald test for $H = 0$:43.3222, p value = 0.0000; F-statistic on Wald test for $H = 1$:15458, p value = 0.0000; *Ho: H* = 0 (Monopoly); *Ho: H* = 1(Perfect Competition); *Ho:* 0 < *H* < 1 (Monopolistic Competition).

REFERENCES

[1] M. Brownbridge, "The Impact of Public Policy on the Banking System in Nigeria," 1996.

[2] L. Weill, "On the Relationship between Competition and Efficiency in the EU Banking Sectors," *Kredit und Kapital*, Vol. 37, No. 3, 2003, pp. 329-352.

[3] S. Claessens and L. Laeven, "Financial Dependence, Banking Sector Competition, and Economic Growth," World Bank Policy Research Working Paper, No. 3481, 2005.

[4] A. Prasad and S. Ghosh, "Competition in Indian Banking," IMF Working Paper, 2005.

[5] L. Weill, A. Pruteanu-Podpiera and F. Schobert, "Banking Competition and Efficiency: A Micro-Data Analysis on the Czech Banking Industry," *Comparative Economic Studies*, Vol. 50, No. 2, 2008. pp. 253-273.

[2]Shaffer 1982, Molyneux etal 1994, Prasad and Gosh 2005, Buchs and Mathisen 2005 among others.

[6] J. A. Bikker and K. Haaf, "Competition, Concentration and Their Relationship: An Empirical Analysis of the Banking Industry," *Journal of Banking and Finance*, Vol. 26, No. 11, 2002, pp. 2191-2214.

[7] S. Claessens and L. Laeven, "What Drives Bank Competition? Some International Evidence," *Journal of Money Credit and Banking*, Vol. 36, No. 3, 2004, pp. 563-583.

[8] D. Denvil, "Testing for Competition in the Jamaican Banking Sector: Evidence from Bank Level Data," Financial Stability Unit, Bank of Jamaica, 2002.

[9] T. Buchs and J. Mathisen, "Competition and Efficiency in Banking: Behavioural and Evidence from Ghana," IMF Working Paper, International Monetary Fund, 2005.

[10] A. M. Simpasa, "Competitive Conditions in the Tanzania Commercial Banking Industry," *African Development Review*, Vol. 23, No. 1, 2011, pp. 88-98.

[11] Y. Sun, "Recent Developments in European Bank Competition," International Monetary Fund Working Paper, 2011.

[12] J. A. Bikker and L. Spierdijk, "How Banking Competition Changed Overtime," Tjalling C. Koopmans Research Institute, Discussion Paper Series, No. 08-04, 2008.

[13] G. Alessandro and R. Kevin, "Bank Competition and Efficiency in the FYR Macedonia," *South-Eastern Europe Journal of Economics*, Vol. 2, 2008, pp. 145-167.

[14] S. Shaffer, "A Non-Structural Test for Competition in Financial Markets," In: *Proceedings of a Conference in Bank Structure and Competition*, Federal Reserve Bank of Chicago, Chicago, 1982.

[15] P. Molyneux, Y. Altunbas and E. Gardener, "Efficiency in European Banking," Wiley, Chichester, 1996.

[16] O. De Bandt and Philip E. Davis, "Competition, Contestability and Market Structure in European Banking Sectors on the Eve of EMU," *Journal of Banking and Finance*, Vol. 24, No. 6, 2000, pp. 1045-1066.

[17] J. C. Panzar and J. N. Rosse, "Testing for Monopoly Equilibrium," *Journal of Industrial Economics*, Vol. 35, No. 4, 1987, pp. 443-456.

[18] A. Kuotsoyiannis, "Modern Microeconomics," International Edition, Macmillian Press Ltd., London, 2003.

[19] C. A. Northcott, "Competition in Banking: A Review of the Literature," Bank of Canada Working Paper, 2004-24, 2004.

[20] J. M. Wooldridge, "Introductory Econometrics: A Modern Approach," South-Western College Publishing, Cincinnati, 2000.

[21] R. S. Pindyck and D. L. Rubinfeld, "Econometric Models and Economic Forecasts," McGraw-Hill, Singapore City, 1997.

[22] K. S. Pesaran and Y. Shin, "Testing for Unit Roots in Heterogeneous Panels," *Journal of Econometrics*, Vol. 115, No. 1, 2003, pp. 53-74.

[23] W. H. Greene, "Econometric Analysis," 6th Edition, Prentice-Hall, Upper Saddle River, 2008.

[24] R. C. Hill, W. E. Griffiths and G. C. Lim, "Principles of Econometrics," 3rd Edition, John Wiley and Sons, Inc., New York, 2007.

[25] A. Levin, C. F. Lin and C. Chu, "Unit Root Tests in Panel Data: Asymptotic and Finite Sample Properties," *Journal of Econometrics*, Vol. 108, No. 1, 2002, pp. 1-24.

[26] B. Baltagi, Eds., "Root Test for Panel Data," In: *Advances in Econometrics, Vol.* 15: *Nonstationary Panels, Panel Cointegration, and Dynamic Panels*, JAI Press, Amsterdam, pp. 161-178.

[27] G. S. Maddala and S. Wu, "A Comparative Study of Unit Root Tests with Panel Data and a New Simple Test," *Oxford Bulletin of Economics and Statistics*, Vol. 61, No. S1, 1999, pp. 631-652.

[28] I. Choi, "Unit Root Tests for Panel Data," *Journal of International Money and Finance*, Vol. 20, No. 2, 2001, pp. 249-272.

[29] K. Hadri, "Testing for Stationarity in Heterogeneous Panel Data," *Econometric Journal*, Vol. 3, No. 2, 2000, pp. 148-161.

[30] B. Casu and C. Girardone, "Does Competition Leads to Efficiency? The Case of EU Commercial Banks," Discussion Paper, Essex Finance Centre, 2007.

[31] L. G. de Rozas, "Testing for Competition in the Spanish Banking Industry: The Panzar-Rosse Approach Revisited," Documentos de Trabajo, No. 0726, 2007.

5

Economic Integration, Tax Erosion, and Decentralisation: An Empirical Analysis

Francesca Gastaldi[1], Paolo Liberati[2], Antonio Scialà[3*]
[1]Department of Economics and Law, Sapienza Università di Roma, Rome, Italy
[2]Department of Economics, Università Roma Tre, Rome, Italy
[3]Department of Law, Università Roma Tre, Rome, Italy

ABSTRACT

This paper addresses the issues of whether and how economic integration can affect the ability of the central governments to raise tax revenues and lead to a greater decentralisation of the public sector. To this purpose, a country-specific measure of tax erosion is derived. That is used as a determinant of the degree of fiscal federalism. We find that an increase of economic integration causes a decline of the implicit tax rates on mobile capital and the process of tax erosion positively contributes to the growth of public sector decentralisation.

Keywords: Economic Integration; Tax Erosion; Fiscal Federalism; Implicit Tax Rates; Tax Competition

1. Introduction

The economic literature that investigates the impact of international tax competition on public finance variables mainly suggests that economic integration may introduce constraints on national public policies (among many, [1-3]).[1] In these cases, however, the public sector is usually considered as a monolithic entity and the impact of economic integration is analysed as if states were organised on a unitary basis. On the other hand, those studies that investigate the link between decentralisation and government size rarely consider that economic integration can affect the vertical structure of the public sector, dealing with this issue as if states were closed[2].

This paper tries to build a bridge between these two separate strands of literature, addressing in a unified empirical framework with the relationships among economic integration, national tax revenues and fiscal federalism.[3] In particular, we maintain the hypothesis that economic integration can to some extent erode the size of central tax revenues and indirectly lead to a greater decentralisation of the public sector. In particular, we postulate that since economic integration may constrain the ability of the central governments to raise additional tax revenues and increase the marginal efficiency cost of taxation, those governments may have some incentives to act strategically, by shifting tax powers to lower government levels.

In order to test our argument, we develop an econometric strategy in two stages, using a sample of OECD countries. In the first stage, economic integration is used as a determinant of the level of taxation, as measured by the *implicit tax rates* (*ITR*) developed by [6] and updated by [7]. In the second stage, a measure of tax erosion given by the elasticity of *ITRs* with respect to economic integration is calculated and used as a determinant of the decentralisation of the public sector.

The results of our empirical analysis show that in the first stage economic integration actually affects the ability of central governments to raise tax revenues from mobile tax bases, while it does not produce comparably significant effects on other tax bases. In the second stage, our measure of tax erosion is then found to have a sig-

---

*Corresponding author.

[1]In what follows, we will use the terms "economic integration" and "economic openness" interchangeably, to mean a country's exposure to foreign trade and financial flows.

[2]A notable exception to this artificial division of interests is [4], who finds (among EU countries) that greater economic integration may be positively associated to a greater decentralisation through the increasing demand for productive local public goods that would be stimulated by economic openness. In this case, however, the level of decentralisation in each country is *directly* related to its degree of economic integration, which amounts to assume that two countries that exhibit the same economic openness would experiment the same constraints on public finance variables despite potentially remarkable differences in their pre-existing tax and spending levels.

[3]For a theoretical setting in this direction, see [4], and [5].

nificant relationship with the degree of decentralisation, supporting the hypothesis that economic integration can be associated to a higher degree of fiscal federalism.

The paper is organised as follows. Section 2 briefly reviews the existing literature on the links between economic integration and tax revenues and between economic integration and decentralisation. The empirical strategy is presented in Section 3, while Section 4 discusses the main results of the empirical analysis. Section 5 concludes.

2. Economic Integration, Tax Revenues, and Decentralisation

2.1. Economic Integration and Tax Revenues

Whether economic integration is potentially able to affect national tax and spending policies is an open issue.[4] The literature on tax competition suggests that capital taxation would be lower with greater international capital mobility, as overtaxed capital might sanction undesirable public policies by exit national borders.[5]

In an extreme version of this model—that has become popular as the race-to-the-bottom hypothesis—capital mobility would cause tax revenues to disappear in the attempt of governments to create favourable conditions for investments, a feature that has led many authors to define tax competition as "harmful".[6] In a milder version, governments would be "disciplined" to a more efficient use of economic resources, the reason why this outcome is also referred to as the efficiency hypothesis in the spirit of [15]. Both cases would fall into what [16] calls the capital flight hypothesis and both, in principle, would lead, in open economies, to lower optimal tax rates on mobile factors, which means that economic openness may to some extent increase the marginal efficiency cost of public funds on mobile tax bases.[7]

On the other hand, some authors argue that citizens in countries with a large exposure to international trade and capital flows try to demand additional public spending (the compensation hypothesis) to cushion the additional risk embodied in opening markets (e.g., unemployment or larger income volatility).[8] However, this possibility must ultimately lead to a growth of taxation (and/or debt) to finance the additional supply of public spending. Whether this additional demand of public spending can easily be accommodated by additional taxes is however controversial, as national governments in integrated economies experience various constraints on the tax side

of the public budget, not least because markets complain about a growth of taxes to finance what they consider unproductive public spending.[9]

This variety of theoretical positions hardly finds a synthesis on the empirical side, not least because of a tiny empirical evidence investigating the relationship between economic integration and tax levels. Some empirical studies give indirect support to the compensation hypothesis;[10] others reinforce the intuition that economic integration is a stressing factor for public finances.[11]

These studies are however hardly comparable. Firstly, the existing literature does not agree on a common indicator of the tax burden, swinging from statutory tax rates to forward-looking or backward-looking effective tax rates (with various possibilities of normalisation), or to measures of tax burden based on tax ratios.[12] Results may therefore be different as the indicators measure different things. Secondly, existing studies usually do not distinguish between capital taxes on mobile and immobile tax bases, which are instead crucial to capture the influence of capital mobility. Thirdly, economic integration is more often modelled as trade integration, disregarding outward and inward flows of foreign direct investments.[13] As a matter of further complication, countries included often differ in number and, more importantly, by geographical areas. Some analyses are confined to OECD countries, others extend over this subset, including transitional and less developed countries. Finally, the period covered only rarely is updated to very recent times also for recent studies, with the consequence that results might be severely biased by not considering those years where economic integration has actually developed most.[14]

2.2. Economic Integration and Decentralisation

The relationship between economic integration and decentralisation is even less generously investigated; the existing studies only allow some speculations. First, the extension of the compensation hypothesis to local governments provides a straightforward link between the two

---

[4]See the review by [2] and, more recently, [8].

[5]For example, [9] show that if capital cannot be taxed with the residence principle (that would guarantee capital export neutrality), it is optimal for a small economy to tax labour only.

[6]This is the "fiscal termites" argument by [10] and [11]. See also [12], [13] and [14].

[7]See [17] and [18].

[8]See [19].

[9]As a result of economic integration, some authors argue that public spending would be more oriented towards privately productive public goods (e.g. infrastructures, training programmes, human capital) and less towards transfers and social welfare expenditures. See [20] and [21].

[10]See, for example, [16,22-27].

[11]See [28-34].

[12]For a detailed treatment of this issue, see [7].

[13]While this might have been an innocuous assumption in the past, the liberalization of capital markets in many advanced countries—especially in Europe in the Nineties—does not legitimate to disregard capital integration (CI) anymore. As suggested by [2] (p. 314), even though there are reasons to believe that countries with higher trade shares tend to be countries with greater capital mobility, trade openness and capital mobility are two distinctively different concepts.

[14]In particular, a large part of the empirical evidence stops around the first half of the Nineties, a period in which capital liberalisation is not likely to have explained all its effects, as many countries (especially in Europe) have abolished capital controls in that period.

variables. Since the shield provided by social spending against additional risk is thought to be best served by centralised fiscal arrangements (e.g. [35]), the consequential outcome is that economic integration should increase the size of central governments and reduce the size of local governments, especially if regions are specialised in production.[15]

Second, since economic integration may reduce the cost of secession by part of small regions (e.g. [37] and [38]), exit threats may become more credible (and cheaper) in an integrated world. In turn, this may lead to an increase of the number of states, or to a larger decentralisation of existing countries in the case where requests for more autonomy are met by national governments. In the same vein, if fiscal decentralisation is interpreted as a backstop to avoid the inefficiency costs associated to secession, as in [39], more economic integration should lead to more decentralised countries.[16] As before, in this case central governments would be willing to pay local governments more to avoid secession, for example, by increasing unconditional grants or by devolving more powers to sub-central units.

A third explanation tends to highlight the role of economic integration as a fiscal discipline device. In this case, economic integration would impose harder budget constraints on local governments (see [41]), reduce the "deficit bias" empirically observed in more decentralised countries—originated by either implicit or explicit bailout guarantees from the central governments[17]—and favour the implementation of a market-preserving federalism (e.g. [43] and [44]).[18]

A fourth explanation is based on the existence of opportunistic behaviour by part of either government level involved in the process. In particular, the existing literature has focused on the case where central governments may offload public expenditures to local governments. Economic integration, for example, command fiscal balance[19], may increase the domestic cost for central governments of pursuing redistributive aims[20], favour more

decentralisation on a political ground, and shift responsibilities to lower government levels.[21]

If one assumes that the most powerful pressure to maintain fiscal balance comes from capital markets, the argument that the central governments may have incentives to offload tax powers and public spending to local governments ends up to be the argument advanced in this paper that more economic integration may lead to change the vertical structure of the public sector. It is to the empirical test of this argument that the next section is devoted.

3. Empirical Strategy and Data

In order to analyse the relationship between economic integration, tax erosion and decentralisation, we follow a two-stage empirical strategy based on two hypotheses:

Hypothesis 1

Economic integration would erode the tax revenues raised by central governments on mobile capital (more generally on mobile tax bases).

Hypothesis 2

Tax erosion experienced by central governments leads to an increase of public sector decentralisation.

A theoretical intuition of the implications of these two hypotheses can be gained by making recourse to the concept of the Marginal Efficiency Cost of Funds (MECF) developed by [50]. As argued above, the central government may try to shift tax responsibilities to other government levels whenever it faces higher marginal efficiency costs in raising its own additional tax revenues. To this purpose, suppose that a central government collects tax revenue R_C according to the following scheme:

$$R_C = t_r Y_r \left(t_r \right) + t_{nr} Y_{nr} \left(t_{nr} \right) \qquad (1)$$

where t_r is the tax rate applied on the "resident" tax base Y_r and t_{nr} is the tax rate on the "non-resident" tax base Y_{nr}, where "resident" and "non resident" can be here interpreted as relatively immobile and mobile tax bases, respectively. Now, the efficiency cost of collecting funds either from resident or non-resident tax bases depends on the level of additional tax revenue that can be obtained by increasing the corresponding tax rate. To this purpose, define:

$$MR_r \equiv \frac{dR}{dt_r} = Y_r \left(t_r \right) + t_r Y_r' \left(t_r \right) \qquad (2)$$

$$MR_{nr} \equiv \frac{dR}{dt_{nr}} = Y_{nr} \left(t_{nr} \right) + t_{nr} Y_{nr}' \left(t_{nr} \right) \qquad (3)$$

---

[15]See also [36].

[16]Nonetheless, as [36] pointed out, central governments may try to "buy" the loyalty of voters by direct spending, admitting the possibility that economic integration would increase (more) the size of central governments. However, local voters might be more effectively "bought" by increasing either the size of—possibly unconditional—grants or the amount of taxes devolved to local territories. Reference [40] also provides a framework of horizontal competition among local governments in which taxpayers have wide information and comparison opportunities of local public policies.

[17]See, for example, [42].

[18]However, hard budget constraints for sub-national governments may not be socially optimal, as under some circumstances socially efficient projects may not be undertaken (see, [45]).

[19]This hypothesis is known as the *domestic balance* hypothesis. See [16].

[20]To some extent, the reason is the same as that predicted by [46] when perfect mobility is assumed. In this latter case, redistribution is a hardly tenable function for local governments and unstable equilibria may originate. See also [47].

[21]The origin of the *shifting hypothesis* can be traced back to the literature on regulation authorities. See, for example, [48]. Reference [49], for example, argue that strategic behavior may be followed by central governments when facing increasing pressures to maintain fiscal balance, in particular by offloading expenditures and deficits to local governments.

as the marginal revenue that can be obtained by moving either t_r or t_{nr}, with

$$Y_r'(t_r) = \frac{dY_r}{dt_r}.$$

Equations (2) and (3) can be interpreted as the sum of the "tax rate effect" $(Y_r(t_r))$ and of the "tax base effect" $(t_r Y_r'(t_r))$. In particular, one could also rewrite

$$MR_j = Y_j - (Y_j - MR_j),$$

$j = r, nr$, by which the marginal revenue is defined by the "potential tax base" (Y_j) minus the "leak" represented by $(Y_j - MR_j)$.

Now, by normalising both (2) and (3) by the potential tax base Y_r and Y_{nr}, respectively, one can get the marginal revenue *per* unit of tax base:

$$\frac{MR_j}{Y_j} = 1 + \varepsilon_{Y_j, t_j} \qquad (4)$$

where $j = r, nr$ and

$$\varepsilon_{Y_j, t_j} = \frac{t_j Y_r'}{Y_j}.$$

It is clear that when $\varepsilon_{Y_j, t_j} = 0$, one unit of tax base gives dt_j units of additional tax revenues. By (4), the definition of the marginal efficiency cost of fund arises by taking its inverse:

$$MECF_j = \frac{Y_j}{MR_j} = \frac{1}{1 + \varepsilon_{Y_j, t_j}} \qquad (5)$$

The general principle follows from (5) that the MECF will be greater for more elastic tax bases, while it will be smaller in the case of less elastic tax bases. Since it can be assumed that tax bases that may migrate are more elastic to tax rates, it will be that $\left| \varepsilon_{Y_{nr}, t_{nr}} \right| > \left| \varepsilon_{Y_r, t_r} \right|$ and $MR_{nr} < MR_r$ (i.e. the marginal revenue that can be obtained by taxing non-residents is lower as part of the tax base would disappear). This latter condition implies $MECF_{nr} > MECF_r$, i.e., a higher $MECF$ on more mobile tax bases, signalling growing difficulties in using those tax bases (Stiglitz, 2003).

Thus, if the central government has a target level of tax revenue, it has some convenience to shift taxation from mobile to immobile tax bases, as this minimises the "leak" of tax revenues. Thus, growing economic integration may encourage, on an efficiency ground, a shift of taxation on less mobile ("resident") tax bases (e.g., labour or immovable properties). Now, since the most mobile tax bases are usually assigned to central governments and immobile tax bases are instead widely used by local governments, growing economic openness may entail a change in the vertical structure of taxation among government levels.

Of course, this may occur at different speeds in various countries, but there is some consensus that economic integration, in recent years, may have accelerated a shift of power away from politics and towards economics. As recently observed ([51], p. 13), the power of politics (to be extended to the power of taxation) has weakened because of several interrelated reasons. First, economic integration has enhanced the number of tradable goods and services in the financial sector (i.e., the most mobile production factor). Second, to the extent that multinational corporations are the primary owners of mobile production factors, they enjoy a strengthened leverage with respect to territorial actors (i.e. those owning relatively immobile production factors like land and labour). Third, markets have outgrown states in size, which implies that states have growing difficulties to regulate and tax markets unless political institutions are adjusted accordingly.

These external pressures would therefore beg the question of whether one can expect a reallocation of public goods provision among government levels. Presumably, global economic pressures have increased the necessity to shift resource allocation beyond national frontiers ([51], p. 26) and reinforced the case to devolve both stabilization and redistributive functions to supranational governments.[22] At the same time, they might have forced states to devolve to sub-national governments all matters that they can efficiently deal with, especially with regard to the allocation function.

In this latter case, decentralisation of taxation and spending powers may provide a mixed outcome. On the one hand, it may favour a better correspondence between spending and taxes at local level (the benefit principle of taxation); it may reduce the domestic costs of redistribution by insulating redistributive local spending and taxation from global pressures; and efficiency may improve because of incentives for local governments to behave more competitively.[23] On the other hand, decentralisation may be opportunistically used to distribute the tax collecting points on a territorial basis, by this way promoting tax illusion, and to strategically shift external constraints to local governments in various institutional forms (e.g., Internal Stability Pacts in the European countries). Thus, whether decentralisation is actually pursued in the presence of growing economic integration, depends on the balance between political advantages and disadvantages. As such, it is a matter of empirical evidence, which is embodied in our hypothesis 2.

For an empirical assessment of the two hypotheses, we

---

[22]One exploited argument to limit national redistributive policies is that they are perceived as being responsible for reducing incentives to work and to invest (e.g., [52]).

[23]The absence of competition among governmental units, for example, was at the base of the pioneering contribution by [53] on the European integration.

have built an unbalanced panel of 16 OECD countries for a total of 469 observations (see **Table A.1** in **Appendix**). Data are taken by a number of sources: the main source for all tax variables is OECD, while for the degree of economic integration we have made recourse to data from the International Monetary Fund. Real income at PPP is finally taken by the Penn World Tables (see **Table A.1**).

Hypothesis 1 is tested in the first stage of an econometric procedure, where economic integration enters as an explanatory variable of tax levels as measured by the implicit tax rates. In particular, the first stage consists of estimating the following equation by a feasible generalised least squares (FGLS) controlling for heteroskedasticity and panel-specific first-order autocorrelation:[24]

$$\lgs\left(ITR_{i,t}^h\right) = \alpha^h + \beta_1^h \lgs\left(ITR_{i,t-1}^h\right) + \beta_2^h \ln\left(OPEN_{i,t}\right)$$

$$+ \beta_3^h \left(\ln\left(OPEN_{i,t}\right)\right)^2 + \sum_{i=1}^{N} \theta_i^h d_i \ln\left(OPEN_{i,t}\right)$$

$$+ \sum_{p=1}^{P} \eta_p \ln\left(X_{i,t}^p\right) + e_{i,t}$$

$$(6)$$

where $\lgs\left(ITR_{i,t}^h\right)$ is the logistic transformation of the implicit tax rate falling on the tax base h in country i at time t, where h is, alternatively, labour income, consumption, immobile capital, and mobile capital.[25] It is worth noting that the distinction between tax rates on immobile and mobile capital remedies the often observed practice, in empirical studies, of including taxes on corporations and on immovable properties under the same heading of "capital tax rates". Indeed, the expected reactions of these two effective tax rates to economic integration may be significantly diversified and would require to be separately measured. Even though, in principle, implicit tax rates on all taxes might decline with increasing economic openness (what we have defined as the process of tax erosion), one can expect a larger decline of implicit tax rates on the most mobile tax bases. As a consequence, when the power to tax these tax bases is concentrated in the hands of the central government, this would mainly entail an erosion of the central government tax revenues.

The other variables in Equation (6) have the following meaning. Economic openness $\left(\ln\left(OPEN\right)\right)$ is defined

as the sum of exports, imports, and both inward and outward foreign direct investment as a share of GDP, aimed at capturing the degree of potential mobility in the most comprehensive way;[26] $d_i \ln\left(OPEN_{i,t}\right)$ is an interaction term between a country dummy and the variable $\ln\left(OPEN\right)$, which will prove useful to calculate country-specific elasticities; X is a vector of control variables including: population and per capita income in US\$, to control for demographic and wealth; general government *expenditures* as a percentage of GDP, to control for government size; $ITR_{i,t}^k$ for $k \neq h$, to control for the existing tax structure; and a vector of year dummy variables, to control for time effects. In addition, a standard measure of the total fiscal burden has also been considered, approximated by the ratio between total tax revenues and GDP.

When Equation (6) produces statistically significant coefficients, a set of country-specific elasticities of implicit tax rates with respect to economic integration can be derived. In particular, by indicating with $k \neq h \hat{\beta}_j^h \left(j \in \{2,3\}\right)$ and $\hat{\theta}_i^h \left(i \in \{1 \cdots N\}\right)$ the estimated value of the parameters in (6), the elasticities $\hat{E}_{i,t}^h$ will be given by:

$$\hat{E}_{i,t}^h = \hat{\beta}_2^h + 2\hat{\beta}_3^h \ln\left(OPEN_{i,t}\right) + \hat{\theta}_i^h d_i \qquad (7)$$

Equation (7) is particularly important for our argument. More specifically, $\hat{E}_{i,t}^h > 0$ would imply that implicit tax rates will increase with economic integration, while $\hat{E}_{i,t}^h < 0$ would imply the opposite. In a static perspective, tax erosion will emerge only when this latter condition is satisfied, which means that a country is at a stage where a further growth of economic integration would reduce the effective tax burden on the specific tax base h. However, in a dynamic perspective, tax erosion cannot be excluded by $\hat{E}_{i,t}^h > 0$, provided that $\hat{E}_{i,t}^h$ follows a decreasing pattern over time. In this case, even though the tax burden on h grows with economic integration, the decreasing rate of growth over time would signal a process of tax erosion.[27]

Equipped with the elasticities estimated in the first stage, the second stage of the econometric procedure provides a test of hypothesis 2, in order to verify the impact of $\hat{E}_{i,t}^h$ on the degree of decentralisation. To this purpose, the following equation is estimated:

$$\Delta_t \ln\left(D_i\right) = \gamma^h + \delta_1^h \Delta_{t-1} \ln\left(D_i\right) + \delta_2^h \Delta_{t-2} \ln\left(D_i\right)$$

$$+ \varphi^h \Delta_t \hat{E}_i^h + \sum_{q=1}^{Q} \psi_q^h \Delta_t \ln\left(Z_i^q\right) + u_{i,t}$$

$$(8)$$

---

[24]The null hypothesis of no panel-level heteroskedasticity is rejected. A test of first-order autocorrelation *within* each panel has been performed via the time-series cross-section equivalent of the standard Lagrange multiplier test. Results of the test are not reported in table.

[25]Full details of this procedure are given in [7] and summarised in **Table A.1**. For mobile capital, two different methods have been used to calculate the appropriate tax bases: a) *net operating surplus of corporations* computed with the OECD methodology (OM2); b) *net operating surplus of corporations* computed as in [6] taking into account the correction proposed by [54] (OMM2). In both cases only corporations are considered.

[26]See [55] for an application of these measures. This comprehensive measure aims at giving a synthetic indication of the total international exposure of a country. For this reason, *OPEN* takes into account both trade and investment indicators and, indirectly, their different growth rates over the last decades.

[27]Reference [56], for example, have argued that if capital owners shift capital out of high-tax jurisdictions, governments may be forced to increase the effective tax burden on capital in order to maintain the same revenue from an eroding tax base.

where, for a generic variable x, $\Delta_t x = x_t - x_{t-1}$; D is the degree of decentralisation as measured by the ratio between local and total public spending; Z is a vector of control variables that are a subset of the control variables included in the first stage regression and $\hat{E}_{i,t}^h$ is the previously estimated elasticity.[28] Note that in this second stage regression, system-GMM estimators are used, to take into account dynamics and possible endogeneity issues. A negative sign of φ^h is what we are looking for to support hypothesis 2 for each tax base h.

4. Results

4.1. The First Stage Relationship between Economic Integration and Implicit Tax Rates

Table 1 reports a set of five regressions (with a Feasible Generalised Least Squares method), experimenting Equation (6) first on a global measure of tax burden (total taxes over GDP, in column A) and then on specific measures of implicit tax rates. In particular, the same model has been estimated considering ITR on mobile capital (tKS_OMM2 in column B), on labour income (tL_O in column C), on consumption (tC_E in column D) and on immobile capital (tKK_OM2 in column E). In all cases, the list of regressors includes the one-period lagged dependent variable, to take into account the persistency of tax variables. The other explanatory variables are the same across regressions, including a vector of interaction terms between economic integration and country dummy variables and a vector of year dummy variables (whose coefficients are not reported in table). As noted above, the set of control variables includes $ITR_{i,t}^k$ for $k \neq h$.

To our aims, the key finding involves the sign of the coefficients of economic integration (OPEN), with a negative sign supporting a process of tax erosion (hypothesis 1). Our results show that this process has statistical significance only for taxes on mobile capital (column B). The coefficients of OPEN and OPEN2 are both negative, signalling that growing economic integration may not only generate a downward pressure on implicit tax rates on mobile capital, but also that this pressure may grow at increasing rates. The coefficients of $ITR_{i,t}^k$ also show that the implicit tax rate on mobile capital is inversely related to the implicit tax rate on labour. This suggests that when economic integration leads to a reduction of the tax burden on mobile tax bases, part of the compensating effect is likely to fall on labour, rather than on other tax bases. This conclusion is reinforced by the results in columns B and C, where implicit tax rates on

labour and mobile capital have an opposite path in both cases.

The outcomes reported in columns C to E, instead, suggest that the other implicit tax rates (on labour, consumption and immobile capital) are not directly affected by economic integration. It means, as expected, that the main impact of economic integration falls on taxes on mobile capital; and that the other tax bases are natural candidates to backstop the tax erosion induced by economic integration. Unlike other studies on the same topic, it is particularly important that these results are captured after separating ITRs on mobile and immobile capital. The result that only specific tax bases react to economic integration could also partially explain why the coefficients of OPEN are not statistically significant when the regression is run using total tax revenues over GDP as a dependent variable (column A). Indeed, these comprehensive measures of tax burden may conceal opposite patterns of tax revenues collected on different tax bases, giving the wrong impression that nothing is happening.

As tax erosion cannot be supported for other tax bases, the only meaningful set of elasticities of ITRs with respect to economic integration can be estimated for mobile capital $\left(\hat{E}_{i,t}^{KS}\right)$. This is done in Table 2, where country-average elasticities are calculated. Elasticities are either positive or negative and, with the exception of Austria, all of them are statistically significant at 1 per cent level. As discussed above, from a static perspective, a negative elasticity is a sufficient condition to state that a process of tax erosion has already taken place, the meaning being that the implicit tax rate would fall when economic integration grows. A positive sign, instead, would signal that growing levels of openness may be consistent with a growth of implicit tax rates.

A negative sign (calculated at the average level of openness) appears only in three countries (Germany, Italy and the Netherlands) and may be partially justified by the fact that, for most countries, our dataset extend from 1973 to 2005, with only the last decade particularly buoyant in terms of flows of trade and foreign direct investments. In other terms, a process of erosion may be in place that is only observed since few years or will be more likely observed in the next years. To capture the possible presence of this trend in the period observed, one can consider a dynamic perspective, where what actually matters is not the point estimate of the elasticities, but their change over the time span.

To this purpose, the last column of Table 2 reports the difference between the elasticity measured in the first and in the last year in which each country is observed in the dataset. The overwhelming prevalence of negative signs (with the exception of Canada) indicates that, even when positive, elasticities decrease over time, i.e., ITRs on mobile capital grow slowly when economic integra-

---

[28]Following [57] the latter requirement generates consistent standard errors from the estimation of Equation (8), which includes the "generated" regressor $\hat{E}_{i,t}^h$. See, in particular, the theorems 3.iii, 4 and 5.

Table 1. Economic integration and implicit tax rates: A panel analysis.

Method	FGLS		FGLS		FGLS		FGLS		FGLS	
Dependent Variable	tax_GDP		tKS_OMM2		tL_O		tC_E		tKK_OM2	
	A		**B**		**C**		**D**		**E**	
Regressors	Coefficients	Sig. level	Coefficients	Sig. level	Coefficients	Sig. level	Coefficients	Sig. level	Coefficients	Sig. level
$tax\_GDP_{(t-1)}$	0.886	***								
$tKS\_OMM2_{(t-1)}$			0.707	***						
$tLO_{(t-1)}$					0.896	***				
$tC\_E_{(t-1)}$							0.878	***		
$tKK\_OM2_{(t-1)}$									0.840	***
OPEN	−0.060		−0.5438	***	−0.073		0.036		0.178	
$OPEN^2$	−0.032	*	−0.2420	***	−0.034		0.007		0.084	
lggov	−0.003		−0.0110		−0.004		−0.003		0.014	
lpopulation	−0.030	***	−0.1242	**	−0.031	**	−0.042	***	0.154	***
linc_us2	0.073	**	0.1870		0.045		0.019		−0.092	
tKS_OMM2					−0.039	***	0.025	***	0.121	***
tL_O			−0.2521	***			0.022	*	0.109	**
tC_E			0.1781	***	0.032				0.105	*
tKK_OM2			0.0955	***	0.026	***	0.002			
dOPEN_AU	0.044		0.2692	*	0.009		0.042		−0.099	
dOPEN_DEN	0.007		0.9264	***	0.094		−0.060		−0.566	***
dOPEN_FIN	0.031		0.5314	***	0.007		−0.009		−0.160	
dOPEN_FR	−0.046	**	0.1497	**	−0.028		−0.061	**	−0.008	
dOPEN_GE	−0.015		0.0223		−0.051		−0.053	*	0.240	***
dOPEN_GR	0.018		0.4065	***	−0.002		−0.025		−0.047	
dOPEN_IT	−0.031		0.1213		−0.096	***	−0.050	**	0.159	**
dOPEN_NL	−0.044		0.3999	*	−0.134		0.055		−0.043	
dOPEN_PO	0.044		0.4509	*	0.077		−0.022		−0.240	
dOPEN_SW	−0.010		0.5230	***	−0.024		0.000		−0.177	
dOPEN_UK	−0.015		0.3616	***	0.077	**	−0.073	***	−0.249	***
dOPEN_AUS	0.049	**	0.3312	***	0.067	**	0.014		−0.251	***
dOPEN_CAN	0.027		0.5197	***	0.072	*	−0.002		−0.399	***
dOPEN_NOR	0.087	*	0.8026	***	0.117	*	−0.030		−0.329	*
dOPEN_SP	−0.005		0.3150	***	0.001		−0.033		−0.119	
Constant	−0.679	*	−1.489		−0.332		−0.153		0.410	
Year dummy variables	Yes		Yes		Yes		Yes		Yes	
Number of observations	452		452		452		452		452	
Number of countries	16		16		16		16		16	
$Wald\ chi^2$	(53) 31474.94 ***		(56) 5735.36 ***		(56) 28640.89 ***		(56) 71214.84 ***		(56) 16914.24 ***	
Panels	Heteroskedastic Panel-specific AR(1)		Heteroskedastic Panel-specific AR(1)		Heteroskedastic Panel-specific AR(1)		Heteroskedastic Panel-specific AR(1)		Heteroskedastic Panel-specific AR(1)	

Note: *** 1% significance level; ** 5% significance level; * 10% significance level; *ggov, population, inc_us2* are introduced in logarithms. *tax_GDP, tKS_OMM2, tKK_OM2, tC_E, tL_O* are logistic transformations of the original variables. Source: authors' elaborations.

Table 2. The elasticity of implicit tax rates.

Country	Mean elasticity	S.E.	Sig. level	First year observed	Last year observed	Difference
Australia	0.435	0.014	***	0.559	0.323	−0.236
Austria	0.016	0.016		0.124	−0.205	−0.329
Canada	0.256	0.022	***	0.303	0.368	0.065
Denmark	0.657	0.015	***	0.730	0.537	−0.192
Finland	0.298	0.018	***	0.377	0.184	−0.193
France	0.067	0.016	***	0.207	−0.073	−0.280
Germany	−0.153	0.016	***	0.022	−0.357	−0.379
Greece	0.482	0.025	***	0.569	0.454	−0.115
Italy	−0.061	0.012	***	0.044	−0.161	−0.204
Netherlands	−0.095	0.014	***	0.021	−0.266	−0.286
Norway	0.548	0.006	***	0.549	0.492	−0.058
Portugal	0.185	0.012	***	0.307	0.217	−0.091
Spain	0.304	0.027	***	0.517	0.138	−0.378
Sweden	0.254	0.018	***	0.440	0.108	−0.332
United Kingdom	0.184	0.009	***	0.261	0.149	−0.113
United States	0.316	0.019	***	0.606	0.162	−0.444
Total	0.153	0.015	***			

Note: *** 1% significance level; ** 5% significance level; * 10% significance level. Source: authors' elaborations.

tion grows. For five countries (Austria, France, Germany, Italy, and the Netherlands), elasticities start on the positive and end up on the negative side, signalling that an erosion process has developed. In all other cases, the smaller positive values indicate that growing economic integration has entailed a progressively lower additional tax burden. In other words, a decreasing trend of positive elasticities is a signal that the ability to extract tax revenues from mobile capital is declining over time and eventually evolve towards erosion. Thus, our estimates (and our measure of economic openness) seem to correctly pick some important characteristics of the process of economic integration and this is actually what is perceived in **Figure 1**. Here, both the estimated values of the elasticities and a polynomial trend of order two are included in each graph. With very few exceptions, it is clear that, in the period observed, the trend of $\hat{E}_{i,t}^{KS}$ is declining in most countries.

4.2. The Second Stage Relationship between Elasticities and Decentralisation

The estimation of $\hat{E}_{i,t}^{KS}$ allows us to move towards the second stage of the analysis, whose aim is to investigate whether the process of tax erosion at the central level may cause second-round effects on the vertical structure of the public sector. As discussed in Section 3, our maintained hypothesis is that, following growing constraints on the action of the central government, the process of tax erosion would stimulate fiscal decentralisation. At

this stage, our method of estimation shifts towards a GMM technique, where changes of the relevant variables are considered. This method would more properly take into account that the dependent variable is persistent over time, that some regressors may be endogenous, and that time-invariant country characteristics may be correlated with the explanatory variables. All these issues may be addressed by moving either to a difference-GMM ([58]) or to a system-GMM ([59] and [60]).

Results are reported in **Table 3**. Column A gives the outcome of the difference-GMM by [58]. The sign of φ^{KS} is negative as expected. Thus, lower values of the elasticities (*i.e.*, a more intense tax erosion) are associated to greater decentralization levels. This implies that, regardless of its initial sign, the change of the elasticity would foster a process of decentralisation, where taxes on less mobile tax bases are possibly applied to compensate the lower tax revenues raised on mobile tax bases. This may also explain why economic integration does not affect taxes on immobile capital, as a large share of these taxes are already used by local governments to secure tax revenues from competitive pressures and to backstop the tax erosion affecting mobile tax bases used by central governments.

Our preferred explanation is that when central governments find mounting difficulties in managing tax bases, they are more incline to decentralise all competencies local governments can efficiently deal with in agreement with the subsidiarity principle. This allows central governments to reduce the size of public spending, by contemporaneously shifting external constraints to local governments in various institutional forms, of which, for example, Internal Stability Pacts introduced in many European countries may be the most visible form. Following this line of reasoning, the degree of decentralisation would increase when economic integration grows, as a result of a deliberate choice of the central government to share tax and spending constraints with other government levels and therefore with other political constituencies.

Column B replicates the difference-GMM by taking into account that our panel is unbalanced and that the first-differencing transformation may magnify gaps. Following [58], we re-estimate the difference-GMM using an orthogonal transformation ([61]), by which the average of all future available observations is subtracted to the current observation. Again, the coefficient of the elasticity is negative and statistically significant.

Since in both cases of difference-GMM, the validity of instruments is supported by AR and Sargan tests, it would not be required to improve the estimation by performing a system-GMM. However, as a further robustness check, column C shows the corresponding outcome. System-GMM uses the equation in levels and the equa-

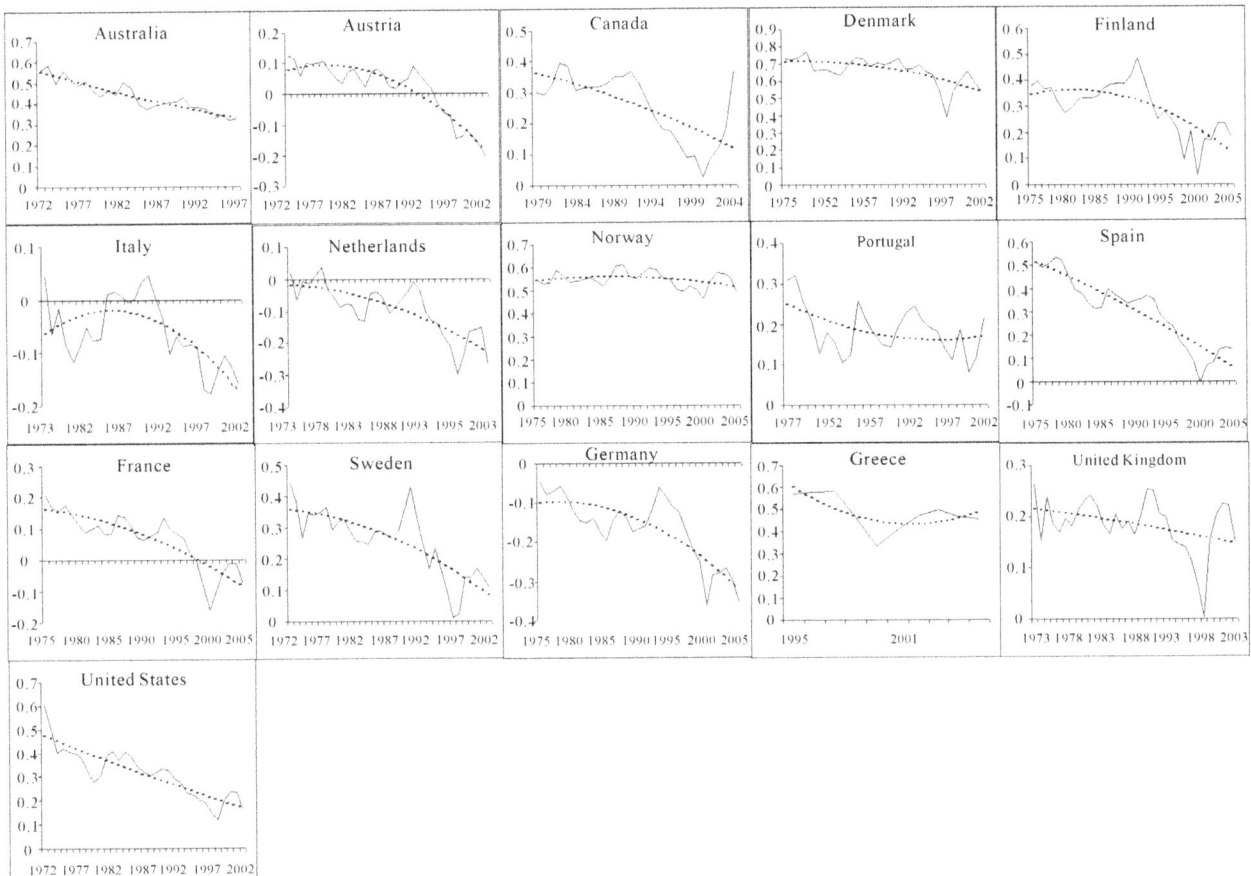

Figure 1. Elasticities of the ITR on mobile capital with respect to economic integration (source: authors' elaborations).

Table 3. Tax erosion and decentralisation.

Method	A) Difference-GMM		B) Difference-GMM		C) System-GMM	
Dependent Variable	lloc		lloc		lloc	
Regressors	Coefficients	Sig. level	Coefficients	Sig. level	Coefficients	Sig. level
$lloc_{(t-1)}$	0.9411	***	0.9550	***	0.5905	***
$lloc_{(t-2)}$	−0.0324		−0.0426		−0.1891	
lggov	0.0015		0.0011		0.0004	
lpopulation	−0.0590		−0.0564		0.4048	
linc_us2	0.0381	*	0.0248		0.1270	
E	−0.1029	***	−0.1060	***	−0.1521	***
Constant	−0.2837		−0.1548		−3.1944	**
Number of observations	415		434		434	
Number of countries	16		16		16	
Wald chi²	(6) 3373.1	***	(6) 4227.7	***	(6) 383.4	***
Sargan test (chi²)	424,9		423,2		2,8	
Number of instruments	409		411		569	
No first order autocorrelation	−2.3	**	−10.9	**	−1,8	*
No second order autocorrelation	−0.4		−0.2		0.7	
Transformation	First Difference		Orthogonal			

Note: *** 1% significance level; ** 5% significance level; * 10% significance level; *loc, ggov, population, inc_us2* are introduced in logarithms. Source: authors' elaborations.

tion in difference to obtain a system of two equations and to get additional instruments, with the requirement that the first difference of the instruments used in the level equation should not be correlated with unobserved country specific effects. Since taxes may possibly be correlated with some unobserved effects, we choose to instrument only the difference equation. Column C shows, once again, that the coefficient of the elasticity supports the idea that the degree of decentralisation may increase with economic integration.

5. Concluding Remarks

This paper has empirically investigated two related issues for a sample of OECD countries. First, whether and how the degree of economic openness may affect central government tax revenues. Second, whether and how the process of tax erosion at central level may cause second-round effects on the vertical structure of the public sector.

To address the first issue we have estimated an equation where economic integration enters as an explanatory variable of implicit tax rates (ITRs) of four tax bases (labour, mobile capital, immobile capital and consumption) as well as of a global measure of the tax burden. The results show that the process of tax erosion induced by economic integration has statistical significance only for taxes on mobile capital, and that part of the compensating effect is likely to fall on labour, rather than on other tax bases.

With regard to the second issue investigated in this paper, our results suggest that the increasing difficulties faced by central governments in collecting additional tax revenues from mobile capital would be associated to an increase of the size of sub-central units. Our explanation is that when central governments find mounting difficulties in managing tax bases, they are more inclined to decentralise competencies to local governments and to boost the decentralization process. This would allow them to reduce the size of the central public spending, by strategically shifting external constraints to local governments in various institutional forms.

REFERENCES

[1] I. Grunberg, "Double Jeopardy: Globalization, Liberalization and the Fiscal Squeeze," *World Development*, Vol. 26, No. 4, 1998, pp. 591-605.

[2] G. Schulze and H. W. Ursprung, "Globalization of the Economy and the Nation State," *The World Economy*, Vol. 22, No. 3, 1999, pp. 295-352.

[3] J. Stiglitz, "Globalization and the Economic Role of the State in the New Millennium," *Industrial and Corporate Change*, Vol. 12, No. 1, 2003, pp. 3-26.

[4] D. Stegarescu, "The Effects of Economic and Political Integration on Fiscal Decentralization: Evidence from OECD countries," *Canadian Journal of Economics*, Vol. 42, No. 2, 2009, pp. 694-718.

[5] P. Liberati and A. Scialà, "How Economic Integration Affects the Vertical Structure of Public Sector," *Economics of Governance*, Vol. 12, No. 4, 2011, pp. 385-402.

[6] E. G. Mendoza, A. Razin and L. L. Tesar, "Effective Tax Rates in Macroeconomics: Cross-Country Estimates of Tax Rates on Factor Incomes and Consumption," NBER Working Paper 4864, 1994.

[7] F. Gastaldi, "Globalisation, Capital Mobility and Convergence of Effective Tax Rates," CRISS Working Paper, No. 32, 2008.

[8] F. Gastaldi and P. Liberati, "Economic Integration and Government Size: a Review of the Empirical Literature," *Financial Theory and Practice*, Vol. 35, No. 3, 2011, pp. 327-384.

[9] S. Bucovetsky and J. Wilson, "Tax Competition with Two Tax Instruments," *Regional Science and Urban Economics*, Vol. 21, No. 3, 1991, pp. 333-350.

[10] V. Tanzi, "Taxation in an Integrating World," Brookings Institutions, Washington DC, 1995.

[11] V. Tanzi, "Globalization and the Future of Social Protection," *Scottish Journal of Political Economy*, Vol. 49, No. 1, 2002, pp. 116-127.

[12] D. R. Lee and R. B. McKenzie, "The International Political Economy of Declining Tax Rates," *National Tax Journal*, Vol. 42, No. 1, 1989, pp. 79-83.

[13] P. Kurzer, "Business and Banking: Political Change and Economic Integration in Western Europe," Cornell University Press, Ithaca, 1993.

[14] S. Steinmo, "The End of Redistribution? International Pressures and Domestic Tax Policy Choices," *Challenge*, Vol. 37, No. 6, 1994, pp. 9-18.

[15] G. Brennan and J. Buchanan, "The Power to Tax: Analytical Foundations of a Fiscal Constitution," Cambridge University Press, Cambridge, 1980.

[16] D. Swank, "Global Capital, Political Institutions and Policy Change in Developed Welfare States," Cambridge University Press, Cambridge, 2002.

[17] A. Razin and E. Sadka, "Efficient Investment Incentives in the Presence of Capital Flight," *Journal of International Economics*, Vol. 31, No. 1-2, 1991, pp. 171-181.

[18] R. H. Gordon, "Can Capital Income Taxes Survive in Open Economies?" *Journal of Finance*, Vol. 47, No. 3, 1992, pp. 1159-1180.

[19] D. Rodrik, "Why Do More Open Economies Have Bigger Governments?" *Journal of Political Economy*, Vol. 106,

No. 5, 1998, pp. 997-1032.

[20] M. Keen and M. Marchand, "Fiscal Competition and the Pattern of Public Spending," *Journal of Public Economics*, Vol. 66, No. 1, 1997, pp. 33-53.

[21] P. Taylor-Gooby, "In Defence of Second-Best Theory: State, Class and Capital in Social Policy," *Journal of Social Policy*, Vol. 26, No. 2, 1997, pp. 171-192.

[22] D. Cameron, "The Expansion of the Public Economy: A Comparative Analysis," *American Political Science Review*, Vol. 72, No. 4, 1978, pp. 1243-1261.

[23] E. Huber, C. Ragin and J. Stephens, "Social Democracy, Christian Democracy, Constitutional Structure, and the Welfare State," *American Journal of Sociology*, Vol. 99, No. 3, 1993, pp. 711-749.

[24] G. Garrett, "Capital Mobility, Trade, and the Domestic Politics of Economic Policy," In: R. Keohane and H. Milner, Eds., *Internalization and Domestic Politics*, Cambridge University Press, New York, 1996, pp. 79-107.

[25] D. Quinn, "The Correlates of Change in International Financial Regulation," *American Political Science Review*, Vol. 91, No. 3, 1997, pp. 531-552.

[26] M. Hallerberg and S. Basinger, "Internationalization and Changes in Tax Policy in OECD Countries: The Importance of Domestic Veto Players," *Comparative Political Studies*, Vol. 31, No. 3, 1998, pp. 321-353.

[27] A. Dreher, "The Influence of Globalization on Taxes and Social Policy—An Empirical Analysis for OECD Countries," *European Journal of Political Economy*, Vol. 22, No. 1, 2006, pp. 179-201.

[28] D. Rodrik, "Has Globalization Gone Too Far," Institute for International Economics, Washington DC, 1997.

[29] D. Swank, "Funding the Welfare State: Globalization and the Taxation of Business in Advanced Market Economies," *Political Studies*, Vol. 46, No. 4, 1998, pp. 671-692.

[30] F. Heinemann, "Does Globalization Restrict Budgetary Autonomy: A Multidimensional Approach," ZEW Discussion Paper No 29, 1999.

[31] D. Swank and S. Steinmo, "The New Political Economy of Taxation in Advanced Capitalist Democracies," *American Journal of Political Science*, Vol. 46, No. 3, 2002, pp. 642-655.

[32] L. Bretschger and F. Hettich, "Globalisation, Capital Mobility and Tax Competition: Theory and Evidence for OECD Countries," *European Journal of Political Economy*, Vol. 18, No. 4, 2002, pp. 695-716.

[33] H. Winner, "Has Tax Competition Emerged in OECD Countries? Evidence from Panel Data," *International Tax*

and Public Finance, Vol. 12, No. 5, 2005, pp. 667-687.

[34] P. Schwartz, "Does Capital Mobility Reduce the Corporate-Labor Tax Ratio?" *Public Choice*, Vol. 130. No. 3-4, 2007, pp. 363-380.

[35] W. Oates, "Fiscal Federalism," Harcourt Brace Jovanovich, New York, 1972.

[36] G. Garrett and J. Rodden, "Globalization and Fiscal Decentralization," In: M. Kahler and D. Lake, Eds., *Governance in a Global Economy: Political Authority in Transition*, Princeton University Press, Princeton, 2003, pp. 87-109.

[37] A. Alesina and E. Spolaore, "On the Number and Size of Nations," *Quarterly Journal of Economics*, Vol. 112, No. 4, 1997, pp. 1027-1056.

[38] A. Alesina and R. Wacziarg, "Openness, Country Size and Government," *Journal of Public Economics*, Vol. 69, No. 3, 1998, pp. 305-321.

[39] P. Bolton and G. Roland, "The Breakup of Nations: A Political Economy Analysis," *Quarterly Journal of Economics*, Vol. 112, No. 4, 1997, pp. 1057-1090.

[40] P. Salmon, "Decentralisation as an Incentive Scheme," *Oxford Review of Economic Policy*, Vol. 3, No. 2, 1987, pp. 24-43.

[41] L. R. De Mello Jr., "Globalization and Fiscal Federalism: Does Openness Constrain Subnational Budget Imbalances?" *Public Budgeting and Finance*, Vol. 25, No. 1, pp. 1-14.

[42] A. Alesina and R. Perotti, "Economic Risk and Political Risk in Fiscal Unions," *The Economic Journal*, Vol. 108, No. 449, 1998, pp. 989-1008.

[43] Y. Y. Qian and B. R. Weingast, "Federalism as a Commitment to Rreserving Market Incentives," *Journal of Economic Perspectives*, Vol. 11, No. 4, 1997, pp. 83-92.

[44] Y. Qian and G. Roland, "Federalism and the Soft Budget Constraint," *The American Economic Review*, Vol. 88, No. 5, 1998, pp. 1143-1162.

[45] M. Besfamille and B. Lockwood, "Bailouts in Federations: Is a Hard Budget Constraint Always Best?" *International Economic Review*, Vol. 49, No. 2, 2008, pp. 577-593.

[46] C. M. Tiebout, "A Pure Theory of Local Government Expenditures," *Journal of Political Economy*, Vol. 64, No. 5, 1956, pp. 416-424.

[47] G. Stigler, "The Tenable Range of Functions of Local Governments," Joint Economic Committee on Federal Expenditure Policy for Economic Growth and Stability, Washington DC, 1957.

[48] B. M. Mitnick, "The Political Economy of Regulation," Columbia University Press, New York, 1980.

[49] G. Garrett and J. Rodden, "Globalization and Decentrali-

zation," Leitner Program in International and Comparative Political Economy, New Haven, 2000.

[50] J. Slemrod and S. Yitzhaki, "The Costs of Taxation and the Marginal Efficiency Cost of Funds," *IMF Staff Papers*, Vol. 43, 1996, pp. 172-198.

[51] A. Hülsemeyer, "Globalization and Institutional Adjustment—Federalism as an Obstacle?" Ashgate Publishing Limited, Farnham, 2004.

[52] P. G. Cerny, "Globalization and the Changing Logic of Collective Action," *International Organization*, Vol. 49, No. 4, 1995, pp. 595-625.

[53] B. S. Frey and R. Eichenberger, "FOCJ: Competitive Governments for Europe," *International Review of Law and Economics*, Vol. 16, No. 3, 1996, pp. 315-327.

[54] D. Carey and J. Rabesona, "Tax Ratios on Labor and Capital Income, and on Consumption," In: P. B. Sørensen, Ed., *Measuring the Tax Burden on Capital and Labor*, CESIFO Seminar Series, MIT Press, Cambridge, 2004.

[55] P. Liberati, "Trade Openness, Capital Openness and Government Size," *Journal of Public Policy*, Vol. 27, No. 2, 2007, pp. 215-247.

[56] K. P. Hagen, E. Norman and P. B. Sørensen, "Financing the Nordic Welfare States in an Integrating Europe," In: P. B. Sørensen, Ed., *Tax Policy in the Nordic Countries*, MacMillan, Houndmills, 1998, pp. 138-203.

[57] A. Pagan, "Econometric Issues in the Analysis of Regressions with Generated Regressors," *International Economic Review*, Vol. 25, No. 1, 1984, pp. 221-247.

[58] M. Arellano and S. Bond, "Some Tests of Specification for Panel Data: Monte Carlo Evidence and an Application to Employment Equations," *Review of Economic Studies*, Vol. 58, No. 2, 1991, pp. 277-297.

[59] M. Arellano and O. Bover, "Another Look at the Instrumental Variable Estimation of Error-Components Models," *Journal of Econometrics*, Vol. 68, No. 1, 1995, pp. 29-51.

[60] R. Blundell and S. Bond, "Initial Conditions and Moment Restrictions in Dynamic Panel Data Models," *Journal of Econometrics*, Vol. 87, No. 1, 1998, pp. 115-143.

[61] D. Roodman, "How To Do Xtabond2: An Introduction to 'Difference' and 'System' GMM in Stata," *Stata Journal*, Vol. 9, No. 1, 2009, pp. 86-136.

Appendix

Table A.1. Definition of variables and source.

Main variables [*]	Description	Source
taxKS_O	Taxes on capital in the corporate sector (excluding taxes on immovable properties—OECD definition)	Elaborations on OECD data
OSN_LM	Net operating surplus in the corporate sector—methodology developed by Mendoza et al. (1994) and Carey and Rabesona (2002)	Elaborations on OECD data
tKS_OMM2	Effective tax rate on mobile capital (taxKS_O/OSN_LM)	Elaborations on OECD data
LAB	Taxes falling on labour (personal income taxes, social security contributions)	Elaborations on OECD data
WAGE	Compensation of employees plus wage and payroll taxes	Elaborations on OECD data
tL_O	Effective tax rate on labour (LAB/WAGE)	Elaborations on OECD data
CONS	Sum of all taxes falling on consumption (VAT, excise taxes, etc.)	Elaborations on OECD data
FCH	Final consumption expenditure by households	Elaborations on OECD data
tC_E	Effective tax rate on consumption	Elaborations on OECD data
IMCAP	Taxes falling on immobile capital	Elaborations on OECD data
OS	Operating surplus of the overall economy (definition by Mendoza et al., 1994)	Elaborations on OECD data
tKK_OM2	Effective tax rate on immobile capital (IMCAP/OS)	Elaborations on OECD data
tax_GDP	Tax burden (ratio between total tax revenue and GDP)	Elaborations on OECD data (both total tax revenue and GDP)
OPEN	Degree of economic integration (Numerator: exports + imports + inward FDI + outward FDI; Denominator: GDP)	Elaborations on OECD and International Financial Statistics data
OPEN^2	OPEN squared	
ggov	General government spending over GDP	OECD and Government Financial Statistics, IMF
loc	Local government spending over general government spending	OECD and Government Financial Statistics, IMF
population	Population	OECD
inc_us2	Real income in PPP $	Penn World Tables
E	Elasticity of effective tax rate to economic integration	Authors' calculations

(*) In the empirical section, some variables are used in first difference (indicated by Δ) and lagged (indicated by $_{t-1}$).

6

Banking Sector and Monetary Policy Transmission: Bank Capital, Credit and Risk-Taking Channels

Philippe Gilles, Marie-Sophie Gauvin, Nicolas Huchet
Université de Toulon, LEAD, Toulon, France

ABSTRACT

In the literature, the question of central banks' responsibility for triggering crises is raised when sustainable low interest rates lead to excessive banks' risk exposures. However, such portfolio choices mainly depend on the various returns of assets and on the official interest rate, taking into account that the bank lending channel is affected by the bank capital channel. On the basis of a simple theoretical model including a solvency ratio, we show that during recessions a credit rationing is observed together with a flight to quality; during expansions monetary policy can induce both a fall in credit activity and an increase in financial instability. Then, regulatory capital arbitrages appear and still weaken productive loans. Conclusions can be drawn in terms of prudential policy, as the central bank may be powerless face to banking strategies if the regulatory framework is procyclical.

Keywords: Banking Sector; Credit Channels; Monetary Policy; Prudential Policy

1. Introduction

Some arguments challenge the goals and tools of central banks, which are regarded as being responsible for the outbreak of the 2007-2008 crisis, especially *via* the risk-taking channel. Financial innovations and off-balance sheet activities have led to a new business model and favor regulatory capital arbitrage. Despite the possible role of central banks, such a framework requires an evolution in prudential and regulatory systems.

The aim of this paper is to highlight the evolution of performance and soundness indicators according to the conduct of monetary policy but also market incentives. The underlying idea is to compare banks that use securitization and off-balance sheet activities and banks that prefer the traditional originate-and-hold business model. We are interested in this topic during growth and slowdowns, because of the impact of interest rates, whose level depends on both the price and the growth targets set by central banks. We show how banks' portfolio choices can be oriented towards risky or safety assets, through a theoretical model which presents the aggregate balance sheet of a banking sector. During the ascending phase, banks prefer speculative assets rather than productive funding, while, after the reversal, they rush towards safety assets and also neglect productive credits. In addition, securitization entails new risks and crowds out the traditional credit activity. Arbitrages are explained by net returns of investments (depending on solvency ratios) and by risk perception.

Works presented in the survey (II) have come to the conclusion that price stability is not enough to give financial stability. Besides, recent researches focused on the risk-taking channel and the bank capital channel show that monetary policy can succeed as regards the price target and at the same time promote financial instability. These arguments highlight the questions relative to the prudential regulation and the aims of central banks. Our model (III) tends to show that, one the one hand, productive credit is all the more useless for banks than they don't hold claims but distribute them, on the other hand, it is necessary to assess the impact of bank capital regulation on global risks. Actually solvency ratios give incentives to risky activities, hence financial instability for which central bank is not responsible.

2. Monetary Policy Transmission and Bank's Behavior: A Survey

The official interest rates and their expected trajectory determine nominal interest rates and aggregate demand. The credit channel highlights the role of banks and their reaction concerning monetary policy decisions. The financial accelerator stresses the procyclicality of the financial sector [1,2], the amplification effects [3] and the aims of central banks. A major problem concerns the stabilization of the output, implying a current debate about macroprudential regulation and its linkages with monetary policy. In accordance with the Jackson Hole Consensus, the price stability and the financial stability are complementary and a flexible inflation targeting should be implemented, with the interest rate as a principal tool and the communication as an other one [4][1].

Current models introduce the banking sector in order to identify the main transmission channels of monetary decisions and booms and busts cycles [8-10]. Based on works focused on financial stability goal for central banks [11,12], it is said that there is no consensus about asset prices. The price stability is conducive to financial instability, since it is hard to conciliate an interest rate policy for prices stability and real activity on the one hand, and a banking policy for financial stability (mostly dependent on wealth effects) on the other hand. These arguments sometimes lead to advocate more recurrent rises of interest rates [13,14]. Fahr *et al.* [15] suggest an inflation target based on a middle term to limit financial instability. Besides, Hobijn and Ravenna [16] introduce securitization and underline the importance of the output at the expense of the inflation.

The main outcome of this literature is the relationship between credit activity and financial instability. The bank lending channel only exists if it is costly to issue debts, relative to required reserves: after a monetary policy tightening, to face the reserves decrease banks prefer to reduce credit activity (or to liquidate assets) to the detriment of new debts with a higher interest rate [17]. Then, the bank capital channel draws this principal conclusion: facing the cost of issuing debts, monetary policy tightening is all the more costly that the level of equities is low. Literature on the bank capital channel focuses on the effects of equity ratios on the credit supply [18,19]: if a crisis occurs, distress sales and (growing) risk aversion lead to amplification effects which in turn imply raising equity to comply with capital requirements, and worsen the credit rationing. Moreover, accounting rules (fair value) strengthen the contraction, through a procyclical effect linked to collateral value [20]. Korinek [21] shows that it is impossible to limit the amplification effects if agents are risk-averse (versus risk neutral, [22]). Here, the new business model (from *originate to hold* to *originate to distribute*) leads to an increase in leverage and in regulatory capital arbitrages: this strategy raises the return on equity (ROE), even if non-interest incomes are more volatile than interest incomes. Moreover, this business model entails a weakening of the bank lending channel and a strengthening of the risk-taking channel [23,24], *via* an excessive optimism concerning the other banks' default risk and an overestimation of expected returns [25,26]. So monetary policies can be responsible for crises, because whenever rates remain durably low, they lead agents to take more risks. The risk-taking channel illustrates not only the reduction of the risk aversion, but also the increase in the impact of the monetary policy on financial stability [27].

Actually, the credit channel, the risk-taking channel and the bank capital channel are tightly linked. Equities requirements entail an opportunity cost for banks, which favor at the expense of the productive credit risk-taking and securitization [28]. After the reversal, banks reconstitute their capital ratios and so strengthen the credit crunch. In other words, as regards as assets, preferences depend on the phases of the economic cycle. Speculative assets and/or microeconomic liquidity are preferred during the upward phase and the reversal triggers a preference for macroeconomic liquidity[2]. In fine, choices are always made at the expense of productive loans. These results legitimate recommendations for monetary and macroprudential policies, as a countercyclical action of the central bank to avoid bubbles [30,31]. For instance, a countercyclical capital ratio can limit assets and output volatility [32] while price targeting could be realized with fewer variations of interest rates [33]. However, such macroprudential recommendations cannot work if the microprudential regulation entails rise in risk-taking. As showed by Blum [34], a capital ratio can reduce the supply of productive credit and at the same time promote speculative assets. Our model highlights possible harmful aftermath of microprudential regulation that should be taken into account during debates on monetary policy. Actually, the new proposal of the Basel Committee on Banking Supervision is better than previous, for example thanks to the introduction of a leverage ratio, but it still maintain procyclical effects and risk measurement by bankers themselves. We show that monetary and microprudential policies can favor risky assets at the expense of productive loans, and underline the weakening of the credit channel and the rise in financial instability. Securitization and off balance sheet activities reduce the costs of equities but increase risks.

3. Analytical Framework

The interactions among banks' portfolio choices depend on monetary policy and can be harmful for credit activity, whatever the phase of the cycle (I and II). In t_0 the banking sector's aggregate balance sheet is composed of I_i assets

---

[1]Asset prices can be a good prevision tool and so an element of the monetary policy rule, if they contain information about expectations and future inflation [5,6]. Nevertheless, included in a rule, asset prices become endogenous and so counterproductive ([7], *cf.* Goodhart's law).

[2]The microeconomic liquidity [29] depends on the market capacity to absorb great volumes with no impact on prices, and on the market resilience, that is to say the rapidity with which prices get back to their initial level after a random shock. According to the macroeconomic liquidity, an asset is liquid if it can be used as a reserve if needed, so it can't lose value. In 2008, a mortgage does not meet the standards of this second definition.

depending on portfolio choices, in order to maximize profit. Liabilities are divided into equities K_{t_0}, which correspond to a share α_i of assets $\left(\alpha_i < [1 - \alpha_i]\right)$, and the debts D_{t_0} (cf. **Table 1**).

In t_1 the Central Bank (whose function is to maximize the welfare: maximization of GDP and minimization of inflation), can change the official interest rate (the aggregate balance sheet is known), and banks make their portfolio choices. A decrease (increase) in the official interest rate is associated to perspectives of rise (contraction) in growth and credit and entails an expansion (reduction) of the aggregate balance sheet of the banking sector, with a new structure, with probabilities p and $(1 - p)$. In t_2 the volume of assets of the banking sector depends on previous choices in t_1 from the initial situation t_0. The growth of assets relies on the net supply of funding ρ_i (or net demand of assets). It can be equal to the (exogenous) demand $\left(\rho_i = 1\right)$, more $\left(\rho_i > 1\right)$ or less $\left(0 < \rho_i < 1\right)$. It includes a yield R_i for assets I_i. In case of excess demand (supply), the volume of assets (recorded with fair value rules) is raised (decreased) because of a wealth effect which is included through a coefficient μ_i:

$$I_{it_2} = I_{it_0}\left[1 + R_i + \rho_i \mu_i\right] \tag{1}$$

$\mu_i > 0$, with, for I_i assets:

$$\mu_i \begin{cases} < 1, \text{ si } \rho_i < 1 \\ > 1, \text{ si } \rho_i > 1 \\ = 1, \text{ si } \rho_i = 1 \end{cases} \tag{2}$$

$0 < R_i < 1$. It is a net return, that is to say the difference between the yield of the claim r_i and the bank's funding cost, which at least corresponds to the interest rate of the central bank r_{BC}:

$$R_i = r_i - r_{BC} \tag{3}$$

A high (low) variance σ_i^2 implies that I_i asset is riskier (less risky). About liabilities in t_2:

$$K_{t_2} = \alpha_i I_{it_0}\left[1 + \rho_i \mu_i\right] \tag{4}$$

$$D_{t_0} = \left(1 - \alpha_i\right) I_{it_0}\left[1 + \rho_i \mu_i\right] \tag{5}$$

There is no distribution of benefits, hence new quasi

Table 1. Aggregate balance sheet of the banking sector in t_0.

Assets	Liabilities
I_{it_0}	$K_{t_0} = \alpha_i I_i$
	$D_{t_0} = \left(1 - \alpha_i\right) I_i$

[3]Note that the model uses a given probability of risk aversion. Making endogenous the coefficient a would constitute an improvement, implying a dynamic study over the cycle.

equities (RAN):

$$RAN = I_{it_0} R_i \tag{6}$$

3.1. Behavioral Equations

The central bank wishes to minimize losses due to the difference between real activity and inflation and their expected levels:

$$\min\left[L = \frac{1}{2}\left(\pi - \pi^*\right)^2 + \theta\left(\text{GDP} - \text{GDP}^*\right)^2 \right] \tag{7}$$

With L the losses of the central bank, π the effective inflation rate, π^* the inflation target, GDP the national income, GDP^* the potential national income (the difference equals to the output gap) and θ the relative weight of the aim on GDP compared to the inflation's one. The tool that satisfies this function is the interest rate complying with the Taylor rule:

$$r_{BC} = \pi + r^r + b\left(\pi - \pi^*\right) + c\left(\text{GDP} - \text{GDP}^*\right) \tag{8}$$

With r^r the real interest rate and $b > 0, c > 0$. When output growth and inflation are too high, the Central Bank increases the interest rate r_{BC} and conversely. So the latter is crucial to assess the banking sector reaction to monetary policy.

Banks maximize profit:

$$\max\left[U\left(R_P, \sigma_P\right) = R_P - a\sigma_P^2 \right] \tag{9}$$

With P the assets portfolio, R_P its net yield:

$$\left(R_P = \sum_{i=1}^{N} R_i \right),$$

and a the risk aversion coefficient. The latter depends on the cycle: $p\left(a = a^{\mathrm{I}}\right) = p$ and $p\left(a = a^{\mathrm{II}}\right) = 1 - p$, with $a^{\mathrm{I}} < a^{\mathrm{II}}$ since risk aversion is higher during recessions[3]. Over several periods, banks are supposed to be risk neutral [35]. $a\sigma_P^2$ measures the portfolio risk according to risk aversion.

With [3], we understand how portfolio choices are made according to expectations, which in turn depend on the official interest rate. If banks observe or expect to a rise in interest rates, then they also expect a higher cost of capital. On the opposite, when low interest rates are set, they expect growth and a lower cost of capital. The (I) configuration with low interest rate is conducive to a growth of credits $\left(\rho_i > 0\right)$, while the (II) configuration favors a flight to quality, preventing banks from extending credits and private assets $\left(\rho_i < 0\right)$:

$$\rho_i = f^-\left(r_{BC}\right).$$

3.2. Assets and Accounting Equilibrium

Assuming three types of assets $\left(i = 1, 2, 3\right)$, we present the balance sheet of the banking sector (cf. **Table 2**).

Table 2. Balance sheet of the banking sector.

Assets	Liabilities
I_1	K
I_2	RAN
I_3	D

I_1 is a safety asset (e.g. Treasury Bond), I_2 is backed on a productive project and I_3 is a speculative asset without linkage with real activity. To focus on banks' behavior, we don't specify the maturity of assets. The speculative assets I_3 include issuances by other financial intermediaries in order to increase leverage: Asset Backed Securities (ABS) and Asset Backed Commercial Paper (ABCP). As I_1 is a safety asset, it does not give any yield $(r_1 = r_{BC})$ and does not require any equity. During the expansion phase, I_3 asset gives a higher net yield than I_2 but is also riskier:

$$R_1 = 0 < R_2 < R_3 < 1$$

and:

$$\sigma_1^2 = 0 < \sigma_2^2 < \sigma_3^2 < 1$$

To simplify, the yield/risk ratio for I_2 and I_3 is equal:

$$\left(\frac{R_2}{\sigma_2^2} = \frac{R_3}{\sigma_3^2} \right)$$

Nevertheless, the risk of I_3 is higher, so it requires more equities as regards prudential solvency ratios: $\alpha_1 = 0 < \alpha_2 < \alpha_3$.

The bank portfolio choices depend on the yield of assets but also on the cost of equities: with the hypothesis of an average neutrality of risk aversion, none of the assets I_2 and I_3 is preferred since:

$$\frac{R_2}{\alpha_2} = \frac{R_3}{\alpha_3}$$

and $E(R_2) = E(R_3)$. To diversify risks, banks select a similar growth of these assets: $\rho_2 = \rho_3 = \rho$. But I_1 and I_2 are not recorded with fair value rules $(\mu_1 = \mu_2 = 1)$, unlike I_3: when its demand (by banks) is higher than supply, the "fair value" is sharply increasing $(\mu_3 > 1)$, and conversely $(\mu_3 < 1)$. To simplify: $\mu_3 = \mu$.

Last, I_1 represents an insurance against liquidity risk. It is used as a collateral in case of refinancing operations by the central bank, hence its inclusion for a proportion β of debts:

---

[4]We have (11) + (12) + (13) = (4') + (5') + (6'). The central bank cannot observe the number of the claims but their amount. The equilibrium of the balance sheet is explained as following: the Treasury Bonds I_1, being a share of debts are both in the asset and liability sides. The credits I_2 appear in the balance sheet of the counterparts as deposits. The speculative assets I_3 are also in the liability side since they are issued by other institutions.

$$I_1 \geq \beta D \qquad (10)$$

The aggregate balance sheet of the banking sector is determined as follows[4] (cf. **Table 3**).

Now we can observe the evolution of assets and liabilities, but also performance and resilience indicators, from t_0 to t_2, i.e. during high or low growth.

4. Results: Banks Choices and Transmission of Monetary Policy

The analytical framework highlights incentives produced by the objectives of financial profitability to the detriment of resilience indicators. (I) characterizes a phase of strong growth and (II) a recession: $R_i^I > R_i^{II}, \forall i = 2,3$ and $\rho^I > 1$ et $\rho^{II} < 1$.

Consequently: $(\mu\rho)^I > 1$ and $0 < (\mu\rho)^{II} < 1$.

4.1. Banks Incentives and Stylized Facts

The financial profitability (ROE) can be expressed by the following Results/Equities ratio. From [4'] et [6']:

$$\frac{RAN_{t_2}}{K_{t_2}} = \frac{R_i \left(I_{2,t_0} + I_{3,t_0} \right)}{\alpha_i \left[\left(I_{2,t_0} + I_{3,t_0} \right) + \rho \left(I_{2,t_0} + \mu I_{3,t_0} \right) \right]} \qquad (14)$$

We find:

$$\left(\frac{RAN_{t_2}}{K_{t_2}} \right)^I > \left(\frac{RAN_{t_2}}{K_{t_2}} \right)^{II}$$

Under the condition:

$$R_i^I > \alpha_i \left[1 + \rho \left(1 + \mu\rho \right) \right]^I > \alpha_i \left[1 + \rho \left(1 + \mu\rho \right) \right]^{II} > R_i^{II}.$$

The condition is satisfied as soon as the fixed solvency ratio is lower (higher) than expected yields during ascending (downturn) phase. The observed financial profitability is higher during growth, together with a rise in individual and contagious risks. The first can be approached by a simple solvency ratio (capital/assets). From (4'), (11), (12) and (13):

Table 3. The aggregated balance sheet of the banking sector.

Assets		
$I_{1,t_2} = I_{1,t_0} \left(1 + \rho_1 \right)$		(11)
$I_{2,t_2} = I_{2,t_0} \left(1 + R_2 + \rho \right)$		(12)
$I_{3,t_2} = I_{3,t_0} \left(1 + R_3 + \rho\mu \right)$		(13)
Liabilities		
$K_{t_2} = \alpha_i \left[\left(I_{2,t_0} + I_{3,t_0} \right) + \rho \left(I_{2,t_0} + \mu I_{3,t_0} \right) \right]$		(4')
$RAN_{t_2} = R_i \left(I_{2,t_0} + I_{3,t_0} \right)$		(6')
$D_{t_2} = \left(1 - \alpha_i \right) \left[\left(I_{2,t_0} + I_{3,t_0} \right) + \rho \left(I_{2,t_0} + \mu I_{3,t_0} \right) \right] + I_1$		(5')

$$\frac{K_{t_2}}{I_{1t_2}+I_{2t_2}+I_{3t_2}}$$

$$=\frac{\alpha_i\left[\left(I_{2,t_0}+I_{3,t_0}\right)+\rho\left(I_{2,t_0}+\mu I_{3,t_0}\right)\right]}{I_{1,t_0}\left(1+\rho_1\right)+I_{2,t_0}\left(1+R_2+\rho\right)+I_{3,t_0}\left(1+R_3+\rho\mu\right)} \cdot (15)$$

Giving the variables' specification during states (I) and (II):

$$\left(\frac{K_{t_2}}{I_{1t_2}+I_{2t_2}+I_{3t_2}}\right)^{I}<\left(\frac{K_{t_2}}{I_{1t_2}+I_{2t_2}+I_{3t_2}}\right)^{II}.$$

Here, the increase in individual risk in phase (I) is clearly underscored, with α unchanged. Now, let's observe contagious risks thanks to the leverage (debts/capital). From (4') et (5'):

$$\frac{D_{t_2}}{K_{t_2}}$$

$$=\frac{(1-\alpha_i)\left[\left(I_{2,t_0}+I_{3,t_0}\right)+\rho\left(I_{2,t_0}+\mu I_{3,t_0}\right)\right]+I_{1,t_0}\left(1+\rho_1\right)}{\alpha_i\left[\left(I_{2,t_0}+I_{3,t_0}\right)+\rho\left(I_{2,t_0}+\mu I_{3,t_0}\right)\right]}.$$

(16)

Since $(1-\alpha_i)>\alpha_i$, we have:

$$\frac{D}{K}>1$$

and:

$$\left(\frac{D_{t_2}}{K_{t_2}}\right)^{I}>\left(\frac{D_{t_2}}{K_{t_2}}\right)^{II}.$$

So, (I) make happen a better performance of the banking sector, a decrease in capital adequacy and a higher contagious risk. These indicators reverse in (II). Looking at data on developed countries, we obtain an illustration (**Figures 1** to **3**):

Financial profitability and leverage are increasing before the crisis for the selected countries. Besides, we in-

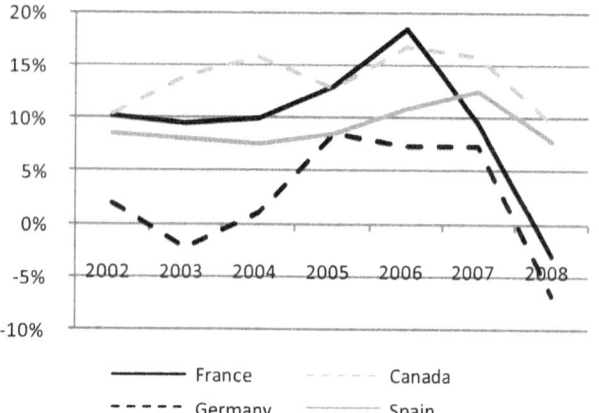

Figure 1. Financial profitability evolution, ROE (caption: OECD, authors' calculations).

troduce the United-States, whose capital ratio is artificially increased by regulatory capital arbitrage (*cf.* post). Here, equities are rather low during growth, and rise after the reversal. Non-performing loans sharply increase in this context (*cf.* **Figure 4**).

Last, the central bank is sensitive to macroeconomic liquidity, defined by the liquidity/assets ratio (independent from the volume of deposits): From (11), (12) and (13):

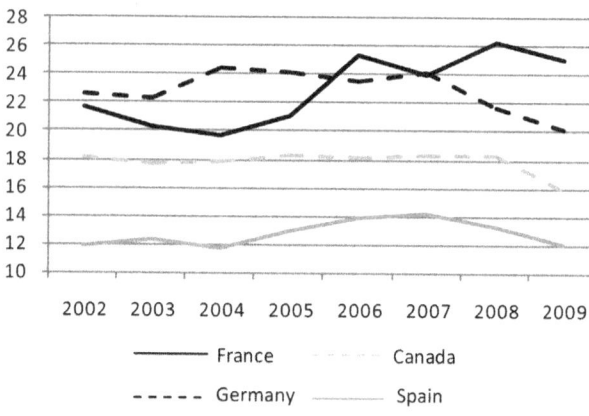

Figure 2. Leverage evolution in % (caption: OECD, authors' calculations).

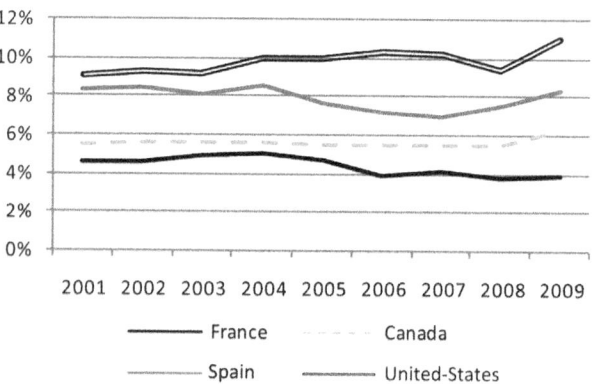

Figure 3. Capital ratio evolution (caption: OECD, authors' calculations).

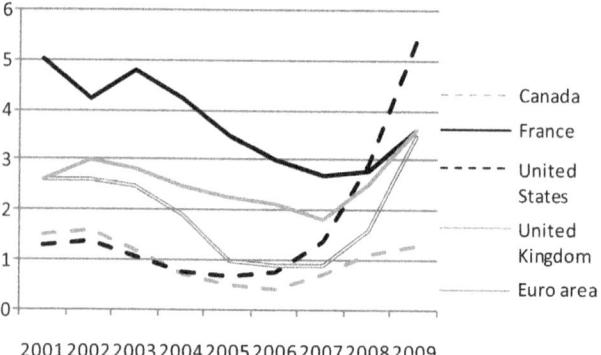

Figure 4. Non-performing loans to the loans portfolio in % (caption: World Bank, authors' calculations).

$$\frac{I_{1t_2}}{I_{1t_2} + I_{2t_2} + I_{3t_2}} \qquad (17)$$

$$= \frac{I_{1,t_0}\left(1+\rho_1\right)}{I_{1,t_0}\left(1+\rho_1\right) + I_{2,t_0}\left(1+R_2+\rho\right) + I_{3,t_0}\left(1+R_3+\rho\mu\right)}$$

get: $\left(\dfrac{I_{1t_2}}{I_{1t_2} + I_{2t_2} + I_{3t_2}}\right)^{\mathrm{I}} < \left(\dfrac{I_{1t_2}}{I_{1t_2} + I_{2t_2} + I_{3t_2}}\right)^{\mathrm{II}}$

During (I), there is a debt increase and a decrease in liquidity ratio. It looks like Minsky's idea [36], that is to say, the linkage between balance sheets evolution and the use of financial innovations leads to financial embrittlement. This result is explained by the difference between micro and macroeconomic liquidity. The asset I_1 is liquid, while I_3 is only liquid if growth is strong (microeconomic liquidity). Indeed, I_3 rapidly drains in the down phase because supply grows faster than demand and accounting rules are procyclical.

4.2. Diversification: Decrease in Productive Assets and Increase in Speculative Assets

Risk aversion changes together with growth and then preconditions portfolio choices. Banks' preferences move towards risky (safety) assets when risk aversion is weak (strong).

$$\frac{I_{3t_2}}{I_{2t_2}} = \frac{I_{3,t_0}\left(1+R_3+\rho\mu\right)}{I_{2,t_0}\left(1+R_2+\rho\right)} \qquad (18)$$

then: $\left(\dfrac{I_{3t_2}}{I_{2t_2}}\right)^{\mathrm{I}} > \left(\dfrac{I_{3t_2}}{I_{2t_2}}\right)^{\mathrm{II}}$

Speculative assets are preferred during (I), while the yield/risk ratio is supposed to be unchanged. As in Adrian and Shin's model [37], these choices are made to the detriment of productive loans: the credit rationing testifies to the limits of the interest rate tool, in a context where financial innovations allow substituting credits by other types of assets. On the opposite:

$$\frac{I_{1t_2}}{I_{2t_2}} = \frac{I_{1,t_0}\left(1+\rho_1\right)}{I_{2,t_0}\left(1+R_2+\rho\right)} \qquad (19)$$

Choices are still unambiguous:

$$\left(\frac{I_{1t_2}}{I_{2t_2}}\right)^{\mathrm{I}} < \left(\frac{I_{1t_2}}{I_{2t_2}}\right)^{\mathrm{II}}$$

Safety assets are preferred in (II), which corresponds to a flight to quality in a context of high risk aversion (or/and uncertainty). Moreover, this preference is due to the losses caused by the fair value rule for I_3.

Financial markets favor risks' diversification. Conse-quently, even if the interest rate would have no effect on credit, the possibility for banks to choose financial assets supplants the credit channel. Banks are exposed to market risk $\left(\sigma_3^2 > \sigma_2^2\right)$, which provides higher returns $\left(E\left(R_3\right) > E\left(R_2\right)\right)$ and profits $\left(RAN\right)$ (Risk-taking channel). This situation is observed when the high amount of equities linked to I_3 (bank capital channel) is offset by a wealth effect under "fair value" rule.

A simple Taylor rule can entail financial instability because of a weakening of the financial accelerator concerning non-financial sector, for which loans require high equities without wealth effects coming from accounting rules. This result doesn't match with the increase in the credit until the subprime crisis, but this paradox can be explained by the growing share of securitized mortgage loans.

4.3. Securitization and Off-Balance Sheet: Financial Instability and Flight to Quality

According to the Equation (16), bank leverage increases during the upward phase in order to improve profitability. We observe this trend for European banks, which have a higher leverage in 2007 than American banks: the gap is explained by off-balance sheet activities. These changes regarding to the business model have to be taken into account, as it implies a risk transfer and stresses the role of consolidated balance sheets. Securitized assets are not backed to a productive project, so they are contained in I_3, whose characteristics change. The cost of protection (i.e. Credit Default Swap [CDS]'s premium g) decreases the return R_3. To simplify, we assume that this premium equalizes net returns of I_2 and I_3:

$R_3 = r_3 - r_{BC} - g = R_2$.

The demand of funding is increased by the introduction of the shadow banking system. In these conditions, we assume that price effects entailed by accounting standards are higher: $\mu' > \mu$. During (I), I_3 are even more preferred than without securitization, since the wealth effect μ' is reinforced but also because there are no required equities (off balance). Consequently, prudential regulation is weaker: $\alpha_3' = 0 < \alpha_2$. The **Table 4** presents the consolidated balance sheet of the banking sector.

The growth of the balance sheet between t_0 and t_2 entails a modification of its composition in favor of I_3. These assets are linked to Special Purpose Vehicles (SPV), which are registered in offshore financial centers, where regulatory (and fiscal) requirements are less binding. Following a positive growth shock in t_1, this business model ("originate and distribute": OD) gives results in t_2, that we compare with the "originate and hold" (OH) system.

On the one hand, we show that $RAN_{OD}^{\mathrm{I}} < RAN_{OH}^{\mathrm{I}}$ and $K_{OD}^{\mathrm{I}} < K_{OH}^{\mathrm{I}}$. On the other hand:

Table 4. Consolidated balance sheet of the banking sector.

Assets	
$I_{1_{t_2}} = I_{1_{t_0}}(1+\rho_1)$	(11')
$I_{2_{t_2}} = I_{2_{t_0}}(1+R_2+\rho_2)$	(12')
$I_{3_{t_2}} = I_{3_{t_0}}(1+R_2+\rho_3\mu')$	(13')
Liabilities	
$K_{t_2} = \alpha_2\left(I_{2_{t_0}}+\rho_2 I_{2_{t_0}}\right)$	(4'')
$RAN_{t_2} = R_2\left(I_{2_{t_0}}+I_{3_{t_0}}\right)$	(6'')
$D_{t_2} = (1-\alpha_2)\left(I_{2_{t_0}}+\rho_2 I_{2_{t_0}}\right)+I_{3_{t_0}}+\rho_3\mu' I_{3_{t_0}}+I_1$	(5'')

$$\left(\frac{RAN}{K}\right)^{I}_{OD} > \left(\frac{RAN}{K}\right)^{I}_{OH}$$

Financial profitability (ROE) increases because of the higher volume of assets entailed by the shadow banking system and the wealth effects linked to I_3. This result is no longer valid if the returns of I_3 are lower than those of I_2 [5].

In addition, we have:

$$\left(\frac{I_1}{I_1+I_2+I_3}\right)^{I}_{OD} < \left(\frac{I_1}{I_1+I_2+I_3}\right)^{I}_{OH}$$

The liquidity ratio decreases because liquid assets I_1 represent a share β of debts and because I_3 are transferred towards SPV: liquidity provided by non-banks highlights the question of the money creation. The collapse of the liquidity ratio is also explained by the high growth of I_3, which requires fewer equities.

Then, we show that: $K^{I}_{OD} < K^{I}_{OH}$ and:

$$\left(I_1+I_2+I_3\right)^{I}_{OD} > \left(I_1+I_2+I_3\right)^{I}_{OH}$$

The decrease in equities is more important:

$$\left(\frac{K}{I_1+I_2+I_3}\right)^{I}_{OD} < \left(\frac{K}{I_1+I_2+I_3}\right)^{I}_{OH}$$

But, as the simple solvency ratio doesn't include off-balance sheet activities, a "buffer" rapidly appears:

[5]Financial profitability is the product of leverage and return on assets. Since (14), the leverage permits to increase the financial profitability. We also show that the ROE is raised if banks securitize their assets, but this result is not available if the return becomes inferior to the productive assets' one, as for Calmès and Théoret [38]. The fall in the ROE is available in a context of great competition or a decrease in distributed benefits.

[6]Indeed, the Fed increases its interest rate from 1 to 5.5% between 2004 and 2006. In this case, savings from the rest of the world entailed a decrease in long term interest rates [40]. Adrian and Shin [37] show that a monetary policy tightening is able to limit the credit activity according to the rise of interest rates but also according to the term structure of interest rates.

$$\left(\frac{K}{I_1+I_2}\right)^{I}_{OD} > \left(\frac{K}{I_1+I_2+I_3}\right)^{I}_{OH}$$

Consequently, the securitization permits a reduction of individual risks but also a rise in contagious risk [39].

Indeed:

$$\left(\frac{D}{K}\right)^{I}_{OD} > \left(\frac{D}{K}\right)^{I}_{OH}$$

This is explained not only by the rise in indebtedness $\left(D^{I}_{OD} > D^{I}_{OH}\right)$ but also by the decrease in equities $\left(K^{I}_{OD} < K^{I}_{OH}\right)$. Yet, a bank can decrease its leverage by going out activities from its balance sheet: this ratio is lowered if the funding of I_3 assets is excluded. Consequently, the latter (artificially) becomes lower than the traditional business model's one. If expectations about assets prices growth become widespread, the bullish movement becomes self-sustaining (bandwagon effect): the rise in interest rate is not enough to reverse the model dynamics in t_1 and turns to a recession. The weakening of the credit channel implied by market and by off-balance sheet activities is due to less productive projects funding, more financial instability and less interest rate efficiency [6].

Securitization entails a deeper leverage and a lower macroeconomic liquidity. The reversal is more harmful if leverage is high; microeconomic liquidity disappears following a distrust about ABS; the illiquidity forces banks to sell assets; informational asymmetries are higher and toxic claims progressively come back to the banking sector; the rise in official interest rate deteriorates the solvency of borrowers (graphic 4). This implies an easing in monetary conditions [41], without inflation because refinancing operations will be repaid. Moreover, in a context of recession, liquidity is decreasing because of a drop in credits and in deposits. So, the high rise of the monetary base can happen without great changes in inflation expectations (**Figure 5**). Besides, the credit risk increases for the central bank due to assets buyouts on secondary markets. The flight to quality is different if public assets are riskier: in the euro zone, banks resort to the deposit facility (**Figure 6**).

The new business model reinforces previous results about productive credit and financial instability, and the official interest rate is less effective. Unfortunately, the shadow banking system is more attractive if bank solvency regulation is stronger. In case of a crisis accompanied by a deterioration of public securities, the central bank can restore the functioning of money markets but not the quality of intermediation.

5. Conclusions

In this model, a growth phase is the outcome of low ef-

Figure 5. Break-even point in euro-zone (OAT 4.25% April 2019-OAT€₁ 2.25% July 2020) (caption: INSEE, authors' calculations).

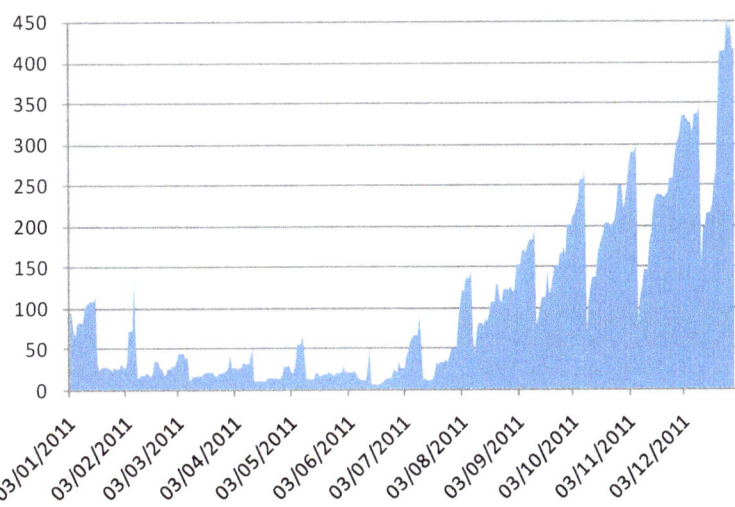

Figure 6. Depositfacilities in euro-zone, end of 2011, Millions of € (caption: ECB, authors'calculations).

fective (and expected) interest rates, considering high net yields. The reversal occurs when banks expect a rise in (nominal) interest rates and/or when official interest rates actually increase. By substituting investors by banks and productive investments by financial assets, this mechanism is described by Minsky: the debt reduction entails a decrease in credits and securities. Instability risks are increased, and the credit channel is less important since productive loans are less rewarding. The usual financial accelerator is weakened but it is still effective through procyclical wealth effects. Given that bank loans are not anymore the only source of money creation, monetary policy could be less focused on the consumption prices indice and more sensitive to financial instability risks.

Securitization and off-balance sheet activities also contribute to the weakening of the credit channel and to the strengthening of the risk-taking channel, with a bigger consolidated balance sheet in the upward phase and relatively more microeconomic liquidity (provided by the shadow banking system). Banks implement strategies to avoid prudential requirements (regulatory capital arbitrage). During the upward phase, due to the investors' search for yields, a possible improvement of monetary policy is linked to macroprudential supervision, for example thanks to a countercyclical solvency ratio. Further, our model highlights the necessary cooperation between central banks and microprudential supervisors, especially if solvency ratios sometimes explain risk exposures. Basel Committee's last recommendations will improve the assessment of credit and market risk, and provide liquidity and leverage ratios. First, these modifications could be harmful in Europe regarding the context of sovereign debt crisis, since it motivates banks to reduce the amount of their assets to comply with prudential requirements. Second, even though it is an improvement, it does not change incentives for banks. In this sense, a banking union is desirable, as the choice of the European central bank (not the European Banking Authority) to implement it.

REFERENCES

[1] B. Bernanke, M. Gertler and S. Gilchrist, "The Financial Accelerator and the Flight to Quality," *The Review of Economics and Statistics, Symposium on Developments in Business Cycles Research*, Vol. 78, No. 1, 1996, pp. 1-15.

[2] B. Bernanke, M. Gertler and S. Gilchrist, "The Financial Accelerator in a Quantitative Business Cycle Framework," In: M. Woodford and J. Taylor, Eds., *Handbook of Macroeconomics*, Elsevier, Amsterdam, 1999, pp. 1341-1393.

[3] N. Kiyotaki and J. Moore, "Credit Cycles," *Journal of Political Economy*, Vol. 105, No. 2, 1997.

[4] B. Bernanke and M. Gertler, "Should Central Banks Respond to Movements in Asset Prices?" *The American Economic Review*, Vol. 91, No. 2, 2001, pp. 253-257.

[5] A. Filardo, "Should Monetary Policy Respond to Asset Price Bubbles? Some Experimental Results," Federal Reserve Bank of Kansas Working Papers, 2001, Paper No. 01-04.

[6] S. G. Cecchetti, H. Genberg and S. Wadhwani, "Asset Prices in a Flexible Inflation Targeting Framework," National Bureau of Economic Research Working Paper, 2002, Paper No. 8970.

[7] G. Levieuge, "Monetary Policy with Financial Information," *Review of Political Economy*, Vol. 113, No. 2, 2003, pp. 233-254.

[8] M. Brunnermeier and Y. Sannikov, "A Macroeconomic Model with a Financial Sector," Working Paper Research, National Bank of Belgium, 2009.

[9] A. Gerali, S. Neri, L. Sessa and F. Signoretti, "Credit and Banking in a DSGE Model of the Euro Area," *Journal of Money Credit and Banking*, Vol. 42, No. 6, 2010, pp. 107-141.

[10] C. Meh and K. Moran, "The Role of Bank Capital in the Propagation of Shocks," Bank of Canada Working Paper, 2010, Paper No. 08-36.

[11] D. Kohn, "Monetary Policy and Asset Prices Revisited," *Cato Journal*, Vol. 29, No. 1, 2009, pp. 31-44.

[12] C. Walsh, "Using Monetary Policy to Stabilize Economic Activity," *Jackson Hole Symposium on Financial Stability and Macroeconomic Policy*, 2009.

[13] R. Rajan, "Has Financial Development Made the World Riskier?" NBER Working Paper, 2005, Paper No. 11728.

[14] W. White, "Is Price Stability Enough?" BIS Working Papers, 2006, Paper No. 205.

[15] S. Fahr, R. Motto, M. Rostagno, F. Smet and P. Tristani, "A Monetary Policy Strategy in Good and Bad Times, Lessons from the Recent Past," European Central Bank Working Paper, 2011, Paper No. 1336.

[16] B. Hobijn and F. Ravenna, "Loan Securitization and the Monetary Transmission Mechanism," Work in Progress. http://ic.ucsc.edu/~fravenna/home/Hobijn_ravenna.pdf

[17] L. Gambacorta and D. Marques-Ibanez, "The Bank Lending Channel. Lessons from the Crisis," BIS Working Papers, 2011, Paper No. 1335.

[18] S. V. den Heuvel, "Does Bank Capital Matter for Monetary Transmission?" *Economic Policy Review*, 2002, pp. 259-265.

[19] V. Bouvatier and L. Lepetit, "Bank Provision Channel and Credit Market Cyclicality," *Economic Review*, Vol. 62, 2011, pp. 67-85.

[20] G. D' Ariccia, D. Igan and L. Laeven, "Credit Booms and Lending Standards: Evidence from the Subprime Mortgage Market," IMF Working Paper, 2008, Paper No. 106.

[21] A. Korinek, "Systemic Risk-Taking, Amplification Effects, Externalities, and Regulatory Responses," European Central Bank Working Paper, 2011, Paper No. 1345.

[22] A. Krishnamurthy, "Collateral Constraints and the Amplification Mechanism," *Journal of Economic Theory*, Vol. 111, No. 2, 2003, pp. 277-292.

[23] M. Ciccarelli, A. Maddaloni and J.-L. Peydro, "Trusting the Bankers: A New Look at the Credit Channel of Monetary Policy," European Central Bank Working Paper, 2010, Paper No. 1228.

[24] Y. Altunbas, L. Gambacorta and D. Marqués-Ibanez, "Securitization and the Bank Lending Channel," European Central Bank Working Paper, 2007, Article ID: 838.

[25] G. Jiménez, J. S. Salas, S. Ongena and J-L. Peydro, "Hazar-Dous Times for Monetary Policy: What Do Twenty-Three Million Bank Loans Say about the Effects of Monetary Policy on Credit Risk-Taking?" Banco de Espana Working Papers, 2009, Paper No. 0833.

[26] Y. Altunbas, L. Gambacorta and D. Marqués-Ibanez, "Does Monetary Policy Affect Bank Risk-Taking," European Central Bank Working Paper, 2010, Paper No. 1166.

[27] C. Borio and H. Zhu, "Capital Regulation, Risk-Taking and Monetary Policy: A Missing Link in the Transmission Mechanism?" BIS Working Papers, 2008, Paper No. 268.

[28] C. C. Riportella, R. S. Medina and A. T. Ponce, "What Drives Bank Securitization? The Spanish Experience," *Journal of Banking and Finance*, Vol. 34, No. 11, 2010, pp. 2639-2651.

[29] J. Tirole, "Liquidity Shortages : Theoritical Underpinnings," *Review of Financial Stability*, No. 11, 2008, pp. 57-69.

[30] P. Weill, "Leaning against the Wind," *Review of Economic Studies*, No. 74, 2007, pp. 1329-1354.

[31] W. White, "Should Monetary Policy 'Lean or Clean'?" Federal Reserve Bank of Dallas, Globalization and Monetary Policy Institute Working Paper, 2009, Paper No. 34.

[32] F. Covas and S. Fujita, "Time-Varying Capital Requirements in a General Equilibrium Model of Liquidity Dependence," Federal Reserve Bank of Philadelphia Working Papers, 2009, Paper No. 09-23.

[33] P. N' Diaye, "Countercyclical Macro Prudential Policies in a Supporting Role to Monetary Policy," IMF Working

Paper, 2009, Paper No. 09/257.

[34] J. M. Blum, "Why 'Basel II' May Need a Leverage Ratio Restriction," *Journal of Banking and Finance*, Vol. 32, 2008, pp. 1699-1707.

[35] A. Korinek, "Systemic Risk-Taking, Amplification Effects, Externalities, and Regulatory Responses," European Central Bank Working Paper, 2011, Paper No. 1345.

[36] H. Minsky, "Can 'It' Happen Again? Essays on Instability and Finance," M. E. Sharpe, New York, 1982.

[37] T. Adrian and H S. Shin, "Monetary Cycles, Financial Cycles, and the Business Cycle," Federal Reserve Bank of New-York Staff Reports, 2010, Paper No. 421.

[38] C. Calmès and R. Théoret, "The Impact of Off-Balance-Sheet Activities on Banks Returns: An Application if the ARCH-M to Canadian Data," *Journal of Banking and Finance*, No. 34, 2010, pp. 1719-1728.

[39] R. Nijskens and W. Wagner, "Credit Risk Transfer Activities and Systemic Risk: How Banks Became Less Risky Individually but Posed Greater Risks to Financial System at the Same Time," *Journal of Banking and Finance*, Vol. 35, No. 6, 2011, pp. 1391-1398.

[40] F. Warnock and V. Warnock, "International Capital Flows and US Interest Rates," NBER Working Paper, 2006, Paper No. 12560.

[41] C. Bastidon, P. Gilles and N. Huchet, "Amplification Effects and Unconventional Monetary Policies," *Theoretical and Applied Economics*, Vol. XIX, No. 2, 2012, pp. 13-30.

7

A Comparison of Three-Stage DEA and Artificial Neural Network on the Operational Efficiency of Semi-Conductor Firms in Taiwan

Hsiang-Hsi Liu[1], Tser-Yieth Chen[1], Yung-Ho Chiu[2], Fu-Hsiang Kuo[3]
[1]Graduate Institute of International Business, National Taipei University, New Taipei City, Taiwan
[2]Department of economics, Soochow University, Taipei City, Taiwan
[3]Department of Information Management, Chaoyang University of Technology, Taichung City, Taiwan

ABSTRACT

In this study, the data envelopment analysis (DEA), three-stage DEA (3SDEA) and artificial neural network (ANN) are employed to measure the technical efficiency of 29 semi-conductor firms in Taiwan. Estimated results show that there are significant differences in efficiency scores among DEA, 3SDEA and ANN analysis. The advanced setting of the three stages mechanism of DEA does show some changes in the efficiency scores between DEA and ANN approaches. We further find that the environmental factor is still a significant variable to explain technical efficiency in Taiwan, irrespective of whether a DEA, 3SDEA or ANN approach is used.

Keywords: Data Envelopment Analysis; Three-Stage DEA; Artificial Neural Network; Semi-Conductor Industry

1. Introduction

In this paper, we compare traditional data envelopment analysis (DEA), three-stage data envelopment analysis (3SDEA) and artificial neural network analysis (ANN) to estimate technical efficiency indices, and to explore the effect of environmental factors (Fried, Lovell, Schmidt and Yaisawarng, 2002) [1] on technical efficiency for policy purposes in the semi-conductor sector. We focus on the efficiency assessment since we believe that efficiency and/or performance will become strategic variables in tackling the increasing competitive pressure and structural changes within this industry. We incorporate an operation mechanism and employ DEA, 3SDEA and ANN approaches to our analysis since we consider that the unpredictability of market demand and supply makes the semi-conductor companies' input-output relationship vary.

The semi-conductor industry is a promising knowledge-intensive industry, which is characterized by large capital, high-quality talent, longer reward and profit for R & D activities, therefore semi-conductor companies must be accountable for the R & D efforts they provide (Chiesa and Toletti, 2003) [2]. In the 1980s, a push for accountability was undertaken in United States and all semi-conductor companies faced the task of allocating scarce resources among high risk and high return R & D activities. Semi-conductor companies are concerned with efficiency, and current tight economic conditions have further highlighted the importance of those concerns. In the 1990s, Taiwan government declared the Technology Industry Establishment Promotion Decree which emphasized the importance of the semi-conductor industry as critical in the development of Taiwan's manufacturing industry. The government also included the semi-conductor industry in the ten emerging focus industries in 1998. Under this climate of focus, Taiwan started to increase operational efficiency in the semi-conductor industry, and to place extra funds into the supply market. The objective of this focus was to increase quality of life and reduce financial uncertainty. Taiwan's semi-conductor companies have also confronted accountability issues in the 2000s with administrators bringing some revolutionary changes.

A semi-conductor firm may be viewed as an enterprise in which the professional staff provides the operating conditions for converting quantifiable resources (inputs) into patents and revenues (outputs). However R & D expense faces budget constraints, and whether or not there is a price tag attached, firms need to choose among competing expenditure options. The efficiency of semi-conductor companies is a critical issue in the development of the technology industry while operational inefficiency increases uncertainty owing to fluctuations in the financial environment. The issues of market risk emerge

A Comparison of Three-Stage DEA and Artificial Neural Network on the Operational Efficiency of Semi-Conductor Firms in Taiwan

71

when we evaluate the operating efficiency of semi-conductor companies (Kliger and Sarig, 2000) [3]. Due to the continued rapid improvement of semi-conductor technology, it is expected that logistics management has become an increasingly important segment of the semi-conductor industry. Therefore, major issues in this study focus on the effect of factory location as part of the firm's logistics management, when the carriage cost is viewed as an important input in Taiwan. Changes in the financial and political environment will undoubtedly affect a firm's location decision.

The research intensity and factory location present a useful reference indicator to the investor and legalistic institution (Garner, 1999) [4]. Thus, incorporating the environmental effects of the research intensity and factory location into the performance evaluating system of semi-conductor companies can obviously improve the effectiveness of the evaluation results because the invisible external and internal environment factors are included in the evaluating system in order to fit actual situations in the semi-conductor companies (Larsen, 2006) [5]. We then employ a three-stage data envelopment analysis method to evaluate semi-conductor company performance in order to tailor the multi-input and multi-output industry setting. To avoid the difficulty in making a subjective choice for the inputs and outputs of the DMUs (decision making unit), the artificial neural network (ANN) can be proposed to choose the inputs and outputs of DMUs which are more related to its operating efficiencies.

The purpose of this paper is to measure the resource utilization efficiency of semi-conductor companies in Taiwan applying three-stage DEA model and artificial neural network analysis on a sample of 29 semi-conductor companies during the period from 2001 to 2006 (Data sample refers to **Appendix 1**). This period of data is employed due to avoiding the one-off shock effect in overall efficiency evaluation. Hopefully the empirical results of this study can provide useful information for firms and government agencies to do decision-making about the improvement of operational efficiency.

The reminders of this paper are organized as follows. Section 2 presents a review of the relevant literature. Section 3 describes the methodology of the three-stage DEA and ANN approaches. Section 4 describes the data employed and its characteristics. Section 5 presents the empirical results. The paper then provides the concluding remarks in Section 6.

2. Literature Review

In this section, we firstly introduce the non-parametric programming approach of DEA and the extended 3SDEA to evaluate efficiency and then propose the alternative programming approach of ANN. The DEA ap-

proach uses a mathematical programming technique to construct a piecewise linear frontier and it can be referred to as a non-parametric programming approach (Charnes, Cooper and Rhodes, 1978 [6]; Banker, Charnes and Cooper, 1984 [7]). DEA allows researchers to avoid specification of a given functional form or error structure, and many researchers have focused on estimating the technical efficiency and scale efficiency of DMUs by utilizing this technique (Oral and Yolalan, 1990 [8]; Favero and Papi, 1995 [9]; Schaffnit, Rosen and Paradi, 1997 [10]; Fukuyama, Guerra and Weber, 1999 [11]). The DEA model used to evaluate the efficiency in the semi-conductor industry is found in Liu and Wang (2008) [12], Chen and Chen (2007) [13], and Chen and Yeh (2005) [14], while Schaffnit, Rosen and Paradi (1997) [10] present a best practice analysis of bank branches based on a DEA assurance region (DEA-AR) model containing output multiplier constraints, with standard transaction and maintenance times, in order to evaluate allocative efficiency.

The three-stage DEA was first proposed by Fried and Lovell (1990) [15]. Fried, Schmidt and Yaisawarng (1999) [16] then extended three-stage DEA and focused on estimating the environmental variables which influence the input slacks variables. Fried, Lovell, Schmit and Yaisawarng (2002) [1] further compare the efficiency based on the first stage DEA and the third stage DEA; they argue that the three-stage DEA is better than the one-stage DEA adjusting inputs and considering the individual environmental effect and statistical white noise. Greasley (2005) [17] employed a three-stage DEA and simulation to guide operating units to improved performance. The model compared the performance of the current and benchmark process designs. Athanassopoulos and Curram (1996) [18] compared DEA and artificial neural network (ANN) mechanisms to facilitate a definition of efficiency measures from the two methods. Wang (2003) [19] further compared the DEA, stochastic frontier analysis (SFA) and ANN and argued ANN can obtain a similar valid effect of DEA proposed by Charnes, Cooper and Rhodes (1978) [6]. Pendharkar and Rodger (2003) [20] compared the performance of the ANN and DEA by using the "efficient" and "inefficient" training data subsets. It may be useful to screen training data on the screened examples to approximately satisfy the monotonicity property. Liao (2004) [21] proposed an effective procedure on the basis of the artificial neural network (ANN) and the data envelopment analysis (DEA) to optimize the multi-response problems. A case study of improving the quality of hard disk drivers in Su and Tong (1997) [22] is resolved by the proposed procedure and yields a satisfactory solution. Pendharkar (2005) [23] illustrated that a DEA-based data screening of training data improves forecasting accuracy of an ANN using real-world health care and software engineering data. Santin (2008) [24] showed how ANN is a valid semi-parametric alternative for fitting empirical production functions and measuring technical efficiency. For the application of ANN in the semi-conductor industry, some results are shown in Wang, Su and Hsieh (2007) [25] and Buddefeld, Grosspietsch, Hosticka and Klinke (1991) [26]. These results demonstrate that DEA-ANN methods offer an useful range information regarding the assessment of performance.

This paper then extends the basic deterministic DEA method to incorporate the three-stage DEA mechanism in order to obtain a more similar comparison base between artificial neural network programming and three-stage DEA approaches.

3. The Three-Stage DEA and ANN Approaches

3.1 Three-Stage DEA Approach

In the DEA approach, Charnes, Cooper and Rhodes (1978) [6] initiated the data envelopment analysis method. They proposed an operational framework for the estimation of productive efficiency (the CCR model) which demonstrated that the mechanism for calculating DEA scores can be formulated as a linear programming problem. We denote $Y_{j \cdot n}$ as the n-th output of the j-th DMU and $X_{j \cdot m}$ as the m-th input of the j-th DMU. If a DMU employs M inputs to produce N outputs, the score of j-th DMU, E_j, is a solution from the linear programming problem,

$$\text{Max } E_j : \sum_{n=1}^{N} U_n Y_{j \cdot n}$$

$$s.t. \sum_{m=1}^{M} V_m X_{j \cdot m} = 1$$

$$\sum_{n=1}^{N} U_n Y_{r \cdot n} - \sum_{m=1}^{M} V_m X_{r \cdot m} \le 0, \forall r$$

$$U_n, V_m \ge 0, \forall n \text{ and } m$$

where $n = 1, 2, \cdots, N, m = 1, 2, \cdots, M, r = 1, 2, \cdots, j, \cdots, R$, and U_n and V_m give the weights associated with each output and input. The technical efficiency of each DMU is calculated by using the ratio of a weighted sum of output to a weighted sum of input. Here the input usage of a DMU is radial contracted to the best practice frontier (*i.e.*, isoquant), and the DMU is assumed to continue using its original production process (*i.e.*, production ray). The distance between the actual performance of the DMU and the best-practice frontier provides a measure of the relative inefficiency of the DMU. The DEA best-practice frontier is constructed from piecewise linear combinations of all available DMUs with each DMU being assigned a positive weight when constructing the best-

practice frontier of the N-th DMU. DMUs with positive weights are used to construct the best-practice frontier and a unique set of weights is determined when calculating the efficiency for each DMU. These weights generate the theoretical best-practice DMU, against which a DMU is compared when calculating that particular DMU's technical efficiency. The weights assigned to the DMUs in order to calculate the technical efficiency of the N-th DMU are then used to calculate the cross-efficiencies of the remaining N-1 DMUs, if necessary. Notably, the pure technical efficiency can be derived through the condition of variable returns to scale. We can add $\sum_{r=1}^{R} \lambda_r = 1$ to the former model to make the famous BCC model (Banker, Charnes and Cooper, 1984) [7], which provides valuable information about the cost-benefit evaluation. We can calculate the pure technical efficiency score from the BCC model, and then the scale efficiency score can be derived from the technical efficiency and pure technical efficiency scores in that the technical efficiency score is equal to the multiplication of pure technical efficiency and scale efficiency scores (Fare, Grosskopf and Lovell, 1985) [27].

We employ the three-stage DEA model (Fried, Lovell, Schmidt and Yaisawarng, 2002) [1] in order to decompose the environmental and statistical noise effects from the efficiencies and further estimate the real efficiency of each DMU. Under this consideration, it can obtain an objective operating efficiency measure given the identical external environment conditions.

In the first stage, we employ the DEA method together with the output and input variables to estimate the efficiency values and also obtain input slacks given that the environmental variables are controlled; a type of deterministic model where the statistical noise is still allowed. As to the second stage, let the dependent variable be the slack variable on each factor input, and the independent variable be the environmental variable. We can set up four types of regressions on the input slack variables as follows,

$$S_{it} = \begin{cases} Z'_{it} \beta + V_{it}, & \text{if } S_{it} > 0 \\ 0, & \text{if } S_{it} = 0 \end{cases} \quad (6)$$

where S_{it} represents the slack value of each input of i-th DMU within period at $t, i = 1, \cdots, n, t = 1, \cdots, T, Z$ is the vector $k \times 1$ and the first element is set as one. Comparing to the intercept item, other $k - 1$ elements represents the environmental variable of i-th, and β is the corresponding coefficient vector and $V_{it} \sim N(0, \sigma^2)$ is the random error item. We can estimate Equation (6) by the Tobin fixed effect model with the pooled data, and obtain the consistency estimator of coefficient estimate. Thus, we can divide the effect on the input variables into

A Comparison of Three-Stage DEA and Artificial Neural Network on the Operational Efficiency of Semi-Conductor Firms in Taiwan

73

the environmental variables, managing X-inefficiency, and random error item. Based on the method of adjusted input variable suggested by Fried *et al.* (2002) [1], one can keep each DMU facing the identical operating environment and opportunity by way of uplifting the data of input variables. The adjusted equation is shown as follows:

$$\chi_{it}^{A} = \chi_{it} + \left[\max_{it} \left(Z_{it}' \hat{\beta} \right) - Z_{it}' \hat{\beta} \right] + \left[\max_{it} \left(\widehat{v_{it}} \right) - \widehat{v_{it}} \right] \quad (7)$$

where χ_{it}^{A} represents the t-th adjusted data of specific input variable of i-th DMU and χ_{it} represents the original data of specific input variable of i-th DMU. $\max_{it} \left(Z_{it}' \hat{\beta} \right)$ is the maximal fitted value within the whole sample, representing the worst operating environment, and vice versa. Similarly, $\max_{it} \left(\widehat{v_{it}} \right)$ is the largest residual within the whole sample, representing the worst fortune and/or opportunity, and vice versa. If the coefficient of environmental variables is negative in the regression on the input slack variable, it represents the beneficial managing environment, given that it can reduce the factor surplus in the sample business. Similarly, firms with smaller residuals represent that it encountered good luck and results in a reduction of the factor surplus. In this circumstance, each DMU faces an identical managing environment in order to reflect the actual operating efficiency through the adjustment of the second stage.

In the third stage, we employ the original DEA model to estimate the operating efficiency by way of the adjusted input variable from the second stage and the original output value from the first stage. It other words, we repeat the procedure of the first stage except that we use the adjusted input variable from the second stage (Equation (7)). At this time, we have decomposed the effects on the environmental conditions and statistical noise effects from efficiencies and obtain the real efficiency of each decision making unit. Notably, Fried, Schmit and Yaisawarng (1999) [16] and Fried, Lovell, Schmit and Yaisawarng (2002) [1] recognize that a firm's technical efficiency will be influenced by the outside environment. They suggest that one should evaluate the effect on the change of input slack variable by the environment variable.

3.2 The ANN Approach

Alternatively, the artificial neural network analysis (ANN) is concerned with the simple simulation or training function base, and focuses on an establishment of the training sample based on previous experience under the assumption that back-propagation network mechanism based on rational economic behavior. In general, ANN model or procedure is specified by network topology, node characteristics and training or learning rules. It is an interconnected set of weights that contains the information or knowledge generated by the model. There are many varieties of connections under study; here in our study we discuss only one type of network which is called the multilayer perception (MLP). The composition of MLP has three main components: input layer, hidden layer and output layer, and can be illustrated in **Figure 1**.

In this study, as it is explained later, the DMU evaluation variables such as number of stuff employed (NSE), expense of fixed assets (EFA), R & D expenses (RD), net business revenues (NBR), ratio of income before tax (RI) and earnings per share (EPS) are defined as the components (X_j) in input layer of ANN system, the technical efficiency which generated according to DEA results are defined as the components (Y_j) in output layer.

Our ANN is composed of a large number of simple processing units, each interacting with others via excitatory or inhibitory connection (**Figure 1**). Distributed rep-

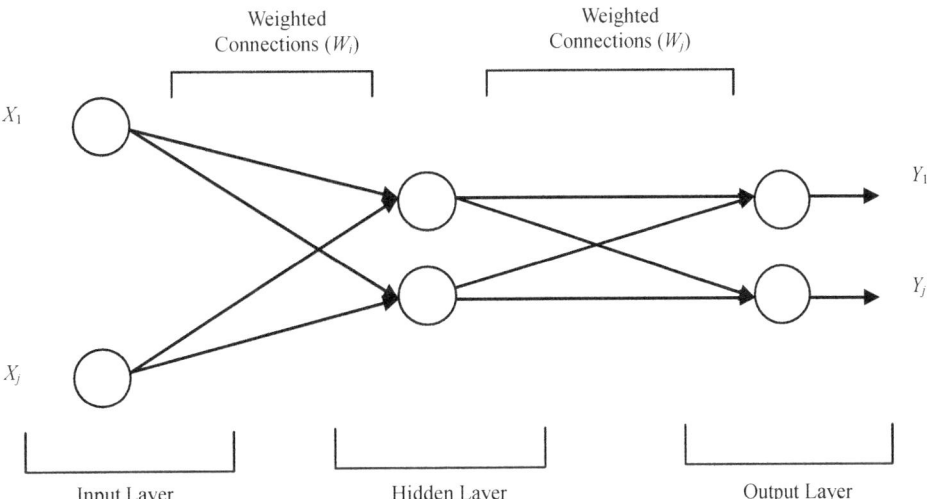

Figure 1. Framework of ANN (X_j refers to input values and Y_j refers to output values).

resentation over a large number of unit together with interconnectedness among processing units, provide an error tolerance. Three different layers can be distinguished. The input layer is responsible for receiving information from the outside environment and transferring it to the hidden layer. In the hidden layer, a neuron will assign a series of weights to the input, cope with the information via a training process, and then forward the results with weights to the output layer.

As indicated in **Figure 1**, a typical three-layer feedforward model used for forecasting purposes. In this study, the input nodes are the observations of NSE, EFA, RD, NBR, RI and EPS while the output provides the forecast for the future values of efficiencies for DMUs. Hidden nodes with appropriate nonlinear transfer functions are used to process the information received by the input nodes. The MLP's most popular learning rule is the error back-propagation algorithm. Back-propagation learning is a kind of supervised learning introduced by Werbos (1974) [28] and later developed by Rumelhart and McClelland (1986) [29]. The algorithm uses a learning set, which consists of input desired output pattern pairs. Each input-output pair is obtained by the offline processing of historical data. These pairs can be used to adjust the weights in the network to minimize the mean squared error (MSE) which measures the difference between the real and the desired values over all output neurons and all learning patterns. After computing MSE, the back-propagation step computes the corrections to be applied to the weights. Under this process we determine how close the actual output to new situations is. In the learning process the values of interconnection weights are adjusted so that the network produces a better approximation of the desired output.

According to this procedure, the values of interconnection weights related to inputs, outputs and their efficiency scores of each DMUs can be obtained. Since the structure of ANN is suitable to made concave functions with multidimensionality, therefore it can be used in creating efficient frontier functions and estimating efficiencies of DMUs (Wang, 2003) [19]. Based on this network design and process, we can farther compute the efficiency scores of each DMUs through the inputs and outputs which have the relative higher value of interconnecttion weights.

4. The Data

We employ the institution functions of the firm in this paper, which is in line with the competitive semi-conductor industry in Taiwan. This can also effectively benefit a firm's operations and improve a semi-conductor firm's efficiency. In accordance with this approach, we specify three types of firm's output, namely the net business revenues (business revenues after tax), ratio of gross

income before tax, ratio of net income after tax, ratio of business profit, turnover of accounts payable, and earnings per share. The first four types of output constitute the main activities of semi-conductor firms; with the last two representing an extended source of revenue for firms (Chiesa and Toletti, 2003) [2]. The input measures based on the above output entail operating resources. We select the following three input factors: number of staff employed, expense of fixed assets, and R & D expenses.

It should also be noted that the ratio of net income after tax is sourced as a ratio of gross income before tax, the ratio of net income after tax being their main element. One of these needs to be excluded in order to avoid a multicollinearity problem in the DEA model. The results of our correlation analysis also support the high correlation phenomenon between these two variables, with a correlation coefficient of 0.919. We then choose the ratio of net income before tax for further analysis.

Next, we determine the relationships between inputs and outputs. The DEA model requires definitions of inputs and outputs so that when inputs are added, outputs will increase. We employ a correlation analysis to test for isotonicity (*i.e.*, the positive direction of the relationship between inputs and outputs). According to the results of the inter-correlation analysis, it is clear that the correlation coefficients between our chosen outputs and inputs are all positive.

Third, we have further utilized correlation analysis to determine the appropriate inputs/outputs in accordance with this approach (Golany and Roll, 1989) [30]. The less correlation between inputs and outputs is neglected since it is weak production oriented. Ratio of business profit and turnover of accounts payable are excluded in the further analysis. Thus, we specify three types of firm output, namely net business revenues (NBR), ratio of gross income before tax (RI) and earnings per share (EPS). Three types of input, namely number of staff employed (NSE), expense of fixed assets (EFA), and R & D expenses (RD) are included. The summaries of the data are provided in **Table 1**.

The official report from the Commission on National Corporations of the Ministry of Economic Affairs provides a rich source of data on the operations of all of Taiwan's semi-conductor firms. We have gathered the requisite data for 29 companies, which represent 90 per cent of the domestic companies in Taiwan, covering the period 2001 to 2006. Please note that we chose the time span of 2001 to 2006 because the Taiwanese government first included the semi-conductor industry into the ten emerging important industries in 2000 and we evaluated the promotion performance in the first six-year periods. We employed MATLAB 7.0 software to solve the artificial neural network programming problem and we used Frontier-41 software to run the three-stage DEA analysis.

A Comparison of Three-Stage DEA and Artificial Neural Network on the Operational Efficiency of Semi-Conductor Firms in Taiwan

75

5. Empirical Results

5.1 The Mean of Efficiency Values in the DEA, Three-Stage DEA and ANN

As indicated in **Table 2**, we can observe that the calculated mean technical efficiency between 2001 and 2006 was 0.825 by traditional DEA. Relative to their production frontier, semi-conductor companies operated efficiently with actual activities 20% above the maximum activity levels during 2001-2006. As for technical efficiency in each year, we then find that it was 0.866 in 2001, with a gentle uplift to 0.892 in 2002, and 0.911 in 2003, followed by a steep decline to 0.844 in 2004. It is clear that average technical efficiency slumped in 2005 (0.708) relative to 2004. We also find that the mean technical efficiency score of 0.708 and 0.732 during the period 2005-2006 was lower than during the periods 2001-2004, at 0.866, 0.892, 0.911, and 0.844 respectively. The technical efficiency score (TE) equals the product of the pure technical efficiency (PTE) and the scale efficiency (SE) scores, and the relative magnitudes of these scores provide evidence of the source of the inefficiencies. Similar results can be found when PTE and SE scores are analyzed. The PTE score of 0.972, 0.944, 0.973 and 0.933 over the period 2001 to 2004 was also

higher than the 0.759 in 2005 and 0.829 in 2006; while the SE scores of 0.891, 0.945, 0.936, 0.905 during the period 2001 to 2004 were not higher than the 0.933 and 0.833 in 2005-2006.

We further find that the mean pure technical efficiency scores of semi-conductor companies (0.901) were lower than the mean scale efficiency score (0.915) during the 2001 to 2006 period. This seems to suggest that pure technical inefficiency has a greater significance than scale inefficiency as a source of inefficiency within all inefficient semi-conductor companies. Thus, given input prices, the effects on technical inefficiency could be attributed to the inappropriate incorrect choice of the initial input combinations, rather than the returns of scale. The reason is that semi-conductor companies increase their own scope or mass investment, and that the resource allocation issue is neglected. Semi-conductor companies suffer higher operating costs on the account that they produce goods without optimal production efficiency. Similar results can be found when periods of data are used for 2005 to 2006, with the respective mean pure technical efficiency scores (0.759; 0.829) being lower than the respective mean scale efficiency scores (0.933; 0.883).

The mean technical efficiency scores of an ANN ap-

Table 1. Summary of the descriptive statistics of the input and output data.

Years	Number of staff employed	The expense of fixed assets	R & D expenses	Net business revenues	Income rate before tax	Earnings per share
	Person	Billion	Billion	Billion	Billion	Dollar
2001-2002	1915	193.10	206.45	182.61	32.19	3.02
2003-2004	2279	288.09	496.90	237.88	43.72	9.30
2005-2006	2123	247.38	372.42	214.19	38.77	6.61
Large	4451	558.04	770.10	442.64	79.06	12.62
Small	1250	130.88	223.31	128.52	23.67	4.36

Note: All monetary values are in NT$ billion. The data consists of thirty-nine domestic commercial semi-conductor companies and the seven years' data. The data consists of seven large-sized semi-conductor companies, and twenty-two small-sized semi-conductor companies.

Table 2. The mean of efficiency values in the DEA, three-stage DEA and ANN during the year of 2001-2006.

Year	Traditional (original) DEA			Three-stage DEA			ANN		
	TE	PTE	SE	TE	PTE	SE	TE	PTE	SE
2001	0.866	0.972	0.891	0.907	0.966	0.939	0.431	0.689	0.622
2002	0.892	0.944	0.945	0.916	0.943	0.971	0.444	0.654	0.678
2003	0.911	0.973	0.936	0.940	0.980	0.959	0.428	0.670	0.643
2004	0.844	0.933	0.905	0.910	0.948	0.960	0.437	0.633	0.663
2005	0.708	0.759	0.933	0.617	0.663	0.931	0.525	0.710	0.717
2006	0.732	0.829	0.883	0.668	0.802	0.833	0.507	0.688	0.763
AEV	0.825	0.901	0.915	0.826	0.884	0.934	0.462	0.674	0.681

Notes: TE: technical efficiency; PTE: pure technical efficiency; SE: scale efficiency; AEV: average efficiency value. The results of sensitivity analysis of year 2001 data are reported here, and the similar results are also obtained when 2001-2007 data are employed.

proach in **Table 2** is 0.462, implying that semi-conductor companies could have produced the same level of output using 46% of the input actually used. Using the three-stage DEA approach, we find that the three-stage DEA efficiency scores (0.826) are on average higher than that of ANN scores (0.462). Similar results are also obtained when the regular DEA technical efficiency is employed. The three-stage frontier (and/or traditional DEA frontier) of semi-conductor companies is naturally a "soft" frontier, at which the output observations of semi-conductor companies are in some cases allowed to cross the envelope, allowing us to make more observations closer to this frontier. However, the ANN frontier is a "hard" frontier for any given figures, and the envelope is located far from the three-stage frontier. Hence, the three stage DEA frontier may be crossed by a few efficient semi-conductor companies, but most semi-conductor companies (95% or more) are still assumed to fall on or beneath the frontier. That is, the efficiency scores of 3SDEA are higher than ANN. Similar results are also obtained when pure technical efficiency and scale efficiency are analyzed. We further find that the average pure technical efficiency and scale efficiency are 0.674 and 0.681 from the artificial neural network analysis (ANN), which are significantly lower than the result gained from the three-stage DEA approach (0.884; 0.934), or the traditional DEA (0.901; 0.915) (**Table 2**).

We then employ a Tobit regression model in the second stage in order to obtain a consistency estimator by solving the intercept issue of data. The intercept issue of data occurred due to the value of slack variables being less than zero, which is not permitted. As indicated in the second column in **Table 3**, we find that there are positive and significant coefficients in a number of semi-conductor companies' location. There is also a positive result for R & D intensity and the slack variable of the number of staff employed; it shows that the input of the number of staff employed should increase; however, it does not need to be adjusted constantly

due to the negative and insignificant coefficient displayed by the number of years that the business has been run for. As to the third column in **Table 3**, the inputs of R & D expenses should increase because there are positive and significant coefficients in a number of semi-conductor companies' location, and R & D intensity in the regression of the slack variable of R & D expense. Additionally, there is a negative and significant coefficient of establishment years in the regression of the slack variable of R & D expense. It shows that more years of establishment is beneficial to the semi-conductor companies in order to deduce the extraneous inputs of R & D expense. The decrease in the inputs of R & D expense is attributed to a benevolent operating environment. Additionally, as to the second columns in **Table 3**, the inputs of fixed assets and R & D expense should be increase especially when the company operates in more than one country because there are positive and significant coefficients of location in the regressions of the slack variable of fixed asset and R & D expense; however, one does not adjust the fixed asset and R & D expense due to the insignificant coefficients of the number of semi-conductor companies location, and establishment years on the slack variable of personnel expense.

Based on the estimated adjusted inputs from the second stage and the original outputs from the first stage, we can estimate the technical efficiency again using DEA. Among the estimated technical efficiency in this stage, one can reflect the actual operating efficiency, representing the results on the removal of the environmental factor and statistical noise effects. **Table 4** lists the polished efficiency of the 29 semi-conductor companies in Taiwan.

5.2 Testing Efficiency Differences for DEA, Three-Stage DEA and ANN Approach

Based on **Table 4**, our results are identical with those of Fried, Lovell, Schmit and Yaisawarng (2002) [1]. The

Table 3. The estimated results of to bit regressions in the second stage.

Independent variable	Dependent variable: slack variable of		
	The numbers of staff employed	The expenses of fixed assets	R & D expenses
Intercept	6.2992	942.8320	−0.6012
	(0.7240)	(0.9470)	(−0.0450)
Location	4.5849**	71.7644	7.6427***
	(2.5340)	(0.3460)	(2.7480)
Establishment years	−0.3446	12.2296***	−0.6652*
	(−1.4340)	(2.5160)	(−1.8010)
R & D intensity	17.5395**	3082.8900***	19.6375*
	(2.5050)	(3.8390)	(1.8240)

Notes: ***, **, *Representing the significance of 1%, 5%, 10%, respectively. Log likelihood = −595.6005.

Table 4. Numbers of semi-conductor companies with efficient efficiency and economies of scale during 2001-2006.

Year	Traditional DEA			Three-stage DEA			ANN		
	TE	PTE	SE	TE	PTE	SE	TE	PTE	SE
2001	9	22	10	13	22	13	3	4	4
2002	10	18	10	14	18	14	0	0	1
2003	12	25	12	15	25	16	0	1	0
2004	8	18	8	14	19	14	5	11	5
2005	9	12	9	9	14	8	5	11	5
2006	10	15	11	8	14	8	4	8	4
Average	9.67	18.33	10.00	11.57	17.86	11.57	2.83	5.83	3.16

Year	Traditional DEA			Three-stage DEA			ANN		
	CRS	DRS	IRS	CRS	DRS	IRS	CRS	DRS	IRS
2001	10	19	0	13	11	5	3	0	26
2002	10	16	3	14	5	10	0	5	24
2003	12	15	2	16	8	5	0	0	29
2004	8	19	2	14	12	3	5	12	12
2005	9	12	8	8	14	7	5	16	8
2006	11	13	5	8	13	8	4	19	6
Average	10.00	15.67	3.33	12.17	10.50	6.33	2.83	8.67	17.50

Notes: TE: technical efficiency; PTE: pure technical efficiency; SE: scale efficiency; AEV: average efficiency value. CRS = constant return to scale; DRE = decreasing returns to scale; IRS = increasing returns to scale.

number of efficient semi-conductor companies, with the technical efficiency that equals unity, is higher during the three-stage DEA (13 DMUs) than that of the first stage DEA (9 DMUs) in 2001. Similar results are also obtained when scale efficiency is analyzed. We further find that the majority of sample semi-conductor companies belong to the stage of decreasing returns to scale (DRS). The number of firms with constant returns to scale during 2001-2006, is also higher during the three-stage DEA (12.17 DMUs) than that of the first stage DEA (10.00 DMUs).

The percentage of decreasing returns to scale firms during 2001-2004 is 65.5%, 55.2%, 51.7%, and 65.4% respectively. The source of the inefficient semi-conductor companies mostly arise from scale inefficiency. Similar results are also obtained when 2005-2006 data is analyzed. We can derive that the semi-conductor companies are shifting from decreasing returns to scale (DRS) to increasing returns to scale (IRS) through the adjustment of the effects on the environment and rand effort in the three-stage DEA. This implies that the production scale of the firms have adjusted and are close to the optimum scale.

Two Banker's asymptotic DEA efficiency tests have been used to test for inefficiency differences between two different efficiency scores (Banker, 1996 [31];

Banker and Chang, 1995) [32]. Firstly, we assume that the two inefficiencies $(1 - \theta_a$ and $1 - \theta_b)$ follow the exponential distribution. The test statistic

$$\left[\sum_r (1 - \theta_{ar}) / N_a \right] \Big/ \left[\sum_r (1 - \theta_{br}) / N_b \right]$$

is evaluated relative to the F-distribution with $(2N_a, 2N_b)$ degrees of freedom. Secondly, we assume that the two inefficiencies $(1 - \theta_a$ and $1 - \theta_b)$ follow the half-normal distribution. The test statistic

$$\left[\sum_r (1 - \theta_{ar}) / N_a \right] \Big/ \left[\sum_r (1 - \theta_{br}) / N_b \right]$$

is evaluated relative to the F-distribution with (N_a, N_b) degrees of freedom. Another two traditional test procedures, Welch's mean test and Mann-Whitney test have also been used to test for comparison on inefficiency differences between the different efficiency scores. For Welch's mean test, the test statistic, under the assumption of unequal variances, is given by,

$$\left(\bar{X}_a - \bar{X}_b \right) \Big/ \sqrt{\left(\sigma_a^2 / N_a \right) + \left(\sigma_a^2 / N_a \right)}$$

which follows the t-distribution of freedoms calculated as,

$$\left[\left(\sigma_a^2 / N_a \right) + \left(\sigma_b^2 / N_b \right) \right] \Big/ \left\{ \left[\left(\sigma_a^2 / N_a \right)^2 / (N_a - 1) \right] + \left[\left(\sigma_b^2 / N_b \right)^2 / (N_b - 1) \right] \right\}$$

where $\bar{X}_a$ and $\bar{X}_b$ and σ_a^2 and σ_b^2 are the sample means and variances of the inefficiencies. In the Mann-Whitney test, the test statistic Z-value is calculated by

$$Z = \left[U - E(U) \right] / \left[\sqrt{V(U)} \right]$$

and U is the lower figure between the calculated magnitudes of U_a and U_b,

$$U_a = N_a N_b + N_a \left(N_a + 1 \right) / 2 - W_a;$$

$$U_b = N_a N_b + N_b \left(N_b + 1 \right) / 2 - W_b;$$

$$E(\mu) = N_a N_b / 2$$

and

$$V(\mu) = N_a N_b \left(N_a + N_b + 1 \right) / 12$$

where W_a and W_b are the rank sums of each selected sample. In our case, one of N has large sample sizes ($N >$ 15); we can generate a Z-value and refer to the standardized normal distribution to test the null hypothesis.

We apply four tests: Banker's two asymptotic DEA tests, Welch's mean test and Mann-Whitney test in our study. All tests show that there is a significant difference among the average efficiency scores of ordinary DEA vs. ANN methods (see the third column, **Table 5**), and 3SDEA versus ANN methods (see the fourth column, **Table 5**). Moreover, the advanced setting of the three-stages mechanism of DEA does not change the instinctive differences of DEA mechanisms. Derived results can be obtained when DEA and 3SDEA are compared and efficiencies obtained within these two approaches are not different as confirmed in four kinds of tests (see the fifth column, **Table 5**). Estimated results show that there are significant differences in efficiency scores between three-stage DEA and ANN. Similar results are also obtained when the efficiencies of regular DEA and ANN are compared. Identical to the results of Fried, Lovell, Schmit and Yaisawarng (2002) [1], we find that different approaches (DEA versus ANN) will result in different results when they are employed in similar methodology-

cal framework. The advanced setting of the three-stage mechanism of DEA does not change the instinctive differences between DEA and ANN approaches.

6. Concluding Remarks

In this study, ordinary (original) DEA, three-stage DEA, and artificial neural network (ANN) approaches are employed to compare the technical efficiency of 29 semi-conductor companies in Taiwan. The six-year data set 2001-2006 is employed, which avoids the one-off shock effect in the overall efficiency evaluation. Estimated results show that there are significant differences in efficiency scores between three stages DEA and ANN. Similar results are also obtained when the efficiencies of regular DEA and ANN are compared. Identical to the results of Fried, Lovell, Schmit and Yaisawarng (2002) [16], we find that different approaches (DEA vs. ANN) will produce different results when they are employed in similar methodological framework. Furthermore, the advanced setting of the three-stage mechanism of DEA does not change the instinctive differences between DEA and ANN approaches. The results are comparable as a whole; however, ANN approach produces a more robust frontier and identifies more efficient units since more good performance patterns are explored. Furthermore, ANN approach provides worse performers the guidance on how to improve their performance in different efficiency ratings. The neural network approach requires no assumptions about the production function (the major drawback of the parametric approach) and it is highly flexible.

We also find that the environmental factors still provide a significant variable to explain the technical efficiency in the efficiency model, irrespective of whether DEA, 3SDEA or ANN approach is employed. Nevertheless, future research with neural networks in the efficiency analysis is suggested. The possible directions include weight restrictions and cross-industry compare-sons and, etc.

Table 5. Summaries of efficiency difference test results.

Classification	Test Procedure	DEA vs. ANN	3SDEA vs. ANN	DEA vs. 3SDEA
Semi-conductor er's asymptotic	Exponential Type	3.3112[**1]	3.3046[**]	1.0018
DEA tests[2]	Half-normal Type	10.9649[**]	10.9170[**]	1.0035
Traditional efficiency	Welch test[3]	8.5732[**]	7.2751[**]	0.0060
Tests	Mann-Whitney test[4]	−5.2831[**]	−5.9791[**]	−0.8542

Notes: 1). [**]Represents significance at the 0.05 level and [*]represents significance at the 0.10 level. 2). As to semi-conductor's asymptotic DEA tests, there are six tests performed: the exponential type, a) DEA vs. ANN (=0.3943/0.1191 = 3.3112), b) 3SDEA vs. ANN (=0.3943/0.1193 = 10.9170), c) DEA vs. 3SDEA (=0.1193/0.1191 = 1.0018); the half-normal type, d) DEA vs. ANNA (=0.1554/0.0142 = 10.9649), e) 3SDEA vs. ANN (=0.1554/0.1423 = 10.9170), f) DEA vs. 3SDEA (=0.0142/0.0141 = 1.0035). 3). As to Welch efficiency tests, there are also three tests performed: a) DEA vs. ANN (=0.2752/0.0321 = 8.5732), b) 3SDEA vs. ANN (=0.2750/0.0378 = 7.2751), c) DEA vs. 3SDEA (=0.0002/0.0331 = 0.0060). 4). As to Mann-Whitney efficiency tests, there are also three tests performed, that is, a) DEA vs. ANN of technical efficiency ((490 − 495) − 162)/31.61 = −5.2831, b) 3SDEA vs. ANN of technical efficiency ((−27 − 162)/31.61 = −5.9791), c) DEA vs. 3SDEA of technical efficiency ((135 − 162)/31.61 = −0.8542). Note that 162 and 31.61 are the calculated average and the standard deviation of the selected sample.

A Comparison of Three-Stage DEA and Artificial Neural Network on the Operational Efficiency of Semi-Conductor Firms in Taiwan

79

Based on the analytical results, the semi-conductor companies in Taiwan should take output factors and the business environment as important factors for improving operating performance. The empirical results also show that the three-stage DEA efficiency is different from the ordinary (first stage) DEA efficiency. Each semi-conductor company of average technical efficiency and scale efficiency in the three-stage DEA is better than in the first stage DEA. Compared with the first stage DEA, the numbers of semi-conductor companies for technical efficiency and scale efficiency values which are equal to one increased. The development of the business environment can enhance technical and scale efficiencies. To decompose environmental and statistical noise effects from efficiencies could estimate real efficiency of every decision making unit. The conclusions of these empirical results may provide some information to identify not only the efficiency of semi-conductor companies but also give evidence to promote the operating efficiency via adapting or adjusting the effects of environmental situations as indicated in this article.

REFERENCES

[1] H. O. Fried, C. A. K. Lovell, S. S. Schmidt and S. Yaisa-warng, "Accounting for Environmental Effect and Statistical Noise in Data Envelopment Analysis," *Journal of Productivity Analysis*, Vol. 17, No. 1, 2002, pp. 157-174.

[2] V. Chiesa and G. Toletti, "How Biotechnology Changes Pharma R & D: A Managerial Perspective," *International Journal of Biotechnology*, Vol. 5, No. 2, 2003, pp. 125-136.

[3] D. Kliger and O. Sarig, "The Information Value of Bond Ratings," *The Journal of Finance*, Vol. 6, No. 12, 2000, pp. 2879-2902.

[4] B. A. Garner, "Black's Law Dictionary," West Publishing Co., New York, 1999.

[5] P. T. Larsen, "Merrill's Dublin-Based Financial Holding Company Is Planning to Expand in Areas," *Financial Times*, Vol. 10, No. 1, 2006, pp. 15-16.

[6] A. Charnes, W. W. Cooper and E. Rhodes, "Measuring the Efficiency of Decision Making Units," *European Journal of Operational Research*, Vol. 2, No. 12, 1978, pp. 429-444.

[7] R. D. Banker, A. Charnes and W. W. Cooper, "Some Models for Estimation of Technical and Scale Inefficiencies in Data Envelopment Analysis," *Management Science*, Vol. 30, No. 12, 1984, pp. 1078-1092.

[8] M. Oral and R. Yolalan, "An Empirical Study on Measuring Operating Efficiency and Profitability of Bank Branches," *European Journal of Operational Research*, Vol. 46, No. 2, 1990, pp. 282-294.

[9] C. A. Favero and L. Papi, "Technical Efficiency and Scale Efficiency in the Italian Banking Sector," *Applied Economic*, Vol. 27, No. 3, 1995, pp. 385-395.

[10] C. Schaffnit, D. Rosen and J. C. Paradi, "Best Practice Analysis of Bank Branches: An Application of DEA in a Large Canadian Bank," *European Journal of Operational Research*, Vol. 98, No. 2, 1997, pp. 269-289.

[11] H. Fukuyama, R. Guerra and W. L. Weber, "Efficiency and Ownership: Evidence from Japanese Credit Cooperatives," *Journal of Economics and Business*, Vol. 51, No. 4, 1999, pp. 473-487.

[12] F. H. F. Liu and P. H. Wang, "DEA Malmquist Productivity Measure: Taiwanese Semi-Conductor Companies," *International Journal of Production Economics*, Vol. 112, No. 1, 2008, pp. 367-376.

[13] T. Y. Chen and L. H. Chen, "DEA Performance Evaluation Based on BSC Indicators incorporated: The Case of Semi-Conductor Industry," *International Journal of Productivity and Performance Management*, Vol. 56, No. 4, 2007, pp. 335-357.

[14] C. J. Chen and Q. J. Yeh, "A Comparative Performance Evaluation of Taiwan's High-Tech Industries," *International Journal of Business Performance Management*, Vol. 7, No. 1, 2005, pp. 16-32.

[15] G. D. Ferrier and C. A. K. Lovell, "Measuring Cost Efficiency in Banks: Econometric and Linear Programming Evidence," *Journal of Econometric*, Vol. 46, No. 2, 1990, pp. 229-245.

[16] H. O. Fried, S. S. Schmidt and S. Yaisawarng, "Incorporating the Operating Environment into a Nonparametric Measure of Technical Efficiency," *Journal of the Productivity Analysis*, Vol. 12, No. 2, 1999, pp. 249-267.

[17] A. Greasley, "Using DEA and Simulation in Guiding Operating Units to Improved Performance," *The Journal of the Operational Research Society*, Vol. 5, No. 6, 2005, pp. 727-740.

[18] A. D. Athanassopoulos and S. P. Curram, "A Comparison of Data Envelopment Analysis and Artificial Neural Networks as Tools for Assessing," *Journal of the Operational Research Society*, Vol. 47, No. 8, 1996, pp. 100-117.

[19] S. H. Wang, "Adaptive Non-Parametric Efficiency Frontier Analysis: A Neural-Network-Based Model," *Computers & Operations Research*, Vol. 30, No. 2, 2003, pp. 279-296.

[20] P. C. Pendharkar and J. A. Rodger, "Technical Efficiency-Based Selection of Learning Cases to Improve Forecasting Accuracy of Neural Networks under Monotonicity Assumption," *Decision Support Systems*, Vol. 36, No. 1, 2003, pp. 117-136.

[21] H. C. Liao, "A Data Envelopment Analysis Method for Optimizing Multi-Response Problem with Censored Data in the Taguchi Method," *Computers & Industrial Engineering*, Vol. 46, No. 4, 2004, pp. 817-835.

[22] C. T. Su and L. I. Tong. "Multi-Response Robust Design by Principal Component Analysis," *Total Quality Management*, Vol. 8, No. 3, 1997, pp. 409-420.

[23] P. C. Pendharkar, "A Data Envelopment Analysis-Based Approach for Data Preprocessing," *IEEE Transactions on*

Knowledge & Data Engineering, Vol. 17, No. 10, 2005, pp. 1379-1388.

[24] D. Santin, "On the Approximation of Production Functions: A Comparison of Artificial Neural Networks Frontiers and Efficiency Techniques," *Applied Economics Letters*, Vol. 15, No. 7, 2008, pp. 597-600.

[25] J. T. Wang, C. T. Su and H. T. Hsieh, "A Framework for Determining MIMO Process Parameters by a Neuro-DM & ACO Approach," *International Journal of Production Research*, Vol. 45, No. 15, 2007, pp. 350-365.

[26] J. Buddefel, K. E. Grosspietsch, B. J. Hosticka, R. Klinke and G. Wagner, "An Intelligent Sensor Integrated Preprocessing Facility for Neural Networks," *Microprocessing and Microprogramming*, Vol. 32, No. 3, 1991, pp. 335-342.

[27] R. Fare, S. Grosskopf and C. A. K. Lovell, *"The Measurement of Efficiency of Production,"* Kluwer Academic Publishers, Boston, 1985.

[28] P. I. Webos, "Beyond Regression: New Tools for Prediction and Analysis in the Behavior Science," Ph.D. Thesis, Harvard University, Cambridge, 1974.

[29] D. E. Rumelhart and J. L McClelland, "Parallel Distributed Processing: Exoloration in the Microstructure of Cognition," MIT Press, Cambridge, 1986.

[30] B. Golany and Y. Roll, "An Application Procedure for DEA," *Omega*, Vol. 17, No. 3, 1989, pp. 237-250.

[31] R. D. Banker, "Hypothesis Tests Using Data Envelopment Analysis," *Journal of Productivity Analysis*, Vol. 7, No. 1, 1996, pp. 139-159.

[32] R. D. Banker and H. Chang, "A Simulation Study of Hypothesis Tests for Differences in Efficiencies," *International Journal of Production Economic*, Vol. 39, No. 1-2, 1995, pp. 37-54.

A Comparison of Three-Stage DEA and Artificial Neural Network on the Operational Efficiency of Semi-Conductor Firms in Taiwan

81

Appendix 1: Data samples of the study

DMU	Full name of companies
Sis	Silicon Integrated Systems Corp.
Realtek	Realtek Semiconductor Corp.
Sunplus	Sunplus Technology Corp.
Weltrend	Weltrend Semiconductor Inc.
MediaTek	MediaTek Inc.
Elan	ELAN Microelectronic Corp.
Esmt	Elite Semiconductor Memory Technology Inc.
Novatek	Novatek Microelectronics Corp.
Ali	Ali Corp.
Ame	Analog Microelectronic Inc.
Sq	Service & Quality Technology Corp.
Syntek	Syntek Semiconductor Ltd.
Myson century	Myson Century Inc.
Etron	Etron Technology, Inc.
Tm	TM Technology, Inc.
Sonix	Sonix Technology Corp.
Issi	Integrated Silicon Solution, Inc.
Tontek	Tontek Design Technology Ltd.
Avid	AVID Electronics Corp.
Genesys	Genesys Logic, Inc.
Ptc	Princeton Technology Corp.
Est	EST Technology Integration Corp.
Anpec	Anpec Electronics Corp.
Holtek	Holtek Semiconductor Inc.
Gsharp	Gsharp Corp.
Prolific	Prolific Technology Inc.
Cmedia	Cmedia Electronics Inc.
Ene	ENE Technology Inc.
Apec	Advanced Power Electronics Corp.

8

Is Agricultural Production Spillover the Rationale behind CAADP Framework? Spatial Panel Model Approach

John Ulimwengu[1], Prabuddha Sanyal[2]
[1]International Food Policy Research Institute, Washington DC, USA
[2]Sandia National Laboratory, Albuquerque, USA

ABSTRACT

The creation of a union is often rationalized on grounds of moving the equilibrium toward the first best solution whenever independent policies generate spillovers. This arises as a common agenda can significantly reduce the scope of free-riding behavior among member countries. In addition, cross-border externalities arising out of higher levels of market integration entails countries to agree on policy coordination. The present study explores the extent and magnitude of agricultural production spillover that might validate the adoption of a common agriculture agenda among African countries. Overall, our results suggest the presence of positive and significant agricultural production spillover. No evidence of *beggar-thy-neighbor* or negative spillover policies was found; on average, each country received 2.5 percent growth as a result of spillover. Our results also suggest that convergence dynamics is much stronger when spillover is accounted for, which provides a rationale for a common agenda such as CAADP.

Keywords: CAADP; Agricultural Growth; Spatial Panel Model; Spillover; Convergence

1. Introduction

The majority of poor people in Africa lives in rural areas and depends directly or indirectly on agriculture for their livelihoods. Sustainable poverty alleviation strategies should thus focus on improving agricultural productivity. As pointed by [1], policy reforms undertaken by many African countries between the mid-1980s and the second half of the 1990s have played an important role in improving agriculture's performance. The trend of total factor productivity (TFP) suggests a remarkable recovery in the performance of Sub-Saharan Africa's agriculture during the 1984-2003 period after a long period of poor performance and stagnation in output.

However, to sustain high productivity growth in agriculture in the future, African countries in general and Sub-Saharan countries in particular will need well designed and better coordinated policies to improve the productivity of smallholder farmers who constitute the backbone of agricultural sector in Africa. Such common policy agenda should cover market and trade opportunities at domestic, regional, and international levels by providing appropriate incentives including infrastructure for improved market access. Infrastructure remains poor in most Sub-Saharan African (SSA) countries with the consequence that many SSA countries are often poorly integrated and characterized by a low level of competetion [2].

The lack of market integration implies that production shortfalls cannot easily be reversed via intraregional, interregional or international trade which may explain why the incidence of food emergencies remains high in many countries of the region. As a result, even where food production increases in some areas, food emergencies might not be averted in nearby zones due to the deficiencies in the structure and distribution of local markets and their lack of coordination with national and international distribution systems [3,4]. Therefore, there is a need for organizations such as the New Partnership for Africa's Development (NEPAD), and regional economic communities (RECs) to initiate coordinated actions to improve access to public services and markets, hold governments' accountable, make markets work for both the public and private sector, and address collective issues facing smallholder farmers. The main question then becomes: how to design and implement collective agricultural agenda aimed at lifting people out of poverty and hunger through improved agricultural productivity.

In order to address the above question, it is important to note that there are two broad strands of thought on the potential role of agriculture in Sub-Saharan African countries. The first view emphasizes the role of agricultural development within a market-based economic framework [5-7]. In contrast, the second school of thought highlights the potential of growth and poverty reduction through the rural off-farm sector or manufacturing exports [8,9]. Regardless of how agriculture is viewed, agricultural development and poverty reduction goals cannot be achieved simultaneously unless more attention is given to the agricultural sector in terms of both policy and investments. For many African countries, agriculture growth will remain the platform for initiating both forward and backward linkages to the rest of the economy in the coming decades, and thus will have strong spillover effects in raising agricultural productivity and incomes [10]. As a result, strategies and policies that aim at reducing food insecurity and poverty in the medium to long-term should not only focus on addressing these issues within the agricultural sector alone, but also through its interactions with the rest of the economy.

Adoption of common agricultural policies has the potential to exploit the continent's abundant natural resources and achieve significant economies of scale, thereby making the sector globally competitive. In addition, by addressing access to interregional and intraregional trade for smallholder farmers, improvement of technology through sustainable natural resource management practices, and the fragility of different eco-systems in the region, common agricultural policies can strengthen the role of farmers' organizations and improve productivity and incomes of smallholder farmers. However, there are also significant costs associated with common agricultural policies, as member countries lose part of their sovereignty in engaging in a common process of setting up policies and strategies. In addition, overlaps in memberships, mandates, objectives and protocols are also likely to generate "unhealthy multiplication and duplication of efforts" that leads to implementation challenges of two or more programs trying to address the same set of issues [11]. Moreover, regional integration through RECs remains inefficient and to a large extent resource constrained owing to "the substantial gaps between what is written in treaties and what happens on the ground" [12].

In theory, adoption of a common agenda should improve the efficiency of policy outcome whenever independent policies generate spillovers [13]. This arises as a common agenda can significantly reduce the scope of free-riding behavior among member countries. The present study seeks to determine whether there is evidence of the presence of spillovers that might justify the adoption of CAADP agenda among sub-Saharan African countries. We also explore possible impact of the presence of agri-cultural production spillover on spatio-temporal dynamics of agricultural production among sub-Saharan African countries.

This paper is organized as follows: In the next section, we provide the current trends and challenges facing agricultural development in Africa while highlighting few areas where cross-country externalities can arise. Section three discusses the conceptual framework of the role of spatial externalities and the priority areas of cooperation for regional, international and national bodies. Section IV formulates the spatial econometric model used in the study, provides the main results of the study and a discussion based on the results of the rationale of a common agricultural policy. The final section provides some concluding thought of how best to rationalize common agriculture strategy for Africa that can ensure the unification of programs, activities and functions of regional and national agencies.

2. Issues Facing Agricultural Development in Sub-Saharan Africa and Policy Responses

The considerable homogeneity of production conditions over extensive areas of irrigated land with similar agro-ecological conditions, presence of factor and product markets, and a supportive institutional environment fostered rapid adoption of new technologies and created large productivity gains, in what is coined as the "green revolution" [14]. In contrast, the situation in Africa is different owing to the complexity of the constraints specific to the region, such as small and fragmented markets, heterogeneous agro-climatic zones, lower accessibility of services (including agricultural extension and advice, credit, storage infrastructures etc), and unsustainable natural resource management practices [15]. In addition, there are extensive market and government failures in agriculture. While market failure prevents the private sector to actively engage in market activities, in contrast government failures prevent the private sector from undertaking any investment projects that yield higher returns in the future.

Agricultural sector in SSA relies heavily on small scale farming. The general consensus is that smallholder farmers' and other small and medium enterprises in the rural non-farm economy cannot compete alone in global markets. They need to cooperate with other large agro-business enterprises so as to achieve competitiveness through cluster development [16]. Linkages through contract farming can produce positive spillovers through higher supply, better planning cycles and limited exposure to fluctuations in international markets [17].

Following the Berg report in the early 1990s, it was recognized that improving agricultural policies were critical for achieving higher agricultural growth. Key areas of reform included the following:

- reforming incentive structures to ensure better prices for smallholder farmers;
- opening up agricultural marketing systems to allow for competition;
- rehabilitating marketing infrastructure, rural roads, and irrigation equipment;
- making improvements in crop and livestock research and pest control.

The above areas of Structural Adjustment Programs (SAPs) were less focused on an agricultural strategy and more centered on short-term macro-economic stabilization. However, the second phase of SAPs (1985-1998) was more proactive with increasing attention given to agricultural market reforms. These reforms included the following:

- liberalization of agricultural input and output prices by reducing or removing subsidies on inputs such as fertilizers;
- doing away with pan-seasonal and pan-territorial prices;
- reducing overvalued exchange rates;
- removing government regulatory controls in input and output markets;
- privatization by withdrawing marketing boards from pricing and marketing activities and restructuring public enterprises [18,19].

The limitations of SAPs in terms of strategy formulation and implementation for the agricultural sector are as follows: 1) lack of emphasis on the importance of supporting market institutions and infrastructure; 2) lack of participation and ownership in the design and implementation of SAPs by governments and other stakeholders such as civil society and farmers; 3) minimal private sector response; 4) limitations with ex-ante policy conditionality; 5) limited or lack of agricultural supply response; and 6) failure of SAPs (SAP1 and SAP2) to make a meaningful impact on growth and poverty reduction.

A decade into SAPs, Africa was still lagging behind—thus, Poverty Reduction Strategy Papers (PRSPs) were initiated to lay out macroeconomic and social programs and policies to be pursued by a country over a 3 or 5 year period in order to promote growth and reduce poverty. A review of several completed PRSPs suggests that while countries acknowledge the important role of agriculture in accelerating "pro-poor" growth, agricultural policies of the SAP era have largely been maintained [20]. Despite the shortcomings of the SAP reforms, the second generation of reforms brought to the attention of policy makers the factors that undermined agricultural productivity growth and strongly emphasized the role of agriculture as an engine of growth for most African countries. The PRSP rhetoric on the importance of agriculture was, however, not matched by increased investments in the sector (by both governments and donors)—agricultural research and development, extension services, and rural infrastructure development were widely neglected.

3. NEPAD's Vision for Agricultural Growth in Africa[1]

In adopting the Comprehensive Africa Agriculture Development Programme (CAADP), African governments set for their countries a collective goal of achieving a 6percent agricultural growth rate, as a key strategy toward achieving the Millennium Development Goal of halving the poverty rate by 2015 from its 1990 level. They also opted for a partnership framework to mobilize the required funding to achieve the above growth rate, including the allocation by national governments of a budget share of at least 10% to the agricultural sector. Finally, CAADP also reflects an option for evidence and outcome based planning and implementation in support of an inclusive sectoral review and dialogue process, in line with the broader NEPAD peer review and accountability principle. **Figure 1** presents an overview of CAADP functions and key players.

In promoting CAADP, the NEPAD framework has developed a vision of agriculture-led development in Africa that seeks to eliminate hunger and reduces food insecurity through an expansion of agriculture-led exports. As described below, CAADP framework is built around the four main technical pillars:

1) Expanding the area under sustainable land management and reliable water control systems. Pillar 1 objectives are as follows: a) To revert fertility loss and resource degradation, and ensure broad-based and rapid adoption of sustainable land and forestry management practices in the small-holder as well as commercial sectors; and b) To improve management of water resources while expanding access to both small-scale and large-scale irrigation.

2) Improving rural infrastructure and trade-related capacities for market access. The objectives of pillar two are as follows: a) To accelerate growth in the agricultural sector by raising the capacities of private entrepreneurs, including commercial and smallholder farmers, to meet the increasingly complex quality and logistical requirements of markets (domestic, regional and international) focusing on selected agricultural commodities that offer the potential to raise rural (on- and off-farm) incomes; and b) A regulatory and policy framework that would expand regional trade and cross-border investments through the creation of regional economic actors

(3) Increasing food supply and reducing hunger. The objectives of pillar three are as follows: a) A well-managed and regionally coordinated food reserves and early warning systems at the national level that would allow

---

[1]See for example [21].

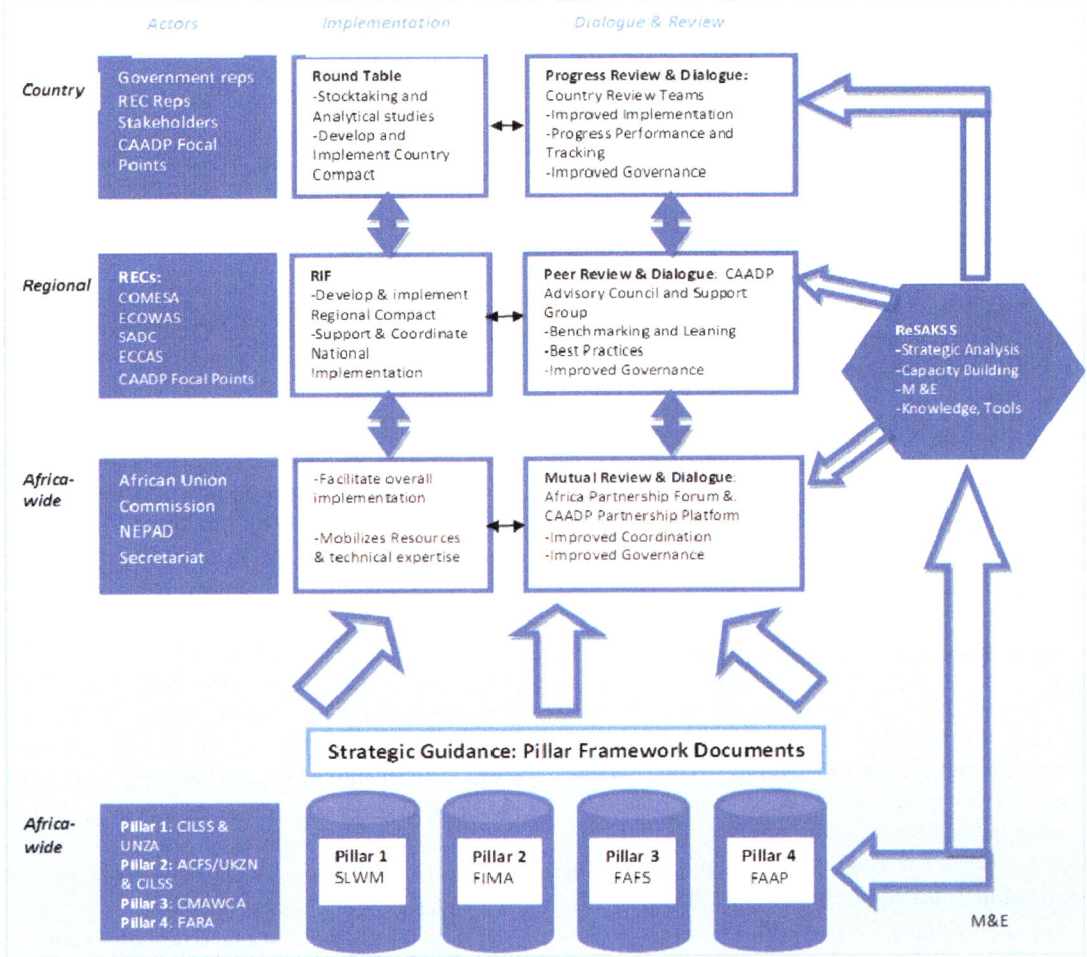

Source: [21]; Notes: CAADP: Comprehensive Africa Agriculture Development Program; NEPAD: New Partnership for Africa's Development; RECs: Regional Economic Communities; RIF: Regional Implementation Framework; M&E: Monitoring and Evaluation; CMAWCA: Conference of Ministers of Agriculture of West and Central Africa; CILSS: Permanent Inter-State Committee for Drought Control in the Sahel; ACFS/UKZN: African Center for Food Security at the University of KwaZulu Natal; UNZA: University of Zambia; FARA: Forum for Agricultural Research in Africa; SLWM: Sustainable Land and Water Management; FIMA: Framework for the Improvement of Rural Infrastructure and Trade-Related Capacities for Market Access; FAFS: Framework for African Food Security; FAAP: Framework for African Agricultural Productivity; ECOWAS: Economic Community of West African States; COMESA: Common Market for East and Southern Africa (COMESA); SADC: Southern African Development Community; ECCAS: Economic Community of Central African States; and ReSAKSS: Regional Strategic and Knowledge Support Systems.

Figure 1. Overview of CAADP implementation functions and processes caption.

African countries to respond in a timely and cost-effective manner to food emergency crises; b) To reduce malnutrition in school-going children through diet supplementation with a complete meal that is adequate in carbohydrates, fat, protein, vitamins and minerals, and to expand local demand and stimulate production by smallholder farmers; and c) To develop an African nutrition initiative to meet countries' broader nutritional challenges in a way that takes account of the complex and multisectoral nature of the problem and possible solutions.

4) Expand agricultural research, and technology dissemination and adoption. The objectives of pillar four are as follows: a) To achieve rapid flow of technologies suitable in the African context that are responsive to the

constraints and opportunities facing farmers; b) To mobilize the large potential of cassava that can contribute to food security and income generation among African countries; c) Contribute to food security and poverty reduction, and ensure sustainable resource management, in the rice sector of ten Eastern, Central and Southern African countries through broad-based access to high-yielding New Rice for Africa (NERICA) rice lines, other improved varieties, and accompanying technologies; and d) To safeguard the future contribution of Africa's fish sector to poverty alleviation and regional economic development, in particular through i) improved management of natural fish stocks; ii) development of aquaculture production; and iii) expansion of fish marketing and trade.

Cross-cutting Areas: The CAADP framework also addresses three clusters of critical issues that cut across the four CAADP pillars. These are: academic and professional training to upgrade skills in the agricultural sector; information and knowledge systems to support sector strategy and policy formulation and implementation; and alignment of country Poverty Reduction Strategy Papers (PRSPs) with CAADP priorities and objectives.

At the country level, the Comprehensive Africa Agricultural Development Programme (CAADP) implementation process aligns national agricultural sector policies, strategies, and investment programs with CAADP principles, pillars and targets. In particular, the process is focused on achieving a 6 percent national agricultural growth rate and allocating 10 percent of national budgets to the agriculture sector. The process builds on ongoing country efforts and is led by national governments and key stakeholders, with coordination by the regional economic communities (RECs)

4. Analytical Framework and Empirical Model

Following [22], we present a framework of a common agenda where a group of countries decide together on the provision of certain public goods and policies because of spillovers originating from neighboring countries.

Consider a group of N countries with the population size normalized to 1; the utility function of the representative individual of country i is given by

$$U_i = c_i + \alpha_i H(g_i) \qquad (1)$$

where g_i is the per capita and total level of government spending in country i, c_i is private consumption and $H_g(\cdot) > 0$, $H_{gg}(\cdot) < 0$. The parameter $\alpha_i > 0$ captures how much a representative individual of country i values public consumption relative to private consumption.

If all N countries decide on a common agenda in the form of a union, the utility function of the representative individual in member country i is as follows:

$$U_i = c_i + \alpha_i H\left(g_i + \rho \sum_{j=1, j \neq i}^{N} g_j\right) \qquad (2)$$

where $\rho \in [0,1]$ represents the spillover effects from other countries' government spending on the "home" country. Furthermore, if each country has a balanced budget, $g_i = t_i \in [0,y]$, then the utility function becomes

$$U_i = y - g_i + \alpha_i H\left(g_i + \rho \sum_{j=1, j \neq i}^{N} g_j\right) \qquad (3)$$

where y is income, t_i are lump sum taxes raised in country i.

If every country acts independently, taking as given the spending of all the other countries, the first order

conditions with respect to g_i is given by

$$\alpha_i H_{g_i}\left(g_i + \rho \sum_{j \neq i} g_j\right) = 1 \qquad (4)$$

In the case of collective action, where each country takes into account other countries' expenditures endogenously, the optimality condition for each country is given by:

$$\alpha_i H_g\left(g_i + \rho \sum_{j \neq i} g_j\right) = 1 - \rho \sum_{j \neq i} \alpha_j H_g\left(g_j + \rho \sum_{k \neq i} g_k\right) \qquad (5)$$

It follows that unless $\rho = 0$, the Nash equilibrium from the first order condition "Equation (4)" is inefficient because countries' behaviors do not account for the effect of their decisions on other countries. The solution $g^*(\alpha_i)$ from the system "Equation (5)" is efficient because it incorporates spillover effects. As pointed out by [1], this first best policy requires that the union dictates a different policy for each country and that the policy preferences of every country are known and verifiable. Although these conditions seems highly unrealistic in practice, the CAADP agenda has provisions that meet these conditions: 1) CAADP is built around common goals in terms of agricultural growth, poverty reduction, and agricultural investment but the actual design of agricultural strategies is left to individual countries; 2) the CAADP peer-review mechanisms allows for regular verification of countries' policy preferences.

If $\rho = 0$, the welfare outcomes with common agenda and without common agenda are qualitatively equivalent. In this case independent policy setting is more efficient than collective action given the cost of union participation.

The purpose of the paper is therefore to estimate ρ. We use an unconstrained spatial Durbin model for panel data as described below. Given geographical proximity between countries, each country's agricultural production can be expressed as a Cobb-Douglas:

$$y_i = A_i \exp(u_i) \prod_{r=1}^{P} s_r^{\beta_r} \qquad (6)$$

where A_i represents country i's total factor productivity; $u_i = \rho w_{ij} u_i + \varepsilon_i$ is an autoregressive (AR) spatial error term; ε is an error term with mean zero and constant variance; ρ represents substantive agricultural spatial spillover; β represent elasticity of production with respect to input s; w_{ij} are elements of the spatial weight matrix W that describes geographical proximity among countries. For convenience, matrix W is row-standardized.

Since we do not observe policy interactions between countries, we specify the production function as a spatial error model. As a result, replacing u with $u(I - \rho W)^{-1} \varepsilon$, Equation (6) yields a spatial Durbin model (SDM) in log linear form:

$$y = \rho W y + S\beta + WS\theta + \iota_n \alpha + \epsilon \quad ^2 \qquad (7)$$

where y is a $n \times 1$ vector of observations on agricultural production for each country; S is a nxk matrix of observations on p $(r = 1, \cdots, p)$ agricultural inputs for each of the n countries; ι_n is nx1 vector of ones.

As pointed out by [23], the spatial Durbin model nests most models used in applied spatial econometrics literature: 1) if $\theta = 0$, Equation (7) becomes a spatial autoregressive (SAR) model that includes a spatial lag of agricultural production from related countries, but excludes these countries' agricultural inputs; 2) if $\theta = -\rho\beta$, it becomes a spatial error model (SEM); 3) if $\theta = 0$ and $\rho = 0$, it is a non-spatial least-squares agricultural production model that assumes countries' productions are independent. [23] shows that Equation (7) can be rewritten as

$$y = \sum_{r=1}^{p} K_r(W) x_r + V(W)\iota_n \alpha + V(W)\varepsilon \qquad (8)$$

where $\qquad K_r(W) = V(W)(I_n\beta_r + W\theta_r)$

and $\qquad V(W) = (I_n - \rho W)^{-1}$.

It follows that the derivative of y_i with respect to s_{jr} can be derived as follows:

$$\frac{\partial y_i}{\partial s_{jr}} = K_r(W)_{ij} = (I_n - \rho W)^{-1} \times (I_n\beta_r + W\theta_r) \qquad (9)$$

For the own derivative of the *ith* country, [24] shows that

$$\frac{\partial y_i}{\partial s_{ir}} = K_r(W)_{ii}, \qquad (10)$$

where $K_r(W)_{ii}$ captures the impact on country i from a change in s_r of country i himself.

Empirical inference of model (7) is conducted using tests presented in Appendix A. The presence of spillover has the potential to affect growth convergence. The NEPAD's CAADP targets are for each country to achieve at least six percent agricultural growth rate every year;

this indicates that at some point African countries will achieve a convergence stage where least agricultural growing economies will catch-up with fast agricultural growing economies.

To test the potential for agricultural growth convergence, we adapt the β-convergence approach [24] which suggests that on average, poor countries grow faster than the rich ones (less-developed regions would be catching-up with more advanced regions). In other words, β-convergence implies a negative correlation between growth rates of per capita agricultural production and its initial levels. **Table 1** presents spatial and non-spatial specifications used to test for convergence.

4.1. Descriptive Analysis and Measurement of Variables

The Panel data were collected on 48 countries in Sub-Saharan Africa from 1961 to 2006.

Traditional inputs are from FAOSTAT website (http://faostat3.fao.org/home/index.html) and Fuglie (2008). It includes agricultural output, fertilizers, livestock, tractors, labor and land quality. The summary statistics is presented in **Table 2** with means, standard errors, minimum, and maximum values of the variables (output, traditional inputs, land quality, and inefficiency changing variables).

Agricultural Gross Production (constant 1999-2001, US$1000, smoothed using Hodrick-Prescott filter with $\lambda = 6.25$) is used as a measure of agricultural production [25]. Fertilizer use is measured as the quantity of fertilizer plant nutrient consumed (tones of N P_2O_5 plus K_2O). Agricultural land is measured as the sum of pasture land and permanent crops in thousand hectares (not quality adjusted). Agricultural labor is measured as the number of persons (male and female) economically active in thousands. The livestock variable is the number of Cattle Equivalent-Aggregate using Hayami-Ruttan weights [25]. The farm machinery is the number of agricultural tractors in use.

Table 1. Spatial and non-spatial model for convergence.

	Unconditional	Conditional
Non-spatial	$\frac{1}{T}\ln\left(\frac{p_{it}}{p_{i0}}\right) = \alpha + \beta\ln(p_{i0}) + \mu_i + \varepsilon_i$, p_{it} is per capita agricultural production, μ_i denotes country specific effect, T is the length of period under consideration, $\varepsilon_i \sim iid(0, \delta_\varepsilon^2)$	$\frac{1}{T}\ln\left(\frac{p_{it}}{p_{i0}}\right) = \alpha + \beta\ln(p_{i0}) + \gamma X_{it} + \mu_i + \varepsilon_i$, X_{it} represents the set of agricultural inputs for country i in period t
Spatial	$\frac{1}{T}\ln\left(\frac{p_{it}}{p_{i0}}\right) = \alpha + \beta\ln(p_{i0}) + \mu_i + \varepsilon_i$ $\varepsilon = \rho W\varepsilon + u$, $\varepsilon u \sim iid(0, \delta_u^2)$	$\frac{1}{T}\ln\left(\frac{p_{it}}{p_{i0}}\right) = \alpha + \beta\ln(p_{i0}) + \gamma X_{it} + \varepsilon_i$

Notes: the convergence speed is given by $\tau = -\ln(1 - \hat{\beta}T)/T$.

---

[2]The complete form of the model with time and country subscripts is: $y_{it} = \rho \sum_{j=1}^{N} w_{ij} y_{jt} + x_{it}\beta + \sum_{j=1}^{N} wx_{ijt}\theta + \mu_i + \varepsilon_{it}$.

Table 3 presents the number of countries by growth range and sub-periods over 1961-2006. Across sub-periods, the majority of countries have achieved 4 percent growth rate or less. However, the results suggest different trends across both locations and time. The highest number of countries (10) with negative growth rates is observed during the 1971-1980 sub-period. This corresponds to the period where exchange rates in some countries became overvalued in order to make imports cheaper and raise the price of exports. However, the overvaluation of the exchange rate discouraged exports of primary commodities, which included the exports of agricultural crops. High population growth rates, growing urban populations, and overvalued exchange rates promoted an increase in food imports while the price of non-tradables increased relative to food imports [26]. Over the 1991-2006 sub-period, 29 out of 47 countries achieved growth rates ranging from 1 to 4 percent (see Appendix B for complete list of agricultural growth rates by countries and sub-periods). As shown in **Figure 2**, the West African region registered the highest growth rate during the period 1999 to 2005—the growth rate of this region was 5 percent compared to the African average of 3.3 percent.

4.2. Estimation Results

Regression results are presented in **Table 4** . Overall, except for machinery, production elasticities with respect to countries own inputs are positive and significant: 0.689 (land), 0.034 (fertilizer), 0.379 (labor), and 0.430 (livestock). The results suggest the presence of significant externalities or neighboring country production effects on own countries' agricultural production, with the elasticity of agricultural production with respect to neighboring countries' being be 0.039 over the 1961-2006 period. In other words, on an average, a one percent increase (decrease) in agricultural production in neighboring countries increased (decreased) agriculture production in the home country by 0.039 percent. After a sharp decline during 1971-1980, the neighboring country' effect increased to 0.179 during 1991-2006—the period in which the NEPAD's CAADP agenda has been adopted by African leaders.

With respect to inputs, we found negative and significant effect of neighbors' elasticity of labor during the period 1981-1990 (−0.019). Although negligible, this implies that an increase (decrease) in the use of agricultural labor in neighboring countries has the potential to lead to a decrease (increase) in agriculture production in the home country. This finding makes sense if one assumes fixed labor supply and spatial mobility of agricultural labor among Sub-Saharan African countries. Negative significant externalities are found for machine use in 1971-1980.

This finding suggest that by increasing the use of other agricultural inputs such as fertilizer, land and water, there

is a risk that if left uncoordinated intensive mechanization by one country can lead to a decrease in production in neighboring countries. On an average, the pace of agricultural mechanization in Sub-Saharan Africa has been slow due to the high costs of implementation and low effectiveness of modern agricultural equipment [27]. Government-run tractor programs in the 1960s and early 1970s were largely ineffective as a result of management failures, shortfalls of government financial support and poor supporting infrastructures [28].

Table 2. Descriptive statistics.

Variable	Obs.	Mean	SE	Minimum	Maximum
Production	2162	1254.9	2072.0	5.9	12251.7
Land	2162	20.2	25.6	0.0	113.1
Fertilizer	2162	34.0	107.4	0.0	720.3
Labor	2162	3.0	3.9	0.0	18.7
Machine	2162	5.5	19.7	0.0	134.9
Livestock	2162	5282.3	8597.1	7.3	43568.5

Table 3. Distribution of countries by growth range and sub-periods.

	1961-70	1971-80	1981-90	1991-2006
<0.0	4	10	5	4
0.1-2.0	6	17	15	16
2.1-3.0	15	7	8	13
3.1-4.0	14	7	10	3
4.1-5.0	5	4	3	7
5.1-6.0	1	1	4	3
>6.0	2	1	2	1
Total	47	47	47	47

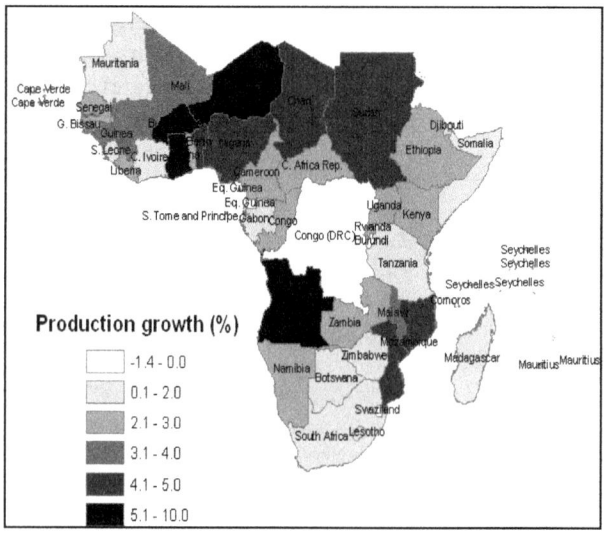

Figure 2. Agricultural production growth (1991-2006).

Table 4. Regression results.

	All		1961-1970		1971-1980		1981-1990		1991-2006	
	Coefficient	SE	Coefficient	SE	Coefficient	SE	Coefficient	SE	Coefficient	SE
Neighbors' outputs elasticities										
Spatial lag	0.039[a]	0.021	0.275[a]	0.048	−0.021	0.064	0.062[b]	0.047	0.179[a]	0.037
Own inputs elasticities										
Land	0.689[a]	0.024	0.664[a]	0.050	0.874[a]	0.077	0.495[a]	0.037	0.641[a]	0.063
Fertilizer	0.034[a]	0.003	0.025[a]	0.006	0.023[a]	0.007	0.010	0.007	0.011[a]	0.004
Labor	0.379[a]	0.020	0.561[a]	0.078	0.378[a]	0.068	0.501[a]	0.059	0.478[a]	0.054
Machine	0.004	0.006	0.008	0.008	−0.016	0.019	0.110[a]	0.021	−0.046[b]	0.019
Livestock	0.430[a]	0.014	0.112[a]	0.034	0.311[a]	0.045	0.400[a]	0.033	0.404[a]	0.033
Neighbors' inputs elasticities										
Land	−0.003	0.008	0.008	0.007	0.000	0.012	0.005	0.009	−0.001	0.009
Fertilizer	−0.001	0.004	0.000	0.004	0.004	0.007	−0.003	0.005	0.001	0.005
Labor	0.000	0.008	0.005	0.008	−0.001	0.013	−0.019[b]	0.009	0.010[b]	0.008
Machine	−0.007	0.005	−0.003	0.004	−0.013[c]	0.007	−0.005	0.005	0.004	0.005
Livestock	0.012	0.009	−0.010	0.007	0.014	0.012	0.008	0.010	−0.014	0.010
#Obs.	2162		470		470		470		752	
LM robust test	15.5	p-value = 0.00	36.7	p-value = 0.00	0.8	p-value = 0.36	5.8	p-value = 0.02	44.8	p-value = 0.00

Notes: [a], [b], [c] mean significant at 1%, 5%, and 10% respectively.

In the literature, there are two terms that are used to characterize policy spillover effects: 1) beggar-thyneighbor policies: These are policies that attempt to remedy the economic problems in one country through mechanisms that tend to worsen the problems of other countries [29]; 2) prosper-thy-neighbor policies: These are policies that generate positive spillovers of a neighboring country's agricultural production on own countries production [30].

Using agricultural growth rates as an outcome of agricultural policies, the results reported in **Figure 3** suggest that on an average, no country witnessed negative spillovers due to its neighbors. In contrast, on an average, each country attained 2.5 percent growth rate as a results of spillover from neighbors. Even countries with negative actual agricultural growth rate such as Equatorial Guinea (–0.5 percent), Swaziland (–0.6 percent), DRC (–1.4 percent) and Burundi (–0.2 percent), benefited from positive spillover growth rates of 1.8 percent, 2.5 percent, 2.5 percent and 3.1 percent, respectively. Ethiopia (4.4 percent), Uganda (4.4 percent), Nigeria (4.4 percent), Comoros (3.7 percent), and Zambia (3.5 percent) are the top beneficiaries from the production effects of its neighbors.

4.3. Convergence Results for Per-Capita Agricultural Growth

The results confirm the potential for convergence of per-capita agricultural growth among Sub-Saharan countries. Both spatial and non-spatial specifications support the hypothesis that countries lagging in terms of per capita agricultural growth are catching up with the leading countries. As shown in **Figure 4**, the potential for convergence is much higher when spatial spillover is accounted for. In addition, the use of agricultural inputs in the production function specification substantially improves convergence.

Figure 5 presents the speed of convergence by model specifications. It appears that incorporating spatial and conditional specifications lead to higher speed of convergence than non-spatial and unconditional specifications respectively. This confirms the important role of spatial spillover in achieving a common agenda such as the six percent growth target under CAADP agenda.

5. Conclusions and Implications

Both theory and empirical evidence clearly suggest that

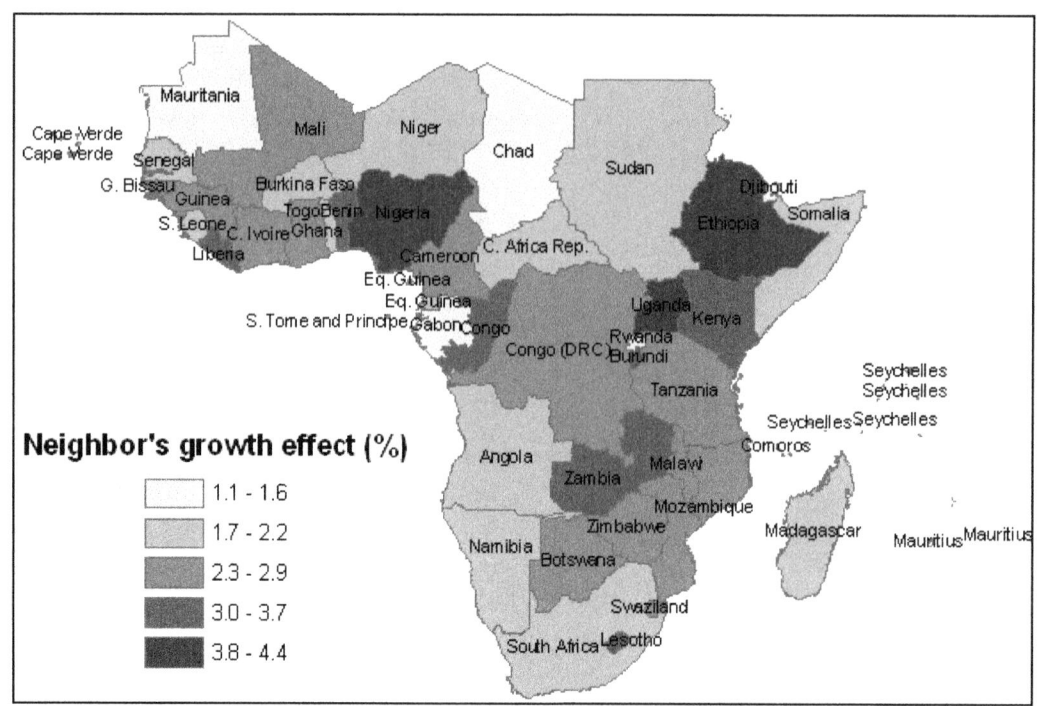

Figure 3. Agricultural growth effects from neighboring countries (%).

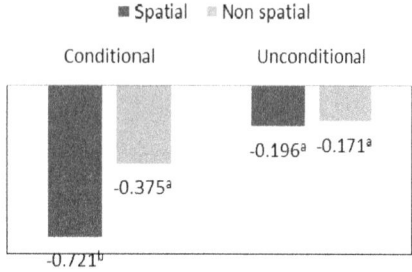

Notes: a,b means significant at 1%, and 5% respectively.

Figure 4. β-convergence.

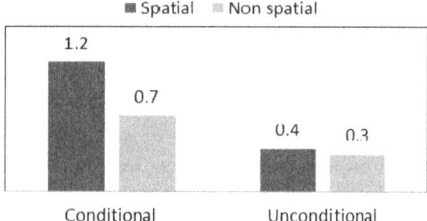

Figure 5. Speed of convergence.

geographical proximity can generate spillovers which ultimately affect agricultural growth dynamics across countries. The creation of a common union is often rationalized on grounds of moving the equilibrium toward the first best solution whenever independent policies generate spillovers. This arises as a common agenda can significantly reduce the scope of free-riding behavior among member countries. In addition, cross-border externalities

arising out of higher levels of market integration requires countries to agree upon policy coordination relative to the option of breaking ranks.

Using a Spatial Durbin Model for panel data, the present study examined the extent and magnitude of agricultural production spillover that might validate the adoption of CAADP agenda among Sub-Saharan African countries. Overall, our results suggest the presence of positive agricultural production spillovers. No evidence of *beggar-thy-neighbor* or negative spillover policies was found. On an average, each country received 2.5 percent growth as a result of spillover. Finally, our results suggest that convergence dynamics is much stronger whenever spillover is accounted for which provides a rationale for a common agenda such as CAADP.

Our results have clear implications for policies that require coordinated interventions by donors and countries. First, bringing in countries to pursue a common agricultural policy agenda will require coordinated actions in the provision of a public good, such as international agricultural research. Second, monitoring such coordinated actions will require an institutional setting (such as the NEPAD and the RECs) for sustained consistency. Finally, the adoption of a common agricultural policy is one way of making foreign aid work better. Donors can fund a common agricultural agenda continent-wide that can move the equilibrium toward the first best solution whenever independent policies generate spillovers. Such coordination will help in guiding strategies and investments to achieve sustainable growth, poverty reduction, and food and nutrition security.

REFERENCES

[1] A. N. Pratt and B. Yu, "An Updated Look at the Recovery of Agricultural Productivity in Sub-Saharan Africa," IFPRI Discussion Paper No. 787, Washington DC, 2008.

[2] FAO, FAOSTAT Database, 2006. http://faostat3.fao.org/home/index.html

[3] FAO (Food and Agriculture Organization of the United Nations), "Agriculture's Contributions to Economic and Social Development," *The Electronic Journal of Agricultural and Development Economics*, Vol. 1, No. 1, 2004, pp. 1-5.

[4] NEPAD Secretariat, CAADP, "CAADP Country Level Implementation Process," *Concept Note Prepared by the NEPAD Secretariat Based on the Outcome of the NEPAD Implementation Retreat*, Pretoria, 24-25 October 2005. http://fsg.afre.msu.edu/mgt/caadp/country_implementation_process_concept_notev21.pdf

[5] H. P. Binswanger-Mkhize and A. F. McCalla, "The Changing Context and Prospects for Agricultural and Rural Development in Africa," International Fund for Agricultural Development and African Development Bank, Rome and Tunis, 2009.

[6] R. Stringer and P. Pingali, "Agriculture's Contributions to Economic and Social Development," *Journal of Agricultural and Development Economics*, Vol. 1, No. 1, 2004, pp. 1-5.

[7] DFID, "Agriculture and Poverty Reduction: Unlocking the Potential," DFID Policy Paper, London, 2003.

[8] F. Ellis, "A Livelihoods Approach to Migration and Poverty Reduction," Paper commissioned by DFID, London, 2003.

[9] M. Fafchamps, F. Teal and J. Toye, "Towards a Growth Strategy for Africa," Centre for the Study of African Economies, University of Oxford, Oxford, 2001.

[10] T. Reardon, J. Bergegué and Escobar, G., "Rural Nonfarm Employment and Incomes in Latin America: Overview and Policy Implications," *World Development*, Vol. 29, No. 3, 2001, pp. 395-409.

[11] UNECA (United Nations Economic Commission for Africa) Economic Report on Africa, "Accelerating Africa's Development through Diversification," Addis Ababa, Ethiopia, 2007.

[12] A. Wambo, "Regional Integration in Africa and Its Implications for Rural Development," UN Economic Commission for Africa Report No. 2, Addis Ababa, 2006.

[13] F. Etro, "International Policy Coordination with Economic Unions," Harvard University Manuscript, Boston, 2001.

[14] A. D. Janvry and E. Sadoulet, "Agriculture for Development in Africa: Business-as-Usual or New Departures," *Journal of African Economies*, Vol. 19, Suppl. 2, 2010, pp. ii7-ii39

[15] A. Dorward, S. Fan, J. Kydd, H. Lofgren, J. Morrison, C. Poulton, N. Rao, L. Smith, H. Tchale, S. Thorat, I. Urey and P. Wobst, "Institutions and Economic Policies for Pro-Poor Agricultural Growth," DSGD Discussion Paper No. 15, IFPRI and Centre for Development and Poverty Reduction, Washington DC and London, 2004.

[16] J. A. Berdegué, "Cooperating to Compete. Peasant Associative Business Firms in Chile," Published Doctoral Dissertation, Wageningen University and Research Centre, Department ofSocial Sciences, Communication and Innovation Group, Wageningen, 2001.

[17] K. Felgenhauer and P. Labella, "Global Agro-Food Supply Chain: Is there space for Africa?" In: Turning African Agriculture into a Business: A Reader, OECD Development Center, Paris, 2008.

[18] M. Kherallah, C. Delgado, E. Gabre-Madhin, N. Minot and M. Johnson, "Reforming Agricultural Markets in Africa: Achievements and Challenges," Johns Hopkins University Press, Baltimore, 2002.

[19] T. S. Jayne, J. Govereh, A. Mwanaumo, J. K. Nyoro and A. Chapoto, "False Promise or False Premise? The Experience of Food and Input Market Reform in Eastern and Southern Africa," *World Development* Vol. 30, No. 11, 2002, pp. 1967-1985.

[20] X. Diao, P. Hazell, D. Resnick and J. Thurlow, "The Role of Agriculture in Development: Implications for Sub-Saharan Africa," Research Report 153, International Food Policy Research Institute, Washington DC, 2007.

[21] O. Badiane, S. Odjo and J. Ulimwengu, "Emerging Policies and Partnerships under CAADP: Implications for Long-Term Growth, Food Security, and Poverty Reduction," IFPRI Discussion Paper No. 1145, 2011. http://www.ifpri.org/sites/default/files/publications/ifpridp01145.pdf

[22] A. Alesina, I. Angeloni and F. Etro, "The Political Economy of International Unions," NBER Working Paper No. 8645, Cambridge, 2001. http://cdi.mecon.gov.ar/biblio/docelec/harvard/hier/1939.pdf

[23] J. P. Lesage and M. M. Fisher, "Spatial Growth Regressions: Model Specification, Estimation and Interpretation," *Spatial Economic Analysis*, Vol. 3, No. 3, 2008, pp. 275-304.

[24] R. J. Barro and X. Sala-i-Martin, "Economic Growth Theory," MIT Press, Cambridge, 1995.

[25] K. O. Fuglie, "Is a Slowdown in Agricultural Productivity Growth Contributing to the Rise in Commodity Prices?" *Agricultural Economics*, Vol. 39, No. s1, 2008, pp. 431-441.

[26] C. L. Delgado, "Agricultural Diversification and Export Promotion in Sub-Saharan Africa," *Food Policy*, Vol. 20, No. 3, 1995, pp. 225-243.

[27] P. L. Pingali, Y. Bigot and H. P. Binswanger, "Agricultural Mechanization and the Evolution of Farming in Sub-Saharan Africa," Johns Hopkins University Press, Baltimore, 1987.

[28] G. C. Mrema, D. Baker and D. Kahan, "Agricultural

Mechanization in Sub-Saharan Africa: Time for a New Look," Agricultural Management, Marketing and Finance Occasional Paper 22, Rome, 2008.

[29] J. Robinson, "Essays on the Theory of Employment," Blackwell, Oxford, 1937.

[30] G. Corsetti and P. Pesenti, "Welfare and Macroeconomic Interdependence," *Quarterly Journal of Economics*, Vol. 116, No. 2, 2001, pp. 421-46.

Appendix A: Spatial Regression Model Tests

Tests of spatial correlation:

The Moran's I for regression residuals is given

$$I = \frac{n}{S_0} \frac{e'We}{e'e}$$

where e is the $(n \times 1)$ vector of OLS residuals.

There are several tests with well-designed alternative hypotheses:

1) Lagrange Multiplier test for spatial error;

$$LM_\lambda = \frac{1}{T}\left(\frac{e'We}{s^2}\right)^2$$

where $s^2 = e'e/n$, is the maximum likelihood variance and $T = tr\left(W'W + W^2\right)$, with tr being the matrix trace operator.

2) Lagrange Multiplier test for spatial lag;

$$LM_\rho = \frac{1}{nJ_{\rho \cdot \beta}}\left(\frac{e'Wy}{s^2}\right)^2$$

where $J_{\rho \cdot \beta} = \left[(WXb)' M (WXb) + Ts^2\right]/ns^2$ is part of

the ML estimated information matrix, b is the vector of OLS estimated parameters, and

$$M = \left[I - X\left(X'X\right)^{-1} X'\right].$$

We also use robust tests developed by Anselin *et al.* (1996):

3) Robust Lagrange Multiplier test for spatial error;

$$LM_\lambda^* = \frac{1}{T - T^2\left(nJ_{\rho \cdot \beta}\right)^{-1}}$$

$$\times \left(\frac{e'We}{s^2} - T\left(nJ_{\rho \cdot \beta}\right)^{-1} \frac{e'Wy}{s^2}\right)^2,$$

where $s^2 = e'e/n$, is the maximum likelihood variance and $T = tr\left(W'W + W^2\right)$, with tr being the matrix trace operator.

4) Robust Lagrange Multiplier test for spatial lag;

$$LM_\rho^* = \frac{1}{nJ_{\rho \cdot \beta} - T}\left(\frac{e'Wy}{s^2} - \frac{e'We}{s^2}\right)^2.$$

These tests asymptotically follow a χ^2 distribution with one degree of freedom.

Appendix B: Agricultural Growth Rates by Countries and Sub-Periods

Countries	1961-1970	1971-1980	1981-1990	1991-2006
Angola	3.4	−3.0	0.3	5.4
Benin	2.1	2.2	5.9	4.0
Botswana	3.8	−0.2	3.4	0.0
Burkina Faso	3.8	1.1	6.2	5.7
Burundi	2.1	0.8	3.0	−0.2
Cameroon	3.1	2.6	2.0	2.4
Cape Verde	5.4	4.7	3.6	1.9
C. Africa Rep.	4.6	1.9	1.8	2.5
Chad	−1.1	3.6	6.0	2.0
Comoros	1.2	0.8	2.5	4.3
Congo	2.3	1.6	2.2	1.2
Congo (DRC)	1.9	1.1	1.6	2.1
C. Ivoire	2.0	1.8	3.0	−1.4
Djibouti	4.8	10.2	7.4	1.3
Eq. Guinea	2.9	−6.4	4.8	−0.4
Ethiopia	2.3	1.5	0.8	2.8
Gabon	−2.3	2.3	4.5	2.6
Gambia	1.8	3.5	1.9	1.5
Ghana	2.5	−2.5	3.9	4.8
Guinea	3.0	−0.8	2.3	7.1
G. Bissau	1.9	1.5	1.1	3.8
Kenya	3.1	3.6	4.6	2.3
Lesotho	1.6	1.5	1.5	0.8
Liberia	4.3	2.2	−1.3	2.7
Madagascar	2.9	1.5	1.6	1.4
Malawi	3.3	4.4	1.8	3.8
Mali	3.3	2.0	3.7	3.2
Mauritania	1.7	0.7	1.6	1.4
Mauritius	2.3	1.0	3.0	0.6
Mozambique	3.3	−0.5	0.2	4.3
Namibia	3.4	1.7	−0.8	2.4
Niger	2.6	3.5	1.6	5.4
Nigeria	4.6	−1.5	5.7	4.2
Rwanda	6.5	3.4	2.2	2.7
S. Tome and Principe	3.1	1.2	2.0	1.5
Senegal	−0.4	−2.5	−1.5	4.7
Seychelles	−1.4	5.7	5.6	2.4
S. Leone	2.4	−0.2	−0.5	1.8
Somalia	3.9	2.5	1.2	0.5
South Africa	2.6	3.5	1.2	1.5
Sudan	3.6	2.7	−0.1	4.5
Swaziland	4.6	4.2	2.2	−0.6
Tanzania	3.9	3.0	2.7	1.7
Togo	2.7	1.3	3.3	2.9
Uganda	7.5	−2.5	3.8	2.1
Zambia	2.3	3.6	3.0	2.5
Zimbabwe	3.6	4.3	3.0	0.4

9

Demand Growth versus Market Share Gains: Decomposing World Manufacturing Import Growth

M. Ataman Aksoy[1], Francis Ng[2]
[1]International Trade Department, World Bank, Washington DC, USA
[2]Trade and International Integration Team (DECTI), Development Research Group, World Bank, Washington DC, USA

ABSTRACT

This paper decomposes manufacturing import growth rates in a selected set of large industrial and developing countries (five industrial and eight developing) and measures the relative contributions of domestic demand and market share changes for two separate periods 1991/92-2001/02 and 2001/02-2007/08. It also shows the shares of imports both from the rest of the world and from developing countries for aggregate and three digit manufacturing sectors. Import growth is much higher during the 2000s driven by higher demand growth rates. While market share changes explain most of the growth during the 1990s, its contribution is relatively smaller during the 2000s. Imports from developing countries have grown much faster both in industrial and developing country markets driven primarily by market share changes. However, more than half of market share gains by developing countries are caused by the exports of China which accounts for more than 70 percent of market share gains of developing countries in our sample countries during the 2000s. Despite rapid growth, developing country's share in the gross absorption of the sample countries is still very low and can expand substantially even if demand growth is much lower in the near future.

Keywords: Global Manufacturing Export Growth; Industrial and Developing Country Import Growth; Decomposition of Growth; Demand Growth; World Market Share Changes; Market Penetration; Gross Manufacturing Production and Outputs; Trade Pattern and Growth

1. Introduction

Within the last few decades, global manufactured goods trade has grown very fast. This growth has been driven both by liberalization of trade regimes across the globe and high demand growth rates especially among developing countries and especially during the 2000s. Trade liberalization has also contributed to global trade expansion. As trade barriers have fallen, increased production sharing and specialization have led to expansion of both exports and imports. These developments have led to increased import shares in almost all countries. While much of liberalization has been unilateral, there are also greater uses of regional agreements.

Recent developments suggest world demand decreases (or slower demand growth) for the near future and it would be difficult to recreate the rapid demand growth of 2000s. Yet the import penetration and growth of both imports and exports should continue if the liberalized trade regimes are maintained and improved. Thus it is important to have some understanding about the relative contribution of market share changes (created because of more liberal trade regimes) and import increases caused by the increases in demand. It is also important to separate 1990s when demand growth was lower from the 2000s when demand growth was much higher.

This paper decomposes import growth rates for a set of large industrial and developing countries (five industrial and eight developing) and measures the relative contributions of domestic demand and market share changes for two separate periods 1991/92-2001/02 and 2001/02-2007/08 (using 2-year averages to minimize the annual fluctuations in trade and output production). It also shows the changes in the shares of imports both from the rest of the world and from developing countries for aggregate and three digit manufacturing sectors. Import shares and their changes show the relative magnitude of the openness in key industrial and developing countries and its change over the last two decades. Canada, France, Germany, Japan, and United States were selected as the industrial countries, and China, Brazil, India, Korea Republic, Malaysia, Mexico, South Africa, and Turkey were selected as the developing countries[1].

Most of the market share analyses have been carried out using only exports, and testing whether the exports of a specific country have expanded at the same rate as world exports [1-6] etc. These exercises take the world trade growth as given and estimate the relative performance of counties against this trend, and not what determines that trend. The contribution of market share changes versus demand increases in explaining trade growth has not received much attention[2]. One simple way of analyzing this issue is to see whether the growth of imports in selected markets are driven by the demand increases or they have expanded by gaining market shares in the importing countries. This can be done by estimating the shares of imports in domestic absorption and then measuring the changes in these shares. These changes in shares show the contributions of share changes while import increases under constant market shares show the contribution of demand increases. This decomposition can also shed light on the likely outcomes for world trade growth under different global demand growth scenarios [7,8].

A related issue involves the role of developing (especially emerging market) countries in world manufacturing trade. Many have also argued that developing country exports are taking a big share of the markets in industrial countries and that within manufacturing a significant portion of production is moving from industrial to developing countries. Some have even argued that this development is leading to deindustrialization of many industrial countries. Along with the decomposition exercise, this paper also estimates the magnitude of developing country exports (aggregate and 3 digit) within the domestic absorption and production in these selected countries (both industrial and developing) and their evolution over the last two decades.

Finally, the study analyzes two periods with very different trade growth rates. World trade growth in current US dollars accelerated for all countries during 2001/02-2007/08 period but the acceleration of export growth of developing countries was greater and reached 18.2 percent per annum during this period. As a result developing countries have increased their market share of global manufactured exports and imports from about 20 and 35 percent in 1991/92 to 44 and 46 percent in 2007/08 respectively.

Section B explains the methodology and the data. In Section C, the shares of total imports from the rest of the world and their decomposition are analyzed separately

for the selected industrial and developing countries. Section D focuses on exports from developing countries to industrial and other developing countries, and extends the analysis to 3-digit ISIC sectors. Very rapid growth of China, especially during the 2000s distorts most of the conclusions and analyses in the previous sections. The impact of China is discussed throughout the text in but given its importance, Section E summarizes its impact on world trade. Section F provides the main results and implications from this empirical analysis. Conclusions are presented in Section G.

The main findings in this paper show that world demand growth is very different during 1990s and 2000s. Demand growth has accelerated during the 2000s. While market share changes explain most of the growth during the 1990s, its contribution is relatively smaller during the 2000s. Even without demand growth, continued liberal trade regimes could generate 3 - 5 percent per annum manufacturing trade growth caused by market share changes.

Imports from developing countries have grown much faster both in industrial and developing country markets. Despite the rapid growth, their share in the absorption of the sample countries is still very low and can expand substantially even if demand growth is much lower in the near future. However, most of this share increase is driven by China. Furthermore, China is among few countries which have reduced its share of imports from other developing countries. Future manufacturing trade growth will depend on the evolution of trade patterns of China as much as other economic developments.

2. Methodology and Data

The total gross absorption (demand) in each country is estimated as gross production in manufacturing, minus exports plus imports, for the beginning and end years. Gross production is taken from UNIDO database [9] and checked against other sources for consistency[3]. All gross production data is converted to US dollars at the current average exchange rates, to make them consistent with trade data from UNSD COMTRADE [10] which is denominated in US dollars (see [11]). These are nominal US dollar values which include US dollar inflation and changes in the real exchange rates of local currencies against the US dollar[4]. Canada, France, Germany, Japan,

---

[1]It would be desirable to undertake this analysis for aggregate developing and industrial countries but manufacturing production data is not available in the same format and definitions for many countries. Sample countries account for more than 50 percent of world trade (**Table 1**).

[2]This decomposition was undertaken for selected industrial countries for the 1990s (World Bank 2005).

[3]UNIDO is the only agency that publishes manufacturing gross output series. In many cases, these numbers were compared to other national sources to ascertain the similarity of movements.

[4]There is a significant appreciation of the US dollar against the currencies of most of the other countries during the late 1990s and depreciation during the 2000s. This appreciation underestimates the domestic production and demand growth in US dollars and overestimates the share of imports, which are denominated in US dollars. Opposite takes place during US dollar depreciations. Thus, nominal US dollar measurement would underestimate real growth during the 1990s and overestimate it during the 2000s.

and United States were selected as the industrial countries, and China, Brazil, India, Korea Republic, Malaysia, Mexico, South Africa, and Turkey were selected as the developing countries.

Import growth in these countries is decomposed into changes due to demand increases and changes due to market share changes. The contribution of demand changes is estimated assuming a constant share of imports in gross domestic demand between the two time periods, *i.e.* the market shares do not change. The market share changes are then estimated as the difference between the actual import growth rate and the import growth rate under a constant market share assumption. The periods of 1991/92, 2000/01, and 2007/08 are used as benchmarks to estimate the growth rates and import shares. Two year averages are used to minimize the annual fluctuations in output and trade. 2007/08 is used as the final year both due to data availability, and more importantly, it is the last year before the global financial crisis. The analysis of the impacts of the crisis on trade values requires a separate study.

This simple method has some limitations. First, it assumes that the income elasticity of demand for specific products exported by a group of countries is identical to the average income elasticity for the sectors as a whole. This bias decreases as the number of products exported increases and as product categories get narrower. Second, it assumes that market share changes are independent of demand growth. Normally, one would expect that when the rate of growth of demand accelerates, there would be spillovers to imports that will increase the import shares. This relationship was tested using the both the detailed 3-digit subsector information using imports and exports from developing countries and aggregate global imports for the selected 13 countries. The relationship between the market share changes and demand changes were not significant across industries and countries[5]. (See **Annex Table 1**).

The developments in our sample countries (key players in world trade) do not exactly mimic total world trade developments but are quite close. In **Table 1**, key growth rates for world trade and the sample countries are presented. Major difference between all countries and our sample is that our sample of developing countries had a lower share of total imports in 1991/92 than total developing countries (at 24.3 percent versus 34.6 percent) and had much higher rate of import growth than total developing countries (11.5 percent p.a. versus 6.2) during the

1991/92-2001/02 period. The rest of the growth rates are not identical but not sufficiently different to create major differences of interpretation.

3. Aggregate Import Growth Decomposition

3.1. Industrial Countries

Tables 2 and *3* show the share of imports, import growth rates and their decomposition for the selected industrial and developing countries respectively[6]. Totals are weighted averages.

There is one important difference between the first period 1991/92-2001/02 and the second one 2001/02-2007/08. Industrial countries' demand growth almost quadrupled from 1.6 percent p.a. to 5.8 percent p.a. Market share changes moved in the opposite direction but only declined to 3.8 percent p.a. from 4.8 percent p.a. Average import growth, which is the sum of demand and market share changes, accelerated from 6.4 percent to 9.6 percent per annum.

Along with the acceleration of demand growth during the second period, relative contribution of demand and market share changes to import growth got reversed. During the first period, except for France, the contribution of market share changes to import growth is much larger than the contribution of demand growth. France has actually import substituted during this period and reduced its share of imports. During the second period, demand increase rate has almost quadrupled and, except for Japan, the contribution of demand growth has been higher then market share changes. But even with higher contribution from demand growth, the role played by market share changes is highly significant and explains almost forty percent of total import growth even during the second period. Market share changes for Japan during both periods, and Germany during the first period, explain bulk of import growth. So if the market shares had stayed the same, and imports only grew at the same rate as domestic demand, the import growth rate in these five countries would have been only 1.6 percent p.a. during the first period and about 6 percent p.a. during the second. Conversely, even in the absence of any demand growth, imports would have increased 4.8 percent p.a. during the first and 3.8 percent p.a. during the second period; very respectable trade growth rates for rich countries.

---

[5]The disaggregated estimation was done at the 3-digit ISIC level correlating the 22 sub-sector import growth rates and corresponding import growth rates due to market share changes, with country dummies. At the aggregate level the relationship was negative but not significant (**Annex Table 1**). Market share changes are negative correlated with demand increases across countries and periods.

[6]**Annex Table 2** also shows the impact of exports from partners that had a special trading arrangement during the 1990s and 2000s. For the US and Canada imports from NAFTA countries are presented separately to see the impact of NAFTA and for France and Germany the imports from EU are separated. In the annex tables, EU is further separated into the first 15 and 12 countries that joined later. For the developing countries, imports from EU for Turkey, and from US and Canada for Mexico, are also presented separately.

Table 1. Growth of manufacturing imports and their market shares in world and sample countries.

Country Group	Partner	Manufacturing Imports (current US dollar in billions)/a			Annual Import Growth (%)		Market Share of Manufacturing Imports (%)		
		1991/92	2001/02	2007/08	91/92-01/02	01/02-07/08	1991/92	2001/02	2007/08
World	World	2421	4553	8921	6.5	11.9	100.0	100.0	100.0
	Developing countries	838	1533	4084	6.2	17.7	34.6	33.7	45.8
	Industrial countries	1582	3020	4838	6.7	8.2	65.4	66.3	54.2
Developing countries/b	World	485	1443	3943	11.5	18.2	20.1	31.7	44.2
	Developing countries	218	612	2171	10.9	23.5	9.0	13.4	24.3
	Industrial countries	267	830	1772	12.0	13.5	11.0	18.2	19.9
Industrial countries/c	World	1935	3110	4978	4.9	8.2	79.9	68.3	55.8
	Developing countries	620	921	1913	4.0	13.0	25.6	20.2	21.4
	Industrial countries	1315	2190	3065	5.2	5.8	54.3	48.1	34.4
Sample Countries									
World totals	World	1210	2421	4707	7.2	11.7	100.0	100.0	100.0
	Developing countries	294	870	2105	11.5	15.9	24.3	35.9	44.7
	Industrial countries	916	1551	2602	5.4	9.0	75.7	64.1	55.3
Developing countries/d	World	222	580	1519	10.1	17.4	18.3	23.9	32.3
	Developing countries	55	176	684	12.3	25.4	4.6	7.3	14.5
	Industrial countries	166	403	834	9.3	12.9	13.8	16.7	17.7
Industrial countries/e	World	988	1841	3188	6.4	9.6	81.7	76.1	67.7
	Developing countries	239	693	1420	11.3	12.7	19.7	28.6	30.2
	Industrial countries	750	1148	1768	4.4	7.5	61.9	47.4	37.6

Notes: /a Manufacturing import is defined as products in SITC 5 + 6 + 7 + 8-68 in revision 3 and it is based on importers import from the specific markets in two-year averages of 1991-92, 2001-02, and 2007-08. /b Industrial countries are based on traditional IMF definition, including EU15, United States, Canada, Japan, Australia, New Zealand, Iceland, Norway, and Switzerland. /c Developing countries include all countries except 23 industrial countries in the world. /d Sample of developing countries includes Brazil, China, India, Korea Rep., Malaysia, Mexico, South Africa, and Turkey. /e Sample of industrial countries includes Canada, France, Germany, Japan, and United States. Sources: Computations based on UN COMTRADE Statistics (trade data) and UNIDO database (production data).

Table 2. Global manufacturing imports of industrial countries from 1991/92 to 2001/02 and 2001/02 to 2007/08.

Country	Share of World Imports in Domestic Demand (%)			Annual Import Growth from World (%)		Annual Import Growth Due to			
						1991/92-2001/02		2001/02-2007/08	
	1991/92	2001/02	2007/08	91/92-01/02	01/02-07/08	Demand Change	Market Share Change	Demand Change	Market Share Change
Canada	32.5	47.1	46.6	6.6	8.4	2.7	3.9	8.6	−0.1
France	31.1	28.2	38.5	3.8	12.5	3.1	0.8	6.8	5.1
Germany	22.4	34.3	38.5	3.0	12.8	−1.3	4.3	10.6	2.1
Japan	4.0	8.9	13.0	6.7	9.1	−1.3	8.1	2.4	6.7
United States	12.6	20.9	23.6	9.1	7.6	3.7	5.4	5.4	2.2
Total: above industrial co.	13.5	21.5	26.6	6.4	9.6	1.6	4.8	5.8	3.8

Note: Data is based on two-year averages of 1991-92, 2001-02, and 2007-08. Source: Based on UN COMTRADE Statistics (trade data) and UNIDO database (production data).

Table 3. Global manufacturing imports of developing countries from 1991/92 to 2001/02 and 2001/02 to 2007/08.

Country	Share of World Imports in Domestic Demand (%)			Annual Import Growth from the World (%)		Annual Import Growth Due to			
						1991/92-2001/02		2001/02-2007/08	
	1991/92	2001/02	2007/08	91/92-01/02	01/02-07/08	Demand Change	Market Share Change	Demand Change	Market Share Change
Brazil	5.7	14.3	13.7	11.5	17.0	1.6	9.9	17.8	−0.8
China	15.8	20.5	13.4	12.7	22.1	9.8	2.9	30.9	−8.9
India	7.6	12.1	17.0	10.4	30.2	5.4	5.0	23.0	7.2
Korea, Rep.	18.8	20.1	23.5	5.5	15.9	4.8	0.7	13.0	3.0
Malaysia	53.1	58.1	45.8	7.3	9.2	6.3	1.0	13.6	−4.4
Mexico	42.3	78.4	69.6	15.2	7.7	8.3	6.9	9.8	−2.2
South Africa	16.1	20.1	27.0	3.1	19.9	0.8	2.3	14.2	5.7
Turkey	17.2	30.0	31.0	7.9	24.2	2.1	5.8	23.6	0.6
Total: above developing co.	17.2	25.4	18.7	10.4	17.6	6.2	4.2	23.7	-6.1

Note: Data is based on two-year averages of 1991-92, 2001-02, and 2007-08. Sources: Computations based on UN COMTRADE Statistics (trade data) and UNIDO database (production data).

The share of imports in domestic demand varies by country. In 2007/08, Canada had the highest share at about 47 percent followed by Germany and France at above 39 percent. Japan had the lowest at 13 percent. Despite two decades of increasing import shares for these five countries, their average import share in domestic demand have only increased to about 27 percent by 2007/08. Of this 27 percent, about 11 percent is attributable to imports from countries with preferential agreements (**Annex Table 2**). Thus, after a period of very rapid growth and liberal trade regime, import shares of the industrial countries, excluding imports from countries with preferential agreements, was only 16 percent. On the other hand, all five countries have experienced significant import share increases during the last two decades.

The definition of gross absorption used in this paper is not a very common concept. **Annex Table 3** shows the import and exports as a share of gross domestic production which as a measure is more familiar. In this table there are few anomalies. Japan, which had a reputation of a major exporter during the pre-1990 period, had only 12 percent of its output exported and only imported 4 percent of its output equivalent in 1991/92. After two decades of very low domestic demand growth and export led expansion, its exports only reached 23 percent of output by 2007/08, which is less than a quarter of its output. Its imports only reached 11 percent of its output leading to larger trade surpluses as a percentage of its manufacturing output. Germany shows even a greater export orientation during the 2000s. Both its import and output shares in output increased but the increase in its export shares

are much greater and leading to large trade surpluses[7]. By 2007/8, Germany exported almost half of its output, highest among large industrial countries.

3.2. Developing Countries

Developing country import behavior in some ways is similar to that of the industrial countries. Import growth rates accelerate from already high rates of 10 percent p.a. during the first period to almost 18 percent p.a. during the second. The acceleration of demand growth is much more dramatic; from an average of 6.2 percent growth per annum during to first period to almost 24 percent p.a. during the second, much higher than that of industrial countries. During the first period, demand growth is high in Mexico and China and low in Brazil, Turkey and South Africa. During the second period, demand growth accelerates in almost every country, reaching 31 and 23 percent per annum respectively in China and India.

During the first period, import shares increase in all our sample countries. Some are very dramatic, such as Turkey and Mexico caused by joining NAFTA for Mexico and EU for Turkey. Other developing countries such as and Brazil also have high rates of import share increases.

The second period is different from the first beyond the rapid acceleration in demand growth. The average contribution of market share changes for developing countries are negative, suggesting that there has been

[7]Its trade surplus originates primarily with the EU-27 partners. They import 30 percent of Germany's manufacturing output but export only 19 percent of Germany's output equivalent.

import substitution within the manufacturing sector despite trade liberalizations. While China accounts for most the import substitution[8], even without China, the net markets share changes in Malaysia, and Mexico are also negative and large[9]. The differences between other developing countries that have increasing import shares, and China, Mexico and Malaysia that have decreasing import shares, suggest further differentiation.

Mexico and Malaysia had manufacturing sectors that had significant assembly operations using mostly imported components and thus had very high import shares. Malaysia had these industries starting in the 1980s. Mexico expanded the "Maquiladores" after it joined NAFTA in 1994. In 2001/02, Malaysia had an import share of 58 percent while for Mexico this share reached 78 percent. While Chinese manufacturing does not fit this definition fully, it also had a large export sector that was based on imported components with relatively lower value added [12-16]. During the 2000s, these three countries must have increased domestic supply of components and reduced the share of imports. Many of the imported components and intermediaries might have started to be produced domestically because of larger domestic demand for them and larger scale suppliers might have invested in these countries to be close to their markets. Or alternatively some goods for final demand might have started to be locally produced.

If these three countries, China, Mexico, and Malaysia are excluded from our developing country list; market share changes in the remaining developing countries are quite similar to developments in industrial countries. **Figure 1** shows average market share changes and demand increases for the three groups of countries. First group is the five industrial countries. The second group is the three import substituting countries of China, Mexico and Malaysia. The third group is the other five large developing countries (India, Brazil, Korea Republic, South Africa, and Turkey).

Import substituting countries (including China, Mexico, and Malaysia) have much higher import growth rates during the first period with little market share changes and during the second period a faster demand growth rate with reductions in import shares. Other developing countries group (Brazil, India, Korea Republic, South Africa, and Turkey) has higher demand increases than industrial countries (much higher during the second period) but rather similar market share change rates. Industrial countries have market share changes of 4.8 and 3.8 percent p.a. during the first and second period respectively and the other developing country group has an average market share changes of 3.6 and 2.6 percent p.a. It is possible

to argue that for most large countries, ceteris paribus, one can expect 3 - 5 percent trade expansion even if there are no increases in demand. The role of increases in import shares can be seen more clearly in **Figure 2**.

While the import substituting group shows large fluctuations driven primarily by China, the other two groups show steady increases in import shares. Other developing country group was slightly less open than industrial countries in 1991/92; this difference has continued during the second period and industrial countries continue to be more open. Again, one can assume that the other developing countries will continue to increase their import shares rates along with the industrial countries generating some trade growth even in the absence of demand growth.

4. Market Shares of Developing Country Exports

4.1. Industrial Countries

One of the important developments during the last few decades has been the rapid expansion of exports from developing countries both to the industrial countries and to other developing countries (see [17,18]). This has led to fears that industrial countries were being de-industrialized and most of manufacturing production would be taken over by the developing countries. There are also arguments that recent deceleration of growth in industrial

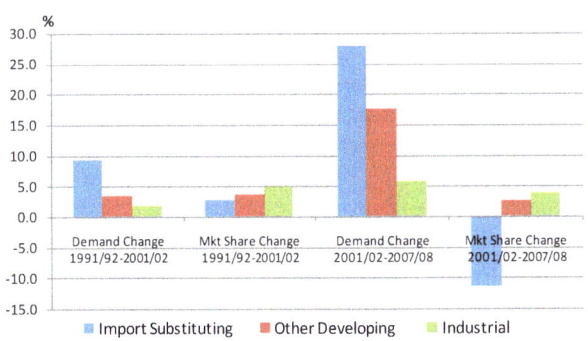

Figure 1. Import growth decomposition.

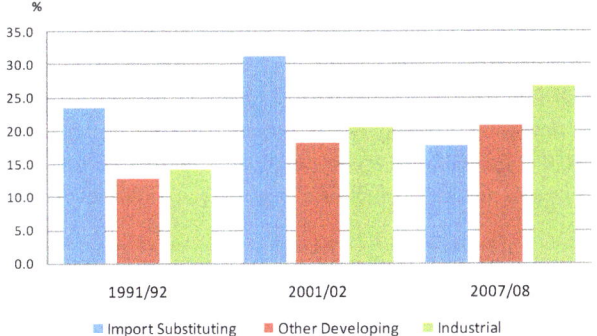

Figure 2. Import shares.

---

[8]Developments in China will be analyzed in Section E in greater detail.
[9]Brazil also has a very slight decrease in its import shares but the decrease is very small.

countries would lower the export and output growth of developing countries and the developments of last two decades might not be replicated. **Tables 4** and **5** show behavior of manufacturing imports from developing countries for our sample of industrial and developing countries.

Table 4 shows the shares of imports from developing countries in the total gross absorption (demand) of the five industrial countries, growth rate of these imports, and the decomposition of the import growth between demand and market share changes. Import growth rates from developing counties (about 11 and 13 percent p.a.) are much higher than their import growth rates from the rest of the world shown in **Table 2**. Import growth rates from developing countries are almost identical for the two periods while world trade growth has doubled during this time. Especially during the first period when the demand increases in industrial countries amounted to only 1.6 percent per annum, imports from developing countries increased by more than 11 percent p.a. Most of the import growth was caused by market share changes rather than demand increases. During the second period, despite higher demand growth, market share changes are still greater than demand changes. For this group of industrial countries, market share changes explain the bulk of the growth of imports from developing countries[10]. Of course, market penetration of almost 10 percent p.a. is much more disruptive and politically more sensitive.

Despite the rapid import growth caused by market penetration, by the end of the second period, the share of imports from developing countries in domestic absorption of this set of industrial countries was only about 12 percent. This 12 percent also includes the 12 countries that joined EU after 1992[11]. Of the remaining 88 percent, 14 percent came from exports of other industrial countries; while the rest (74 percent) came from domestic production. If China is excluded, the share of developed country imports goes down to 6.8 percent. Excluding China and developing countries included in regional trade arrangements such as EU and NAFTA reduces the share of all other developing countries to only 4.3 percent. The share of imports from developing countries is lower in Japan and France compared to the other three countries (see **Annex Table 4**).

It is possible to interpret the changes in market shares of developing countries in two ways. One is to highlight the fast growth and argue that market shares have tripled over two decades, which is a very dramatic increase which

cannot be sustained. Furthermore, developing countries have expanded their exports through primarily replacing domestic production.

On the other hand, the shares of developing country exports (including China and EU 12 countries) in total demand of these industrial countries were less than 12 percent at the end of almost two decades of very rapid import growth. So small changes in market shares of developing countries in the markets of industrial countries over the next decades can drive the export growth from developing countries at very high rates even if their absolute absorption growth rates decline significantly over the next decades. The shares are still small enough so that fast growth of exports can be accomplished without significant production losses by the industrial countries.

This aggregate picture masks large differences in market penetration in different sub-sectors. **Table 5** shows the market shares and the decomposition of import growth from all developing countries into the five Industrial countries by selected 22 3-digit sub-sectors. These 3-digit ISIC in Revision 3 sub-sectors range from very capital intensive, such as rubber and glass, to very labor intensive such as garments and footwear.

There are significant differences in market shares among different industries, arising from comparative advantage as well as differences in protection. There are two sets of subsectors that have reached high import penetration rates in 2007/08. First set includes the traditional labor intensive subsectors such as wearing apparel (70.3 percent), leather (71.4 percent), and textiles (40.2 percent). The second are the more recent labor intensive sectors such as office machinery (53.9 percent) and radio, television etc (36.5 percent). These are mostly classified as high technology products but their nominal growth rates have also been very low. These are the sectors where developing countries have gained significant market shares. On the other extreme sectors such as, tobacco (1.1 percent), paper (3.5 percent), publishing (2.7 percent), and food processing (5.3 percent) have low import shares.

In this set of subsectors, market share increases dominate import growth. In both periods and for almost all the subsectors, contribution of market share changes is greater than the contribution of demand growth. That is the reason for rapid import growth despite very low demand increases for many of the labor intensive subsectors. For example, for garments and footwear, despite negative and very low demand increases, imports have increased substantially purely on the basis of market share increases.

Market share gains are significant in almost all sectors including many of the high technology sectors such as machinery, medical precision equipment, and the like.

---

[10]EU-12, the countries which joined European Union after 1990 and Mexico for US and Canada are included in the developing country numbers. They do not change the general picture as shown in **Annex Table 4**.

[11]If they are excluded the shares of other developing countries are only 10 percent.

This suggests that the rise of South in gaining competitiveness in sectors have the domain of industrial countries is significant and is continuing (Akyuz, 2012).

Finally, while the growing competitiveness of developing countries is impressive, a significant portion of the increases in market shares are driven by the exports from China (see details in Section E). This is especially prevalent in the 2000s where more than 70 percent of market share gains are due to increases in imports from China.

4.2. Developing Countries

One of the most important developments of the last two decades is the growth of south-south trade (see [19-25]). All developing country imports from all developing counties increased at a slower rate than their imports from industrial countries during the 1990s but these were reversed during the 2000s where their imports from developing countries grew at almost 25 percent versus 14 percent per annum growth for their imports from industrial countries. By 2007/08 they were importing more from other developing countries than they were from industrial countries (see figures on **Table 1**).

Narrowing the data to our sample of seven developing countries the results are slightly different. Their import growth rates from other developing countries are higher than their import growth rates from industrial countries in both periods. However, they still import more from industrial countries than they do from other developing countries (see **Table 1**). Their imports from industrial countries were 16.8 percent of their total absorption in 2001/02 while their imports from other developing countries were only 8.8 percent (see **Tables 3** and **6**). By 2007/08, these ratios were only 9.7 and 9.0 percent respectively. Our sample of developing countries have significantly reduced relative share of their imports from

industrial countries and maintained their imports from developing countries. Thus, the sample developing countries' import structure has become more balanced between industrial and other developing countries.

Acceleration of import growth from other developing countries to about 25 percent p.a. during the second period is especially dramatic. In all countries excluding China, share of imports from developing countries increased substantially along with higher import growth rates. In China also, import growth has increased to 25 percent per annum but the demand increase has been much higher than the import growth rates leading to declining shares of imports from developing countries in domestic demand. During the first period, excluding China and Malaysia, the contribution of market share changes are greater than demand increases. Even in the second period when demand increases dominate, absolute contributions of market share changes reach almost double digit levels in six out of eight countries. Thus China and to less extent Malaysia are an exception to the general trend of increasing share of imports from developing countries. While it has reduced its share of imports from other developing countries it has increased the share its exports in other developing countries and a significant part of the increase in the share of imports from developing countries is driven by the exports of China (see details in the next Section E). Without China, the increase in the shares of developing countries in out sample countries have also increased but at much slower rates.

Table 7 shows the disaggregated imports of our developing country sample from all developing countries by three digit industries. Again in many of the sectors the share of imports from developing countries is very low. For industrial countries the significant market shares are concentrated in two distinct sets of industries, traditional

Table 4. Industrial country imports of manufacturing goods from developing countries during 1991/92 to 2001/02 and 2001/02 to 2007/08.

Country	Share of Developing Country Imports in Domestic Demand (%)			Annual Import Growth from Developing Co. (%)		Annual Import Growth Due to			
						1991/92-2001/02		2001/02-2007/08	
	1991/92	2001/02	2007/08	91/92-01/02	01/02-07/08	Demand Change	Market Share Change	Demand Change	Market Share Change
Canada	3.5	7.6	11.7	10.9	16.8	2.7	8.2	8.6	8.2
France	4.3	5.0	9.6	6.5	19.1	3.1	3.4	6.8	12.3
Germany	3.8	9.9	13.9	8.5	17.2	−1.3	9.8	10.6	6.6
Japan	1.5	4.8	8.2	11.1	12.3	−1.3	12.4	2.4	9.8
United States	4.3	9.9	13.1	12.8	10.4	3.7	9.1	5.4	5.4
Total: above Industrial Co.	3.3	8.1	11.8	11.3	12.7	1.6	9.7	5.8	6.9

Note: Data is based on two-year averages of 1991-92, 2001-02, and 2007-08. Source: Computations based on UN COMTRADE Statistics (trade data) and UNIDO database (production data).

Table 5. Industrial countries' manufacturing imports from developing countries by sector during 1991/92 to 2001/02 and 2001/02 to 2007/08.

| | | Share of Imports from Developing Countries in Domestic Demand (%) | | | Annual Import Growth in Industrial Countries (%) | | Annual Import Growth Due to | | | |
| | | | | | | | 1991/92-2001/02 | | 2001/02-2007/08 | |
ISIC	Manufacturing Sector (Rev. 3)	1991/92	2001/02	2007/08	91/92-01/02	01/02-07/08	Demand Change	Market Share Change	Demand Change	Market Share Change
15	Food and beverages	2.4	3.7	5.3	5.3	11.3	0.8	4.5	4.7	6.6
16	Tobacco products	0.1	0.5	1.1	22.7	12.7	1.8	20.9	0.6	12.1
17	Textiles	9.2	25.0	40.2	8.5	8.7	−1.9	10.3	0.4	8.3
18	Wearing apparel, fur	23.2	51.1	70.3	6.7	6.3	−1.4	8.1	0.8	5.5
19	Leather, leather products and footwear	28.1	54.8	71.4	6.9	8.1	−0.1	6.9	3.4	4.7
20	Wood products (excl. furniture)	4.3	7.3	9.3	7.7	8.6	2.1	5.7	4.5	4.2
21	Paper and paper products	0.6	1.9	3.5	13.1	14.5	1.0	12.1	3.0	11.4
22	Printing and publishing	0.3	1.5	2.7	13.5	13.5	−3.1	16.6	2.5	11.0
23	Coke, refined petroleum products, nuclear fuel	2.3	6.4	9.6	13.0	23.5	2.0	11.0	15.4	8.1
24	Chemicals and chemical product	1.7	3.6	7.0	10.6	19.8	2.2	8.4	7.5	12.4
25	Rubber and plastics products	1.5	4.8	9.4	14.5	17.5	1.8	12.7	5.2	12.3
26	Non-metallic mineral products	1.7	4.9	6.7	12.2	11.5	1.2	11.0	5.7	5.7
27	Basic metals	4.9	8.6	15.3	5.1	23.2	−0.6	5.6	11.9	11.3
28	Fabricated metal products	1.2	3.6	6.4	13.7	17.0	1.9	11.8	6.4	10.6
29	Machinery and equipment n.e.s.	1.4	6.0	14.4	14.6	23.6	−1.4	16.0	6.9	16.7
30	Office, accounting and computing machinery	6.3	35.5	53.9	18.5	7.7	−0.3	18.8	0.5	7.2
31	Electrical machinery and tools	1.8	15.4	22.4	15.4	12.5	−7.1	22.5	5.7	6.8
32	Radio, television and communication equipment	5.6	22.0	36.5	13.9	12.5	−0.6	14.6	3.4	9.1
33	Medical, precision and optical instruments	3.1	8.6	13.8	14.3	13.7	3.0	11.3	5.2	8.6
34	Motor vehicles, trailers, semi-trailers	1.1	5.5	8.7	18.6	11.4	1.0	17.6	3.3	8.1
35	Other transport equipment	0.8	4.1	7.3	18.7	15.0	1.2	17.5	4.4	10.6
36	Furniture; manufacturing n.e.s.	10.4	21.6	35.1	12.2	11.9	4.3	7.9	3.2	8.7

Note: Data is based on two-year averages of 1991-92, 2001-02, and 2007-08. Source: Based on UN COMTRADE Statistics (trade data) and UNIDO database (production data).

and new labor intensive activities. But unlike the imports of industrial countries, the shares of imports in total demand are quite low in traditional labor intensive sectors of textiles, garments and leather products. In developing countries share of imports are high only the new labor intensive subsectors such as office machinery, and radio and television; similar to industrial countries.

The contribution of market share changes is much higher during the first period where demand increases are lower. During the second period, demand increases overwhelm the market share changes and very high import growth rates are achieved by mostly by demand increases. In machinery related (29 to 34) subsectors, market share changes has played a more important role.

Table 6. Developing country's manufacturing imports from developing countries during 1991/92 to 2001/02 and 2001/02 to 2007/08.

| | Share of Developing Countries Imports in Domestic Demands (%) | | | Annual Import Growth from Developing Countries (%) | | Annual Import Growth Due to | | | |
| | | | | | | 1991/92-2001/02 | | 2001/02-2007/08 | |
Country	1991/92	2001/02	2007/08	91/92-01/02	01/02-07/08	Demand Change	Market Share Change	Demand Change	Market Share Change
Brazil	0.9	3.8	6.0	16.8	27.2	1.6	15.2	17.8	9.4
China	8.1	10.2	7.7	12.3	24.8	9.8	2.6	30.9	−6.1
India	2.1	4.6	8.8	14.0	36.9	5.4	8.6	23.0	13.9
Korea, Rep.	2.9	6.0	10.1	12.7	23.2	4.8	7.9	13.0	10.3
Malaysia	15.3	24.0	24.0	11.2	13.6	6.3	4.9	13.6	0.0
Mexico	3.3	11.1	20.1	22.3	21.3	8.3	14.0	9.8	11.5
South Africa	2.2	4.6	10.4	8.8	30.7	0.8	7.9	14.2	16.5
Turkey	3.0	7.1	13.1	11.5	36.7	2.1	9.4	23.6	13.1
Total: above developing co.	4.6	8.6	9.0	13.0	24.7	6.2	6.9	23.7	1.0

Note: Data is based on two-year averages of 1991-92, 2001-02, and 2007-08. Sources: Based on UN COMTRADE Statistics (trade data) and UNIDO database (production data).

Table 7. Developing country's manufacturing imports from developing countries by sector during 1991/92 to 2001/02 and 2001/02 to 2007/08.

| | | Share of Developing Countries Imports in Domestic Demands (%) | | | Annual Import Growth in Developing Countries (%) | | Annual Import Growth Due to | | | |
| | | | | | | | 1991/92-2001/02 | | 2001/02-2007/08 | |
ISIC	Manufacturing Sector (Rev. 3)	1991/92	2001/02	2007/08	91/92-01/02	01/02-07/08	Demand Change	Mkt Sh Change	Demand Change	Mkt Sh Change
15	Food and beverages	2.5	3.7	4.0	10.0	21.1	5.5	4.5	19.9	1.3
16	Tobacco products	0.2	0.2	0.4	−0.7	29.2	3.7	−4.4	13.3	15.9
17	Textiles	5.5	12.0	7.4	9.1	10.2	0.9	8.2	19.6	−9.4
18	Wearing apparel, fur	2.1	7.0	6.4	16.4	20.0	3.2	13.2	21.8	−1.8
19	Leather, leather products and footwear	2.7	11.1	14.2	13.1	17.6	−1.9	15.0	12.9	4.6
20	Wood products (excl. furniture)	11.9	14.6	6.4	8.1	11.2	6.0	2.1	27.6	−16.4
21	Paper and paper products	2.7	6.8	4.1	17.1	12.7	6.7	10.4	22.5	−9.8
22	Printing and publishing	1.0	2.6	2.9	17.5	15.6	6.7	10.8	14.0	1.5
23	Coke, refined petroleum products, nuclear fuel	5.9	11.1	13.2	15.7	28.1	8.6	7.1	24.4	3.7
24	Chemicals and chemical products	4.3	9.4	10.7	14.2	23.8	5.6	8.6	21.3	2.5
25	Rubber and plastics products	1.9	3.7	5.0	14.3	26.6	6.8	7.5	20.1	6.5
26	Non-metallic mineral products	1.3	2.3	2.1	10.8	21.3	4.5	6.3	23.5	−2.2
27	Basic metals	5.0	8.9	8.4	11.5	30.1	5.2	6.3	31.5	−1.4
28	Fabricated metal products	1.9	3.7	3.6	11.3	28.6	4.1	7.2	29.3	−0.7
29	Machinery and equipment nes	2.6	5.1	6.9	11.2	31.0	3.8	7.4	24.6	6.4

Continued

30	Office, accounting and computing machinery	1.5	18.2	48.9	30.7	22.0	1.6	29.2	3.5	18.5
31	Electrical machinery and tools	2.0	5.1	13.3	20.3	26.8	9.7	10.7	8.1	18.6
32	Radio, television and communication equipment	2.9	15.0	32.2	22.0	26.3	3.5	18.5	11.2	15.1
33	Medical, precision and optical instruments	6.4	14.6	40.6	15.4	43.5	6.3	9.1	21.0	22.5
34	Motor vehicles, trailers, semi-trailers	1.0	2.2	4.4	16.6	31.7	7.5	9.1	17.6	14.1
35	Other transport equipment	2.8	5.2	4.8	8.7	14.4	2.2	6.6	16.1	-1.7
36	Furniture; manufacturing n.e.s.	3.8	25.6	17.1	14.4	29.4	-5.4	19.8	38.5	-9.0

Note: Data is based on two-year averages of 1991-92, 2001-02, and 2007-08. Source: Based on UN COMTRADE Statistics (trade data) and UNIDO database (production data).

5. Impact of China

China is one of the outliers in out sample of countries. It has the highest rate of demand growth throughout the two periods reaching 31 percent per annum during the second period. Its trade has also increased at very high rates. For our sample of countries, it has become the world's largest manufacturing goods exporter and third largest importer. It accounted for almost 31 percent of exports from all developing countries (14 percent of world exports) in 2007/08. This ratio was 18 percent in 2001/02 and only 14 percent in 1991/02. China has an even bigger share of 44 percent in 2007/8 of all developing country exports to industrial countries. Without China, the share of developing country exports in total absorption of our sample of industrial countries is only 6.8 percent (see **Table 8**).

China's production has increased at rates even higher than its trade growth; about 31 percent p.a. during the second period. Thus the shares of both exports and imports have decreased as a share of output during this period. Its share of exports as a percentage of gross output increased from 16.2 in 1991/2 to 24.2 percent 2001/02, and then decreased to 21.4 percent in 2007/08. Its share of imports in total production has increased from 15.7 percent in 1991/92 to 19.5 percent in 2001/02, but decreased to 12.2 percent in 2007/08 (see **Annex Table 3**). Thus the dramatic increase in production was not led by international trade but by domestic demand and import substitution. Its imports and exports are distributed equally between the industrial and developing countries.

Table 8 shows the performance of developing countries with and without China for our sample countries. This table revises two important conclusions reached in this paper. First, most of market share gains attained by the developing countries in the markets of industrial countries are driven by exports from China where, China accounts for 72 percent of market share gains during the 2000s. In terms of annual markets share gains, all developing countries excluding China increased their market shares in the markets of industrial countries only at 3 percent p.a. The ratio for China for the same period was 14 percent p.a.

Second, China also accounts for the bulk of the increases in South-South trade during the 2000s. China accounts for 82 percent of the market share gains of developing countries in the markets of our 7 large developing countries. Without China, market share gains of all developing countries in our sample would be 2.4 percent p.a. versus 20.5 p.a. for China. This relationship holds true for all countries in our sample. Thus, these generalizations about south-south trade need to be reanalyzed and China has to be treated separately.

6. Results and Implications

In this study we analyzed the pattern of manufacturing trade for a group of large industrial and emerging market countries. Our basic hypothesis that a significant portion of import growth have been caused by increases in the market penetration of imports holds true for most countries and products. In the slower growth period between 1991/92 and 2001/02, most of the import growth is caused by market share changes. During the second period (2001/02-2007/08) where demand growth accelerates, contribution of market share changes decreases relatively but is still quite high for industrial countries. For the developing countries, the average contribution of market share changes becomes negative driven primarily by the substantial import substitution undertaken by China, and to a lesser degree, by Malaysia and Mexico.

For the industrial countries, share of imports in domestic demand has increased consistently, reaching an average of 27 percent in 2007/08. Their imports from developing countries have increased at a faster rate throughout this period but only reached 12 percent in 2007/08. And if the imports from China are excluded, the

Table 8. Manufacturing imports of industrial and developing countries with and without China from 1991/92 to 2001/02 and 2001/02 to 2007/08.

| Country Group | Share of Imports in Domestic Demands (%) | | | Annual Import Growth (%) | | Annual Import Growth due to | | | |
| | | | | | | 1991/92-2001/02 | | 2001/02-2007/08 | |
	1991/92	2001/02	2007/08	91/92-01/02	01/02-07/08	Demand Change	Market Share Change	Demand Change	Market Share Change
Industrial Countries (5)									
From Developing without China	2.7	5.7	6.8	9.6	8.8	1.6	8.0	5.8	3.0
From China	0.6	2.4	5.1	17.0	20.0	1.6	15.4	5.8	14.2
Developing Countries (7)									
From Developing without China	2.7	5.5	6.2	11.8	18.7	4.1	7.7	16.3	2.4
From China	0.3	1.8	4.9	23.8	36.9	4.1	19.7	16.3	20.5
All Sample Countries (12)									
From Developing without China	2.7	5.7	6.7	9.8	10.4	1.9	7.9	7.5	2.9
From China	0.5	2.3	5.0	17.6	22.5	1.9	15.7	7.5	15.0

Note: Data is based on two-year averages of 1991-92, 2001-02, and 2007-08. Sources: Based on UN COMTRADE Statistics (trade data) and UNIDO database (production data).

share of imports from developing countries was only 6.8 percent. This suggests that there is ample capacity to for the imports to increase even if demand in industrial countries does not increase significantly.

Trade penetration in the developing country sample behaves somewhat differently. Import shares go up during the first period where most countries adopt trade liberalization programs. Average share of imports increases from about 17 percent of domestic absorption to 25 percent. During the second period, there is a large decrease in average import shares to about 19 percent and if China is excluded, the shares still decline but much less. Significant production increases and import substitution explain this difference.

The shares of imports of developing countries from developing countries are much lower but the import growth rates are much higher, double digits for both periods. The contribution of market share changes is much larger during the first period and much greater than the contributions of demand except for China and Malaysia. During the second period, the results are mixed but, except for China and Malaysia, the contribution of market share changes to import growth is in double digits per annum. Despite these high growth rates, the share of imports from developing countries in total demands of these selected developing countries reached only 9 percent in 2007/08. Very low import shares in China explain part of low shares but given the much higher overall import shares in many of these countries, there is a significant potential for developing countries to in-

crease the share of their exports going to other developing countries.

Furthermore, the share of production going to exports and imports have changed somewhat for all these countries. In this context, it is important to note some of the differences among similar countries. In 1991/92 Germany had a lower share of imports and exports (27 and 21 percent) than France (31 percent for both). But by 2007/08 Germany had restructured its manufacturing sector in such a way that its export and import to output ratio had increased to 49 and 32 percent while these ratios had become 37 and 39 percent respectively for France. Japan has also increased its export and import ratios from 11 and 4 percent in 1991/02 to 23 and 11 percent in 2007/08. As explained in Section E, China is the only economy where trade to output ratios had declined during the 2000s. India also had seen declines in its export to output ratio but its import share has increased significantly.

Relative sizes of the value of gross production have also changed during this period. USA had the by far the largest value of manufacturing output in 1991/92 and was followed by Japan and Germany whose outputs were 84 and 43 percent of the United States level. By 2007/08, output in Japan had come down to 51 percent of the USA level and Germany's output had stayed at about 44 percent. Germany's apparent export success is not caused by faster increases in its output but by restructuring its output for exports. The absolute value of its exports was almost 25 percent more than the exports from USA despite its value of output being only 44 percent of the USA level.

All other countries have increased their output as compared to United States. Of course China has had the greatest output increase. The value of its manufacturing output was only 13 percent of the USA level in 1991/02 and increased to 109 percent in 2007/08. India's output increased threefold to reach 12 percent; Korea twofold to 18 percent of the US level. It is important to note that Korea's manufacturing sector was 30 percent bigger than India's. Finally, France has seen its manufacturing sector grow faster than other industrial countries in our sample.

Finally, the success of developing countries in increasing their shares in the markets of both industrial and developing countries are driven primarily by China. Without China, the market share gains of other developing countries are much less significant. Similarly, China accounts for more than 80 percent of market share changes of developing countries in the markets of other developing countries.

7. Conclusion

These findings and developments suggest the following. First, world demand growth is very different during 1990s and 2000s. Demand growth has accelerated during the 2000s. A significant portion of trade growth for the sample countries has been caused by market share changes in 1990s. While demand increases are very important in explaining the acceleration of trade growth during the 2000s, market share changes still play an important role. Second, imports from developing countries have grown much faster both in industrial and developing country markets. Despite the rapid growth, their shares in the absorption of the sample countries are still very low and can expand substantially even if demand growth is much lower in the near future. Future trade growth from developing countries would still be high due to very low existing shares both in the markets of industrial and other developing countries. Finally, a significant part of the future developments would be driven by China. If China continues to reduce its import shares and increase its export shares, the result would affect all the countries negatively and would, in the long run, creating an environment where liberal trade regimes becomes to be threatened. So the most important question would be whether, China would continue with its declining trade shares or follow the other countries in having greater import shares. Future manufacturing trade growth will depend on the evolution of trade patterns of China as much as other economic developments.

8. Acknowledgements

We would like to thank Baris Sivri and Zeynep Ersel for their contributions to an earlier version of this paper. Yilmaz Akyuz made useful comments/questions of our numbers which led to significant revisions. The findings, interpretations, and conclusions expressed in this paper are entirely those of the authors. They do not necessarily represent the views of the World Bank, its Executive Directors, or the countries it represents.

REFERENCES

[1] B. Balassa, "Trade between Developed and Developing Countries: The Decade Ahead," OECD Economics Studies, No. 3, Autumn 1984.

[2] A. K. Fosu, "Export Composition and the Impact of Exports on Economic Growth of Developing Countries," Economics Letters (Netherlands), Vol. 34, No. 1, 1990, pp. 67-71.

[3] F. Ng and Y. Alexander, "Major Trade Trends in East Asia: What Are their Implications for Regional Cooperation and Growth?" Policy Research Working Paper, No. 3084, World Bank, Washington DC, 2003.

[4] F. Ng and Y. Alexander, "Open Economies Work Better: Did Africa's Protectionist Policies Cause Its Marginalization in World Trade?" World Development, Vol. 25, No. 6, 1997, pp. 889-904.

[5] J. Mayer, "Export Dynamism and Market Access," Journal of Economic Integration, Vol. 19, No. 2, 2004, pp. 289-316.

[6] G. Hanson and R. Raymond, "China and the Recent Evolution of Latin America's Manufacturing Exports," In: D. Laderman, M. Olarreaga and E. Perry, Eds., Chapter 5 in China's and India's Challenge to Latin America: Opportunity or Threat? World Bank, Washington DC, 2009.

[7] M. A. Aksoy, Z. Ersel and B. Sivri, "Demand Growth versus Market Share Gains: Decomposing Export Growth in the 1990s," Mimeo, World Bank, Washington DC, 2003.

[8] M. A. Aksoy, "The Evolution of Agricultural Trade Flows," In: A. Aksoy and J. Beghin, Eds., Chapter 2 in Global Agricultural Trade and Developing Countries, World Bank, Washington DC, 2005.

[9] United Nations Industrial Development Organization, "UNIDO INDSTAT3 Industrial Statistics Database," UNIDO, Vienna, 2011.

[10] UNSD, "Commodity Trade Database (COMTRADE through WITS)," United Nations Statistical Office, New York, 2011.

[11] A. Nicita and O. Marcelo, "Trade, Production and Protection Database: 1976-2004," World Bank Economic Review, Vol. 21, No. 1, 2007, pp. 165-171.

[12] Y. Akyuz "Export Dependence and Sustainability of Growth in China," China and World Economy, Vol. 19, No. 1, 2011, pp. 1-23.

[13] H. L. Kee and H. Tang, "Domestic Value-Added in Chinese Exports," World Bank Development Research Group, Internal Paper, World Bank, Washington DC, 2011.

[14] R. Koopman, Z. Wang and S.-J. Wei, "How Much of Chinese Exports Is Really Made in China? Assessing Domestic Value-Added When Processing Trade Is Pervasive," The National Bureau of Economic Research Working Paper, No. 14109, NBER, Cambridge, 2008.

[15] J. Dean, K. C. Fung and Z. Wang, "How Vertically Specialized Is Chinese Trade?" US ITC Economics Working Paper, No. 2008-09-D, US International Trade Commission, Washington DC, 2008.

[16] X. Chen, L. Cheng, K. C. Fung and L. Lau, *et al.*, "Domestic Value-Added and Employment Generated by Chinese Exports: A Quantitative Estimation," Munich Personal RePEc Archive (MPRA) Paper, No. 15663, 2008.

[17] D. Herzer, "What Does Export Diversification Do for Growth? An Econometric Analysis," *Applied Economics (UK)*, Vol. 38, No. 15, 2006, pp. 1825-1838.

[18] J. Madsen, "Innovation and Manufacturing Export Performance in the OECD Countries," *Oxford Economic Papers*, Vol. 60, No. 1, 2008, pp. 143-167.

[19] World Bank, "Global Economic Prospects," World Bank publication, World Bank, Washington DC, 2004, 2005 and 2007.

[20] Y. Akyuz, "The Staggering Rise of the South?" Research Papers 44, South Centre, Geneva, 2012.

[21] P.-C. Athukorala, "South-South Trade: An Asian Perspective," ADB Economics Working Paper, No. 265, Asian Development Bank, Manila, 2011.

[22] R. M. Stern, "Comparative Advantage, Growth, and the Gains from Trade and Globalization (World Scientific Studies in International Economics)," 1st Edition, World Scientific Publishing Company, Singapore City, 2011.

[23] IMF, "New Growth Drivers for Low-Income Countries: The Role of BRICs," IMF Strategy, Policy and Review Department, International Monetary Fund, Washington DC, 2011.

[24] Organisation for Economic Co-operation and Development, "South-South Trade: Vital for Development," Policy Brief, OECD Observer, 2006.

[25] United Nations Conference on Trade and Development, "Trade and Development Report," UNCTAD, Geneva, 2002 and 2005.

Annexes

Annex Table 1. Correlation coefficients of manufacturing growth and demand/ market share changes between 1991/92 to 2001/02 and 2001/02 to 2007/08.

	Correlation Coefficient					
	Import Growth vs Demand Changes		Import Growth vs Mkt Share Changes		Demand Changes vs Mkt Share Changes	
Country Group (no. of countries)	1991/92-2001/02	2001/02-2007/08	1991/92-2001/02	2001/02-2007/08	1991/92-2001/02	2001/02-2007/08
All selected countries (13)	0.146	0.381	0.773	0.471	−0.515	−0.636
Developing countries (8)	0.032	0.284	0.769	0.468	−0.615	−0.715
Industrial countries (5)	0.344	0.505	0.710	0.838	−0.417	−0.048

Note: Correlation coefficient is computed as manufacturing import growth versus global demand and market share changes in ISIC 2-digit manufacturing sector across countries in the period averages of 1991/92 to 2001/02 and 2001/02 to 2007-08. Sources: Computations based on UN COMTRADE Statistics (trade data) and UNIDO database (production data).

Annex Table 2. Global manufacturing imports of industrial and developing countries (with and without China & FTAs).

	Share of World Imports in Domestic Demands (%)			Annual Import Growth (%)		Annual import growth Due to			
						1991/92-2001/02		2001/02-2007/08	
Reporter	1991/92	2001/02	2007/08	91/92-01/02	01/02-07/08	Demand Change	Mkt Share Change	Demand Change	Mkt Share Change
Industrial Countries									
Canada	32.5	47.1	46.8	6.6	8.4	2.7	3.9	8.6	−0.1
Canada, excl. NAFTA	7.1	7.7	12.2	3.5	17.2	3.1	0.5	7.5	9.7
France	31.1	28.2	38.5	3.8	12.5	3.1	0.8	7.5	5.1
France, excl. EU15	8.1	10.1	14.9	7.2	14.1	4.5	2.7	8.4	5.6
France, excl. CEEC12	7.9	9.1	12.7	6.4	12.9	4.5	2.0	8.4	4.5
Germany	22.4	34.3	38.5	3.0	12.8	−1.3	4.3	10.6	2.1
Germany, excl. EU15	7.1	16.9	21.0	7.6	14.6	−1.2	8.8	11.1	3.5
Germany, excl. CEEC12	6.6	12.7	15.8	5.4	14.7	−1.2	6.6	11.1	3.6
Japan	4.0	8.9	13.0	6.7	9.1	−1.3	8.1	2.4	6.7
United States	12.6	20.9	23.6	9.1	7.6	3.7	5.4	5.4	2.2
United States, excl. NAFTA	9.6	15.0	18.1	8.4	8.8	4.3	4.1	4.6	4.2
Total above industrial co.	13.5	21.5	26.6	6.4	9.6	1.6	4.8	5.8	3.8
Total above, excl. China	12.9	19.1	21.5	5.6	7.9	1.6	4.1	5.8	2.1
Total above, excl. FTAs	7.1	12.4	15.9	7.4	10.2	2.5	4.9	4.9	5.4
Total above, excl. FTAs &China	6.5	10.0	10.8	6.0	7.1	2.5	3.5	4.9	2.3
Developing Countries									
Brazil	5.7	14.3	13.7	11.5	17.0	1.6	9.9	17.8	−0.8
China	15.8	20.5	13.4	12.7	22.1	9.8	2.9	30.9	−8.9
India	7.6	12.1	17.0	10.4	30.2	5.4	5.0	23.0	7.2
Korea, Rep.	18.8	20.1	23.5	5.5	15.9	4.8	0.7	13.0	3.0
Malaysia	53.1	58.1	45.8	7.3	9.2	6.3	1.0	13.6	−4.4
Mexico	42.3	78.4	69.6	15.2	7.7	8.3	6.9	9.8	−2.2
Mexico, excl. NAFTA	12.5	24.5	34.1	15.9	16.1	9.4	6.5	8.7	7.4
South Africa	16.1	20.1	27.0	3.1	19.9	0.8	2.3	14.2	5.7
Turkey	17.2	30.0	31.0	7.9	24.2	2.1	5.8	23.6	0.6

Continued

Turkey, excl. EU15	6.3	11.5	16.2	8.5	30.8	1.6	6.9	20.4	10.3
Total above developing co.	17.2	25.4	18.7	10.4	17.6	6.2	4.2	23.7	−6.1
Total above, excl. China	17.8	29.1	26.9	9.3	14.8	4.1	5.2	16.3	−1.5
Total above, excl. FTAs	14.7	20.5	16.8	9.8	19.6	6.0	3.8	24.5	−4.8
Total above, excl. FTAs & China	14.2	20.5	22.0	8.0	17.6	4.3	3.7	15.1	2.6

Note: Data is based on two-year averages of 1991-92, 2001-02, and 2007-08. Source: Based on UN COMTRADE Statistics (trade data) and UNIDO database (production data).

Annex Table 3. Exports and imports as a percentage of gross value of manufacturing production.

Country	Exports in Manufacturing Production (%)			Imports in Manufacturing Production (%)		
	1991/92	2001/02	2007/08	1991/92	2001/02	2007/08
Industrial Countries						
Canada	27.7	44.0	39.6	34.8	49.9	53.1
Canada, excl. NAFTA	3.6	3.9	6.5	7.6	8.1	13.8
France	31.1	29.1	37.2	31.2	27.8	39.3
France, excl. EU15	9.7	11.7	16.1	8.1	10.0	15.3
France, excl. CEEC12	9.3	10.4	13.9	7.9	9.0	13.0
Germany	26.9	42.8	49.4	21.1	29.9	31.7
Germany, Excl. EU15	8.6	20.1	25.0	6.7	14.7	17.3
Germany, Excl. CEEC12	7.9	16.3	19.4	6.2	11.1	13.0
Japan	11.3	15.9	23.1	3.7	8.2	11.4
United States	10.9	14.5	17.1	12.8	22.5	25.6
United States, excl. NAFTA	7.3	8.9	11.4	9.8	16.2	19.7
Total above industrial countries	15.7	21.5	27.6	13.1	21.5	26.2
Total above, excl. China	15.4	20.8	25.9	12.6	19.1	21.2
Total above, excl. FTAs	8.8	11.7	15.5	6.9	12.4	15.6
Total above, excl. FTAs & China	8.5	11.0	13.9	6.4	10.0	10.7
Developing Countries						
Brazil	7.8	12.0	11.6	5.5	14.7	14.1
China	16.2	24.2	21.4	15.7	19.5	12.2
India	10.7	16.4	15.0	7.3	11.5	17.3
Korea, Rep.	23.3	28.4	33.0	17.8	18.0	20.6
Malaysia	46.9	62.4	49.2	60.1	52.1	43.0
Mexico	33.0	77.5	67.8	49.2	81.8	73.9
Mexcio, excl. NAFTA	4.9	7.9	10.0	14.5	25.5	36.2
South Africa	7.6	16.5	19.8	17.8	21.0	29.6
Turkey	12.1	28.2	27.8	18.3	30.8	32.4
Turkey, excl. EU15	4.7	13.2	15.1	6.6	11.8	17.0
Total above developing countries	17.1	28.4	23.9	17.3	24.3	17.5
Total above, excl. China	17.5	31.7	28.1	18.0	28.0	26.4
Total above, excl. FTAs	15.2	23.0	21.5	14.7	19.7	15.7
Total above, excl. FTAs, China	14.7	22.1	21.8	14.3	19.8	21.6

Note: Data is based on two-year averages of 1991-92, 2001-02, and 2007-08. Source: Based on UN COMTRADE Statistics (trade data) and UNIDO database (production data).

Annex Table 4. Manufacturing imports of industrial and developing countries from developing countries (with and without China & FTAs).

| Reporter | Share of World Imports in Domestic Demands (%) | | | Annual Import Growth (%) | | Annual import growth Due to | | | |
| | | | | | | 1991/92-2001/02 | | 2001/02-2007/08 | |
	1991/92	2001/02	2007/08	91/92-01/02	01/02-07/08	Demand Change	Mkt Share Change	Demand Change	Mkt Share Change
Industrial Countries									
Canada	3.5	7.6	11.7	10.9	16.8	2.7	8.2	8.6	8.2
Canada, excl. NAFTA	2.8	5.7	9.5	10.1	18.3	3.1	7.0	7.5	10.8
France	4.3	5.0	9.6	6.5	19.1	4.9	1.6	6.8	12.3
France, excl. EU15	4.3	5.0	9.6	6.5	19.1	4.5	2.0	8.4	10.7
France, excl. CEEC12	4.1	4.0	7.4	4.8	18.1	4.5	0.4	8.4	9.7
Germany	3.8	9.9	13.9	8.5	17.2	−1.3	9.8	10.6	6.6
Germany, excl. EU15	3.8	9.9	13.9	8.5	17.2	−1.2	9.6	11.1	6.1
Germany, excl. CEEC12	3.3	5.6	8.8	4.2	19.1	−1.2	5.4	11.1	8.0
Japan	1.5	4.8	8.2	11.1	12.3	−1.3	12.4	2.4	9.8
United States	4.3	9.9	13.1	12.8	10.4	3.7	9.1	5.4	5.0
United States, excl. NAFTA	3.5	7.3	10.5	11.8	11.9	4.3	7.5	4.6	7.3
Total above industrial co.	3.3	8.1	11.8	11.3	12.7	1.6	9.7	5.8	6.9
Total above, excl. China	2.7	5.7	6.8	9.6	8.8	1.6	8.0	5.8	3.0
Total above, excl. FTAs	2.8	6.1	9.4	9.9	13.6	2.5	7.4	4.9	8.7
Total above, excl. FTAs & China	2.2	3.7	4.3	7.0	8.4	2.5	4.6	4.9	3.5
Developing Countries									
Brazil	0.9	3.8	6.0	16.8	27.2	1.6	15.2	17.8	9.4
China	8.1	10.2	7.7	12.3	24.8	9.8	2.6	30.9	-6.1
India	2.1	4.6	8.8	14.0	36.9	5.4	8.6	23.0	13.9
Korea, Rep.	2.9	6.0	10.1	12.7	23.2	4.8	7.9	13.0	10.3
Malaysia	15.3	24.0	24.0	11.2	13.6	6.3	4.9	13.6	0.0
Mexico	3.3	11.1	20.1	22.3	21.3	8.3	14.0	9.8	11.5
Mexico, excl. NAFTA	3.3	11.1	20.1	22.3	21.3	9.4	13.0	8.7	12.7
South Africa	2.2	4.6	10.4	8.8	30.7	0.8	7.9	14.2	16.5
Turkey	3.0	7.1	13.1	11.5	36.7	2.1	9.4	23.6	13.1
Turkey, excl. EU15	3.0	7.1	13.1	11.5	36.7	1.6	9.9	20.4	16.2
Total above developing co.	4.6	8.6	9.0	13.0	24.7	6.2	6.9	23.7	1.0
Total above, excl. China	3.0	7.4	11.1	13.8	24.6	4.1	9.7	16.3	8.3
Total above, excl. FTAs	4.6	8.6	9.0	13.0	24.7	6.0	7.0	24.5	0.3
Total above, excl. FTAs & China	3.0	7.4	11.1	13.8	24.6	4.3	9.5	15.1	9.6

Note: Data is based on two-year averages of 1991-92, 2001-02, and 2007-08. Source: Based on UN COMTRADE Statistics (trade data) and UNIDO database (production data).

10

Growth and Competitiveness of Non-Traditional Agricultural Exports in Zambia

Chibamba Mwansakilwa[1], Gelson Tembo[2], Johnny Mugisha[3]

[1]Research Fellow, Palm Associates Limited, Lusaka, Zambia
[2]Department of Agricultural Economics and Extension, University of Zambia, Lusaka, Zambia
[3]Department of Agribusiness and Natural Resource Economics, Makerere University, Kampala, Uganda

ABSTRACT

This study investigates the determinants of growth and competitiveness of Zambia's flower exports to three main export destinations—the Netherlands, the UK and Germany—using annual time series data from 1990 to 2010. Acknowledging that time series data are often nonstationary, leading to misleading economic analyses, the study employs cointegration and error correction models to establish factors of conditions growth and competitiveness of Zambia's flower exports. The results show that supply and competitiveness of flower exports are positively influenced by domestic flower production, real GDP and population of importing countries, relative depreciation of domestic currency and world export prices. In contrast, exports from competing countries and real interest rates were found to negatively influence flower exports. This seems to suggest that monetary policies and exchange rate regimes that promote trade are required for enhancing and fostering an environment favorable for flower production and exporting. In addition, the replacement of Zambia's flower exports by those from other countries dictates that there must be a quality improvement so the country's exports can compete favorably with those from other countries.

Keywords: Export Horticulture; Growth; Competitiveness; Cointegration; Error Correction Models; Zambia

1. Introduction

Like many African countries' economies, Zambia's economy has continued to be predominantly agriculture based. According to the country's Central Statistical Office [1], of the 56 percent who live in the rural areas [2], 97.4 percent are directly engaged in agriculture for their livelihood[1]. With unemployment at about 50 percent, agriculture is the only potential source of income within the informal sector employing about 85 percent of the 3.4 million people in the labour force [3]. The sector mainly consists of smallholder farmers who make up about 52 percent of the country's farmers and contribute about 80 percent of the nation's staple food, maize [4-6].

However, despite their aggregate contribution to the nation's staple food supply and gross domestic product

(GDP), smallholder farmers still account for over a third of the nation's hungry and poor [7]. Several factors have been cited for the low welfare levels among smallholder farmers including concentration on low-market value staples, low education levels, low productivity, poor health conditions, lack of market access and credit facilities, poor infrastructure and lack of productive assets [5,8,9]. Nevertheless, evidence has shown that those who produce high-value export commodities earn relatively higher incomes than their counterparts who mainly produce cereals [10,11]. For instance, although Zambia's total agricultural production largely consists of cereals, high value agricultural exports make a significant contribution of 40 percent annually to total agricultural output [12]. In addition, [13] reveal that despite the overconcentration on cereal production, high-value fresh produce accounts for about 39 percent of total household income among producing households. The sub-sector has also been characterized by a steady growth over the past two decades, mainly in response to the government's significant support and private investment. In 2006, non-traditional

---

[1]All national development plans from independence to present have identified agriculture as the key for improving rates of growth and diversifying the Zambian economy. See for example, the Fourth National Development Plan and Policy Framework Paper, 1989-93; The Fifth National Development Plan, 2006-2010; and The Sixth National Development Plan, 2011-2015.

agricultural exports increased by about 25 percent over the previous year, recording earnings of more than USD 650 million [10].

Zambia's non-traditional exports have included sugar, cotton lint, horticulture, soya beans and other primary agricultural produce with textile, engineering products, cement and handcrafts being the other products [14]. Other significant export products are fertilizers, hydrated lime, coal, tea, maize, skin leather, asbestos pipes/sheets, groundnuts, mushrooms, fresh eggs and day old chicks, paper, aluminium wires and cables, sorghum, clothing and blankets [11,15]. Of the agricultural commodities, export horticulture, consisting mainly of cut flowers and fresh vegetables, earned the highest foreign exchange over the period 1990-2010 [13]. However, unlike other agricultural exports, export horticulture has declined sharply after reaching the peak in 2006, exhibiting high volatility in both production and export volumes [11,16]. [16] reveal that the share of export horticulture to total non-traditional exports has declined from 11.1 percent in 2003 to about 1.2 percent in 2009 representing a 64 percent (USD 29 million) reduction in the industry's income. This identifies the need to understand the major determinants of the industry's growth and contribution to the nation's export earnings.

A number of studies have considered the impact of export horticulture on poverty in Africa. A national survey by [7] in Zambia has shown that smallholders who produce fresh produce are more likely to move out of poverty compared to their counterparts who mostly produce cereals. The study found farmers who sold horticultural products earning annual mean per capita incomes of USD 183 compared to USD 139 for non-sellers. Similarly, [17] in Kenya found that households involved in export horticulture were better off, particularly in rural areas. They further contend that enabling more households to participate in the sector could reduce poverty substantially. A similar result was found by [18] in Senegal, who also argued that the sub-sector could cut regional poverty by 12 percent and extreme poverty by half. Furthermore, since the industry is highly labour intensive, horticulture production has been proposed as a pro-poor development strategy in many African countries [19]. In Zambia, the sub-sector is believed to be among the government's poverty reduction programs in agriculture that can substantially reduce poverty [10].

According to Medina-Smith [20], countries that have relied on outward oriented development strategies have done better over the medium and long term than inward-looking ones. For agriculture-based economies like Zambia's, such an outward oriented development strategy implies development of traditional agricultural exports and diversification into non-traditional exports of different price elasticities [21]. However, there is a dearth

of empirical evidence on the drivers of export horticulture and producers' responsiveness to changes in price and non-price incentives. A better understanding of the factors affecting horticultural export performance is central in crafting informed decisions and interventions. Most studies have focused on characterizing domestic horticulture supply and value chains, and have not provided information on the important determinants of export horticulture in Zambia [see for example, 11,13,16]. According to [22], deficiencies in information and analysis have led to policy and market failures in developing countries.

The study reported in this paper uses annual time series data from 1990 to 2010 and error correction models to identify determinants of Zambia's flower exports. Overall, the results suggest that in addition to the determinants of production, flower exports are equally determined by policies that affect a country's trade position. Particularly, the results imply that programs, policies and practices that promote trade are clearly required and important ingredient for both farmer export decisions and the competitiveness of the industry.

In the rest of the paper, we first review export horticultural production and export trends in Section 2, followed by a discussion of the determinants of agricultural exports in Section 3. Empirical methods and data sources are presented in Section 4, followed by results and conclusions in Sections 5 and 6.

2. Production and Export Trends of Horticulture in Zambia

Zambia has been exporting horticultural products since the early 1980s. The industry was launched by comercial farmers, who needed foreign currency to import equipment for their main activities, beef, dairy and cereal production [16]. However, the industry only expanded rapidly in the 1990s and early 2000s due largely to an increase in the number of producers, raising export volumes of vegetables and flowers from USD 6 million in 1994 to over USD 33 million in 2001 when the sector employed about 10,000 people [23]. This rapid growth was mainly due to the support of the European Investment Bank (EIB) through the Export Development Project (EDP) which provided long-term credit to some investors and cold storage facilities at airports that allowed producers to import the necessary but locally unavailable inputs, often under subsidized air freight charges [16,24]. At its peak in 2006, the horticulture industry employed over 12,000 people of whom more than 50 percent were women widely engaged in growing and packaging stages of the value chain [13]. At that point the industry was generating annual earnings in excess of USD 50 million [23]. During the same time, about 95 percent of the domestically produced fresh produce was exported to the

EU, with the UK, the Netherlands and Germany, among others, as the main destinations [3,16]. Small quantities were exported to South Africa, Australia and the Far East [10].

Most of these gains have, however, been lost during the past seven years mainly due to the collapse in 2004 of the largest horticultural export company, Agriflora [11]. The bankruptcy of Agriflora not only deprived small-holder farmers who participated under contract with the horticultural firm of reliable income, transport logistics, and technical support but also caused most of them to stop production [13]. This development led to a reduction in the number of people that were employed at every stage in the chain from 16,000 to about 5000, causing output and exports to reduce [10] (**Table 1** and **Figure 1**). In addition, the industry has continued to face other challenges such as exchange rate fluctuations [11], high air freight costs due to high cost of aviation fuel in the country [25] and high operating costs that exceed levels observed in most other countries in the region [4]. The reducing investments in the horticulture industry together with the challenges affecting the industry have continued

Table 1. Production and export trends of horticulture in Zambia, 1990-2010.

Year	Flower Production (metric tons)	Flower Exports (metric tons)	Vegetable Production (metric tons)	Vegetable Exports (metric tons)
1990	210.53	200.00	182.87	168.24
1991	251.46	246.43	308.55	293.12
1992	362.88	312.80	456.60	421.90
1993	644.74	600.90	521.19	509.72
1994	811.45	762.76	700.51	623.45
1995	981.29	944.00	1084.93	1022.00
1996	2053.65	1914.00	2479.74	2264.00
1997	2975.30	2770.00	4221.38	3909.00
1998	4195.52	3562.00	4599.78	5130.00
1999	3490.84	3316.30	4814.98	4530.90
2000	3843.01	3574.00	6724.02	6354.20
2001	4492.06	4186.60	8949.47	8430.40
2002	4239.54	4010.60	9040.00	8588.00
2003	4082.02	3767.70	7907.73	7670.50
2004	4767.21	4362.00	5475.34	5174.20
2005	4234.41	3938.00	7230.77	6862.00
2006	4785.64	4733.00	5790.58	5779.00
2007	4610.39	4260.00	5140.24	5058.00
2008	3564.55	3479.00	1162.47	3396.10
2009	3779.63	3711.60	1172.14	1127.60
2010	2234.25	2191.80	1090.60	1070.60

Source: Based on data obtained from Zambia Export Growers Association (ZEGA).

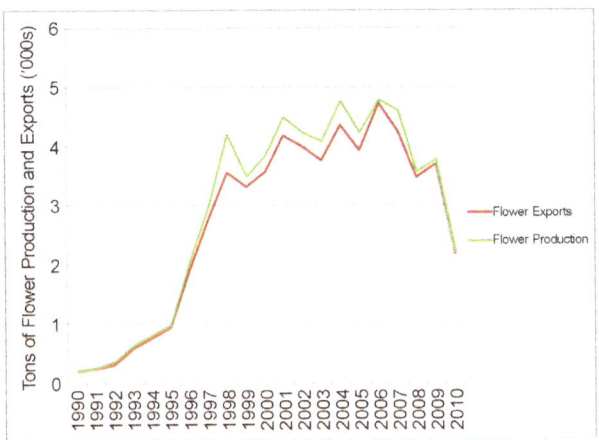

Figure 1. Production and export trends of fresh flowers in Zambia, 1990-2010. (Source: Own estimates using data from Zambia Development Agency, ZDA, and Zambia Export Growers Association, ZEGA).

to adversely affect horticultural production and export constraining its growth and contribution to the economy. According to [25], the area devoted to cut flowers and fresh vegetables in Zambia has stagnated at 140 hectares, compared to Kenya's over a million hectares, because of high lending rates that prohibit most people from venturing into horticulture production. Furthermore, because the industry is largely export oriented, significant financial losses continue to be incurred by exporters each time the currency fluctuates upwards [11,24]. According to [11], financial losses of about 30 percent of export value were incurred because of the appreciation of the Zambian Kwacha against the US Dollar and other major world currencies in 2005.

Furthermore, tightening standards in the EU export destinations in recent years, mainly to control quantity of imports, have also served a major blow to the Zambian horticultural sector, especially among smallholder producers. For instance, it is argued that the cost of compliance to the European retailers' private standards for Good Agricultural Practices (EurepGAP) cut farmers' incomes in half between 2002 and 2006 [26]. As a result, less than 3 percent of the smallholder and commercial farmers involved in supplying foreign markets in 2000 were still doing so in 2006 [23]. [23] reveals that a total of 22 horticultural farms that were involved in production in 2000 had ceased production by 2004 resulting in the loss of about 1440 and 82 hectares of vegetables and flowers, respectively.

3. Determinants of Flower Exports

Empirical studies have identified two main sets of factors that explain the performance of agricultural exports in international trade. One set comprises factors that are external to the individual country, such as volume of growth of world primary commodity markets and producer prices or commodity terms of trade. The other emphasizes variables that are internal to the country, including macroeconomic, production and demographic variables, and policies.

3.1. Impact of Domestic Factors on Flower Exports and Competitiveness

Many researchers have studied the impact of domestic factors on agricultural exports. Most identify production, demographic, macroeconomic variables, and public investments in infrastructure as important factors. For instance, [27], using error correction models, found Nigeria's agricultural exports to be positively influenced by domestic producer prices and negatively by population growth. These findings were consistent with [21] and [28]. [21] also identified relative rainfall amounts, export credit, and improvement in road network as being directly correlated with agricultural exports.

In a study in Egypt to determine factors that influence agricultural exports, [29], using the gravity model approach, found that agricultural exports increase with GDP. These findings are consistent with those by [28] who also found GDP to have a significant positive impact on volume and competitiveness of South Africa's agricultural exports.

While it has been argued that high interest rates attract domestic savings, studies have found high rates to discourage local investments by increasing the cost of capital [30,31]. As a result, [30] argues that monetary policies should ensure appropriate interest rates that break the double-edge effect of interest rate on savers and local investors by both attracting savings mobilization and encouraging domestic investment.

Other studies have assessed the impact of domestic exchange rates on export performance of the agricultural sector. These studies have however produced mixed results. Some show that performance of a country's exports is highly dependent on its exchange rate regime, specifically the real exchange rate, while others do not. The majority of the studies that have observed the dependence of agricultural exports on domestic exchange rate show that the demand for a country's exports increases when its export prices fall in relation to the world prices, that is, when the domestic currency depreciates against major world currencies [29,32]. In contrast, an investigation of the impact of trade liberalization on export volumes by [33] in Uganda found no significant relationship between real exchange rate and volumes of exports.

3.2. Impact of External Factors on Flower Export Growth and Competitiveness

The impact of external factors such as growth in the importing country and quantity of exports from competing countries has been investigated by many. Most studies have found growth in importing countries, world export price, and quantity of exports from competing countries as important in explaining growth and competiveness of agricultural exports [27,28,34]. For instance, [34] found trading partners' income or GDP to be the most important driver of Fiji's exports. Similarly, [28], using gravity models to determine the drivers of South Africa's agricultural exports, found population (physical market size) and GDP (economic market size) of trading partners to positively influence agricultural export growth.

On the other hand, [27] found world export price, quantity supplied by competing countries and population growth of importing countries to significantly affect Nigeria's agricultural exports. Their findings show that quantity exported by competing countries negatively influences a country's agricultural exports. However, the increase in population of an importing country produced mixed results.

4. Methods and Procedures

4.1. Data and Data Sources

This study uses annual time series data from the Ministry of Agriculture and Cooperatives (MACO), Zambia's Central Statistical Office (CSO), Zambia Development Agency (ZDA), Zambia Export Growers Association (ZEGA), the World Bank (WB), *eurostat*, faostat, Food and Agriculture Organization of the United Nations (FAO), Zambia National Farmers Union (ZNFU), Indaba Agricultural Policy Research Institute (IAPRI), Bank of Zambia (BoZ) and selected farmers. The quantitative secondary data collected were complemented by key informative interviews with selected farmers, ZDA and ZEGA.

Data on flower production, domestic producer prices, costs, export quantities and revenues, and destinations of Zambia's flowers exports were collected from ZEGA, EBZ, MACO, ZDA and ZNFU. Data on Zambia's interest and exchange rates, GDP, inflation, population and national staple food (cereal) production were sourced from BoZ, CSO and IAPRI. In addition, data on world producer prices, GDP of importing countries and flower exports from competing countries were collected from the World Bank, FAO and eurostat.

The quality of export statistics in Zambia was however, at best, variable. Therefore, in an effort to ensure data quality, averages of the data collected from the different sources were used. In addition, with the exception of data on flower exports, and domestic real exchange and interest rates, and real exchange rate, all the data on the afore-mentioned production, macroeconomic and demographic variables were used as obtained from the different sources, without processing. Given that Zambia's annual flower exports constitute about 95 percent of domestic flower production [3,16], the quantities of flower exports over the period under study, 1990-2010, were estimated from the annual data of flower production obtained from ZEGA and ZDA. On the other hand, real interest series were estimated from the annual nominal interest rates obtained from BoZ, CSO and IAPRI using the *Fishers's* equation approach. Likewise, real exchange rate series were estimated from annual nominal exchange rates.

4.2. Determining Factors Influencing Supply of Zambia's Flower Exports

To investigate the factors that influence supply of Zambia's flower exports to the three main export destinations—the UK, the Netherlands and Germany an error correction model (ECM) of flower exports, which incorporates both demand and supply factors, was used.

Many authors have noted the increased importance of ECM and co-integration methods in analyses that attempt to describe long and short-run equilibrium relationships simultaneously [see for example, 27,35-37]. According to [36] and [38], an equilibrium relationship exists when variables in the model are co-integrated (a long-run relationship exists between variables). A pre-condition for integration, however, is that the data for each variable involved exhibit similar statistical properties, that is, are integrated to the same order with evidence of some linear combination of the integrated series [27,39-41].

The starting point in the ECM modeling is to assess the order of integration of the variables [27]. The order of integration ascertains the number of times a variable will be differenced to arrive at stationarity [39]. A stationary series has a mean, variance, and auto-correlation that are constant over time [40-43]. The inspection of the order of integration of variables allows the ECM estimation procedure to thoroughly examine the characteristic of time series, helping overcome the problem of spurious or meaningless regression results often associated with non-stationary historical data [31,44]. According to [37] and [39], treating nonstationary series as if they were stationary produces biased OLS results, resulting in misleading economic analysis.

Engel and Granger (1987) [45] present appropriate tests for the stationarity of individual series such as the Dickey-Fuller (DF) and Augmented Dickey-Fuller (ADF) statistics [46]. These tests are based on t-statistics obtained from the estimates of static (long-run) OLS regressions applied to each of the series [41]. This study used the ADF test because of its ability to capture additional dynamics left out by the DF test and ensures that the error term is white noise through the inclusion of

additional lag length [27]. Following Engel and Granger (1987) [45], we define the ADF test procedure as:

$$\Delta X_t = \alpha_0 + \alpha_1 X_{t-1} + \sum_{t=1} b_i \Delta X_{t-1} + e_t , \qquad (1)$$

where ΔX_t is the differenced X_t series, X_{t-1} is first lag of X_t series, ΔX_{t-1} is the first lag of the differenced X_t series; b_i is the constant coefficient and e_t is the error term with mean zero and finite variance. According to the ADF test, the null hypothesis of nonstationarity is rejected if the t-statistic on α_1, which is expected to be negative, is significantly different from the critical values for a given sample size [41].

After the order of integration of the variables has been ascertained, through differencing, the next step is to test for cointegration [27,37][2]. Cointegration is a test of stationarity of the residuals generated from a long-run regression [41]. The main purpose of cointegration analysis is to establish whether the series in the model trend together over time [39]. The analysis therefore helps to discover existence of a tendency for some linear relationships to hold among a set of variables over long periods of time. Several methods of investigating cointegrating relationships exist including Engle and Granger's (1987) [45] residual-based, and Johansen and Juselius' (1990) maximum likelihood tests [47]. Rejection of the null hypothesis that the residuals are nonstationary indicates existence of some cointegrating relationships [37].

The existence of at least two cointegrating vectors among the variables in long-run models implies that an ECM could be estimated to investigate the relationships in the short-run [37]. Therefore, the ECM is estimated when the residuals from the long-run linear combination of nonstationary I(1) series are themselves stationary [27]. The information in the error term from the long-run relationship is used to create a dynamic ECM [39]. The ECM is estimated by capturing all variables in their differenced stationary form, with the exception of the error correction term, which is lagged and given by the residuals from the long-run cointegration equation [39]. The resulting ECM is then used to analyze the impulse response of the dependent variable, annual flower exports in our case, to a stimulus in the explanatory variables in a dynamic setting [27]. A significant error correction term coefficient shows the speed at which the dependent variable adjusts to any deviations from the equilibrium position between itself and each explanatory variable in the previous period confirming the existence of relationships in the short-run between variables.

In addition, a series of estimations are carried out with varying number of lags on explanatory variables in order to achieve parsimonious models [27,37,39]. [48] find that

---

[2]In order to avoid the spurious regression problem, with its related nonstationary pattern of the variables, differencing has become the common method of bringing nonstationary series to Stationarity [55].

accuracy of forecasts from vector auto-regression (VAR) models, including ECMs, varies substantially for alternative lag lengths. As a result, the estimates of a VAR model are inconsistent as are the impulse response functions and variance decompositions derived from the estimated VAR if the lag length used differs from the true lag length [49]. The optimal lag lengths used in the tests in this study were selected by the Akaike Information Criterion (AIC) because it selects true lag lengths more frequently than any other criteria [50]. Following Sargan (1984) [51], and Engle and Granger (1987) [45], the ECM is specified as:

$$\Delta Y_t = \beta_0 + \beta_1 \Delta X_t + \beta_2 \left[Y_{t-1} - \phi X_{t-1} \right] + \varepsilon_t, \quad (2)$$

where the term $\left(\beta_0 + \beta_1 \Delta X_t + \varepsilon_t \right)$ is the equilibrium relationship between Y_t and X_t; $\beta_2 \left[Y_{t-1} - \phi X_{t-1} \right]$ is the error correction term which accounts for deviations of Y_t and X_t from the equilibrium position; β_1 measures the short-term effect X_t has on Y_t; ϕ measures the long-term (equilibrium) effect X_t has on Y_t; β_2 measures the error term correction rate *i.e.* the speed at which Y_t adjusts to any deviation from the equilibrium position between X_t and Y_t in the previous period.

Drawing on the findings of past empirical studies, it was hypothesized that supply of Zambia's flower exports is influenced by domestic flower production [27,52], flower exports from competing countries [27], GDP of an exporting country [28,29] and GDP of an importing country [28,34,53]. It was also postulated that fresh flower exports in Zambia are conditioned by domestic interest rates [30,31], domestic population growth [27], population growth in an importing country [27,28], and domestic and world producer prices [27,28]. Furthermore, Zambia's annual flower exports were assumed to be explained by national staple food production [54], export credit [21] and real exchange rate [32,53,55]. Flower exports were selected in terms of growth in export quantity rather than export value because the latter is influenced by fluctuations in exchange rates resulting from dynamics often outside the agricultural sector [28]. Therefore, the dependent variable in the error correction models was supply of flower exports in metric tons to each of the three importing countries. Following [27] and [39], the estimated ECM was specified as:

$$\Delta X_t = \beta_0 + \beta_1 \Delta Q_t + \beta_2 \Delta Q_{t-1} + \beta_3 \Delta OTHERS_t$$
$$+ \beta_4 \Delta zamGDP_t + \beta_5 \Delta impGDP_t + \beta_6 \Delta rer_t$$
$$+ \beta_7 \Delta zamPOP_t + \beta_8 \Delta impPOP_t + \beta_9 \Delta domPRICE_{t-1}$$
$$+ \beta_{10} \Delta worldPRICE_{t-1} + \beta_{11} \Delta FOOD_t + \beta_{12} \Delta CREDIT_t$$
$$+ \beta_{13} EXRATE_t + \beta_{14} ECM_{(-1)} + \varepsilon_t,$$
$$(3)$$

The definitions and sources of explanatory variables used in Equation (3) are contained in **Table 2**.

Table 2. Definitions and sources of variables in models of flower exports.

Variable Name	Description and Source
X_t	Quantity of flower exports in metric tons (mt). Source is ZEGA and ZDA.
Q_t	Flower production (mt). The source is ZEGA and ZNFU.
Q_{t-1}	Lagged flower production (mt). Variable estimated by lagging current flower production once.
$OTHERS_t$	Total flower exports (mt) from competing countries to each of the three main destinations of Zambia's flower exports. Source is eurostat, World Bank, and FAO.
$zamGDP_t$	Real GDP of Zambia (million dollars). Source is Central Statistics Office (CSO) and Bank of Zambia (BoZ). 100 = 2000.
$impGDP_t$	Real Gross Domestic Product (million dollars) of an importing country. Source is World Bank.
rer_t	Zambia's real interest rates. Calculated using Fisher's equation estimated as: $\left[\{(1+r)/(1+\Pi) - 1\} \right] \cdot 100$, where, r is nominal interest rate obtained from BoZ and Π is national inflation rate obtained from CSO and BoZ.
$zamPOP_t$	Zambia's population. Source is CSO and World Bank.
$impPOP_t$	Population of importing country. Source is eurostat and World Bank.
$domPRICE_{t-1}$	Lagged domestic producer price of flowers (dollars/kg). Source is ZEGA and ZNFU.
$worldPRICE_{t-1}$	Lagged world producer price of flowers (dollars/kg). Source is eurostat, World Bank, and FAO.
$FOOD_t$	Cereal production (mt). Source is CSO and MACO.
$CREDIT_t$	Export credit to the horticulture industry (millions of Zambian Kwacha). Source is EBZ and ZEGA.
$EXRATE_t$	Real exchange rate, computed as $\ln(EXRATE_t) = \left[\ln(\text{nomrate}) + \ln(p) - \ln(pf) \right]$ where nomrate is nominal exchange rate obtained from CSO and BoZ, p is domestic price given by CPI and supplied by CSO, and pf is foreign price given by Producer Price Index (PPI, 1990 = 100) for all commodities for USA. Source: Bureau of Labour Statistics of the US.

The operational definitions of variables used in the model of flower exports (Equation 3) and their hypotheses are described in this section as follows:

Dependent variable

The dependent variable was annual quantity in metric tons (mt) of Zambia's flower exports to each of the three main export destinations, X_t. Three separate error correction models were run with the aim of capturing key variables that affects the supply of flower exports to each of the three trading partners, the UK, the Netherlands and Germany.

Independent variables

It was hypothesized that higher domestic agricultural production increases a country's agricultural exports since surplus production can only be exhausted in the international markets [56]. As a result, both current and lagged flower production, Q_t and Q_{t-1}, were hypothesized to have positive impacts on flower exports.

National cereal production, $FOOD_t$, was hypothesized to have negative effects on quantity of flower exports. While more recent studies have noted positive impact of horticultural production on smallholder farmers' income [17,19], other studies, particularly earlier works, have raised concerns about the microeconomic performance of non-traditional agricultural exports [see for example, 54,57]. Most of such concerns are related to the trade-offs between food and export or cash crops due to the possibility of competition for resources between one another. In the case of Zambia, much of the increase in cereal production in the recent years is largely attributed to significant production and marketing subsidies, averaging 62 percent of total annual agricultural budgets, mostly directed at the nation's staple food crop, maize [58].

Flower exports from competing countries, $OTHERS_t$, was expected to negatively influence Zambia's flower exports to the three countries because of the likelihood to have the absorptive capacity of foreign markets reduced by imports from Zambia's competitors. In a study to establish the key determinants of Nigeria's main agricultural crops, [27] found exports from competing countries to have negative effects on Nigeria's agricultural exports.

Real GDP of an importing country, $impGDP_t$, was hypothesized to positively impact flower exports. Many studies have found export performance of developing countries, especially the growth rate of world trade in primary products, to depend on the growth rate of industrial production in developed countries [24,27,29,53]. Similarly, Zambia's real gross domestic product, zam GDP_t, was hypothesized to have positive impact on export supply of Zambia's flower exports, since increased output often results from and leads to a general growth in the economy's productive and consumption sectors, including agriculture [59].

Domestic interest rate, rer_t, which indicates the cost of capital [37,60], was expected to negatively influence flower exports because of its negative impact on local investment. Many studies have found high interest rates to discourage local investments into even productive sectors by increasing the cost of capital [30,31,61].

Domestic population, $zamPOP_t$, was hypothesized to negatively influence supply of flower exports since increase in population is expected to require corresponding increase in production of staples, something that could

necessitate shifting of resources from exportables. [27] found domestic population to have negative effects on Nigeria's agricultural exports. In contrast, population increase in importing countries, $ZamPOP_t$, was assumed to be ambiguous as the increase in population in export destinations might lead to increased consumption of imports, including primary products from developing countries, or reduced importation due to reduced per capita disposable income among households.

Domestic and world producer prices, $domPRICE_{t-1}$ and $worldPRICE_{t-1}$, were both hypothesized to have positive effects on flower exports since farm gate prices largely determine how households allocate their resources to competing farm enterprises in context of various factors [62]. Many authors have found agricultural exports to be positively influenced by domestic and world producer prices [21,27,28].

The effect of domestic real exchange rate, $EXRATE_t$, on quantity of flower exports was hypothesized to be in two folds. Firstly, depreciation of the local currency was expected to result in high prices of imported inputs such as fertilizers, chemicals, seeds and pesticides [31,37]. This would then mean reduced utilization of purchased inputs among farmers that would invariably lead to low agricultural output, and hence exports [37]. On the other hand, the depreciation of the Zambian Kwacha was also expected to stimulate net exports of agricultural commodities since depreciation of domestic currency make exports cheaper and competitive in international markets [29,37,60]. Therefore, like population of importing countries, the sign for real exchange rate too was considered to be indeterminate, positive or negative.

Export credit, $CREDIT_t$, which was partly taken as subsidy given that recipient farmers pay less than loaned in many respects [16], was expected to positively affect flower exports. It has been argued by many that lack of credit is an important constraint to adoption of yield enhancing technologies [5,8]. Therefore, given the widespread lack of sufficient savings by most smallholder farmers for investments, availability and increase of credit to the sector was expected to positively impact flower exports. Many other studies have found agricultural credit to have positive effects on exports [21,31,63].

Lastly, lagged error correction term, ECM_{-1}, which shows the speed at which the model returns to equilibrium from disequilibrium, was expected to be negative and less than unitary in absolute terms, since instantaneous or 100 percent adjustment was not expected [27,37, 39]. According to [37], a negative sign for the coefficient of the correction term indicates that if flower exports were above the long-run relationship with each explanatory variable, they would decrease and return to equilibrium eventually.

4.3. Determining Factors Influencing Flower Competitiveness

To determine the impact of macroeconomic and production variables on the competitiveness of Zambia's flower exports, an ECM of competitiveness was run using the estimated annual domestic resource cost (DRC) series of flower exports. The domestic resource cost was used to indicate competitiveness of Zambia's flower exports because of limited data on importing countries and its ability to overcome problems of trade distortions, data quality and volatility that often characterizes international agricultural trade [64,65]. The ECM of the factors influencing competitiveness of Zambia's flower exports was specified as:

$$\Delta DRC_t = \beta_0 + \beta_1 \Delta Q_{1t} + \beta_2 \Delta Q_{t-1} + \beta_3 \Delta zamGDP_t$$
$$+ \beta_4 \Delta rer_t + \beta_5 \Delta zamPOP_t + \beta_6 \Delta domPRICE_{t-1}$$
$$+ \beta_7 \Delta worldPRICE_{t-1} + \beta_8 \Delta FOOD_t + \beta_9 \Delta CREDIT_t \quad , \quad (4)$$
$$+ \beta_{10} EXRATE_t + \beta_{11} ECM_{(-1)} + \varepsilon_t$$

The sources of explanatory variables in used in Equation (4) are as defined in Section 4.2 (**Table 2**).

The operational definitions of variables used in the model of flower exports (Equation 4) and their hypotheses are described in this section as follows:

Dependent Variable

The dependent variable used in the competitiveness error correction model was the estimated annual domestic resource cost (DRC_t) of flower exports. The domestic resource cost of flower exports, DRC_t, was estimated using annual historical cost, revenue and macroeconomic data collected from Zambia Export Growers Association (ZEGA), Zambia National Farmers Union (ZNFU), Zambia Development Agency (ZDA), Central Statistical Office (CSO) and selected farmers. Following Monke and Pearson (1989) [66], a reduction in the DRC or a negative effect from an explanatory variable indicated an improvement in competitiveness of Zambia's flower exports.

Independent Variables

Increased flower production was hypothesized to have positive influence on competitiveness of flower exports since fixed costs per unit output decrease as output increases due to the economies of scale [67]. As a result, both current and lagged domestic flower production, Q_t and Q_{t-1}, were expected to both positively influence competitiveness.

Zambia's real GDP, $zamGDP_t$, was expected to positively influence flower competitiveness. [59] have asserted that increased national output or GDP often results from and leads to a general growth in the economy's productive and consumption sectors, including agriculture through forward and backward linkages. In addition, [28] and [29] found the GDP of an exporting country to

have significant positive impacts on both volume and competitiveness of agricultural exports in Egypt and South Africa.

Domestic real interest rates, rer_t, were expected to negatively influence competiveness of Zambia's flower exports because of the negative effects they have on both agricultural production and competitiveness. Following [66], this assumption implied a positive effect of real interest rates on the domestic resource cost (DRC) of flower exports.

We considered the effect of the domestic population, $zamPOP_t$, on flower competitiveness indeterminate, positive or negative. While the increase in domestic population might lead to increased demand for fresh flowers supplied locally, it has potential to reduce horticultural production if the increase in population requires that resources be shifted from exportables to staples to meet increased staple food requirements as a result of high population growth.

Although past studies have produced mixed results, domestic and world producer prices, $domPRICE_{t-1}$ and $worldPRICE_{t-1}$, were hypothesized to have positive effects on flower competitiveness since increase in output prices was expected to lead to increased revenues and savings [62]. Higher savings were in turn expected to lead to increased investments and adoption of innovative technologies which ultimately should increase competitiveness of agricultural exports.

National staple food production, $FOOD_t$, was expected to be negatively related to flower competitiveness because of the likelihood of competition for resources between staples and exportables [57], and the orientation of the Zambian agricultural policy, which mainly favors cereal production [58,68]. The agricultural policy regimes in Zambia have focused mainly on fertilizer subsidies and targeted credit programs to largely stimulate smallholders' productivity in cereal production, mostly maize [58,68].

It was assumed that Export Development Project's (EDP) credit to the horticulture industry, $CREDIT_t$, would influence competitiveness in two folds. Firstly, export credit to the industry was expected to make it possible even for inefficient producers to continue producing given that, in many respects, recipient farmers pay less than loaned. This would invariably reduce competitiveness in the sub-sector. According to [16], farmers under the EDP, in addition to getting free cold storage facilities at major exit points, are allowed in certain instances to import the necessary but unavailable inputs at subsidized freight charges. Many studies have found such government and donor support, with some subsidy elements, to negatively influence competitiveness and efficiency [69-72]. On the other hand, a positive influence of export credit on flower competitiveness was also expected since credit makes it possible even for resource poor famers to adopt yield enhancing technologies [10,12].

The effect of real exchange rate, $EXRATE_t$, on competitiveness of export flowers too was hypothesized to be in two folds. Firstly, depreciation of the local currency was expected to result in high prices of key imported inputs such as fertilizers, chemicals, seeds and pesticides which might lead to high costs of production, and hence reduced competitiveness [37]. However, the high input prices resulting from the depreciation of the Zambian Kwacha might reduce utilization of purchased inputs among farmers, reducing agricultural output and exports in the process [37]. In contrast, depreciation of the Zambian Kwacha was also expected to stimulate net exports of agricultural commodities since depreciation of domestic currency make exports relatively cheaper than before and hence more competitive in international markets [37, 60].

The lagged error correction term, ECM_{-1}, was expected to be negative and less than unitary in absolute terms, since instantaneous or 100 percent adjustment by the model was not expected [37,39]. In addition, a negative sign for the coefficient of the correction term was assumed since it indicated that if flower competitiveness was above the long-run relationship with each explanatory variable, it would decrease and return to equilibrium eventually [37].

5. Results

5.1. Stationarity Tests

The results of the ADF unit root tests are presented in **Table 3**. The results show that of the 23 variables tested for integration (nonstationarity), only flower exports to the Netherlands, flower exports to the UK, flower exports to Germany, population of the Netherlands and Germany, flower production, lagged flower production, export credit, interest and exchange rates, and the DRC of flower exports were stationary in their original levels at 5 percent significance level. The test results therefore strongly support the hypothesis at 5 percent that most time series variables were nonstationary in their original levels. The nonstationary variables were, thus, differenced once or more to arrive at stationarity before using them. As a result, all the series, with the exception of those that were found stationary in their original level form, have two ADF test statistics, one when in nonstationary original form $\left(ADF_t^0\right)$, and the other after attaining stationarity following differencing $\left(ADF_t^d\right)$.

5.2. Cointegration Tests

The results of cointegration tests are reported in **Tables 4** and **5** for competitiveness and export models, respectively. In all the models, Johansen's maximum likelihood

Table 3. Augmented dickey-fuller unit root test for variables used in the horticultural export models of flower supply and competitiveness.

Variables	Test Statistic		Optimal	Order of
	ADF_t^0	ADF_t^d	Lag	Integration
Log of flowers to Netherlands	−3.361		1	I(0)
Log of flowers to UK	−3.476		1	I(0)
Log of flowers to Germany	−3.226		1	I(0)
Log of flowers to Netherlands by others	−1.346	−5.291	0	I(2)
Log of flowers to UK by others	−1.472	−6.281	5	I(2)
Log of lowers to Germany by others	−1.666	−4.261	5	I(3)
Log of real GDP of the Netherlands	−1.564	−4.854	3	I(2)
Log of real GDP of the UK	−0.919	−3.341	2	I(2)
Log of real GDP of Germany	−1.564	−4.854	3	I(1)
Log of population of the Netherlands	−3.050		6	I(0)
Log of population of the UK	9.704	−4.808	0	I(2)
Log of population of Germany	−7.216		2	I(0)
Log of flower production	−3.187		1	I(0)
Log of lagged flower production$_{[-1]}$	−3.325		1	I(0)
Log real GDP of Zambia	−2.340	−3.343	6	I(1)
Log of population of Zambia	−1.627	−3.461	0	I(1)
Log of lagged domestic flower price$_{[-1]}$	−1.085	−3.080	0	I(1)
Log of lagged world flower price$_{[-1]}$	−2.590	−4.813	6	I(2)
Log of cereal production	−2.453	−6.633	2	I(1)
Log export credit	−5.590		1	I(0)
Log real exchange rate	−8.986		6	I(0)
Log real interest rate	−3.704		1	I(0)
Log of DRC of flowers exports	−1.032	−5.458	0	I(1)

Notes: ADF critical values at 1% and 5% levels were −3.750 and −3.000 respectively.

(trace) test results show the presence of at least two cointegrated vectors since the null hypothesis of no cointegrated relationships ($r = 0$) is rejected at both 1 and 5 percent levels, respectively. Similarly, the ADF test statistics of residuals at 5 percent significance level show that the predicted residuals were stationary in their original levels. Therefore, the null hypothesis of no cointegration among variables was firmly rejected on the basis of

Table 4. Cointegration test results for flower competitiveness model.

Test statistic	Test statistic and critical values by null hypothesis			
	$r = 0$	$r \leq 1$	$r \leq 2$	$r \leq 3$
Trace Statistic	697.02	79.47	38.02	18.88
5% Critical Value	68.52	47.21	29.68	15.41
1% Critical Value	76.07	54.46	35.65	20.04
ADF_t^{level} for residual	−5.564 [5]			

Notes: ADF critical values at 1% and 5% levels were −3.750 and −3.000 respectively. [ ] is number of lags. *r* is number of cointegrating relationships given by the maximum rank column of the Johansen tests for cointegration.

Table 5. Cointegration test results for flower export models.

Test statistic	Test result and critical values by null hypothesis			
	$r = 0$	$r \leq 1$	$r \leq 2$	$r \leq 3$
Model 3.5.1: Determinants of Flower Exports to Germany				
Trace Statistic	977.42	354.13	229.11	134.69
5% Critical Value	192.89	156.00	124.24	94.15
1% Critical Value	204.95	168.36	133.57	103.18
ADF_t^{level} for residual			−5.374 [0]	
Model 3.5.2: Determinants of Flower Exports to UK				
Trace Statistic	1588.9968	890.998	289.308	189.9248
5% Critical Value	233.13	192.89	156.00	124.24
1% Critical Value	247.18	204.95	168.36	133.57
ADF_t^{level} for residual	−5.720 [5]			
Model 1.3: Determinants of Flower Exports to UK				
Trace Statistic	920.6490	303.3712	203.7325	116.5819
5% Critical Value	192.89	156.00	124.24	94.15
1% Critical Value	204.95	168.36	133.57	103.18
ADF_t^{level} for residual	−4.930 [6]			

Notes: ADF critical values at 1% and 5% levels were −3.750 and −3.000 respectively. [ ] is the number of lags. *r* is the number of cointegrating relationships given by the maximum rank column of the Johansen tests for cointegration.

both tests. The existence of cointegrating vectors (long-run relationships among variables) implied that dynamic error correction models could be estimated to explain the performance of Zambia's flower exports in the short-run.

5.3. Error Correction Models for Factors Affecting Supply and Competitiveness of Flower Exports

Given that fluctuations in flower exports are largely expected to be more evident in the short-run than in the long-run, analysis focused on estimating dynamic short-run parsimonious export and competitiveness determinant models. **Table 6** presents the results for the models that simulated short-term changes in the quantity

of flower exports to the three main export destinations - the UK, the Netherlands and Germany—in terms of changes in the other variables, and the adjustment towards the long-run equilibrium in each time period. The p-values for the LM test statistic of 0.869, 0.629 and 0.813 suggest that the null hypothesis of no autocorrelation could not be rejected at 1 percent in all the three models. The condition of no autocorrelation between residuals in the three models was strongly supported by

Table 6. Short-run models for factors affecting flower exports to germany, the UK and the Netherlands.

Explanatory variable	Model results by country		
	Germany	UK	Netherlands
	(1)	(2)	(3)
Constant	0.7775** (0.2690)	1.4025** (0.4089)	0.9063** (0.4336)
Log of flower production	0.3870*** (0.0338)	0.2587** (0.0477)	0.2599*** (0.0240)
Log of lagged flower production[−1]	0.0750 (0.1058)	0.0157 (0.1913)	0.1597 (0.4034)
Log of flower exports by others	−0.0680** (0.0141)	−0.0726** (0.0157)	−0.1504** (0.0482)
Log of real GDP of Zambia	0.1247 (0.4155)	0.2696 (0.7556)	0.0036 (0.6515)
Log of population of importing country	11.0564** (2.980)	2.8551*** (0.2478)	6.5674*** (0.7322)
Log of population of Zambia	0.0147 (0.0162)	1.7046 (5.3440)	1.3829 (6.5597)
Log of importing country's real GDP	1.0848 (0.7416)	0.9682** (0.3133)	0.1176** (0.0325)
Log of lagged domestic producer price[−1]	0.1023 (0.0761)	0.0577 (0.1627)	0.0594 (0.1742)
Log of lagged world producer price[−1]	0.9618*** (0.0858)	0.8046** (0.2700)	0.3513** (0.1282)
Log of cereal production	−0.0285 (0.0434)	−0.0037 (0.1209)	−0.0501 (0.1824)
Log of export credit	0.3737** (0.0953)	1.1232*** (0.1172)	0.0893** (0.0185)
Log of real exchange rate	0.1413** (0.0474)	0.0267** (0.0072)	0.1052** (0.0557)
Log of real interest rate	−0.1234** (0.0392)	−0.0274** (0.0107)	−0.0113* (0.0083)
Error correction term[−1]	−0.9800** (0.3082)	−0.1018** (0.0350)	−0.4846** (0.1768)
F-statistic	596.11 (0.000)	352.43 (0.000)	271.29 (0.004)
N(Yrs: 1990-2010)	18	18	18
DW	1.97	1.78	2.17
R^2	0.9280	0.9751	0.9145
LM Test (Prob > chi2)	0.8691	0.6290	0.8131
Hettest (Prob > chi2)	0.9754	0.2484	0.4367

Dependent variable is log of flower exports; Standard errors in parentheses; Significant level: * = 10%; ** = 5%; *** = 1%.

the Durbin-Watson (DW) test statistics which are within the acceptable bound, 1.5 - 2.5 [52]. The p-values (<0.0001 and <0.0037) for the F-statistic indicates that the models were significant at 1 and 5 percent levels, respectively. The models overall had very strong goodness-of-fit each with an R^2 of above 0.90.

The results demonstrate that Zambia's flower exports are positively influenced by domestic production, GDP and population of importing countries, producer prices, export credit and exchange rate depreciation. For instance, the positive coefficients for real exchange of 0.1413, 0.0267 and 0.1052 indicates that a 1 percent increase in exchange rate (decrease in value of the Zambian Kwacha relative to the US Dollar) increased flower exports to Germany, the UK and the Netherlands by about 0.14, 0.03 and 0.11 percent, respectively. The regression results also show that increases in exports from competing countries, domestic cereal production and interest rates negatively influenced flower exports. The percentage decrease in the quantity of the flower exports to the three main destination countries attributed to a percentage increase in each of the three variables is indicated by the negative coefficient for the respective covariates (**Table 6**). Lastly, the coefficients for the error correction term show that there was 98, 10, and 48 percent feedback in the estimated ECMs of flower exports to Germany, the UK and the Netherlands, respectively, from the previous year disequilibrium into the short-run dynamic process. The significant error correction terms in the models confirm the proposed relationship between flower exports to the three countries under study, and the variables considered in the models.

Table 7 present results for the ECM which evaluated the impact of the covariates on competitiveness. The R^2 of 0.7406 indicates that the estimated relationship explained 74.06 percent of the total variation in the competitiveness of flower exports. In addition, all diagnostic tests (LM and DW) show that there was no autocorrelation, the chief source of biasedness in time series analyses. Overall, the findings indicate that flower production, prices and exchange rate depreciation positively impacted while cereal production, export credit and interest rates negatively impacted competitiveness of flower exports. Following Monke and Pearson (1989), [47] a reduction in domestic resource cost (DRC) indicates an improvement in competitiveness. Finally, the significant coefficient of −0.0366 for the correction term implies that there was 3.7% feedback in the competitiveness adjustment model from the previous year disequilibrium into the short-run dynamic process.

On the whole, our results in the two sets of models conform to both our prior expectations and findings by other empirical studies. The positive impact of domestic flower production on flower export supply and competi-

Table 7. Short-run model for factors affecting competitiveness of flower exports.

Explanatory variable	Domestic Resource Cost (DRC$_t$)
Constant	0.8467[*] (0.4576)
Log of Flower production	−0.0162[**] (0.0054)
Log of lagged flower production$_{[-1]}$	−0.0111[**] (0.0042)
Log of real GDP of Zambia	−1.7313 (2.7827)
Log of Population of Zambia	0.0477 (0.0338)
Log of Lagged domestic flower price$_{[-1]}$	−0.0493[**] (0.0174)
Log of Lagged world flower price$_{[-1]}$	−0.0824[**] (0.0274)
Log of cereal production	0.0089[**] (0.0039)
Log of export credit	0.0156[**] (0.0059)
Log of real exchange rate	−0.0263[**] (0.0096)
Log of real interest rate	0.0332 (0.0175)[*]
Error Correction Term$_{[-1]}$	−0.0366[**] (0.0123)
F(10, 9)	31.14 (0.0020)
N (Yrs: 1990-2010)	18
DW(14,20)	2.28
R^2	0.7406
Hettest (Prob > chi2)	0.7730
LM Test (Prob > chi2)	0.1927

Dependent variable is log of domestic resource cost of flowers (DRC$_t$); Standard errors in parentheses; Significant level: [*] = 10%; [**] = 5%; [***] = 1%.

tiveness is consistent with [52] suggesting, in part, that if interventions are to achieve increased flower exports; they should among other things, first increase domestic flower production. According to [67], increasing farm production improves competitiveness and efficiency of the farm sector since fixed costs per unit output decrease as output increase due to economies of scale. Therefore, the decline of flower exports from 2006 onwards did not just result in reduced export revenues but equally resulted in high overhead costs causing a reduction in competitiveness. The positive effect of real GDP and population of importing countries on Zambia's flower exports too conform to other studies which also found economic growth and population increase in foreign markets critical in stimulating a country's agricultural export supply and competitiveness. Explicitly, the result implies that economic and population growth in foreign markets increases demand for a country's agricultural exports suggesting that the decline of the horticultural industry from 2006 onwards could be partly attributed to the poor performance of the global economy during the same period. Both [28] and [34] found GDP and population growth in importing countries to increase agricultural exports. In addition, conforming too to our findings, [21] found agricultural export credit to have significant positive influence on the volume of Cameroon's agricultural exports while [27] and [28] found world producer prices to positively impact agricultural exports in Nigeria and South Africa, respectively. Drawing on this result, it could be equally deduced that the significant decline in investments to the industry following the bankruptcy of the largest horticultural firm, Agriflora, in 2004 largely contributed to the slump the industry continued to record thereafter. Besides, the result recognizes the fragility of the horticulture industry in the country suggesting the need for appropriate, broad-based policy support to ensure sustainability and growth of the industry. Conversely, most studies have consistently found a negative relationship between subsidized credit, like in our case, and agricultural competitiveness [69-72]. Particularly, the negative relationship between subsidized credit and flower competitiveness seem to suggest that while the subsidized credit managed to increase output in the short-run, it failed to sustain the high production recorded in the earlier years of the EU's Export Development Project (EDP) due to resource constraints that followed after the project concluded. Similarly, [27] also found exports from competing countries to reduce Nigeria's major agricultural exports implying that in addition to increasing production, the replacement of Zambia's flower exports to the three principal countries by those from other countries dictate that there must be a quality improvement so the country's exports can compete favorably with those from other countries.

Furthermore, our results on interest and exchange rates in both export and competiveness models are comparable with those of [1,2,31]. The authors also found high domestic interest rates and appreciation of the local currencies to reduce both volume and competitiveness of agricultural exports. The results therefore suggest that the significant appreciation of the Zambian currency during the late 2000s contributed substantially to the decline of the horticultural industry during the same time period. The observed negative impact on supply and competitiveness of flower export due to the appreciation of the local currency could be attributed to the loss of export revenue among exporting producers arising from the increase in value of the domestic currency relative to the major world currencies such as the US Dollar and Euro [29,32,52]. The result could equally be attributed to the decline in competitiveness in the international markets because of high export prices for commodities that arise following an increase in the relative value of a country's currency [37]. On the other hand, the negative impact of interest rates on exports and competitiveness is particularly attributed to the resultant high cost of capital, mainly credit, which makes it difficult for smallholders, especially resource poor ones, to adopt modern and yield enhancing technologies for increased agricultural exports [39]. According to [25], the area devoted to cut flowers and fresh vegetables in Zambia has stagnated at 140 hectares, compared to Kenya's over a million hectares, because of high lending rates (over 35 percent) that prohibit most people from venturing into horticulture production.

6. Conclusions and Policy Implications

Overall, the results suggest that in addition to the determinants of production, flower exports are equally determined by policies that affect a country's trade position. The results in particular imply that relative depreciation of the Zambian currency stimulates agricultural exports. Hence macroeconomic policies that explicitly seek to over-value the Zambian currency are not desirable for the country's agricultural exports. By reducing exporters' revenues and making exportables relatively expensive in the international markets, such anti-trade policies are likely to lead to reductions in both output and competitiveness. In addition, the positive impacts of export credit on supply of flower exports but negative on competitiveness suggest that while subsidized agricultural grants may increase output by enhancing farmers' access to productive inputs, they may also reduce competitiveness by allowing inefficient producers to continue producing. Furthermore, the negative effect of cereal production on both supply and competitiveness of flower exports indicates that food and export crops are not complimentary but competitive with one another for resources, including policy incentives.

These findings seem to identify a strong need for programs, policies and practices that are aimed at enhancing and fostering an environment favorable for both flower production and exporting. First, investments in infrastructure and other broad-based interventions that improve producers' access to crucial but locally unavailable inputs and storage facilities, without distorting markets, are especially needed to help exporting farmers reduce the cost of production and handling. Such market-based interventions have potential to increase production without reducing competitiveness. Second, market determined exchange rate regimes that promote trade are clearly required and important ingredient for both farmer export decisions and the competitiveness of the industry. Third, the results indicate that supports to the agricultural sector in the country need to be appropriately balanced between food and cash crops if both sub-sectors in the sector (agriculture) are to grow. Furthermore, the discernible positive effects of foreign countries' GDP and population on flower exports call for policies that take into consideration the growth in industrial production in the major importing countries—the UK, the Netherlands and Germany.

7. Acknowledgements

This paper is based on earlier work done by the authors with support from the African Economic Research Consortium (AERC) through the Collaborative Masters in Agricultural and Applied Economics (CMAAE) programme. However, the views expressed herein do not necessarily represent the position of any of these organizations. All errors in interpretation are the authors' own.

REFERENCES

[1] CSO, "Agricultural and Pastoral Production Small and Medium Scale Holdings 1997-1998," Structural Type and Post Harvest Data, Government of the Re public of Zambia, Lusaka, 2000.

[2] World Bank, "Zambia Country Report," 2002.

[3] M. Zulu and G. Tembo, "Export Horticulture and Household Welfare: Evidence from Zambia," In Press, *Journal of Journal of Development and Agricultural Economics*, 2013.

[4] C. Chipokolo, "Smallholder Agriculture: Ignored Goldmine," PELUM Zambia, Policy Brief No. 1, 2006.

[5] A. Chapoto, D. Banda, S. Haggblade and P. Hamukwala, "Factors Affecting Poverty Dynamics in Rural Zambia," Food Security Research Project (FSRP), 2011.

[6] T. S. Jayne, N. Mason, W. Burke, A. Shipekesa, A. Chapoto and C. Kabaghe, "Mountains of Maize, Persistent Poverty," Food Security Research Project (FSRP), Policy Synthesis No.48, 2011.

[7] CSO, "National Postharvest Survey," Government of the Republic of Zambia, Lusaka, 2008.

[8] D. K. Chiwele, "Agriculture Development and Food security in Sub-Saharan Africa: Building a Case for More Support: A Case Study of Zambia," RuralNet Associates Limited, Lusaka, Zambia, 2004.

[9] USAID, "Economic Growth: Increased Private Sector Competitiveness in Agriculture and Natural Resources," USAID/Zambia, Lusaka, 2005.

[10] OECD, "Economic Development in Zambia," A Country Study Report, 2007.

[11] A. Sergeant and M. Sewadeh, "Current Status of Zambia's Agricultural Exports," Working Paper, The World Bank, 2006.

[12] MoFNP, "Zambia Poverty Reduction Strategy Paper 2002-2004," Government of the Republic of Zambia, Lusaka, 2002.

[13] Mataa and Hichaambwa, "Video Conference on High Value Agriculture in Eastern and Southern Africa: Small-holders Involvement in Commercial Agriculture in Zambia," 2011.

[14] ZDA, "Promoting Economic Growth and Development," Publicity Brochure, Lusaka, 2012.

[15] Export Board of Zambia (EBZ), "Horticulture/Floriculture Sector Report," Public Brochure, Lusaka, 2005.

[16] M. Hichaambwa, "Developments in the Horticultural supply chains in Zambia," Food Security Research Project (FSRP), Lusaka, 2010.

[17] N. McCulloch and M. Ota, "Export Horticulture and Poverty in Kenya," Institute of Development Studies, University of Sussex, Brighton, 2002.

[18] M. Maertens and J. F. M. Swinnen, "Trade, Standards and Poverty: Evidence from Senegal," *World Development*, Vol. 37, No. 1, 2006, pp. 161-178.

[19] V. Afari-Sefa, "The Micro-Level Distributional Effects of Horticultural Export Value Chains among Smallholders in Southern Ghana," *Research in Agricultural and Applied Economics*, Vol. 2, 2008.

[20] J. E. Medina-Smith, "Is the Export-Led Growth Hypothesis Valid for Developing Countries? A Case Study of Costa Rica," *United Nations Conference on Trade and Development (UNCTAD), Policy Issues in International Trade and Commodities*, (2008).

[21] D. Gbetnkom and S. A. Khan, "Determinants of Agricultural Exports: Case of Cameroon," African Economic Research Consortium Research Paper No. 120, the African Economic Research Consortium (AERC), Nairobi, 2002.

[22] T. N. Benson, J. Minot, Pender, M. Robles and J. Von-Braun, "Global Food Crises: Monitoring and Assessing Impact to Inform Policy Response," International Food Policy Research Institute (IFPRI), Issue Brief 55, Washington DC, 2008.

[23] Zambia Export Growers Association (ZEGA), "Submissions to the National Assembly Committee on Economic Affairs on Factors Influencing the Value of the Zambian Kwacha," 24 August 2006, pp. 3-6.

[24] Zambia Export Growers Association (ZEGA), "Submission of Recommendations to the Ministry of Commerce, Trade and Industry on the Performance of Export Horticulture Industry in Zambia," 30 September 2011, pp. 1-4.

[25] African Agriculture, "Entry Costs in Zambian Horticultural Sector," Public Brochure, 2007.

[26] Agrifood Standards Project, "Impact of EurepGap on Small-Scale Vegetable Growers in Zambia, Fresh Perspectives," No. 6, 2007.

[27] V. Okoruwa, G. Ogundare and S. Yusuf, "Determinants of Traditional Agricultural Exports in Nigeria: An Application of Cointegration and Correction Model," *Quarterly Journal of International Agriculture*, Vol. 42, No. 4, 2003, pp. 427-438.

[28] E. Idsardi, "Determinants of Agricultural Export Growth in South Africa," Paper Presented at the *3rd African Association of Agricultural Economists (AAAE) Conference*, Cape Town, 19-23 September 2010, pp. 1-14.

[29] A. A. Hatab, E. Romstad and X. Huo, "Determinants of Egyptian Agricultural Exports: A Gravity Model Approach," *Journal of Modern Economy*, Vol. 1, 2010, pp. 134-143.

[30] I. Adofu, M. Abula and S. I. Audu, "An Assessment of the Effects of Interest Rate Deregulation in Enhancing Agricultural Productivity in Nigeria," *Current Research Journal of Economic Theory*, Vol. 2, No. 2, 2010, pp. 82--86.

[31] J. D. Amassoma, P. I. Nwosa and A. F. Ofere, "The Nexus of Interest Rate Deregulation, Lending Rate and Agricultural Productivity in Nigeria," *Current Research Journal of Economic Theory*, Vol. 3, No. 2, 2011, pp. 53-61.

[32] E. O. Abolagba, N. C. Onyekwere, B. N. Agbonkpolor and H. Y. Umar, "Determinants of Agricultural Exports," *Journal of Human Ecology*, Vol. 29, No. 3, 2010, pp. 181-184.

[33] L. Kasekende and M. Atingi-Ego, "Impact of Liberalization on Key Markets in Sub-Saharan Africa: The Case of Uganda," *Journal of International Development*, Vol. 11, No. 3, 1999, pp. 411-436.

[34] S. Prasad, "Determinants of Exports in Fiji," Fiji Reserve Bank, Suva, 2000.

[35] N. E. Tambi, "Cointegration and Error Correlation Modelling of Agricultural Export Supply in Cameroon," *Agricultural Economics*, Vol. 20, No. 1, 1999, pp. 57-67.

[36] Z. Psaradakis, M. Sola and F. Spagnolo, "On Markov Error-Correction Models, with an Application to Stock Prices and Dividends," *Journal of Applied Econometrics*, Vol. 19, 2004, No. 1, pp. 69-88.

[37] M. G. U. Khonje, "Food Inflation in Malawi: Implications for the Economy," Master's Thesis, Makerere University, Kampala, 2010.

[38] D. Salvatore and D. Reagle, "Theory and Problems of Statistics and Econometrics," In: McGraw-Hill, Ed., *Schaum's Out- line*, 2nd Edition, McGraw-Hill Companies, Inc., New York, 2002, p. 252.

[39] A. Dlamini, D. Armstrong and T, Nxumalo, "A Cointegration Analysis of the Determinants of Inflation in Swaziland," 2001.

[40] W. H. Greene, "Econometrics Analysis," 4th Edition, Pearson Education, Upper Saddle River, 2003.

[41] D. N. Gujarati, "Basic Econometrics," 5th Edition, McGraw-Hill Companies, Inc., New York, 2004.

[42] G. S. Maddala, "Introduction to Econometrics," 3rd Edition, John Wiley & Sons Pulishers, West Sussex, Chichester, 2006.

[43] D. N. Gujarati and Sangeetha, "Basic Econometrics," 4th Edition, Tata McGraw Hill Education Private Limited, New Delhi, 2010.

[44] T. E. Nwachukwu and F. O. Egwaikhide, "An Error-Correction Model of the Determinants of Private Saving in Nigeria," A Paper Presented at the *African Economic Society (AES) Conference*, Cape Town, 2007.

[45] R. F. Engel and C. W. J. Granger, "Cointegration and Error Correction: Representation, Estimation and Testing," *Econometrica*, Vol. 55, No. 2, 1987, pp. 215-276.

[46] D. A. Dickey and W. A. Fuller, "Likelihood Ratio Statistics for Auto-Regressive Time Series with a Unit Root" *Econometrica*, Vol. 49, No. 4, 1981, pp. 1057-1072.

[47] S. Johansen and K. Juselius, "Maximum Likelihood Estimation and Inference on Cointegration with Applications to the Demand for Money," *Oxford Bulletin of Economic and Statistics*, Vol. 52, No. 2, 1990, pp. 169-210.

[48] R. W. Hafer and R. G. Sheehan, "The Sensitivity of VAR Forecasts to Alternative Lag Structures," *International Journal of Forecasting*, Vol. 5, No. 3, 1989, pp. 399-408.

[49] P. A. Braun and S. Mittnik, "Misspecifications in Vector Autoregressions and their Effects on Impulse Responses and Variance Decompositions," *Journal of Econometrics*, Vol. 59, No. 3, 1983, pp. 319-341.

[50] O. Ozcicek and B. Rouge, "Lag Length Selection in Vector Autoregressive Models: Symmetric and Asymmetric Lags," *Journal of Applied Economics*, Vol. 31, No. 4, 2010, pp. 517-524.

[51] J. D. Sargan, "Wages and Prices in the United Kingdom: A study in Econometric Methodology," In: P. E Hart, G. Mills and J. K. Whitaker Eds., Econometric Analysis for National Economic Planning, Butterworths, London, 1964.

[52] N. Nwachukwu, A. Ifeanyi, Nnanna, N. Jude and I. George, "Competitiveness and Determinants of Cocoa Export from Nigeria," *Report and Opinion*, Vol. 2, No. 7, 2010, pp. 51-54.

[53] M. Kaptui, "Does the Exchange Rate Matter for Kenya's Exports? A Bounds Testing Approach," A Paper Prepared for Presentation at the 2007 *African Econometric Society Conference*, Cape Town, 4-6 August 2007, pp. 11-19

[54] J. Von Braun and E. Kennedy, "Commercialization of Subsistence Agriculture: Income and Nutritional Effects in Developing Countries," Working Papers on Commercialization of Agriculture and Nutrition, IFPRI, Washington DC, 1986.

[55] S. C. Mesike, "Analysis of the Determinants of Rubber Export Supply in Nigeria," Master's Thesis, Ibadan University, Ibadan, 2005.

[56] N. Kumar, "Multinational Enterprises, Regional Economic Integration, and Export-Platform Production in the Host Countries: An Empirical Analysis for the US and Japanese Corporations", *Weltwirtschaftliches Archiv*, Vol. 134, No. 3, 1998, pp. 450-483.

[57] M. Weber, J. Staatz, J. Holtzman, E. Crawford and R. Bersten, "Informing Food Security Decisions in Africa: Empirical Analysis and Policy Dialogue," *American*

Journal of Agricultural Economics, Vol. 70, No. 5, 1988, pp. 1044-1052.

[58] Z. Xu, Z. Guan, T. S. Jayne and R. Black, "Factors Affecting the Profitability of Fertilizer Use on Maize in Zambia," 2009.

[59] S. Sadoulet and A. de Janvry, "Quantitative Development Policy Analysis," The Johns Hopkins University Press, Baltimore, 1995.

[60] J. F. Fabiosa, "Assessing the Impact of the Exchange Rate and its Volatility on Canadian Pork and Live Swine Exports to the United States and Japan," Working paper 02-WP 305, Center for Agricultural and Rural Development, Iowa State University, Ames, 2002.

[61] M. B. Kaabia and J. M. Gill, "Spanish Agricultural Exports Competitiveness: The Role of Macroeconomic Variables," *Cahiers Options Méditerranéennes*, Vol. 57, No. 5, 2001, pp. 81-99.

[62] C. P. Timmer, P. F. Water and R. S. Pearson, "Food Policy Analysis," The Johns Hopkins University Press, Baltimore, 1983.

[63] A. Enoma, "Agricultural Credit and Economic Growth in Nigeria: An Empirical Analysis," *Business and Economics Journal*, Vol. 2010, 2010, Aticle ID: BEJ-14

[64] R. Balance, H. Forstner and T. Murray, "Consistency Tests of Alternative Measures of Comparative Advantage," *Review of Economics and Statistics*, Vol. 69, No. 1, 1987, pp. 157-161.

[65] World Bank, "Ukraine Agricultural Competitiveness," Europe and Central Asia Region, Sustainable Development Unit, 2008.

[66] E. A. Monke and S. R. Pearson, "The Policy Analysis Matrix for Agricultural Development," Outreach Program, 1989.

[67] D. L. Debertin, "Agricultural Production Economics," 3rd Edition, Privately Published, Macmillan Publishing Company, New York, 2004.

[68] J. M. Chizuni, "Food Policies and Food Security in Zambia," *Nordic Journal of African Studies*, Vol. 3, No. 1, 1994, pp. 46-51.

[69] O. Nivievskyi, and S. von Cramon-Taubadel, "The Determinants of Dairy Farming Competitiveness in Ukraine," Paper Presented at the 12*th EAAE Congress*, Gent, 27-30 August 2008, pp. 1-8

[70] K. Giannakas, R. Schoney and V. Tzouvelekas, "Technical Efficiency, Technological Change and Output Growth of Wheat Farms in Saskatchewan," *Canadian Journal of Agricultural Economics*, Vol. 49, No. 2, 2001, pp. 135-152.

[71] A. Rezitis, K. Tsiboukas and S. Tsoukalas, "Investigation of Factors Influencing the Technical Efficiency of Agricultural Producers Participating in Farm Credit Programs: The case of Greece," *Journal of Agricultural and Applied Economics*, Vol. 35, No. 3, 2003, pp. 529-541.

[72] D. Hadley, "Efficiency and Productivity at the Farm Level in England and Wales 1982 to 2002," Report for the Department for Environment, Food and Rural Affairs (DEFRA), London, 2006.

11

Accruals, Persistence of Profits and Stock Returns in Brazilian Public Companies

Renata Turola Takamatsu, Luiz Paulo Lopes Fávero
School of Economics, Business and Accountancy University of São Paulo, São Paulo, Brazil

ABSTRACT

The central aim in this research was to assess investors' accounting information interpretation skills. Therefore, it was assessed how different profit components would affect the future profitability of publicly traded Brazilian companies. Through a sample of all Brazilian public companies listed in Bovespa from 1995 to 2010, the research results demonstrated that current accruals were incapable of explaining future abnormal return behavior in the firms analyzed. In addition, no significant abnormal returns were reached in an accruals-based investment strategy, indicating that investors would be capable of interpreting and pricing accounting data.

Keywords: Accounting Accruals; Persistence of Profits, Stock Returns, Brazil, Panel Data

1. Introduction

Departing from the seminal work by [1], subsequent studies started to show the relation between the data and indicators extracted from financial statements and companies' future performance, proving this association through empirical evidence ([2,3]). According to [4], however, even when used to assess business risks and estimate companies' capital costs, accounting variables have not been sufficiently explored in contemporary academic research. Imperfect understanding about the nature of the financial statement can result in a reduction of capital market agents' ability to: 1) manage resources efficiently, and 2) detect investment alternatives to enhance the possibility of gains. This possible interference between what Accounting informs and what its users understand results in accounting anomalies.

Among the data included in the financial statements, there is a trend for investors, analysts and creditors to recommend some information more recurrently like profit-related information for example. That is so because, despite possible social implications, businesses are primarily based on the owners' conviction that company operations can result in profits. In profit analysis, [5] defend the idea that different profit components entail different implications for company value, frequently found in financial studies, and apparently supported by investment analysts. In general, profits contain cash flow components and accruals, distinguished by different degrees of subjectivity. While the cash flow components comprise revenues and expenses that represent effective inflows or outflows of financial resources during the pe-

riod, accruals are temporary cash flow adjustments, transferring them to the period when they are recognized in the income statement [6]. In that sense, [7] affirms that accruals are based on deferrals, allocations and evaluations, all of which involve a high level of subjectivity.

According to [7], subjectivity and the transitory nature of accruals represent causes for their shorter persistence. Therefore, one may suppose that companies with higher accrual levels during the fiscal year tend to increase the probability of exhibiting a lower persistence level of this profit in the future. The empirical results the author found confirmed the persistence of lower profits associated with accruals, thus supporting traditional authors' arguments that accruals and cash flow components should be considered separately in financial assessments [5].

Investors should consider the reduction in the future profitability level as a result of a shorter persistence of current accruals than cash flow items [8,7], on the other hand, detected negative associations between current accruals and abnormal future returns in the companies. In other words, although empirical evidence indicates that high accrual levels enhance the probability of reductions in future profitability, investors' expectations—reflected in stock prices—demonstrated that they have not incorporated information about the persistence of accruals in their analyses.

Studies that investigated the effect of accruals on profit persistence and company value in general have focused on developed markets like the United States and the United Kingdom [9]. Hence, the number of investigations to study investors' reaction to different profit components in emerging markets is still limited.

A series of distinguished characteristics marks the Brazilian market. Historically, in its institutional environment, fiscal rules have strongly influenced the financial statements. The State issued accounting standards in response to its fiscal and tax needs, what deviates the statements' focus from the provision of useful information to investors and other users [10,11] defends that, in countries where the impact of accounting information is comparatively weaker, like in Brazil, the functional fixing in the final profit reported is less common or less important in stock pricing, which in turn interferes in accrual anomalies.

The above considerations and a transition period in the financial statements, which used to be based on standards, towards a more principle-based accounting, reveal a unique opportunity to analyze investors' ability to interpret Accounting data, particularly the disclosure of profit information. Thus, the general aim of this study was to verify whether accounting anomalies in accruals are detected in the Brazilian capital market. To assess this objective, the research was developed to check whether different profit components influence profit persistence and the market's reactions. The study was conducted based on the method by [7], which served as a reference for further similar studies ([5,12-14]).

The specific aims are to verify whether the current accrual level is related to the profit behavior and market value in future periods and to detect whether investment strategies based on accruals produce statistically significant abnormal returns.

After presenting the research objectives, it is interesting to express the research hypotheses in analytic terms. The first hypothesis, on the persistence of accruals, serves as a premise to evaluate the other hypothesis. Thus:

H_1: The current profits resulting from adjustments to the accrual base of accounting are less persistent than the profits deriving from cash flow components.

The other tests refer to the accrual anomaly itself, that is, that investors would not understand the nature of profits, resulting in asset pricing evaluation errors. Therefore, the second research hypothesis is that:

H_2: The expected profits embedded in current stock prices do not correctly reflect available information on accounting profit.

An extension of the second research hypothesis established refers to the formation of investment strategies. It can be formulated as follows:

$H_{2,1}$: A negotiation strategy based on the profit accrual level produces positive abnormal returns.

Traditional financial literature is based on the semistrong form of the capital market efficiency hypothesis. The premise is that asset prices embed all publicly available information in a logical and instantaneous form, making it impossible for investors to systematically reach extraordinary gains. The empirical results on the anomaly of accruals challenge the market efficiency paradigm in its semi-strong form, suggesting that abnormal returns can be reached through investment strategies based on publicly available information [15].

In other words, if anomalous accruals are detected, it is demonstrated that investment strategies based on accounting data support decision making, allowing capital market agents to detect investment alternatives with a greater possibility of gains. In that sense, investors and financial market portfolio managers will obtain additional empirical evidence and theoretical arguments for the financial statement information efficiency in companies whose stocks are traded on the primary and secondary markets of the São Paulo Stock Exchange (BM&F Bovespa).

2. Theoretical Platform

The theoretical platform can be separated in four subsections. First, a short summary on profit, its elements and importance is presented. Then, financial anomalies are defined, explaining how they challenge the Market Efficiency Hypothesis by [15]. The third subsection discusses the literature on the anomaly of accruals, highlighting the empirical evidence found. Finally, anomalous accruals are treated specifically in the Brazilian environment.

2.1. Accounting Profit

According to [16], profits produced in the framework of accounting accruals represent a measure that summarizes company performance information. Hence, profit information is used in a range of situations, like in the establishment of executive compensation plans, in the prospects of firms that intend to go public, and also by any creditor or investor interested in assessing companies' future performance.

Basically, cash flows and accruals constitute profits. The cash flow components comprise revenues and expenses that corresponded to actual inflows or outflows of financial resources during the period. On the other hand, accruals are temporary cash flow adjustments [6]. The relationship between profits, accruals and cash flow is shown in Equation (1).

$$\text{Profits} = \text{Cash Flow} + \text{Accruals} \qquad (1)$$

Accruals permit compliance with the main foundations of the accrual base of accounting: the revenue realization principle and the matching principles between revenues and expenses in the same period. Cash flows, on the other hand, cannot comply with these principles, as they join revenues and expenses accrued in different periods in the same statement. In that sense, [6] highlight that accruals inhibit potential timing and mismatching problems.

[17] underlines that accrual estimates are based on business administrators' view/expectation of revenues and expenses related to the economic phenomena incurred in the current period. [18] defend that, when adding accruals to operating cash flows, Accounting produces a variable with less noise than operating cash flows alone, as accruals mitigate extreme and temporary variations deriving from modifications in working capital, anticipated payment, accounts receivable and accounts payable.

2.2. Financial Anomalies

In capital market studies, in general, the efficient market hypothesis is assumed in its semi-strong form. [15] generically established that, in efficient markets, the prices of the assets traded fully reflect available information, making it impossible for investors to systematically achieve abnormal returns.

Inquiries about support for the argument in favor of investors' total rationality encouraged the creation of a group of behavioral fans, in which the principle of limited rationality replaced that of limited rationality [19]. Information efficiency constraints, like the concentration and information processing abilities inherent in human nature, imply economic effects called financial anomalies [14].

Financial anomaly can be considered a seemingly unexplained systematic event [20]. Similarly, [21] define financial anomalies as documented standards of price behavior that is inconsistent with the theory of market efficiency. According to [22], despite the strong focus on capital market anomalies, recent researches are almost exclusively focused on behavioral finance, without addressing accounting anomalies.

2.3. Anomaly of Accruals

The seminal research developed by [7] evaluated whether stock prices would reflect the different persistence of cash flow components and accruals. The results demonstrated that cash flow components are more capable of predicting profits for the subsequent period. In the author's model, accruals were subdivided in ten groups (based on the calculated deciles) and the cash flow components and accruals showed persistence coefficients of approximately 0.8 and 0.5.

Based on the estimated regressions and constitution of theoretical portfolios, [7] found that companies in which the income contained a large share of accruals generally exhibited negative abnormal returns in the year after forming the portfolio, mainly during the period when financial statements are presented and accounting income is disseminated. These findings demonstrated that inves-

tors did not understand the different persistence of profit components but focused on the final profit reported, instead of analyzing the different implications of its components in the formation of company income.

In view of the results those authors found, the conjecture was established that the market would be incapable of correctly pricing accrual information. These findings triggered subsequent studies that investigated the anomaly of accruals, which implied the development of new research methods and a considerable range of foci, samples and empirical evidence available on the theme.

The hypothesis established [7] about investors' naïve focus on the final profit accounting reported, without an in-depth understanding about the different properties of its components, was tested by [12,14,23], among others.

[23] explored some cross-sectional characteristics of the accrual anomaly. Based on the premise that this anomaly would result from investors' inability to correctly process the information in the financial statements, the authors investigated whether this inability could be related to investigators' degree of sophistication. Against expectations, the results demonstrated that the association between accruals and subsequent returns was stronger in larger firms. For smaller companies, in which less interest by sophisticated investors was expected, this relation was weaker. These results collide with the hypothesis that the anomaly would derive from market participants' inability to understand relevant information, as it seems improbable that more sophisticated investors, with a comprehensive understanding about the different natures of profit components, would only focus on the bottom line.

Using a method distinct from [12,23] evaluated the functional fixing hypothesis of the final accounting profit. The author demonstrated that the profitability of companies that exhibited extreme accrual levels continued across two consecutive years and that, despite this continuity, companies experienced abnormal returns, suggesting that these returns do not result from the reversal of accruals. Thus, using distinct methods, the findings by [12] and [23] led to the same conclusion, *i.e.* both studies found that the investors' fixation could not be the reason for the accrual anomaly.

[14], however, documented results that are consistent with the hypothesis of the investors' focus on accounting profit, as opposed to the abovementioned evidence. The authors investigated whether investors neglect information on cash generation, assessing the extent to which reported profits arouse excessive optimism. These authors also demonstrated when companies' net operating assets (NOA) are high, that the subsequent growth in profits tends to be low. A strong and negative association between NOA and long-term returns would demonstrate that investors did not analyze information on the amount of NOA adequately, but essentially based their evalua-

tions on accounting profitability. Hence, it is only in later periods, when the large quantity of net operating assets affects company profitability that investors readjusted their evaluations, resulting in the negative return observed through empirical tests.

2.4. Empirical Results Found in the Brazilian Market

The deep review realized by [24] found that, despite the increasing number of international studies on the anomaly of accruals, in Brazil, research on this phenomenon is still incipient, to the extent that [25] are pioneers in their exploration of the theme.

[25] evaluated the first hypothesis [7] established, about the lower persistence of accrual-related profits than that of cash flow items. In a sample of 126 Brazilian companies, with data available for the period 1995-2007, the authors were unable to prove the established hypothesis. When expanding the sample to all assets traded on BM&FBovespa (except for financial companies) between 1990 and 2008, however, [24] obtained indices consistent with international literature. In this study, signs were found that the persistence of accruals is shorter than that of cash flows. No relation was found, though, between high levels of accruals and negative abnormal returns in companies on the Brazilian capital market. Hence, no evidence was detected that accruals would be badly priced by the market, nor even that accrual-based negotiation strategies would provide positive and consistent returns.

3. Research Methods

The methodological procedures adopted in the study are described in this chapter, in which the sample selection criterion is treated in the first subsection. Then, the procedures to detect outliers are explained, as well as the operational definitions of the study variables. Next, the estimated models to investigate the research hypotheses are presented.

3.1. Research Sample

The sample used in this study consisted of Brazilian publicly traded companies with stocks traded on BM&FBovespa between 1995 and 2010, excluding financial companies. As three-monthly observations tend to vary as a result of possible seasonal spreads and accounting principles, we decided to use the companies' annual reports. The financial information used was taken from the Eco-

nomática® database and variables were updated to December 31st 2010, using the Brazilian Institute of Geography and Statistics' (IBGE) Extended Consumer Price Index—IPCA.

To compose the sample, only companies with complete data for all study variables across the study period were considered. In addition, corrective measures were adopted for the outliers. Using box plot graphs, the presence of outliers was evaluated in the dependent variable. Thus, any values beyond the inter-quartile interval were excluded from the sample. On the other hand, to detect outliers in the independent variables, the Mahalanobis distance was used [26]. Hence, the research sample for the first hypothesis included 465 companies, totaling 3166 observations.

Significantly fewer observations were available to assess the second study hypothesis. That was so because the stocks of a range of companies listed on BM&FBovespa are not frequently traded, which makes it impossible to calculate return in the period after the presentation of the financial statements. As a result, less data were available to assess the second hypothesis, resulting in a final sample of 243 companies and 1291 observations.

3.2. Operational Definitions of Variables

The measure used to represent company profits was Earnings before Interest and Taxes—EBIT). The used of the EBIT excludes non-recurrent items, such as extraordinary items, discount operations and special items, as well as non-operating profit (present in statements before law 11.638/2007). Non-recurrent items are problematic, as the information needed to decompose them between cash flows and accruals are not always available. The exclusion of these items permits more consistent access to the persistence of cash flow components and accruals. Profits were standardized in relation to mean total assets [27].

$$\frac{Profits_t}{\frac{1}{2} \times \left(TA_{t-1} + TA_t \right)} \tag{2}$$

where:

$Profits_t$ = Current profits before interests and taxes
TA_{t-1} = Lagged Total Assets
TA_{t-1} = Current Total Assets

Total accruals were calculated through the balance sheet focus ([28]), as demonstrated in Equation (3):

$$Acc = \frac{\left(\Delta CA_{t-(t-1)} - \Delta C_{t-(t-1)} \right) - \left(\Delta CL_{t-(t-1)} - \Delta Deb_{t-(t-1)} - \Delta Tap_{t-(t-1)} \right) - Dep}{\frac{1}{2} \times \left(TA_{t-1} + TA_t \right)} \tag{3}$$

where:

ΔCA = Variation in Current Assets

ΔC = Variation in Cash and cash equivalents

ΔPC = Variation in Current Liabilities

ΔDiv = Variation in Short-term debts

$\Delta \operatorname{Im} p$ = Variation in taxes payable

Dep = Variation in depreciation and amortization expenses

AT_{t-1} = Lagged Total Assets

AT_t = Current Total Assets

The cash flows, on the other hand, were estimated by the difference between profits and accounting accruals, as shown in Equation (4).

$$\text{Cash Flows} = \text{Profits} - \text{Accruals} \qquad (4)$$

Returns were calculated for an annual period. The start of the estimation window was established at the end of the fourth months after closing off the previous year. This procedure assumes a lag between the end of the year and the date on which the financial statements are disseminated [24]. To calculate the returns, the expression described in Equation (5) was used:

$$r = \frac{P_t}{P_{t-1}} - 1 \qquad (5)$$

With P_t and P_{t-1} indicating stock prices on t and t_{-1}, respectively.

The abnormal return was given by the actual return obtained by security R_{it} minus the expected normal return $E(R_{it})$, given X_t, which is the conditioning information for the normal performance model. For a stock i and event date t, the abnormal return (AR_{it}) was defined as shown in Equation (6):

$$AR_{it} = R_{it} - E(R_{it}/X_t) \qquad (6)$$

The expected return was calculated through the financial asset pricing model CAPM. The Beta of each stock was obtained using the Economática database. The risk-free return rate of the economy was represented by the Selic (basic interest rate in Brazilian economy). The proxy of the market return was the Ibovespa index return. The CAPM is expressed in Equation (7):

$$E(R_{it}/X_t) = r_{f,t} + \beta_{i,t} \times (r_{m,t} - r_{f,t}) \qquad (7)$$

To assess the risk, the Beta of the sample companies' stock was estimated. As an alternative, the Ibovespa return was included as a dependent variable. In addition, two additional measures were used: Book-to-Market and return on assets (ROA). Traditional authors like [29] detected that value-related measures like the Book-to-Market ratio were reliable to forecast expected returns on assets. The results were extended and confirmed by [30-32], which included this indicator in their three fac-

tor model. To control for company size, a proxy was used, calculated based on the natural logarithm of total company assets, a variable that was also considered significant to explain stock returns.

To test the influence of the activity sector on the relation between current accruals and future returns, dichotomous dummy variables were inserted to identify the sector each company belongs to (*dsector*). In this case, 20 sectors were considered, following the Economática classification, as displayed in **Figure 1**.

In view of the argument that the investment anomaly would cover the effect of the anomaly of accruals [33], a proxy was included for the Investment activity: Growth in Fixed Assets. Finally, it should be highlighted that the arrival of Law 11.638/2007 changed Corporation Law 6.404/1976. This law and the approval of Accounting Pronouncement 03 obliged publicly traded companies in Brazil to publish the Cash Flow Statement (CFS) as from 2008. This obligation could interfere in investors' ability to separate profit components into accruals and cash flow components.

3.3. Estimated Models

To evaluate whether accruals and cash flow components affect predicted future profits differently, regressions were estimated, considering the sample companies' behavior during the years covered in the analysis. Separating the two main profit components, a possible variation in their persistence was investigated, according to Equation (8):

$$\text{Profits}_{t+1} = \beta_0 + \beta_1 \text{Accruals}_t + \beta_2 \text{CashFl}_t + \varepsilon_t \qquad (8)$$

If the regression demonstrates significant differences between β_1 and β_2, the hypothesis of different prediction powers between the two profit components will be confirmed. In order to actually test the anomaly of accrual, however, a relation needs to be established between stock returns and past accruals. A negative and statistically significant relation between accruals and stock returns during the immediately subsequent period

Sectorial Classification			
Agriculture and Fishing	Electric Energy	Others	Software and Data
Food and Beverages	Funds	Paper and Pulp	Telecommunications
Commerce	Industrial Machinery	Oil and Gas	Textile
Construction	Mining	Chemistry	Transportation and Services
Electro-electronics	Non-Metallic Minerals	Iron and Steel	Vehicles and parts

Figure 1. Sectorial classification according to economática database.

demonstrates investors' inability to understand the reversible property of accruals. To be able to test this relation, control variables were included in the model (Equation (9)), based on [7,23].

$$R_{i,t+1} = \beta_0 + \beta_1 \text{Accruals}_{it} + \beta_2 \text{Book}/\text{Mkt}_{it}$$
$$+ \beta_3 \text{Ibov}_t + \beta_4 \text{POA}_{it}$$
$$+ \beta_5 \text{INV}_{it} + \beta_7 \text{lei}_{it} + \beta_8 \text{Size}_{it} \quad (9)$$
$$+ \sum_{j}^{J-1} \phi \text{Dsector}_{it} + \varepsilon_{it}$$

In this regression model, β_1 measures the ability of accruals to predict future returns. When β_1 is not statistically equal to zero, there are signs that an abnormal return can be reached in a strategy that involves the selection of firms based on the exhibit accruals level.

3.4. Exploring the Anomaly of Accruals

Portfolios were constituted according to the level of accruals the firms exhibited. To evaluate whether companies with a higher level of accruals exhibited significantly lower abnormal returns that companies with low accrual levels, the following was done:

1) Classification of firms according to the level of accruals reported over the years for each year analyzed;

2) Segregation of firms into five portfolios of equal weight, based on the quintiles calculated for each firm;

3) Measurement of abnormal returns for portfolios with low as well as with high levels of accruals;

4) Comparison among returns reached through a test of differences of means.

4. Results and Discussion

This chapter presents the analyses and discussion of results. The first hypothesis established, about less persistent profits related to accruals than to cash flow components, represents a premise for the assessment of the other hypotheses. The other tests refer to the anomaly of accruals itself.

4.1. First Hypothesis—Persistence of Profits

Regression analysis with panel data was used to evaluate the first study hypothesis. First, Chow's test was applied to compare available models for panel data. F-statistics (482, 2, 872) reached 2.26 (Prob > F = 0.000), which permits the rejection of the null hypothesis that the model that would best adapt to the data would be the estimation of the model through the Pooled Ordinary Least Squares —POLS), demonstrating the superiority of the fixed effects model, at a confidence level of 95% (**Table 1**).

The Hausman test offered an objective criterion for the decision between the fixed effect model and the random effect model. Hausman test statistics reached 455.44 (Prob > χ^2 = 0.000), which permitted the rejection of

the null hypothesis, again leading to the conclusion that the most adequate model for the sample under analysis is the fixed effect model.

The regression results demonstrated that the accruals are less persistent than the cash flow components. These differences are perceived in a more transparent way based on the standardized coefficients, in which accruals and cash flows presented standardized coefficients of 0.43 and 0.53, respectively. To evaluate whether the coefficients were statistically different, the hypothesis of equality between the coefficients through the F-test is appropriate. The results of that test proved, at a confidence level of 95%, that the coefficient of the accruals related to profit persistence was significantly different from the coefficient related to the cash flow components, with F-statistics (1, 2699) = 35.73 (Prob > F = 0.000).

The obtained results regarding profit persistence differed from Sloan's findings (1996). In that author's study, the cash flow components and accruals presented persistence coefficients bordering on 0.8 and 0.5, respectively, when calculating regressions in deciles. The coefficients detected in this study, however, are similar to [24]'s findings for the Brazilian reality, showing a persistence coefficient of 0.3945 for the cash flows and 0.3759 for the accruals.

4.2. Second Hypothesis—Effects of Current Accruals on Future Returns

Chow's test was again applied, which permitted the conclusion that the fixed effect model was superior to the minimum least squares models for the study sample with regard to the second model under evaluation. F-test statistics (482, 2, 872) reached 2.26 (Prob > F = 0.000). At a 95% confidence level, this result induces the rejection of the null hypothesis that the model that would best adapt to the data would be the POLS model.

Like in the first model, to identify which of the fixed and random effects models would be the most adequate for the sample data, Hausman's test was performed. As a result of a test statistics equal to 16.75, the null hypothesis was rejected. Thus, the result analysis concentrated on the fixed effects models presented in **Table 2**.

The first variable to be excluded from the model, the least significant in the regression, was exactly the study variable, *i.e.* accruals standardized by total assets. This exclusion leads to the rejection of the second study hypothesis. That is, a negative association between the current accruals and future abnormal returns of the companies under analysis cannot be proven. Thus, as opposed to what was detected in international literature, no empirical evidence was found that, after the arrival of new profit information, investors would revise their expectations, raising stock prices with low accrual levels and generating significant abnormal returns.

Table 1. Panel regression (fixed effects) for future profits.

r²within =	0.1533						
between =	0.7028				F (4.172) =	244.39	
Overall =	0.4154				Prob. > F =	0.0000	

VM_PL	Coefficient	Standardized Coefficient	Standard Error	T	P > |t|	95% confidence interval	
accruals	0.41382	0.43564	0.021497	19.25	0.000	0.371667	0.455973
FCO	0.412106	0.53092	0.018912	21.79	0.000	0.375022	0.44919
Intercept	0.055152	0	0.001781	30.97	0.000	0.05166	0.058645
sigma_u	0.048646						
sigma_e	0.058184						
Rho	0.411425		(variance fraction due to u_i)				

Table 2. Panel regression for future returns (fixed effects).

r²within =	0.1533						
between =	0.7028				F (4.172) =	244.39	
Overall =	0.4154				Prob. > F =	0.0000	

VM_PL	Coefficient	Standardized Coefficient	Standard Error	T	P > |t|	95% confidence interval	
Bktmkt	−0.029	−0.136	0.009	−3.450	0.001	−0.046	−0.013
Roa	0.009	0.174	0.002	5.000	0.000	0.006	0.013
Tm	−0.086	−0.324	0.032	−2.720	0.007	−0.148	−0.024
Ibov	0.735	0.473	0.042	17.660	0.000	0.653	0.816
dummy_ifrs	0.098	0.081	0.040	2.460	0.014	0.020	0.176
_cons	1.183	0.000	0.450	2.630	0.009	0.299	2.067
sigma_u	0.048646						
sigma_e	0.058184						
Rho	0.411425		(variance fraction due to u_i)				

The growth variable was the second variable excluded from the model, resulting in the final model presented. The Book-to-Market and ROA variables were significant and their signs were in line with international literature. The results signaled that, the greater the company's valuation in the market (exhibiting a lower Book-to-Market indicator) and the higher its profitability (with a higher ROA rate), the higher the company's future returns. In addition, the regression results demonstrate that larger companies would present a lower risk of insolvency, which would entail a lower risk and, therefore, a lower risk premium (return).

Investment Strategies Based on Information about Accruals

As an additional way to evaluate the effects of adjustments in the accrual base of accounting in period t on future returns, asset portfolios were constituted based on the accrual levels the companies exhibited [7]. After dividing the companies into five groups, it was evaluated whether firms with a higher level of accruals exhibited significantly lower abnormal returns that companies with a low level. In the assembly of the portfolios, it was considered that each stock portfolio was purchased and maintained for a year, *i.e.* a one-year return was considered for each stock.

The returns of the specific companies and the market index (Ibovespa) were calculated on the stock prices obtained from Economática. The portfolios were reached by adding up the returns of their individual stocks. To compare the mean returns, the t-test for two samples was used, always preceded by the variance analysis between the samples, a premise inherent in the application of the t-test.

According to the t-test, it is observed that the mean returns of portfolios with low accrual levels did not significantly differ from companies with high accrual levels. To reach definitive results on the effect of accruals on returns, however, the expected return part should be removed from the assets, permitting the analysis of the unexpected part only. To estimate the expected return part, the asset pricing model CAPM was used, which incorporates the variability of the security in view of market returns in its analyses.

To compare the abnormal return between the two stock portfolios, in which the first included observations with low accrual levels in the profits, and the second behaviors at the other end, the t-test for two samples was again processed, as indicated in **Table 3**.

Evidence for the purpose of arbitrage and for the development of investment strategies based on accrual information goes against expectations. In the year after the portfolio was established, no positive abnormal returns were identified for the portfolio with low accrual levels, differently from [7]'s findings. On the opposite, the mean return found was negative and statistically lower than the mean returns of companies with high accrual levels. Therefore, based on the analysis of nominal returns, no significant differences were detected between previously constituted portfolios. When the same returns were adjusted to the risk, however, the portfolio of assets with low accrual levels showed a statistically lower abnormal return.

5. Final Considerations

This study investigated the relation between companies' accrual level and the market's perception of publicly available profit information. Literature about accounting users' perception on the different profit components is still incipient, a factor that demands further research to enhance knowledge about the understanding of accounting information in the Brazilian capital market.

The first research hypothesis established was that accruals were less persistent than cash flows. The estimated regression demonstrated that the persistence of the accrual components was significantly lower than the cash flow component, with coefficients of 0.43 and 0.53, respectively. Statistically different coefficients between the cash flow items and the profit components resulting from

adjustments in the accrual bases, besides the shorter persistence of the second item, led to the acceptance of the first hypothesis.

The second hypothesis was established to detect whether Brazilian investors understand the relation demonstrated in the first study hypothesis, *i.e.* that the persistence of accrual-related profits was shorter than that of profits related to cash flow items. Thus, it was evaluated whether they attribute different weights to the accrual components and cash flow components of profits. Among the variables included in the estimated model to explain future stock returns, the accrual variable showed the most limited explanatory capacity, as the statistical tests demonstrated. The lack of statistical significance led to the rejection of the hypothesis, showing that there was no evidence to conclude that the investors did not understand the profit components. In addition, a lack of significant differences among economic sectors was demonstrated, as all coefficients of the dichotomous variables that served to identify the effect of companies' activity sectors were not statistically significant.

Expanding the second hypothesis, it was verified whether negotiation strategies based on the accrual level would produce positive abnormal returns. Through the establishment of portfolios based on accrual information and inter group comparison, additional evidence was obtained, which demonstrated that investment strategies based on accrual information were unable to produce statistically significant abnormal returns.

In summary, in line with [24]'s findings, the results indicate that future stock returns cannot be estimated based on accrual information for Brazilian publicly traded companies, leading to the rejection of the second research hypothesis. That is so because no consistent and statistically significant positive abnormal returns were identified, a necessary condition for an efficient negotiation strategy. This fact reinforces the perception that accruals have little explanatory power and, hence, demonstrates that the anomaly of accruals does not exist for the Brazilian stock market.

In view of evidence on the occurrence of the anomaly of accruals, following [34], this study contributed to current accounting literature by offering additional evidence on market behavior towards accounting information in an emergent country. The incorporation of variables like the proxies for the investment level and for the adoption of IFRS, omitted in other studies, can also be appointed as an additional contribution.

Nevertheless, gaps remain, including the role of investors' level of sophistication and financial asset pricing errors. Departing from the premise that investors do not process relevant information on profit components and overestimate the accrual effect on future profits, it seems probable that this behavior is less recurrent in company

Table 3. Test of mean returns and abnormal returns between different accrual levels.

Measures	Returns		Abnormal Returns	
	Acc1	Acc5	Acc1	Acc5
Mean	0.069033	0. 136051	−0.1355675	−0.0553477
Variance	0.209896	0. 23092	0.1644046	0.1877601
Observations	265	252	265	252
Grouped variance	0.220142		0.1757876	
Hypothesis of difference of means	0		0	
Gl	515		515	
Stat t	−1.62337		−2.1745299	
P (T < = t) two-tailed	0.105123		0.0301198	
Critical t two-tailed	1.964581		1.9645809	

stocks traded by less sophisticated investors. That is so because this type of investor tends to understand accounting information in a less detailed way, mainly profit information, thus revealing a lesser ability to adjust their future profit estimates in function of changes between profit proportions [23].

Another opportunity for research on the effect of accounting information in the Brazilian capital market would be the segregation of accruals into broad categories, according to equity elements, *i.e.* between elements deriving from assets and from liabilities, leveling accruals according to their reliability level [35]. Thus, a link could be established between this reliability and profit persistence, besides permitting assessments of investors' ability to capture and anticipate persistence differences between groups of accruals.

Finally, research that provides results on the presence of the anomaly of accruals in emerging markets is highly relevant. In those markets, weak investor protection reduces the efficacy of accounting information for decision-making purposes. Thus, a general model to evaluate the anomaly of accruals in different countries could capture the effect of institutional differences and the legal regimen (code law/common law), indicating how these factors influence investors' ability to interpret Accounting information.

REFERENCES

[1] R. Ball and P. Brown, "An Empirical Evaluation of Accounting Income Numbers," *Journal of Accounting Research*, Vol. 6, No. 2, 1968, pp. 159-178.

[2] J. A. Ou, "Financial Statement Analysis and the Prediction of Stock Returns," *Journal of Accounting and Economics*, Vol. 11, No. 4, 1989, pp. 295-329.

[3] J. S. Abarbanell and B. J. Bushee, "Fundamental Analysis, Future Earnings, and Stock Prices," *Journal of Accounting Research*, Vol. 35, No. 1, 1997, pp. 1-24.

[4] J. Y. Campbell, C. Polk and T. Vuolteenaho, "Growth or Glamour? Fundamentals and Systematic Risk in Stock Returns," *Review of Financial Studies*, Vol. 23, No. 1, 2005, pp. 305-344.

[5] A. Ali, L.-S. Hwang and M. A. Trombley, "Accruals and Future Stock Returns: Tests of the Naive Investor Hypothesis," Working Paper, Social Science Research Network Electronic Paper Collection, 1999.

[6] P. M. Dechow and I. D. Dichev, "The Quality of Accruals and Earnings: The Role of Accrual Estimation Errors," *The Accounting Review*, Vol. 77, 2001, pp. 35-59.

[7] R. G. Sloan, "Do Stock Prices Fully Reflect Information in Accruals and Cash Flows about Future Earnings?" *The Accounting Review*, Vol. 71, No. 3, 1996, pp. 289-315.

[8] M. T. Bradshaw, S. A. Richardson and R. G. Sloan, "Do Analysts and Auditors Use Information in Accruals?" *Journal of Accounting Research*, Vol. 39, No. 1, 2001, pp. 45-74.

[9] M. Pincus, S. Rajgopal and M. Venkatachalam, "The Accrual Anomaly: International Evidence," *The Accounting Review*, Vol. 82, No. 1, 2007, pp. 169-203.

[10] A. B. Lopes and E. M. Martins, "Teoria da Contabilidade: Uma Nova Abordagem," São Paulo, Atlas, 2005.

[11] I. K. el Mehdi, "An Examination of the Naive-Investor Hypothesis in Accruals Mispricing in Tunisian Firms," *Journal of International Financial Management and Accounting*, Vol. 22, No. 2, 2011, pp. 131-164.

[12] T. Zach, "Evaluating the Accrual-Fixation' Hypothesis as an Explanation for the Accrual Anomaly," Working Paper, Washington University, 2006.

[13] S. P. Kothari, E. Loutskina and V. Nikolaev, "Agency Theory of Overvalued Equity as an Explanation for the

Accrual Anomaly," Working Paper, MIT Sloan School of Management, 2006.

[14] D. A. Hirshleifer, K. Hou, S. H. Teoh and Y. L. Zhang, "Do Investors Overvalue Firms with Bloated Balance Sheets?" *Journal of Financial Economics*, Vol. 38, No. 1, 2004, pp. 297-331.

[15] E. F. Fama, "Efficient Capital Markets: A Review of Theory and Empirical Work," *The Journal of Finance*, Vol. 25, No. 2, 1970, pp. 383-417.

[16] P. M. Dechow, "Accounting Earnings and Cash Flows as Measures of Firm Performance: The Role of Accounting Accruals," *Journal of Accounting and Economics*, Vol. 18, No. 1, 1994, pp. 3-42.

[17] E. Paulo, "Manipulação das Informações Contábeis: Uma Análise Teórica e Empírica Sobre os Modelos Operacionais de Detecção de Gerenciamento de Resultados," Faculdade de Economia, Administração e Contabilidade da Universidade de São Paulo, São Paulo, 2007.

[18] R. Ball and L. Shivakumar, "The Role of Accruals in Asymmetrically Timely Gain and Loss Recognition," *Journal of Accounting Research*, Vol. 44, No. 2, 2006, pp. 243-255.

[19] A. Mussa, E. Yang, R. Trovao and R. Fama, "Hipótese de Mercados Eficientes e Finanças Comportamentais: As Discussões Persistem," *FACEF Pesquisa*, Vol. 11, No. 1, 2008, pp. 5-17.

[20] R. Lafond, "Is the Accrual Anomaly a Global Anomaly?" Working Paper, Sloan School of Management, 2005.

[21] A. Brav and J. B. Heaton, "Competing Theories of Financial Anomalies," *The Review of Financial Studies*, Vol. 15, No. 2, 2002, pp. 575-606.

[22] S. A. Richardson, P. D. Wysocki and I. Tuna, "Accounting Anomalies and Fundamental Analysis: A Review of Recent Research Advances," Working Paper, Social Science Research Network Electronic Paper Collection, 2009.

[23] A. Ali, L.-S. Hwang and M. A. Trombley, "Accruals and Future Stock Returns: Tests of the Naïve Investor Hypothesis," *Journal of Accounting, Auditing & Finance*, Vol. 15, No. 2, 2000, pp. 45-63.

[24] C. M. Cupertino, "Anomalia dos Accruals no Mercado Brasileiro de Capitais," Universidade Federal de Santa Catarina, Florianópolis, 2010.

[25] C. M. Cupertino, J. K. Galimberti, J. R. Costa and C. A. Newton, "Explaining Earnings Persistence: A Threshold Autoregressive Panel Unit Root Approach," *X Encontro Brasileiro de Finanças*, Anais, São Leopoldo, 2009.

[26] L. P. Fávero, P. Belfiore, F. L. da Silva and B. L. Chan, "Análise de Dados: Modelagem Multivariada Para Tomada de Decisões," Campus Elsevier, Rio de Janeiro, 2009.

[27] T. Gabrielsson and H. Giaever, "The Accruals Anomaly in Sweden," *Master Thesis in Finance*, Lund School of Economics and Management, 2007.

[28] P. Hribar and D. W. Collins, "Errors in Estimating Accruals: Implications for Empirical Research," *Journal of Accounting Research*, Vol. 40, No. 1, 2002, pp. 105-134.

[29] S. Basu, "Investment Performance of Common Stocks in Relation to Their Price-Earnings Ratios: A Test of the Efficient Market Hypothesis," *Journal of Finance*, Vol. 32, No. 3, 1977, pp. 663-682.

[30] E. F. Fama and K. R. French, "The Cross-Section of Expected Stock Returns," *The Journal of Finance*, Vol. 47, No. 2, 1992, pp. 427-465.

[31] E. F. Fama and K. R. French, "Common Risk Factors in the Returns on Stocks and Bonds," *Journal of Financial Economics*, Vol. 33, No. 1, 1993, pp. 3-56.

[32] E. F. Fama and K. R. French, "Multifactor Explanation of Asset Pricing Anomalies," *The Journal of Finance*, Vol. 51, No. 1, 1996, pp. 55-84.

[33] J. Zhang, "Two Essays on Empirical Asset Pricing: 1. Forecasted Earnings per Share and the Cross Section of Expected Returns and 2. The Limits to Arbitrage and the Fundamental Value-to-Price Trading Strategies," Doctoral Dissertation in Finance, Hong Kong University of Science and Technology, 2006.

[34] P. M. Dechow and W. L. Ge, "The Persistence of Earnings and Cash Flows and the Role of Special Items: Implications for the Accrual Anomaly," *Review of Accounting Studies*, Vol. 11, No. 2-3, 2006, pp. 253-296.

[35] S. A. Richardson, R. G. Sloan, M. T. Soliman and I. Tuna, "Information in Accruals about the Quality of Earnings," Working Paper, University of Michigan, 2001.

12

Extending the Textbook Dynamic AD-AS Framework with Flexible Inflation Expectations, Optimal Policy Response to Demand Changes, and the Zero-Bound on the Nominal Interest Rate[*]

Sami Alpanda[1][#], Adam Honig[2], Geoffrey Woglom[2]
[1]Canadian Economic Analysis Department, Bank of Canada, Ottawa, Canada
[2]Department of Economics, Amherst College, Amherst, USA

ABSTRACT

Many popular macroeconomics textbooks have recently adopted the dynamic aggregate demand-aggregate supply framework to analyze business cycle fluctuations and the effects of monetary policy. This brings the textbook treatment much closer to the research frontier, although a major remaining difference is the treatment of inflation expectations. Textbook treatments typically assume adaptive expectations for tractability. In this paper, we extend the model presented in Mankiw [1] by incorporating a more flexible form of expectation formation that is determined as a weighted average of past inflation and the inflation target. This brings the treatment closer to rational expectations and allows for a discussion of costless disinflation. Monetary policy is assumed to follow a Taylor rule, but we allow for deviations from the rule to motivate a discussion regarding optimal monetary policy response to demand shocks. We also include a shock to the risk-premium on the interest rate relevant for demand relative to the policy rate set by the Central Bank, and impose the zero-bound on the nominal interest rate in the solution of the model. These features allow for the analysis of the recent financial crisis, monetary policy falling into a liquidity trap, and the desirability of a temporary increase in the inflation target. Finally, we make available an Excel sheet with which students can analyze the effect of shocks to the economy using impulse responses and dynamic aggregate demand-aggregate supply diagrams.

Keywords: Dynamic AD-AS; Inflation Expectations; Optimal Monetary Policy; Liquidity Trap

1. Introduction

For many decades, the teaching of business cycles has been dominated by the investment savings—liquidity money (IS-LM) model whereby monetary policy is summarized using an exogenous level of the money supply (Hicks [2])[1]. Although this model has served well in many respects, it has often created confusion among students regarding the distinction between deflation and disinflation because of its emphasis on the price level rather than the inflation rate. It has also become less relevant as monetary policy is now typically communicated in terms of a short-term interest rate and, in some cases, a medium-run inflation target.

To overcome these drawbacks, many popular textbooks for undergraduate macroeconomics have recently adopted the dynamic aggregate demand-aggregate supply (DAD-DAS) framework to analyze business cycle fluctuations and the effects of monetary policy (c.f. Jones [4]; Mankiw [1]; Mishkin [5]). The change in the treatment of business cycles found in textbooks has paralleled a burgeoning pedagogical literature that presents alternatives to the traditional Keynesian IS-LM/AD-AS framework that are suitable for undergraduates (Bofinger, Mayer, Wollmershäuser [6]; Carlin and Soskice [7]; Kapinos [8]; Romer [9]; Weerapana [10]; Weisse [11]). These developments have brought the undergraduate treatment of business cycle fluctuations much closer to the research frontier where monetary policy is modeled as an interest rate rule and the analysis is undertaken in

---

[*]The views expressed in this paper are solely those of the authors. No responsibility for them should be attributed to the Bank of Canada.
[#]Corresponding author.
[1]Although early expositions of the IS-LM model were static, later versions have discussed dynamic adjustment of the economy to a long-run equilibrium identified with a full-employment level of output. This long-run adjustment is achieved through adjustment in the price level. This also renders the model consistent with long-run neutrality of money as prices increase proportional to the increase in the money supply in the long-run (Abel, Bernanke and Croushore [3]).

the inflation rate-output gap space. At the research frontier, New Keynesian dynamic stochastic general equilibrium (DSGE) models have become the workhorse of business cycle analysis and monetary economics (c.f. Smets and Wouters [12]). In their simplest form, these models can be summarized by three equations: an IS curve relating the output gap to the real interest rate, a Taylor rule summarizing how the nominal interest rate is determined by the Central Bank as a reaction to the prevailing inflation rate and output gap, and finally a Phillips curve expression which relates current inflation to expected inflation and the output gap (c.f. Gali [13]; Clarida, Gali and Gertler [14]). The first two can be combined to obtain an aggregate demand expression in the inflation-output gap space, and the Phillips curve provides the corresponding aggregate supply curve (Kulish and Jones [15]). Although modern variants of these DSGE models feature many layers of complexity, their skeleton is still comprised of these three familiar equations[2].

To achieve the leap from the three-equation DSGE model to simpler models suitable for undergraduates found in textbooks and the recent pedagogical literature, several simplifications are used. Most importantly, inflationary expectations are typically assumed to be determined with adaptive expectations (Jones [4]; Mankiw [1]; Carlin and Soskice [7]; Kapinos [8]; Weisse [11]). This has important implications in terms of generating high inflation persistence with temporary shocks and imposing high output costs to disinflationary programs. Also, in this framework, a positive temporary demand shock leads initially to a positive output gap and a rise in inflation, but then several periods of negative output gaps as the adverse effects of higher inflation on the aggregate supply curve continue to reverberate after the positive impact of demand has subsided. Imposing rational expectations would overcome these issues, but would substantially complicate the analysis and is typically ignored.

In this paper, we extend the DAD-DAS model of Mankiw [1] to include a more flexible form of inflation expectations. In particular, we allow inflation expectations to be determined as a weighted average of past inflation and the inflation target. This brings the treatment closer to rational expectations whereby disinflation can be costless if the decrease in the inflation target is credible. This framework also allows us to consider alternative forms of expectations formation simply by changing the weight, with purely adaptive and near-rational (or

well-anchored) expectations as the limiting cases.

The paper makes several other contributions to the pedagogical literature on dynamic AD-AS models. First, we include a shock to the risk-premium on the interest rate relevant for demand relative to the policy rate set by the Central Bank. The inclusion of risk shocks is becoming standard in medium-scale DSGE models and allows for a discussion of the recent financial crisis (c.f. Bernanke, Gertler, Gilchrist [18]; Gilchrist, Ortiz, Zakrajsek [19]; Alpanda [20]).

Second, we allow for more flexibility in the way monetary policy is conducted by allowing for deviations from the Taylor rule. Our specification allows for monetary policy to fully offset demand shocks as prescribed by optimal policy (Clarida, Gali and Gertler [14]). It also allows for partial offsetting of demand shocks in the short-run and full offsetting in the long-run, which arguably provides for a more realistic description of actual monetary policy. This partial adjustment in the short-run may capture the unwillingness of the Central Bank to change interest rates too quickly. It could also capture the learning process on the part of the Central Bank regarding the extent of the demand shock. The full-offsetting in the long-run also provides a realistic model of the Central Bank's response to permanent demand shocks that reinforces the pedagogical point that competent Central Banks can achieve their objectives in the long-run.

Third, we impose a constraint that the nominal interest rate cannot become negative (*i.e.* the zero-bound on the nominal interest rate). When faced with a large increase in the risk-premium (or a large decline in demand), the Central Bank becomes unable to fully offset this shock due to the zero-bound. We illustrate this *liquidity trap* situation, faced by the Federal Reserve during the recent financial crisis, using simulations from our model[3]. We also show how the adverse developments during a liquidity trap (such as negative output gap and possible deflation) can be partially counteracted by the Central Bank by credibly raising the inflation target only *temporarily*. The temporary increase in the inflation target raises expected inflation and reduces the real interest rate even when the nominal interest rate is stuck at the zero-bound. This reduces the adverse impact of the risk shock on the real interest rate relevant for demand. Note however that the desirability of temporary changes in the inflation target is a point of contention in Central Banks because it could erode the hard-earned credibility of the monetary authority vis-à-vis the long-run inflation target, an issue ignored in our set-up here.

Finally, we make available an Excel sheet with which students can generate impulse response functions of the

---

[2]DSGE models were initiated by the seminal work of Kydland and Prescott [16], which explored the role of productivity shocks in generating business cycles. Since then, these models have been expanded to include multiple shocks and various nominal and real rigidities, and have become commonplace tools in analyzing different sources of economic fluctuations, the impact of fiscal and monetary policy on macroeconomic variables, and in forecasting. See Tovar [17] for a recent discussion of these models and their use in central banks around the world.

[3]Weerapana [10], Bofinger and Debes [21], and Kapinos [22] also present pedagogical treatments of the liquidity trap, although they do not present the impulse responses.

variables in the model to unexpected shocks and also trace the effects of these developments on a DAD-DAS diagram in the inflation rate-output gap space. We also provide a similar analysis in the unemployment rate-inflation rate space using a Phillips curve diagram. Importantly, our Excel sheet allows for simulating the effects of different shocks simultaneously. This enables us to study, among other possibilities, the effects of adverse risk shocks and concurrent changes in the inflation target in order to avoid the liquidity trap[4].

The rest of the paper is organized as follows: Section 2 introduces the model. Section 3 discusses the accompanying Excel sheet and explores the main implications of the model. Section 4 concludes.

2. The DAD-DAS Model

The model is based on the DAD-DAS model in Mankiw [1], although with several important modifications. First, we allow a more flexible form of inflation expectations that depends not only on past inflation, but also on the inflation target. Second, on top of demand and cost-push shocks explored in Mankiw [1], we include a shock to the risk-premium which drives a wedge between the policy rate and the interest rate relevant for demand. Third, we allow monetary policy to deviate from the Taylor rule when the economy is hit with demand-type shocks. Fourth, we impose the zero-bound on the nominal interest rate. Finally, we model the persistence of shocks explicitly and consider the effects of permanent as well as temporary shocks to demand.

The demand side of the model is summarized with an IS equation that reads:

$$Y_t^{gap} = -\alpha \left(r_t - \rho \right) + \varepsilon_t^{demand}, \qquad (1)$$

where Y_t^{gap} is the output gap defined as the percent-difference between actual output and the natural rate of output. ρ is the *natural* real interest rate capturing the real interest rate in the long-run of the model (which would equal the marginal product of capital minus the depreciation rate in the Solow growth model). This long-run real interest rate is set equal to 2% following Mankiw [1][5]. α is an elasticity parameter capturing the sensitiv-

ity of the output gap to changes in the real interest rate, and is set equal to 1 in the benchmark calibration as in Mankiw [1]. When the prevailing ex-ante real interest rate exceeds the long-run natural rate (*i.e.* when the interest rate gap, $r_t - \rho$, is positive), consumption and investment demand are constrained, which results in a negative output gap all else equal. ε_t^{demand} is a demand shock where a positive value would generate a higher output gap for the same real interest rate. This captures variation in consumption, investment or government expenditure demand that is not related to the interest rate gap.

The real interest rate that is relevant for the IS relationship above is defined as the difference of the nominal interest rate and expected inflation, plus a risk-premium shock, ε_t^{risk}, which changes exogenously over time and reflects the wedge between the policy rate set by the central bank and the cost-of-capital and borrowing costs incurred by final demanders[6]:

$$r_t = i_t - E_t \pi_{t+1} + \varepsilon_t^{risk}. \qquad (2)$$

As shown later, risk shocks affect the economy analogously to demand shocks and move inflation and output gap in the same direction.

The short-run aggregate supply is summarized by a New-Keynesian Phillips curve given by:

$$\pi_t = E_{t-1} \pi_t + \phi \cdot Y_t^{gap} + \varepsilon_t^{cost}, \qquad (3)$$

where current inflation is partly determined by past expectations regarding current inflation (because of predetermined prices)[7]. The output gap also affects current inflation as higher output results in an increase in the marginal cost of production. ϕ is an elasticity parameter capturing the sensitivity of inflation to changes in the output gap and is set equal to 0.25 in the benchmark calibration following Mankiw [1]. ε_t^{cost} is a cost-push shock that captures changes in current inflation due to unexpected changes in costs (such as changes in oil prices).

Expectations regarding future inflation are assumed to

---

[4]The Excel workbook accompanying this paper can be downloaded from our websites. Kapinos [8] also provides an accompanying Excel workbook. Our spreadsheet differs in that it allows for the analyses of risk shocks, the simultaneous effects of different shocks, or alternative forms of inflation expectations formation beyond adaptive expectations.

[5]The natural real interest rate is also known as the *Wicksellian* interest rate, and is the real interest rate that would prevail in the absence of nominal rigidities. Shocks that have an impact on the economy regardless of the presence of nominal rigidities (e.g. fiscal policy, productivity shocks etc.) would also alter the natural real interest rate (Woodford [23]) even in the short-run. We abstract from time-variation in the natural interest rate for simplicity, and focus on the *long-run* natural interest rate, which is a constant when the economy is hit only with temporary shocks.

[6]The assumption here that the risk-premium is equal to 0 at the steady-state is without loss of generality.

[7]The expectations term on the right-hand-side of the Phillips curve, which is *past expectations of current inflation*, follows Mankiw [1]. An alternative is to consider *current expectations of future inflation* (multiplied by a discount factor) instead. The latter can be motivated by the price-setting assumption in Calvo [24], where each period a fraction of randomly-selected firms are forced to keep their price the same as in the previous period. A similar expectations term also show up in models using the price-setting environment in Taylor [25] or Rotemberg [26]. For our purposes here, the distinction between these price-setting assumptions is not of major importance as long as the expected inflation term is determined as a combination of past inflation and target inflation One way to motivate past inflation impacting current inflation in these other set-ups mentioned above (even in the presence of rational expectations) is to assume that there is partial inflation-indexation in price-setting (Smets and Wouters [12]).

be based on a mixture of current inflation (capturing adaptive expectations) and the future inflation target of the Central Bank (capturing rational expectations—assuming the target is credible)[8]:

$$E_t \pi_{t+1} = \gamma \cdot \pi_t + (1 - \gamma) \cdot \pi_{t+1}^{\text{target}}, \qquad (4)$$

where γ is a parameter that determines the weight on current inflation in generating expectations about the future. If $\gamma = 1$, then expectations are fully adaptive. If on the other hand $\gamma = 0$, then the expectations are (close to) rational and are based on the inflation target set by the Central Bank.

Monetary policy is summarized by a Taylor rule on the nominal interest rate except when the Taylor rule implies a negative rate in which case the rate is set to 0; hence,

$$i_t = \max \left\{ 0, \rho + E_t \pi_{t+1} + \theta_\pi \cdot \left(\pi_t - \pi_t^{\text{target}} \right) \right.$$
$$\left. + \theta_y \cdot Y_t^{\text{gap}} + \Delta_t^{\text{monet}} \right\} \qquad (5)$$

θ_π and θ_y are response coefficients of the Central Bank to deviations of inflation from its target and the output gap respectively. We set both θ_π and θ_y equal to 0.5 following Taylor [28] and Mankiw [1]. Note that, coupled with the expected inflation term on the right-hand-side, the interest rate rule satisfies the *Taylor principle* that states that the nominal interest rate should be raised more than the increase in expected inflation. This results in an increase in the ex-ante real interest rate and curbs demand when inflation starts to rise. The inflation target is assumed to be initially set at 2% as in Mankiw [1].

Δ_t^{monet} is a term that captures deviations of monetary policy from the Taylor rule[9]. Note that *optimal* monetary policy under full-information would recommend fully offsetting demand-type shocks since they move inflation and output gap in the same direction, and therefore, do not entail a tradeoff between inflation volatility and output gap volatility for the Central Bank. This requires monetary policy to be more active than a Taylor rule in order to shift the DAD curve back (as explained later, strictly following the Taylor rule would only provide a movement along the DAD curve which cannot fully offset a demand-type shock). We therefore model this deviation term as follows:

$$\Delta_t^{\text{monet}} = (1 - \delta) \Delta_{t-1}^{\text{monet}} + \delta \left(\frac{1}{\alpha} \varepsilon_t^{\text{demand}} - \varepsilon_t^{\text{risk}} \right), \qquad (6)$$

where $\delta \in [0,1]$ is a parameter that captures the extent to which the Central Bank offsets demand-type shocks (*i.e.* demand and risk shocks). Setting $\delta = 0$ recovers the benchmark case where the Central Bank strictly follows the Taylor rule (given past deviations are zero). With $\delta = 1$, monetary policy fully offsets demand shocks as prescribed by optimal policy (Clarida, Gali and Gertler [14])[10]. By considering δ to be between 0 and 1, we also allow for partial offsetting of demand shocks in the short-run. Given our lagged deviation term on the right hand side of (6) however, the Central Bank fully offsets demand shocks in the long-run; this arguably provides for a more realistic description of actual monetary policy. This partial adjustment in the short-run may capture the unwillingness of the Central Bank to change interest rates too quickly. It could also capture the learning process on the part of the Central Bank regarding the extent of the demand shocks.

Finally, *Okun's Law* summarizes the relationship between the unemployment rate and the output gap as:

$$u_t - u^n = -\beta Y_t^{\text{gap}}, \qquad (7)$$

where the natural unemployment rate, u^n, is set at 5% and the unemployment rate rises by $\beta = 0.5$ percentage points for every percentage point decline in the output gap. Note that the Okun's Law expression is not central to the determination of equilibrium of the model; it is merely added here as a side equation that can help translate output gap numbers into, perhaps more intuitive, unemployment rates.

2.1. Persistence of Shocks

We assume that risk and cost-push shocks have only temporary effects on the economy. We nevertheless allow these shocks to possibly persist into the future by modeling them as stationary AR(1) processes:

$$\varepsilon_t^i = \omega_i \varepsilon_{t-1}^i + \eta_t^i \qquad (8)$$

where $0 \leq \omega_i < 1$ is the persistence parameter, and η_t^i is the innovation to the shock process for each $i \in \{\text{risk}, \text{cost}\}$.

For demand shocks, we consider the effects of both temporary $\left(0 \leq \omega_t^{\text{demand}} < 1 \right)$ and also permanent shocks (*i.e.* $\omega_t^{\text{demand}} = 1$), the latter capturing permanent changes in private savings behavior or permanent changes in fiscal policy. For the inflation target, we assume that any change announced by the Central Bank is permanent in

---

[8]Note that this expectation equation is not strictly model-consistent, therefore not fully "rational". For example, with $\gamma = 0$, agents always expect next period's inflation rate to be at the target. In the presence of persistent shocks, rational agents would take into account that inflation may stay above the target level for a while. See Blanchard and Kahn [27] for imposing rational expectations to the solution of these models. As noted before, lagged inflation can still impact current inflation in the presence of rational expectations if there is inflation-indexation in price-setting.

[9]Alternatively, these deviations can be viewed as part of the Taylor rule when one acknowledges that the natural real interest rate is not a constant as modeled here, but is time-varying with demand-type shocks.

[10]Note that $1/\alpha$ in front of the demand shock is to change the units of the demand shock from units of the output gap to units of the interest rate. In the benchmark calibration, α is set equal to 1 and hence the deviation from Taylor rule is of the same magnitude as the shocks.

the benchmark case (by setting the number of periods that inflation target, cell C23 in the Excel workbook, to a number equal to or greater than 51). We also allow the change in the inflation target to be temporary, by setting the number of periods that the inflation target is in effect to a number less than or equal to 50.

2.2. Solution of the Model

In this subsection, we first solve the model under the assumption that the zero-bound on the nominal interest rate does not bind. In particular, we derive the dynamic aggregate demand (DAD) and the dynamic aggregate supply (DAS) expressions that characterize equilibrium. We then discuss how the equilibrium is amended to allow for the zero-bound to occasionally bind.

To derive DAD, we first combine Equations (2) and (5) to solve for the interest rate gap:

$$r_t - \rho = \theta_\pi \cdot \left(\pi_t - \pi_t^{\text{target}} \right) + \theta_y \cdot Y_t^{\text{gap}} + \Delta_t^{\text{monet}} + \varepsilon_t^{\text{risk}}. \quad (9)$$

We then plug the above expression into the IS equation in (1) to get:

$$Y_t^{\text{gap}} = -\alpha \left[\theta_\pi \cdot \left(\pi_t - \pi_t^{\text{target}} \right) + \theta_y \cdot Y_t^{\text{gap}} + \Delta_t^{\text{monet}} + \varepsilon_t^{\text{risk}} \right] + \varepsilon_t^{\text{demand}} \quad (10)$$

We then rearrange terms and solve for the output gap in terms of current inflation and various shocks. This yields the DAD expression:

$$Y_t^{\text{gap}} = -\frac{\alpha \theta_\pi}{1 + \alpha \theta_y} \left(\pi_t - \pi_t^{\text{target}} \right) - \frac{\alpha}{1 + \alpha \theta_y} \left[\Delta_t^{\text{monet}} + \varepsilon_t^{\text{risk}} \right] + \frac{1}{1 + \alpha \theta_y} \varepsilon_t^{\text{demand}}, \quad (11)$$

which summarizes an inverse relationship between inflation and the output gap. In particular, an increase in inflation prompts the Central Bank to increase the nominal *and* the real interest rate and cause a reduction in demand. Note that the interest rate is not constant along a DAD curve in this setup. The Central Bank's reaction to inflation developments according to the Taylor rule results in movements along the DAD curve. Changes in demand and risk shocks (or a deviation from the Taylor rule), result in a parallel shift of the DAD curve.

The slope of the DAD curve is partially determined by the Central Bank's response coefficients to inflation and output gap in the Taylor rule. A higher θ_π, the response coefficient to inflation, or a lower θ_y, the response coefficient on output gap, is associated with a flatter DAD curve (with inflation drawn on the y-axis) as the Central Bank becomes less tolerant of inflation variation and more tolerant of output gap variation. Note that if the Taylor principle is violated, e.g. if $\theta_\pi < 0$, then the DAD curve becomes upward-sloping.

To derive DAS, first note that the inflation expectations equation (4) implies

$$E_{t-1} \pi_t = \gamma \cdot \pi_{t-1} + \left(1 - \gamma \right) \cdot \pi_t^{\text{target}}.$$

We plug this into the Phillips curve expression (3) to get the (short-run) DAS expression:

$$\pi_t = \gamma \cdot \pi_{t-1} + \left(1 - \gamma \right) \cdot \pi_t^{\text{target}} + \phi \cdot Y_t^{\text{gap}} + \varepsilon_t^{\text{cost}}, \quad (12)$$

which summarizes a positive relationship between inflation and the output gap. Achieving a higher level of production in the short-run comes at the cost of increased marginal costs which feed into current inflation. This is captured through a movement along the DAS curve. Inflation expectations play a crucial role as well since prices are predetermined and are assumed to be "sticky" for a period. Changes in inflation expectations and the cost-push shock result in a shift of the DAS curve.

Note that the shocks and the inflation target are exogenously determined; therefore, the DAD and DAS equations have only two unknowns: the output gap and the inflation rate. We can solve for the equilibrium values of output gap and inflation as the intersection of the DAD and DAS curves, and then derive the nominal interest rate from the Taylor rule and the real interest rate from Equations (2) and (4). This constitutes the equilibrium when the zero-bound on the nominal interest rate does not bind.

General Solution of the Model When the Zero-Bound can Occasionally Bind

To find the general solution when the zero-bound can occasionally bind, we derive equilibrium in an analogous, but perhaps less intuitive fashion. We first set the nominal interest rate to 0 or the equilibrium value found in the previous subsection under the Taylor rule assumption, whichever one is higher. We then use Equations (1)-(4) to solve for the real interest rate, r_t, in terms of the nominal interest rate, past inflation, and the exogenous variables in the model as:

$$r_t = \frac{1}{\left(1 - \gamma \phi \alpha \right)} \left[i_t - \gamma^2 \pi_{t-1} - \gamma \left(1 - \gamma \right) \pi_t^{\text{target}} - \gamma \phi \left(\alpha \rho + \varepsilon_t^{\text{demand}} \right) - \gamma \varepsilon_t^{\text{cost}} - \left(1 - \gamma \right) \pi_{t+1}^{\text{target}} + \varepsilon_t^{\text{risk}} \right] \quad (13)$$

Equation (1) then yields the equilibrium value of output gap and Equations (3) and (4) yield the inflation rate.

When the zero-bound does not bind, the equilibrium obtained here using Equation (13) is equivalent to the equilibrium obtained in the previous subsection under the Taylor rule. The equilibrium values for the endogenous variables would differ though when the zero interest rate binds. Since past inflation is a *state* variable in the system (*i.e.* a variable that can affect current values), it is important to always take these past inflation figures from the equilibrium obtained from the general solution—even when calculating the equilibrium under the Taylor rule assumption—during the simulation process in Excel.

3. The Excel Sheet and Main Results

In this section, we explain how the accompanying Excel workbook can be used to simulate the DAD-DAS model presented in Section 2. We provide examples as well as a discussion of issues that relate to inflation expectations and duration of shocks.

3.1. Using the Excel Sheet

The Excel workbook in the worksheet called "Model" contains cells (in column C) for the model's structural parameters, $\alpha, \phi, \rho, u^n, \beta$, the monetary policy parameters $\theta_\pi, \theta_y, \pi_{initial}^{target}$ (the last one sets the initial inflation target before any possible changes are made), the shock persistence parameters, ω_i, the share of past inflation in the inflation expectation expression, γ, the share of demand shocks offset by the Central Bank in the short-run, δ, and the number of periods that a change in the inflation target is in effect. All of these parameters can be altered and are highlighted in yellow on the worksheet. The effect of shocks and the inflation target can be analyzed by changing the values of the exogenous variables at time 0 in cells G7:J7, which are also highlighted in yellow.

The structural and policy parameters are set to the same benchmark values as in Mankiw [1].

The model is assumed to be at the steady-state prior to period 0. Period 0 is the impact period when there is an unexpected change in the inflation target or a demand, cost-push, or risk shock hits the economy. The workbook then calculates the future equilibrium values of the endogenous variables, which are also plotted in the worksheets called "Impulse response chart", "DAD-DAS chart", and "Phillips curve chart". The impulse response charts trace the effects of the shock(s) on output gap, inflation and the interest rates over time following the impact period. The DAD-DAS chart captures this dynamic behavior in the output gap-inflation rate space. It plots the initial position of the DAD and DAS curves at the steady-state prior to any shocks and replots these curves with appropriate shifts at the impact period of the shocks. Following these shifts, the diagrams trace out the equilibrium path of output gap and the inflation rate over time using arrows. The Phillips curve chart provides a similar analysis in the unemployment rate-inflation rate space.

3.2. The Effects of Temporary Cost-Push Shocks

In **Figures 1** and **2**, we present the impulse response and the DAD-DAS charts resulting from a 1 percentage point positive cost-push shock with zero persistence (*i.e.*

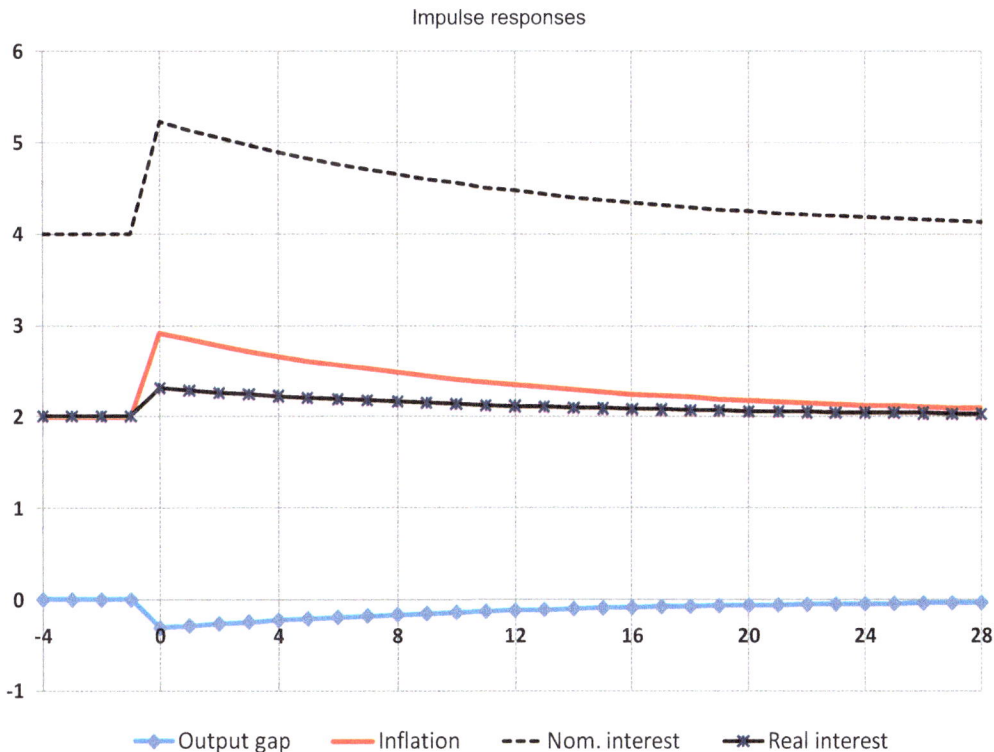

Figure 1. Impulse responses to a +1% cost-push shock with 0 persistence under fully adaptive expectations.

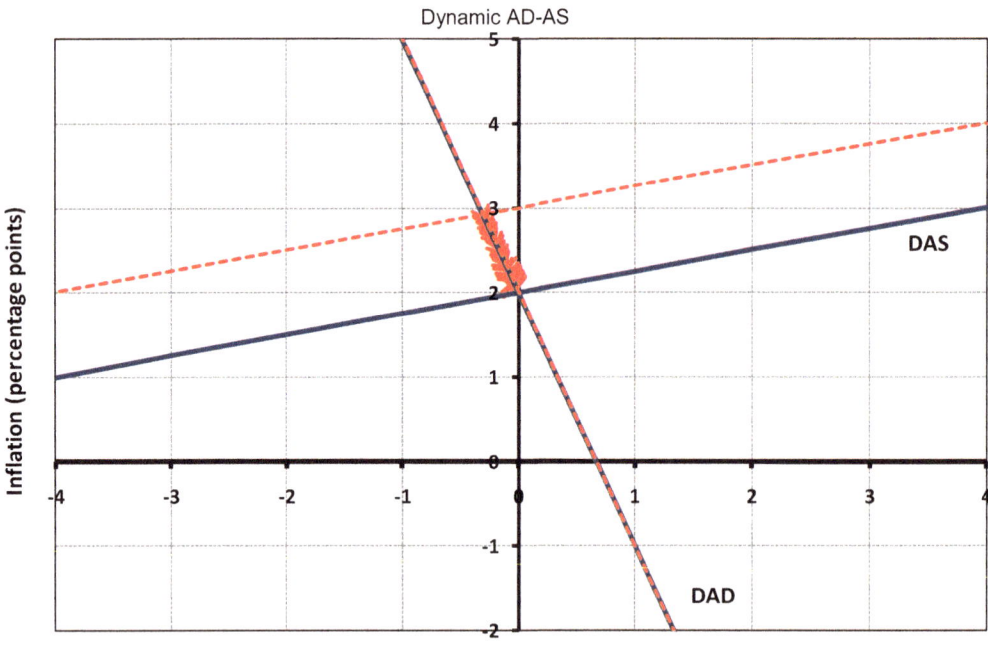

Figure 2. DAD-DAS diagram for a +1% cost-push shock with 0 persistence under fully adaptive expectations.

$\omega_{\text{demand}} = 0$) under fully adaptive inflation expectations (*i.e.* $\gamma = 1$)[11]. The shock can be simulated by changing the value of cell G7 from 0 to 1. The AS curve shifts up by 1 percentage point which leads to an immediate increase in inflation. This prompts the Central Bank to raise the nominal interest rate by more than 1 percentage point, which raises the real interest rate and causes a decline in the output gap. The resulting negative output gap ensures that the increase in inflation in equilibrium at the impact period is less than 1%. Even though the cost-push shock has no persistence, adaptive expectations ensure that inflation remains above target for a prolonged period of time. Over time, inflation slowly declines back to the target (due to the negative output gap), while the output gap increases back to 0 as the initial interest rates are restored.

Note that the adjustment process is much faster, even immediate, when inflation expectations are not adaptive, but fully based on the inflation target. If we set $\gamma = 0$, then the shock's effect lasts only for one period, and the economy reverts back to the steady-state immediately after the impact period. When inflation expectations are formed in part in adaptive fashion and in part based on the target (e.g. $\gamma = 0.5$), then the adjustment process is faster than the case with fully-adaptive expectations, but not immediate.

As argued above, adaptive expectations can result in inflation persistence even when the inflation shock is very temporary[12]. Alternatively, if the cost-push shock is persistent, it will lead to a prolonged period of high inflation and negative output gaps even when inflation expectations are fully based on the inflation target and are not adaptive at all. For example, the impulse responses for output gap and inflation are similar when $\gamma = 1$ and $\omega_{\text{cost}} = 0$ versus when $\gamma = 0$ and $\omega_{\text{cost}} = 0.75$.

3.3. The Effects of Temporary Demand (and Risk) Shocks

In this section, we analyze the effects of temporary demand shocks on the economy under two separate assumptions regarding monetary policy. In the first, we assume that the Central Bank follows the Taylor rule and does not deviate from it as in Mankiw [1]. In the second, we allow the Central Bank to partially or fully offset the demand shocks as implied by optimal policy. Our analysis here also extends to risk shocks which are analogous to demand shocks as implied by the DAD expression in (1.10).

3.3.1. Case I: Central Bank Does Not Deviate from the Taylor Rule

In **Figures 3** and **4**, we present the impulse response and the DAD-DAS charts resulting from a 5 percentage point

---

[11]The specification in (1.6) already assumes that the Central Bank does not deviate from the Taylor rule when hit with cost-push shocks. If the loss function of the Central Bank solely depends on inflation and output gap volatility, there exist Taylor rule coefficients which are consistent with the optimal policy response to a cost-push shock, since the Taylor rule balances the inflation and output gap concerns of the Central Bank.

[12]In the DSGE literature with rational expectations, a similar result can be obtained by assuming that there is inflation indexation in price and wage-setting.

Extending the Textbook Dynamic AD-AS Framework with Flexible Inflation Expectations, Optimal Policy Response
to Demand Changes, and the Zero-Bound on the Nominal Interest Rate

143

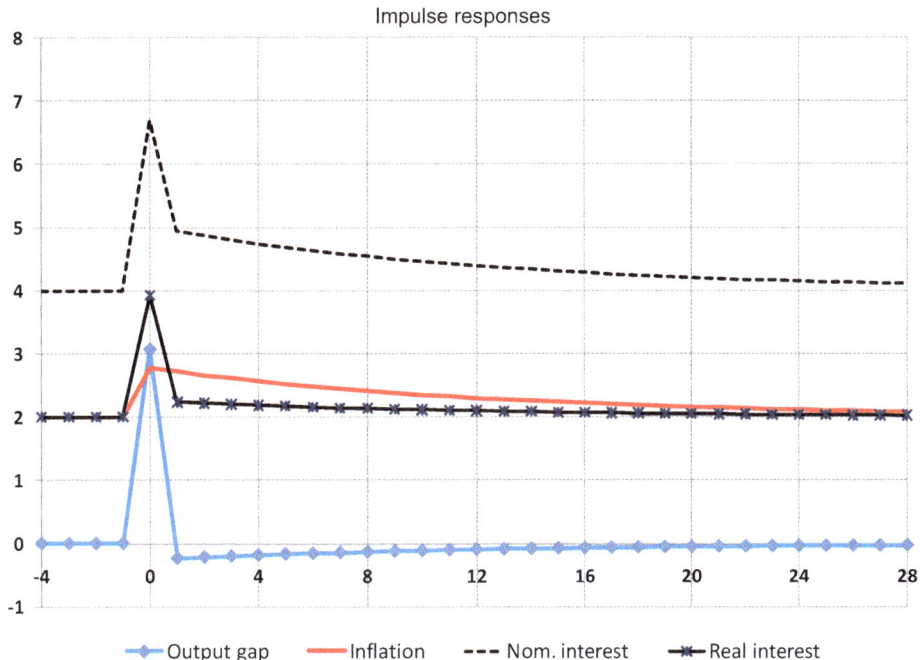

Figure 3. Impulse responses to a +5% demand shock with 0 persistence under fully adaptive expectations and no deviations from the Taylor rule.

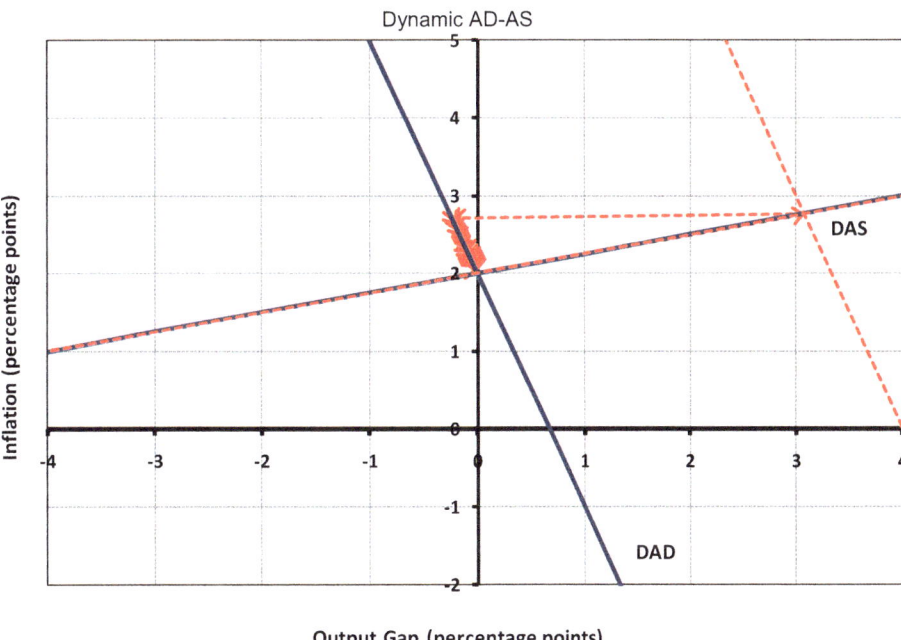

Figure 4. DAD-DAS diagram for a +5% demand shock with 0 persistence under fully adaptive expectations and no deviations from the Taylor rule.

positive demand shock with zero persistence (*i.e.* $\omega_{\text{demand}} = 0$) under fully adaptive inflation expectations (*i.e.* $\gamma = 1$) and the Central Bank not deviating from the Taylor rule (*i.e.* $\delta = 0$). The shock can be simulated by changing the value of cell H7 from 0 to 5. The AD curve shifts to the right by 5 percentage points which leads to an increase in both the output gap and the inflation rate at the impact period. In equilibrium, the output gap increases less than the initial 5% shift. This is because the Central Bank raises the nominal interest rates above and beyond the increase in expected inflation which leads to an increase in the real interest rate and curbs aggregate demand. Right after the impact period, the demand shock reverts back to 0 and the DAD curve shifts back to its original position. Note however that in this example inflation expectations are fully adaptive. The increase in inflation in the impact period becomes entrenched and therefore causes an upward shift in the DAS curve. This results in a negative output gap and an inflation rate that is higher than target, similar to a cost-push shock, right after the impact period. Inflation slowly goes down to target and output gap slowly recovers to zero as time elapses, as was the case with the cost-push shock examined before.

When inflation expectations are based solely on the inflation target (*i.e.* $\gamma = 0$), the model does not generate any negative output gap when hit with a temporary positive demand shock. If the demand shock has no persistence, then the model reverts back to the initial steady-state immediately after the impact period. The reason is that the increase in inflation during the impact period does not feed into future inflation and therefore does not cause any effects on the output gap. If the demand shock is persistent, then the economy goes through periods of above-target inflation and positive output gaps until the effects of the shock die down.

Under fully rational expectations (*i.e.* with model-consistent expectations), inflation expectations would increase above target in the short-run if the shock is persistent. Our model cannot simulate fully-rational expectations with persistent shocks. Nevertheless, the impulse responses obtained would be similar if in our set-up we consider a persistent shock (e.g. $\omega_{demand} = 0.8$) with inflation expectations formed as a combination of past in-

flation and target inflation (e.g. $\gamma = 0.5$). **Figures 5** and **6** plot the impulse responses from a +5% demand shock given the above numbers for the persistence and expectations parameters. The impulse responses imply that the economy experiences positive output gap along with above-target inflation for a prolonged period of time. During the transition, the DAS curve shifts as inflation expectations are partially affected from past above-target inflation.

3.3.2. Case II: Central Bank Offsets the Temporary Demand Shock

Demand shocks do not pose a tradeoff for the Central Bank as they move both inflation and output gap in the same direction. If the Central Bank is averse to fluctuations in inflation and output gap, optimal policy would suggest that the Central Bank should fully offset all demand shocks [14]. Note that the Taylor rule utilized by the Central Bank cannot achieve this automatically. As shown in **Figures 3** and **5**, the Taylor rule indeed recommends an increase in the nominal and real interest rates as a result of a positive demand shock. This ensures that the increase in the output gap is less than the 5 percentage point shift considered. Note however this is merely a movement along the new DAD curve and does not shift the DAD curve back.

As the Central Bank becomes aware of the presence of a positive demand shock, it could do more than the Taylor rule (*i.e.* it could increase the interest rates more than the Taylor rule to shift the DAD curve back faster). In

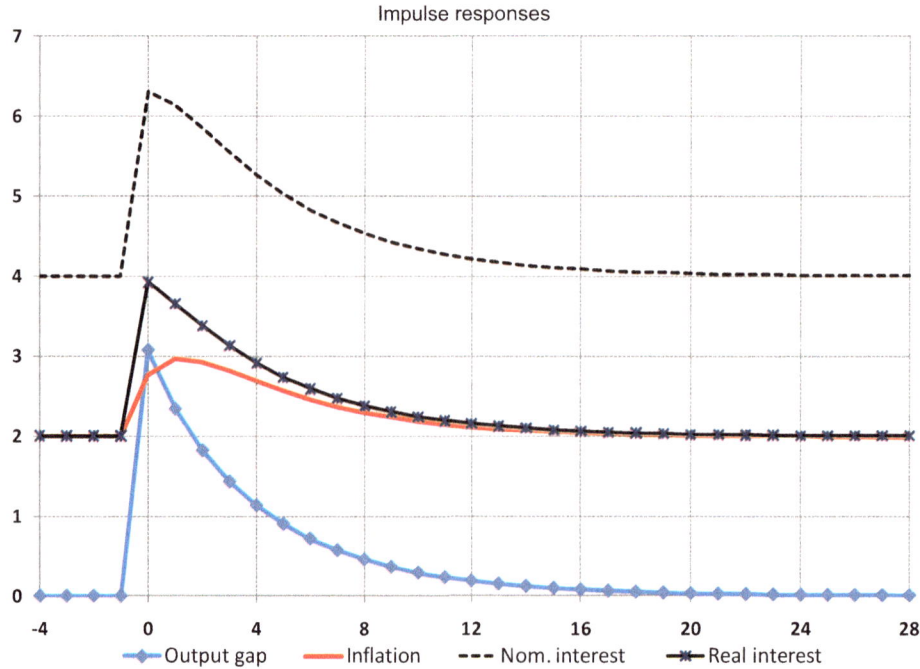

Figure 5. Impulse responses to a +5% demand shock with 0.8 persistence and inflation expectations parameter = 0.5 and no deviations from the Taylor rule.

Extending the Textbook Dynamic AD-AS Framework with Flexible Inflation Expectations, Optimal Policy Response to Demand Changes, and the Zero-Bound on the Nominal Interest Rate

145

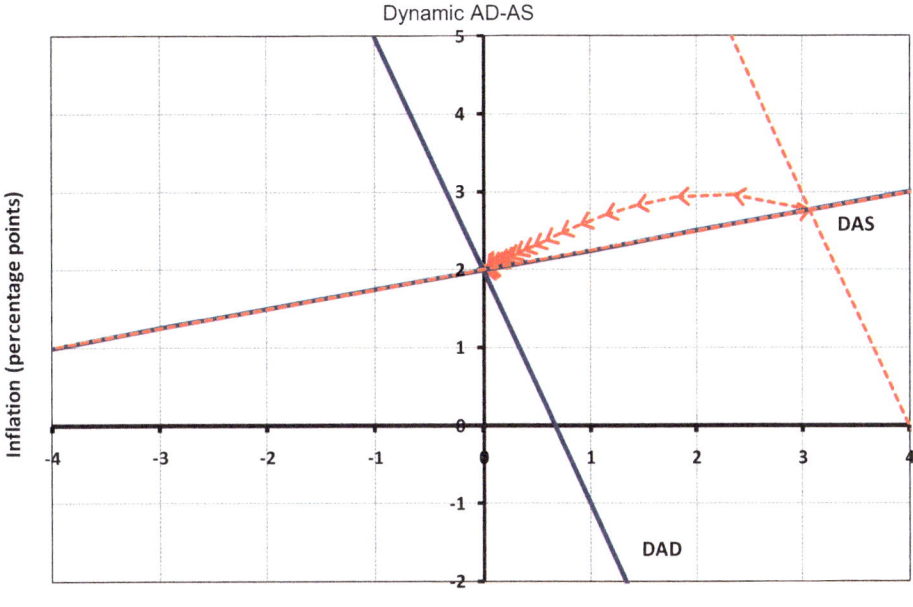

Figure 6. DAD-DAS diagram for a +5% demand shock with 0.8 persistence and inflation expectations parameter = 0.5 and no deviations from the Taylor rule.

our set-up, this could be obtained by setting the parameter relating to the deviation from the Taylor rule, δ, to a value greater than 0. For illustration, we first set this parameter equal to 1 to capture full-offsetting of demand shocks by the Central Bank and consider the same demand shock as before (see **Figure 7**). As shown, both the output gap and inflation stay at their initial steady-state position without any change, but the nominal and real interest rates rise in order to offset the effects of the demand shock[13]. It may be more realistic to assume that the Central Bank would choose to offset demand shocks slowly as it may be unwilling to change interest rates too quickly or may need more time to fully grasp the extent of the demand shock. This gradual offsetting of demand shocks by the Central Bank can be captured by setting δ to a value between 0 and 1.

3.4. The Effects of Permanent Demand Shocks

In this section, we extend our previous analysis to permanent demand shocks. Note however that what we discuss here is also relevant for temporary, but very persistent, demand shocks as well.

In **Figures 8** and **9**, we explore the effects of a 1% permanent increase in demand (which may be as a result of a permanent change in the savings attitudes of households or a permanent change in fiscal policy). Under fully adaptive expectations and the Central Bank strictly following the Taylor rule, the model generates the counterintuitive and incorrect result that the long-run inflation rate is permanently increased as a result of the demand shock. This is despite the fact that there has been no change in the inflation target. The output gap gradually converges to 0 and the real interest rate is permanently increased. The latter is consistent with the Solow growth model's implication that a permanent decline in the overall savings rate would result in a decline in the capital-output ratio and an increase in the real interest rate at the new steady-state and along the transition path. The inconsistency arises from the model's implication regarding long-run inflation.

In our framework, this can be amended by considering a gradual offsetting of the demand shock by the monetary authority (see **Figure 10**). The deviation from the Taylor rule results in a quicker convergence of the output gap to zero and inflation gradually converges back to the target rate of 2%. The real interest rate gradually rises to a permanently higher level as a result of the permanent decline in savings, which also results in a permanent increase in the nominal interest rate.

3.5. Permanent Changes to the Inflation Target and Costless Disinflation

Suppose the Central Bank decides to permanently lower its inflation target to 1%. To simulate this change in the Excel workbook, the value in cell J7 is changed from 2 to

---

[13]If there are only demand shocks, then optimal policy can stabilize both inflation and output gap perfectly with strict inflation-targeting (this is also known as "divine coincidence"). In the presence of supply shocks, optimal policy balances the relative importance that the Central Bank places on these two macroeconomic indicators, which can be achieved via a Taylor rule.

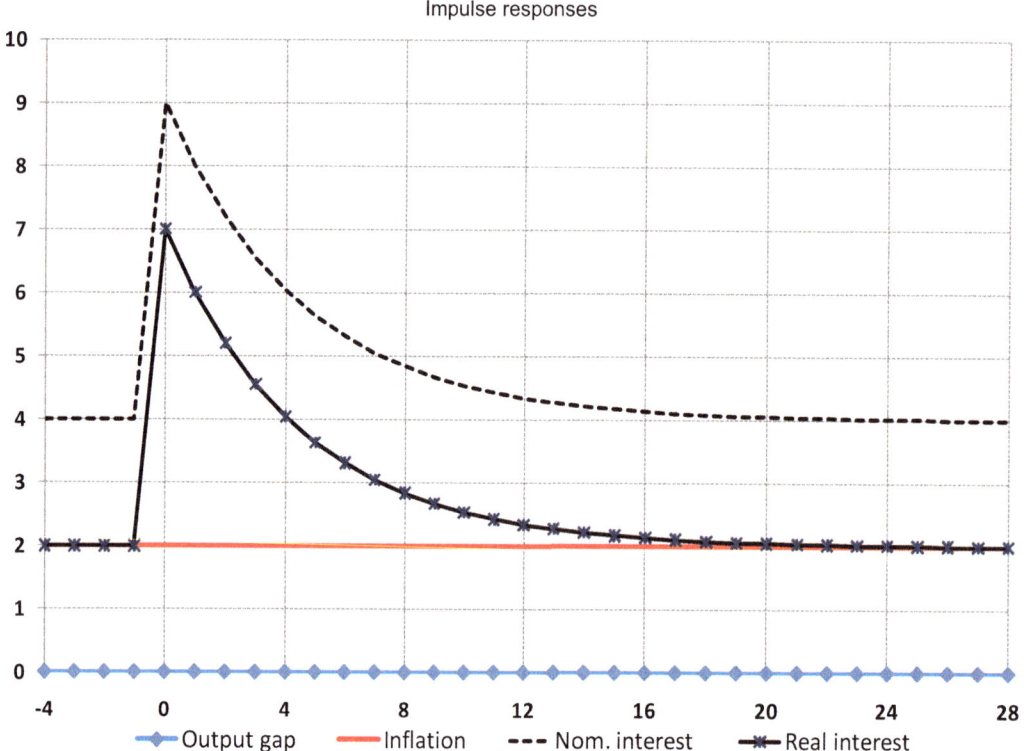

Figure 7. Impulse responses to a +5% demand shock with 0.8 persistence when the Central Bank fully offsets the demand shock (inflation expectations parameter = 0.5).

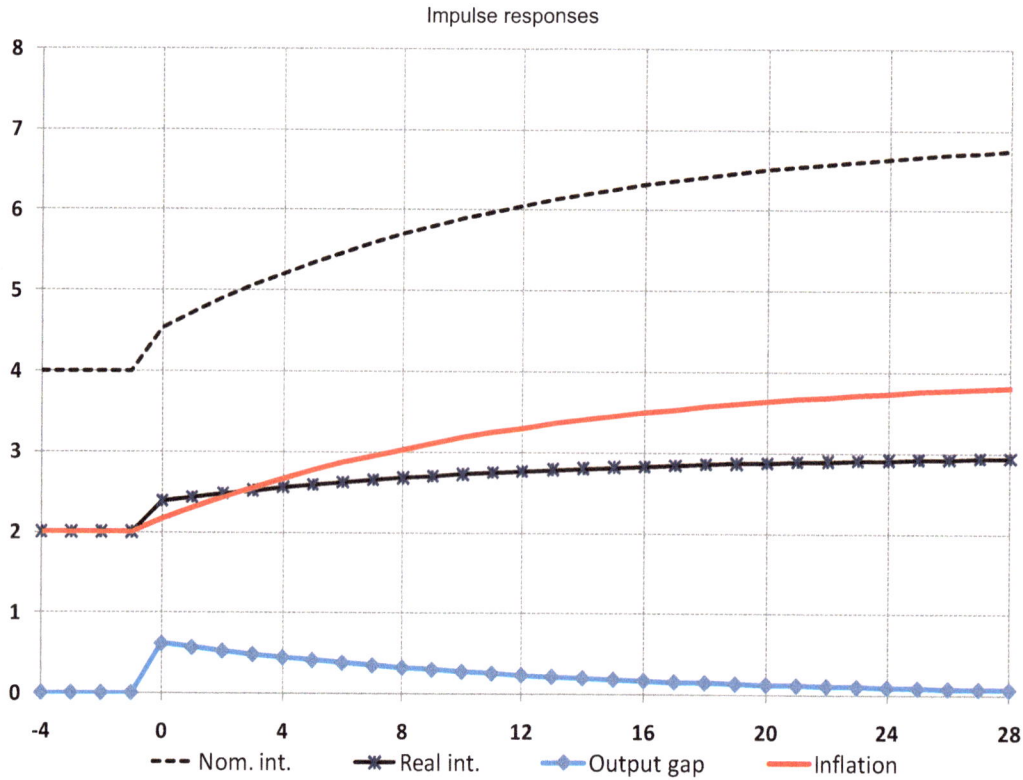

Figure 8. Impulse responses to a +1% permanent demand shock under fully adaptive expectations and no deviations from the Taylor rule.

Extending the Textbook Dynamic AD-AS Framework with Flexible Inflation Expectations, Optimal Policy Response to Demand Changes, and the Zero-Bound on the Nominal Interest Rate

147

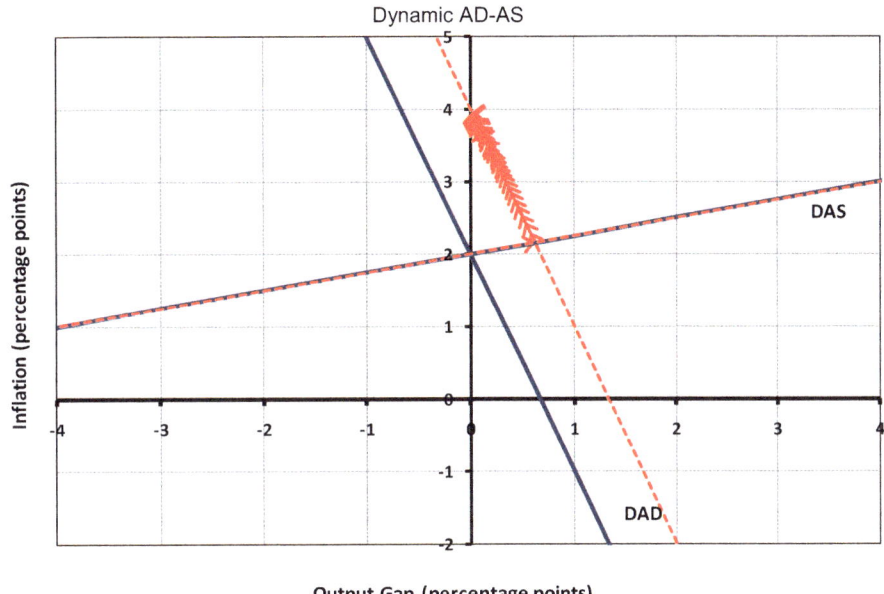

Figure 9. DAD-DAS diagram for a +1% permanent demand shock under fully adaptive expectations and no deviations from the Taylor rule.

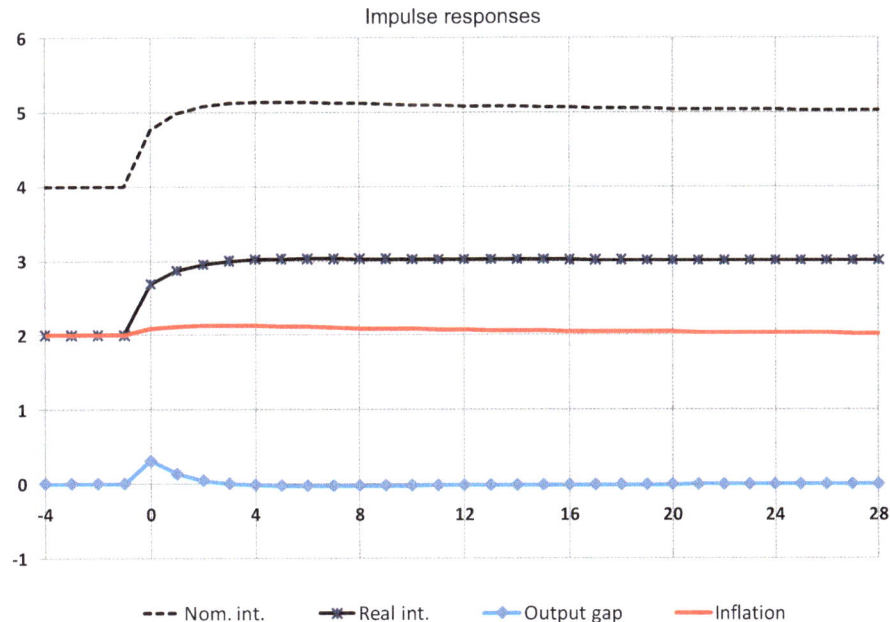

Figure 10. DAD-DAS diagram for a +1% permanent demand shock under fully adaptive expectations and with gradual off-setting of the shock by the Central Bank ($\delta = 0.5$).

1. **Figures 11** and **12** show the resulting impulse responses under the assumption of fully-adaptive inflation expectations (*i.e.* $\gamma = 1$) and expectations that are fully based on the inflation target (*i.e.* $\gamma = 0$), respectively[13].

[13]The *credibility* of the new inflation target is important since if the change in the inflation target is not credible, rational agents will still consider the previous higher inflation rate when forming expectations. In our exposition, we assume that the announced target changes by the Central Bank are credible. The presence of lagged inflation in inflation expectations may also be a proxy for the lack of credibility in the inflation target.

When expectations are adaptive, the change in the inflation target results in a period of negative output gaps along with falling inflation. Since at the time of impact, current inflation (which is close to 2%) is higher than target inflation (equal to 1%), the Central Bank raises the nominal interest rates to reduce demand, which causes the negative output gap. This reduces inflation over time, but the decrease of actual inflation to the target is gradual due to adaptive expectations, and the disinflation process therefore is costly in terms of foregone output. Over time,

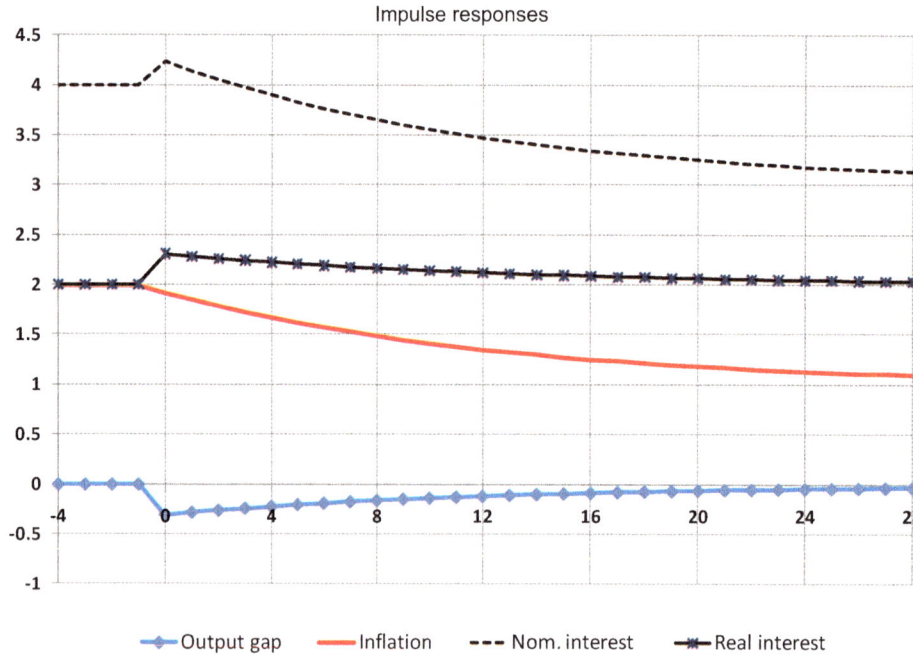

Figure 11. Impulse responses to a permanent decrease in the inflation target from 2% to 1% under fully adaptive expectations.

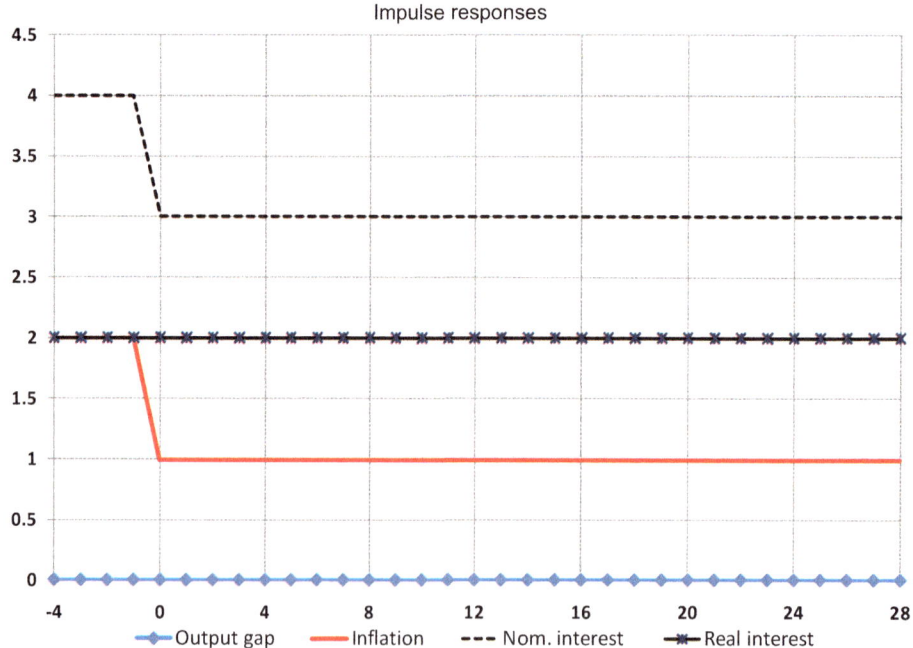

Figure 12. Impulse responses to a permanent decrease in the inflation target from 2% to 1% under inflation expectations fully based on the credible inflation target.

the nominal interest rate declines along with the decline in the inflation rate (*i.e.* the Fisher effect). On the other hand, when expectations are based fully on the (credible) inflation target, the disinflation process is costless in terms of the output gap. Both the inflation rate and the nominal interest rate decline by 1 percentage point immediately as a result of the change in the inflation target, but this does not cause any changes to the real interest

rate or the output gap.

3.6. The Zero-Interest Rate Bound and the Liquidity Trap

As Equation (1.9) indicates, the effects of risk-shocks on inflation and the output gap are analogous to demand shocks. We have included them in our model separately

Extending the Textbook Dynamic AD-AS Framework with Flexible Inflation Expectations, Optimal Policy Response
to Demand Changes, and the Zero-Bound on the Nominal Interest Rate

149

though to point out that the real interest rate implied by Central Bank policy may not reflect the real interest rate relevant for demand. More importantly, there may be times, as in the recent financial crisis, when the increase in risk-premia may result in an increase in the real interest rate relevant for demand despite the decline in the nominal interest rate set by the Central Bank.

In principle, the Central Bank can fully offset the effects of risk shocks with a larger change in the policy rate called for by the Taylor rule. In particular, if the risk shock increases by 7% and shifts the AD curve to the left, immediately lowering the nominal interest rate by 7 percentage points would shift the DAD curve immediately back to its initial position (with no resulting change in the output gap or inflation). A problem arises however if the nominal interest rate cannot be lowered by the full 7 percentage points due to the zero-interest rate bound, a situation known as the "liquidity trap". A full offsetting of the risk shock cannot be achieved in this case and the best that the Central Bank can do is to lower the nominal interest rate to 0. Thus, the economy cannot escape a high real interest rate (including the risk-premium) and a corresponding negative output gap situation even when the Central Bank immediately recognizes and tries to fully offset the risk shock (see **Figure 13**).

During the recent financial crisis, there were discussions regarding *temporarily* increasing the target inflation rate by a few percentage points. This was intended to reduce the downside risks involved with deflation, lower real interest rates even when the nominal interest rate is stuck at 0, and slow down the decline in nominal asset prices. The latter was thought to be crucial in order to

provide relief to homeowners with negative equity in their homes due to the decline in housing prices. In **Figure 14**, we simulate a 4-quarter temporary increase in the inflation target from 2% to 4% on top of the risk shock and the monetary response considered in **Figure 13**. This type of a credible and temporary increase in the target inflation rate dampens the increase in the real interest rate and reduces the severity and the duration of the resulting negative output gap. Note however that such temporary and discretionary changes in the inflation target could erode the hard-earned credibility of Central Banks regarding the long-run inflation target, an issue ignored in our set-up here.

An alternative policy advocated by the Federal Reserve Bank and other Central Banks around the world during a liquidity trap is *Quantitative Easing* (QE). This refers to an increase in liquidity through purchases of government (or at times private) securities by the Central Bank when the interest rate is at the zero-interest rate bound. QE could impact the economy through a devaluation of the currency, a decrease in the long-term interest rates, or a decrease in the risk-premium. Although the first two of these effects cannot be directly incorporated in our setup, QE's effects on risk-premia can be simulated by simultaneously considering a negative risk-premium shock (or decreasing the extent of the risk-premium shock that is currently hitting the economy).

4. Conclusion

In this paper, we extended the DAD-DAS model presented in Mankiw [1] by including more shocks and

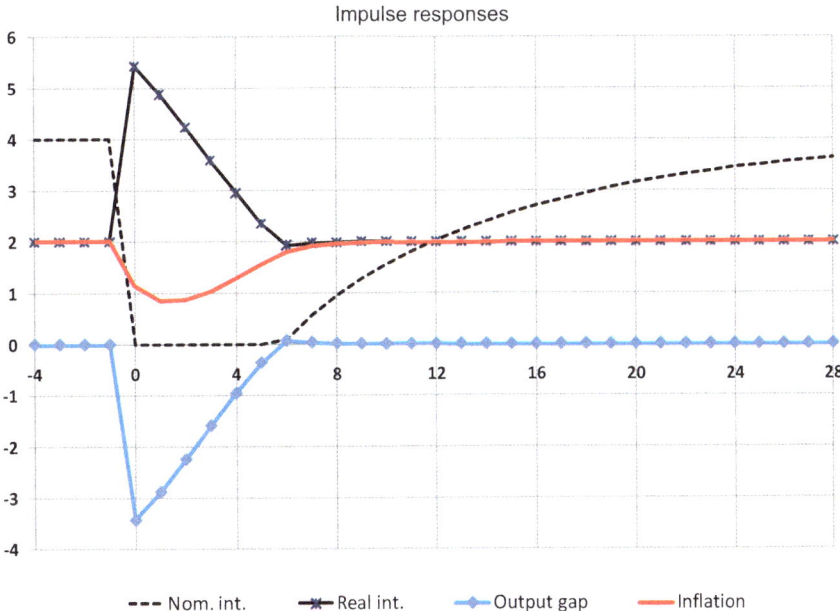

Figure 13. Impulse responses to a +7% risk shock with 0.9 persistence (and $\gamma = 0.5$) when the Central Bank tries to fully offset the effects of the shock ($\delta = 1$), but cannot due to the 0-bound.

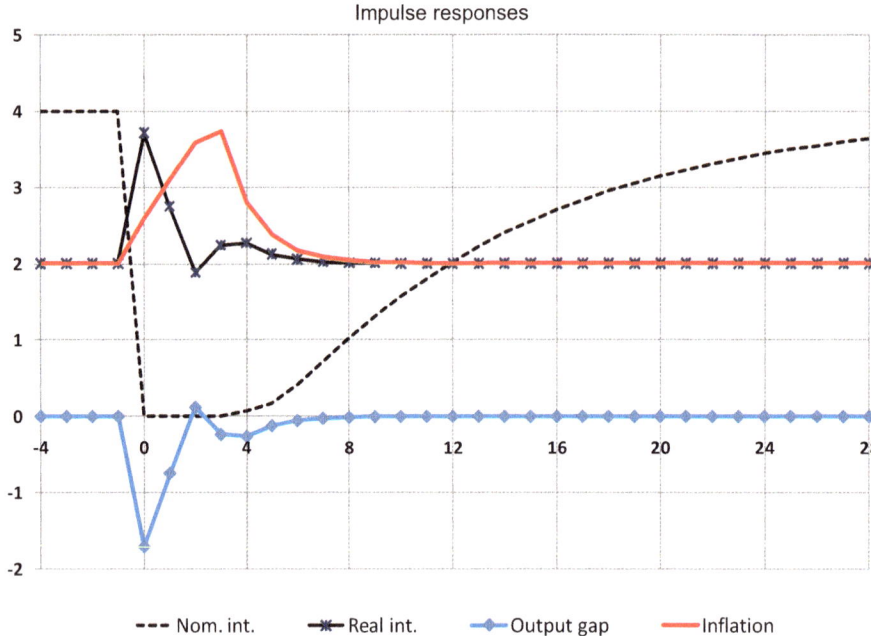

Figure 14. Impulse responses to the situation in Figure 13 along with a 4-quarter temporary increase in the inflation target from 2% to 4%.

flexible inflation expectations. Allowing inflation expectations to be determined as a weighted average of past inflation and the inflation target brings the exposition closer to rational expectations and allows for a discussion of costless disinflation. The inclusion of risk-premium shocks and the zero-bound on the policy rate allows for a discussion on the recent financial crisis and the ensuing liquidity trap. We also allow for deviations from the Taylor rule when setting monetary policy; this motivates a discussion regarding optimal policy response to demand shocks. These modifications to the textbook DAD-DAS model continue the trend of reducing the gap between undergraduate teaching of business fluctuations and the research frontier.

REFERENCES

[1] N. G. Mankiw, "Macroeconomics," 7th Edition, Worth Publishers, London, 2010.

[2] J. Hicks, "Mr. Keynes and the 'Classics': A Suggested Interpretation," *Econometrica*, Vol. 5, No. 2, 1937, pp. 147-159.

[3] A. Abel, B. Bernanke and D. Croushore, "Macroeconomics," 7th Edition, Prentice Hall, Upper Saddle River, 2010.

[4] C. I. Jones, "Macroeconomics," 2nd Edition, W.W. Norton and Co., New York, 2010.

[5] F. S. Mishkin, "Macroeconomics: Policy and Practice," Prentice Hall, Upper Saddle River, 2011.

[6] P. Bofinger, E. Mayer and T. Wollmershäuser, "The BMW Model: A New Framework for Teaching Monetary Economics," *Journal of Economic Education*, Vol. 37,

No. 1, 2006, pp. 98-117.

[7] W. Carlin D. Soskice, "The 3-Equation New Keynesian Model—A Graphical Exposition," *Contributions to Macroeconomics*, Vol. 5, No. 1, 2005, pp. 1-36.

[8] P. Kapinos, "A New Keynesian Workbook," *International Review of Economics Education*, Vol. 9, No. 1, 2010, pp. 111-123.

[9] D. Romer, "Keynesian Macroeconomics without the LM Curve," *Journal of Economic Perspectives*, Vol. 14, No. 2, 2000, pp. 149-169.

[10] A. Weerapana, "Intermediate Macroeconomics without the IS-LM Context," *Journal of Economic Education*, Vol. 34, No. 33, 2003, pp. 241-262.

[11] C. Wiese, "A Simple Wicksellian Macroeconomic Model," *The B.E. Journal of Macroeconomics*, Vol. 7, No. 1, 2007, Article 11.

[12] F. Smets and R. Wouters, "Shocks and Frictions in US Business Cycles: A Bayesian DSGE Approach," *American Economic Review*, Vol. 97, No. 3, 2007, pp. 586-606.

[13] J. Gali, "Monetary Policy, Inflation, and the Business Cycle: An Introduction to the New Keynesian Framework," Princeton University Press, Princeton, 2008.

[14] R. Clarida, J. Gali and M. Gertler, "The Science of Monetary Policy: A New Keynesian Perspective," *Journal of Economic Literature*, Vol. 37, 1999, pp. 1661-1707.

[15] M. Kulish and C. Jones, "A Graphical Representation of an Estimated DSGE Model," Dynare Working Papers Series #3, 2011.

[16] F. Kydland and E. C. Prescott, "Time to Build and Aggregate Fluctuations," *Econometrica*, Vol. 50, No. 6,

1982, pp. 1345-1371.

[17] C. E. Tovar, "DSGE Models and Central Banks," Kiel Institute for the World Economy, Economics Discussion Papers 2008-30, 2008.

[18] B. S. Bernanke, M. Gertler and S. Gilchrist, "The Financial Accelerator in a Quantitative Business Cycle Framework," In: J. B. Taylor and M. Woodford, Eds., *Handbook of Macroeconomics*, Elsevier Science, Amsterdam, 1999, pp. 1341-1393.

[19] S. Gilchrist, A. Ortiz and E. Zakrajsek, "Credit Risk and the Macroeconomy: Evidence from an Estimated DSGE Model," Boston University, Boston, 2009.

[20] S. Alpanda, "Identifying the Role of Risk Shocks in the Business Cycle Using Stock Price Data," *Economic Inquiry*, Vol. 51, No. 1, 2013, pp. 304-335.

[21] P. Bofinger and S. Debes, "A Primer on Unconventional Monetary Policy," CEPR Discussion PAPER: No. 7755, 2010.

[22] P. Kapinos, "Liquidity Trap in an Inflation-Targeting Framework: A Graphical Analysis," *International Review of Economics Education*, Vol. 10, No. 2, 2011, pp. 91-105.

[23] M. Woodford, "Interest and Prices," Princeton University Press, Princeton, 2003.

[24] G. Calvo, "Staggered Prices in a Utility Maximizing Framework," *Journal of Monetary Economics*, Vol. 12, No. 3, 1983, pp. 383-398.

[25] J. B. Taylor, "Aggregate Dynamics and Staggered Contracts," *Journal of Political Economy*, Vol. 88, No. 1, 1980, pp. 1-23.

[26] J. Rotemberg, "Monopolistic Price Adjustment and Aggregate Output," *Review of Economic Studies*, Vol. 49, No. 4, 1982, pp. 517-531.

[27] O. J. Blanchard and C. M. Kahn, "The Solution of Linear Difference Models under Rational Expectations," *Econometrica*, Vol. 48, No. 5, 1980, pp. 1305-1311.

[28] J. B. Taylor, "Discretion versus Policy Rules in Practice," *Carnegie-Rochester Conference Series on Public Policy*, Vol. 39, No. 1, 1993, pp. 195-214.

13

The Breakdown of the Traditional Mechanistic Worldview, the Development of Complexity Sciences and the Pretence of Knowledge in Economics

Andreas Liening

Faculty of Economics, Business Administration and Social Sciences, University of Dortmund, Dortmund, Germany

ABSTRACT

This article is an introduction to complexity theory, which will be discussed using the example of economic science. In this context, a short historical overview is intended to demonstrate why the traditional mechanistic worldview persistently remains a part of economic science and how it led to the development of the theory of complex systems, which, for example, can be subsumed under chaos theory. Furthermore, a simple supply and demand model is employed as an example to discuss this new theory and to describe the characteristics of complexity in comparison with the general mechanistic principle. For this purpose, specially designed software is used for the simulation and analysis of selected complex systems.

Keywords: Bifurcation; Butterfly Effect; Chaos Theory; Complexity Theory; Nonlinear Systems

1. "Run Through" and Introduction

Because the economy is characterized by increasing complexity, many traditional economic explanatory models have increasingly lost their persuasive power. As suggested by numerous traditional models, the economic development of the system as a whole and in specific domains, such as the business sector, are not always characterized by fluent transitions. In fact, discontinuities, jump discontinuities and turbulence occur. Thus, the economy and economy related subareas can be understood as nonlinear, dynamic systems. In this context, complex systems are discussed.

Therefore, it is particularly important to conduct research on new concepts and methods in the field of complex dynamical systems. The research approaches within this domain are increasingly being used in the field of economic science; for example, such an approach may be employed to better understand complex order structures, which are generated by market-based systems.

For example, an examination of the works of the Nobel Prize winner in economics von Hayek reveals that order is not necessarily a result of planning. In this connection, he even postulates a constructivist error [1]. In this context, von Hayek writes as follows:

"It is thus a paradox, based on a complete misunderstanding of these connections, when it is sometimes contended that we must deliberately plan modern society because it has grown so complex. The fact is rather that we can preserve an order of such complexity only of we control it not by the method of "planning", i.e., by direct orders, but on the contrary aim at the formation of a spontaneous order based on general rules" [2].

Following von Hayek, such an order cannot be analyzed adequately with the assistance of mechanistic models that are still frequently applied[1] and are based on lineal[2] cause-and-effect chains and which are thus predictable.

To model complex developments based on realistic scenarios, one must utilize traditional exogenic dysfunctions or random variables. Eventually, abnormal and non-continuous developments are analyzed through the use of methods that seem to be applicable only to linear and

---

[1]Models can be interpreted as material or immaterial systems, which illustrate other systems such that experimental manipulations of the depicted structures and conditions become possible [3].

[2]Lineal systems are conceptions in which the elements of a system are arranged consecutively as a chain. Because feedback loops are missing in this structure, in contrast to non-lineal systems, a predefined performance is executed without reacting to endogenous or exogenous events. Frequently, lineal systems are mathematically linear, whereas non-lineal systems are often non-linear. Therefore, linear systems should be distinguished from lineal systems.

lineal conditions or continuous processes, respectively. For a long time, economics was subordinate to the influence of a mechanistic worldview, which, for example, applied to models whose trajectories[3] tended toward equilibrium and seemed to be predictable and tangible with the assistance of partial analyses.

However, the economic reality is often much more difficult and complex than suggested, for example, by linear models. For instance, it is not possible to explain self-organizing processes separately from equilibrium with the use of linear views. Therefore, Nijkamp and Poot assert the following:

"Our economic world is highly dynamic and exhibits a wide variety of fluctuating patterns. This forms a sharp contrast with our current economic toolbox, which is largely filled with linear and comparative static instruments" [4, p. 25].

Consequently, if you look at economic theory one can say:

"The assumptions of mainstream economics are totally changing" [5, p. 7].

So, the engagement with nonlinear, complex systems may have a decisive role in searching for an expansion of the "economic toolbox." With this approach, it is possible to represent a wide range of economic behavioral patterns and explanatory approaches. Using this method, complexity can be described, analyzed and understood in a manner in which traditional statistical methods would fail[4].

In addition to the theory of self-organization (synergetics) or the theory of thermodynamics, fractal geometry or catastrophe theory, chaos theory in particular must be mentioned [7]. Although these approaches seem to differ greatly from each other, they are all primarily concerned with questions related to the origination and analysis of complex order patterns. Therefore, they can properly be subsumed as a subdiscipline of a theoretical superstructure, which is referred to as a "theory of complex systems" in this context.

Within the scope of its popular scientific upswing in the 1990s, chaos theory became a theory of a new, homogeneous world explanation for the one part—or rather a world transfiguration[5]—whereas the others insulted the representatives of chaos theory as shamans[6]. Today, these advocates of chaos theory continue to search in the structures of remote galaxies or in the ascending wads of the smoke from a cigarette for the power of chaos. The opponents repeatedly question why chaos exists exclusively in the computer and why the "spook" disappears as soon as the computer is shut down.

Consequently, there have been many misunderstandings. It is widely believed that chaos theory is a theory of disorder. As this essay will demonstrate, this belief is entirely misleading. Chaos theory neither disproves determinism nor considers ordered systems impossible. Although chaos theory suggests that the current state of a system may not be predictable, it nevertheless demonstrates that it is generally possible to model the overall characteristics of such a system. Consequently, chaos theory does not emphasize disorder, which is the inherent unpredictability of a system's status; rather, this theory emphasizes the order structures that are inherent to a system—the universal characteristics of homogeneous systems. Nijkamp and Reggiani explain as follows:

"There is 'order in chaos'" [4, p. 12].

The possibility of researching "chaos" and the connected order patterns in complex systems was not imaginable prior to the development of modern computer technology. The multitude of calculations and the different types of visualizations of complex structures were previously unrealizable. Therefore, it is not surprising that this theory gained importance especially at the beginning of the 1990s.

Meanwhile, the euphoria that accompanied chaos theory has again receded, and the number of new popular scientific publications has decreased. However, the number of scientific publications attempting to transfer important aspects of chaos theory to other areas of science has increased. In this regard, economics is not excluded because one expects a better approach to economic reality from chaos theory than, for example, the neoclassical paradigm can render[7].

Regarding these considerations, this article is titled "Econoplexity," which refers to the application of the theory of complex systems to economics. In this article,

---

[3]A trajectory is the development line of a dynamic system. It depicts the course, which begins from a certain starting point and is conducted by a system in the course of its dynamical development in the phase space. Here, the phase space is a space spanned by the time-variant variables of a dynamical system. If the trajectory moves in an "attractive" dynamical state, it is referred to as an attractor, which is a subset of a phase space. There are four types of attractors: fixed point, limit-cycle, limit-tori, chaotic resp. strange attractors.

[4]For more information, cp. e. g. the comment on Grammar Complexity [6].

[5]With regard to popular scientific literature, refer to Bestenreiner [8]. Rosser, for instance, notices: "Chaos theory has no single inventor, but a fad for it followed publication of the best-selling book by the journalist, Gleick (1987), a fad further fueled in the popular mind by Goldblums's portrayal of a 'chaotician' in the film *Jurassic Park*" [7, p. 173].

[6]At this point, an example from an article series in the German SPIEGEL magazine should be mentioned; this magazine is a popular scientific publication along the lines of "cult about chaos—superstition or world explanation" ("Kult um das Chaos—Aberglaube oder Welterklärung") [9-11].

[7]For more information, cp. the comments and bibliographical references in Liening [12]. Especially in the recent past, numerous interesting publications addressing chaos theory and economics have been published. For example, the following monographs are cited: Faggini & Vinci [13], Metcalfe & Foster [14], Trosky [15], Mandelbrot & Hudson [16], Barnett, Deissenberg & Feichtinger [17], Zehetner [18], and Puu [19]. An introduction to chaos theory and some economic applications can be found, for instance, in the work by Baumol & Benhabib [20].

Section 1 presents a short historical overview to demonstrate why the traditional linear causal mechanistic worldview persistently remains a part of economic science, and Section 2 explains how this worldview led to the development of the "theory of complex systems". Section 3 explains the new theory with the assistance of software that was specifically designed to simulate a supply and demand model. Thus, the characteristics of complexity are described briefly.

2. Economic Science Under the Mechanistic Counterbalance, or Economia Non Facit Saltum

2.1. A Short History

The question of what effect natural sciences, particularly the findings of classical mechanics, had on the development of economics is of great relevance for the understanding of economic science because the past influence of mechanistic thinking on economic science continues today. However, it must be critically analyzed with respect to the subject matter and this is done [21].

To enable readers to understand the influence of classical mechanics—and thus of Newtonian Physics—on economic science, this section provides a brief historical review.

An examination of the history of economics reveals that a wide range of economic schools of thought have developed over time and had—or rather have—a more or less important position in the discussion of the development of economic science.

By the middle of the 18th century, Quesnay, one of the forerunners of the classical economic school, developed his "Tableau économique", which graphically illustrates the national economy as a whole. Initially, it was thought that Quesnay was inspired by the process of blood circulation when creating his "Tableau" (see **Figure 1**). However, more recent research has shown that the work of Quesnay is rather a mechanistic analogy and that Quesnay intended to apply the physical findings of Descartes to political economics [21]. In later comments regarding his Tableau, Quesnay underlined the mechanistic and mathematic character of his illustration because he wanted to prove that the functioning of the economic system is similar to that of a machine [22].

Mainzer argues that the school of physiocracy, which was represented by Quesnay, modeled economic development on the natural science-based course of a ball in the firm chutes of a clock; this analogy was commonly used at that time [23]. Thus, Quesnay was among the first economists to apply natural scientific thinking to the economy, and he argued for the self-regulation of the market, which is consistent with findings from this field [24]. The "laissez faire, laissez passé" motto of the physiocrats became well known.

Classical economics, which emerged with Adam Smith, John Stuart Mill and others in the 1770s, replaced physiocracy. Indeed, Smith also advocated for the self-regulation of the market, but he differed from his predecessors in some aspects [25]; particularly, he did not argue in favor of an unlimited "laissez-faire economy"[8]. According to Bürgin, Smith's work, in which the physiocratic motto has been developed into a closed economic concept, can be considered an application of Newtonian physics [26]. However, especially in the case of Smith, economists were at least slightly hesitant to subscribe to the mechanistic view[9]. Nevertheless, similar to that described in Newtonian gravitation theory (which provides for actions at a distance, according to which levitating astronomical objects move into a condition of equilibrium when they interact), Smith claimed that an "invisible hand" [28] coordinates millions of individual plans in such a way that an equilibrium of supply and demand is achieved.

"By preferring the support of domestic to that of foreign industry he [the individual person; the author] intends only his own security; and by directing that industry in such a manner as its produce may be of the greatest value, he intends only his own gain, and he is in this, as in many other cases, led by an *invisible hand* [emphasis added; the author] to promote an end which was no part of his intention [···]. By pursuing his own interest he

Figure 1. Tableau Economique, visualization of the physiocratic concept [26].

---

[8]In the areas in which the market fails, as in the cases of the allocation of public goods and the tendency to form monopolies, *Smith* definitely considers state interventions as justifiable. From the regulation of the banking business to the raising of taxes to reduce the consumption of alcohol, the moral philosopher *Smith* views many possibilities for governmental intervention. However, for the first time in history, *Smith* succeeded in illustrating that *only* by means of individual freedom of action in the economic system is it possible to achieve maximal economic growth and standards of wealth under the prevailing circumstances [27]. For more information, also cp. [28].
[9]The reasons for this hesitation are mentioned in Smith's theory of moral sentiments [29]. Cp. also the explanations by Denis [22].

frequently promotes that of the society more effectually than when he really intends to promote it" [28, p. 485].

The physiocrats and later the classics restricted themselves to the formation of analogies between mechanics and economic science, whereas neoclassical economics, which was initiated by Alfred Marshall and Leon Walras in the middle of the 19th century and continued by Kenneth Arrow, Gérard Debreu and Frank Hahn in this century, effected the concrete formalization of these ideas [30]. Thus, mechanics became more than merely the basis of an analogy with economic science, whose tertium comparationis was the mechanistic functioning of the physical world. Rather, in neoclassical economics, the economic science got under the regulative ideasof mechanics or, as Söllner writes with reference to Mirowski, a revaluation of economic science to the physics of social science occurred [31].

Röpke notes that classical mechanics (and the constructivist form of rationality that explains it) presents the living world as something that consists of rationally determined beings. These beings are controlled by a superior rationality from the outside, and thus, they are beings without an "internal principle of action" (Kant) and are only able to pass on a movement which once has been got from the outside (in the case of Descartes from the creator god). This basic mechanistic-constructivist element of the early enlightenment period has paradigmatically become fundamental to one part of modern economics [32]. Röpke divides this basic mechanistic principle into three areas of economic theory:

- First, on the individual level, the mechanistically influenced theory type can be found in the concept of humankind in economics. The neoclassical homo oeconomicus, with its implicitly used psychology, must be assigned to the field of behaviorism, which is based on the stimulus-response intensification principle[10]. The homo oeconomicus systematically reacts to given action restrictions and their changes. His preferences (wishes, objectives, and motives) are constant. Thus, the action of the homo oeconomicus is considered a reaction that is determined by the environment (*i.e.*, that is externally controlled). It is not considered a spontaneous, self-organizing activity[11].
- Second, the "machine-command-organization" [36], or the "mechanistic organization" [37], is found at the level of businesses. The inner life of businesses and their internal organization, production and contract problems are not of interest in this context. Rather, their members are able to reproduce optimal adaptation reactions according to particular circumstances [37].

- Finally, on the level of the market, one finds clearly definable market structures that are supposed to be historically given and that assign certain behavioral patterns to individual market participants; their change and their evolution remain unconsidered; and their particular macroeconomic efficiency and optimality (with regard to the allocation of scarce resources or other supra-individual objectives) can be shown theoretically and achieved socio-technologically, at least by tendency [37].

Based on the economic principle that the highest possible output must be achieved with the means that are available (or that a given yield target must be achieved with the least possible input), optimal circumstances on the level of individuals, businesses and the market can be achieved or can be assumed to exist with neoclassical assumptions. One may share the opinion of Schlösser, who consistently remarks that a theory of spontaneous social order is not achievable with the neoclassical fiction [35].

In this context, it is interesting that some advocates of neoclassical economics had a technical, natural scientific or mathematic education[12]. For example, Pareto was a trained engineer[13]; Marshall was a mathematician [38], and Jevons studied natural sciences [25]. However, this education alone cannot explain a formalized assumption of the ideas of mechanics applied to neoclassical economics. To answer this question with regard to specific reasons, this paper will offer some comments regarding classical mechanics and its philosophy.

2.2. Regarding Classical Mechanics and Newtonian Physics

The most important principles of mechanics were founded through the use of Newton's "Philosophiae Naturalis Principia Mathematica"[14] (1687) and the principle of continuity by Leibniz[15] (1700), which can be circumscribed by the famous sentence "natura non facit saltus"[16]. These principles, which will be described subsequently, are as follows:
- determinism
- reversibility
- (strong) causality
- the assumption that the whole consists of the sums of its parts

---

[10]For more information regarding (traditional) behaviorism, cp. [33,34].
[11]For a detailed illustration of the neoclassical image of humanity, cp. the critical analysis in [35].

[12]Lentz also indicates that a number of the most prominent advocates initially underwent a technical-natural scientific education [25].
[13]Oltmanns, cited according to [38].
[14]Hawking considers Newton's contributions to be presumably the most important physical publication written by one person alone [39].
[15]Note that Kant characterized Leibniz as a mechanic [40].
[16]Leibniz and Newton were not actually friends and Newton's realism conflicted with Leibniz's realism. Nevertheless, the importance of both scholars for physics and mathematics is indisputable (consider infinitesimal calculus).

• the assumption that complex elements are composed of a multitude of basic elements

With the help of the Newtonian laws, the relationships between factors such as velocity, acceleration, force and mass can be established. For example, one can calculate how long it takes for an apple falling from a tree to touch the ground. Based on these laws, it is also possible to describe the courses of the planets around the sun or the path of a space shuttle back into orbit.

Among other things, the given examples show that classical mechanics can illustrate the time development of physical systems. Newton was the first scientist to be proficient in this art. Based on his work, it is known that any state at any time can be derived if the initial state of a system is known. Consequently, the result is an entirely deterministic worldview. The mathematician Poincaré expresses this result as follows:

"Every phenomenon, however minute, has a cause; and a mind infinitely powerful, infinitely well-informed about the laws of nature, could have foreseen it from the beginning of the centuries"[17].

Laplace's (fictional) demon is regarded as a symbol for this determinism of classical mechanics [42]. Laplace's demon is the institution that has all of the data of the universe at its disposal such that it can predict future developments at any point in time. However, it can also recalculate past developments from the earliest times. Thus, Laplace writes as follows:

"Given for one instant an intelligence which could comprehend all the forces by which nature is animated and the respective positions of the beings which compose it, if moreover this intelligence were vast enough to submit these data to analysis, it would embrace in the same formula both the movements of the largest bodies in the universe and those of the lightest atom; to it nothing would be uncertain, and the future as the past would be present to its eyes" [43, Chapter II].

Thus, determinism and reversibility, or time reversibility, predominate in classical mechanics[18]. Because mechanistic sequences are identically reproducible, time is only the duration of an event that occurs between the beginning and the end of mechanistic processes (thus, until the new equilibrium is reached).

In addition to the abovementioned points, the apparent weak law of causality, according to which the same causes incur the same effects (and thus causality is invariant), is not the only important concept in classical mechanics. In fact, strong causality, which means that similar initial conditions always lead to similar results, is also important.

Descartes, who certainly would not have accepted every aspect of the later Newtonian mechanics[19], is regarded as one of the most important representatives of this mechanistic school of thought. It is not an exaggeration to state that the basic concept of classical mechanics can be traced back to Descartes. In particular, Descartes was interested in the methods that allowed for reliable scientific findings. He applied logic for this purpose, and among numerous rules, he selected four rules that he believed are especially relevant for logic. In this context, the second rule is particularly important. In 1637, Descartes wrote as follows:

"Le second, de diviser chacune des difficultés que j'examinerais, en autant de parcelles qu'il se pourrait, et qu'il serait requis pour les mieux résoudre" [45, p. 30].

In other words, if a problem is too complex to be solved in one step, it should be divided into many subproblems that are sufficiently small to be solved separately. Thus, it is assumed with this analytical notion that the whole consists of the sum of its parts.

Descartes's third rule illustrates that the purpose of scientific thinking is to consistently organize all thoughts in a certain way when researching the truth: the process should begin with the easiest and most comprehensible ideas and gradually progress to obtaining an awareness of more difficult and sophisticated issues. Furthermore, such things that do not automatically form a sequential relationship should be organized in a certain order [45][20]. In principle, Descartes considers it possible to subdivide complex matters into a multitude of basic elements and to recompose them. As a basic principle, scientists since Demokrit and Aristoteles have believed that there is a multitude of simple objects and forces behind the complexity of the world [46]. The entire worldview of classical mechanics is affected by concentration on closed, simple, and frequently linear systems [25]. These systems comprise exactly those characteristics that have been described: the characteristics of determinism, reversibility, and (strong) causality; the assumption that the whole consists of the sum of its parts; and the assumption that complex elements are composed of a multitude of basic elements.

---

[17]Poincaré, cited according to [41].

[18]A system can be considered reversible if it can also proceed in a backward fashion. For instance, Newton's first law states that the law of inertia is reversible such that if there is an equation of a force-free movement at time point t, then a solution at time point-t also exists. Here, the time reversal is expressed by a change of sign in the direction of movement.

[19]For example, according to Newton, the gravitational force of two astronomical objects is inversely proportional to the square of the distance of both bodies. Descartes would have been suspicious of this conception of "action at a distance". He would have preferred a mechanistic explanation such as that which describes contact forces that cause one gear wheel to affect another rather than actions at a distance [44].

[20]Descartes resisted the term "treatise" and insisted on the original title "Discours" because he did not want to teach the method but only wanted to discuss it.

2.3. Analogy between Classical Mechanics and Economic Science

With regard to discovering the reasons for the analogy between classical mechanics and economic science, the following should be noted: economic science is often said to be inexact, or rather unreliable. It is not reliable science in the sense that economic findings have no objective validity. In this regard, the lack of reliable findings in economics was problematic, particularly because during that period economic science belonged to the field of humanities, which was not always viewed positively from a natural scientific point of view.

However, the concepts of mechanics spread quickly due to its practical utility. The fascinating aspect of classical mechanics is that everything is definitely describable, mathematically deducible and predictable when all initial parameters are known. Thus, it is not surprising that the optimism that spread with classical mechanics also influenced other disciplines, including economic science. Thus, classical mechanics could support the endeavor of economists to successfully develop economics into an "exact" science.

According to Dopfer, three fundamental assumptions of classical mechanics found their way into economics:

- A mechanistic whole can be subdivided into its basic elements. These elements can be analyzed individually and recomposed.
- The causalities are invariant, and the relations between the elements can be described by linear functions.
- The same or similar conditions lead to the same or similar dynamic paths of a system [47].

As mentioned above, the classics had already established analogies between economics and mechanics. On the basis of the first assumption, for example, John Stuart Mill writes impressively as follows:

"The order of nature, as perceived at first glance, presents at every instant a chaos followed by another chaos. We must decompose each chaos into single facts. We must learn to see in the chaotic antecedent a multiple of distinct antecedents, in the chaotic consequent a multitude of distinct consequents"[21].

Beyond this analogy, neoclassical economics, which emerged from the "marginalist revolution," applied the ideas of mechanics to mathematical-economic models. This borrowing facilitated the development of the neoclassical equilibrium theory.

Another typical example reflecting the assumption of ideas from mechanics is Marshall's partial analysis. To better analyze complex reality, economists rely on the study of the partial aspects of economic events. This approach corresponds to the first mentioned fundamental assumption of classical mechanics, according to which a whole can be subdivided into its basic elements. These elements can be analyzed individually to obtain an impression of the whole. This concept is also reflected in Marshall's ceteris paribus assumption, according to which one variable is changed whose effects can be examined in a model by holding all of the other relevant factors constant.

Marshall's successor Pareto, after whom the well-known pareto optimum[22] is named, employed many mathematic principles in his economic models. His thoughts also revealed a great affinity for mechanics, as the following sentences demonstrate. With regard to the immediate benefit, for example, the analysis of the exchange in the pure economy corresponds to the analysis of free-falling bodies in physics textbooks. A falling feather does not act more upon the laws of falling bodies than certain acts of exchange act upon the laws of exchange [38].

Dopfer extends this idea further, perhaps even too far, when he quotes Frank Knight, who claims that economic science is a "sister science" of classical mechanics [49].

However, one can follow Dopfer when he states that neoclassical works missed few opportunities to emphasize mechanics as a role model for economics.

3. The Breakdown of Laplace's World View

As demonstrated in the previous chapter, the influence of classical mechanics on economic science, which underwent a concrete formalization in neoclassical economics for the first time, was not insignificant. Even today, the general principle of mechanics influences many economic approaches. These approaches are based on comparative statics—which facilitates the comparison of equilibrium states (e. g. on the basis of different constellations of demand and supply curves)—or in some cases, they are based on linear-dynamical systems, which enable a process-related analysis.

3.1. First Doubts

However, the mechanistic worldview was destabilized at the end of the 19th century and at the beginning of the 20th century. At that time, the French mathematician Henri Poincaré confronted the physical worldview, which had been widely accepted until then, with entirely new findings based on his questions regarding the stability of the solar system.

According to Newtonian physics, few interacting bod-

---

[21]Mill, cited according to [48].

[22]According to Pareto, goods and services in an economy are optimally distributed in situations in which a person can only improve his/her position if he/she takes something from another person. However, until today, it has been questionable whether this idea is actually positive because the optimum situation can be achieved irrespective of how the goods are distributed among the poor and the rich [38].

ies demonstrate predictable behavior. However, Poincaré knew that the Newtonian equations could be solved only approximately and that these equations—also in the case of very minor alterations of the initial conditions—to some extent, bring forward very irregular, chaotic developments.

With respect to the solar system, in the context of observing more than two planets, entirely eccentric orbits, which call the stability of the solar system into question, are possible[23]. In this regard, Poincaré showed that systems that have been stable for a long period of time can become instable without an extraneous cause. At this point, the concept of disorder—chaos—became relevant because it could be initiated by any small interference.

Until this time, chaos was considered as a type of infection that could affect a system from the outside. However, it became clear that a closed system could be described with few equations and could feature unpredictable, chaotic characteristics [46]. Apparently, determinism was questioned because Poincaré aligns coincidence with determinism via long-term unpredictability. He writes as follows:

"A very small cause which escapes our notice determines a considerable effect that we cannot fail to see, and then we say that the effect is due to chance"[24].

However, at this time, few scientists anticipated the importance of his research results; many economists either ignored his results or were simply unaware of them[25]. Despite some subsequent important findings, such as the findings of Birkhoff (USA) in the 1920s or Cartwright and Littlewood (GB) in the 1940s, which were provided by mathematical works in the field of dynamic systems, Poincaré's discoveries were ignored for decades[26].

3.2. The Weather Forecast and the Butterfly Effect

At the beginning of the 1960s, the meteorologist Edward Lorenz made an interesting discovery, which can be considered a practical consequence of Poincaré's findings[27].

Lorenz used his computer to solve non-linear equations for modeling the earth's atmosphere. To verify the result, he repeated the computer calculations. However,

in the second instance, he reduced the accuracy of the computer from six to three decimal places. The result was fundamentally different from that obtained in the first instance. Lorenz discovered that non-linear dynamical systems, such as the weather, react very sensitively to very minimal changes. Thus, he confirmed Poincaré's assumption.

This finding, which became known as the butterfly effect, is expressed as follows: the flapping of a butterfly wing in Hong Kong can cause a hurricane in New York.

Lorenz's investigations demonstrate that unpredictable nature of dynamical systems cannot be observed because some details are not known. Even the most detailed knowledge does not necessarily allow for exact projections in the case of dynamical systems.

However, if this notion is correct, then Laplace's demon (the hypothetical construct that can theoretically predict the future if it knows all initial conditions) is an absurd figure, and the mechanistic worldview must be denied or at least qualified.

In the following section, some aspects of the new approach will be considered in greater detail.

4. Criteria of the New Approach

4.1. Paradigm Shift in Economic Science

Schefold states that new economic ideas are often old ideas that quasi-recur periodically: a mercantilist theory of interest is part of Keynesianism, and the monetary theoretical nominalism of antiquity recurs in this century—not for the first time—due to the rejection of metallism [56].

Moreover, Schmalensee opines that the majority of scientists work on existing theories and approaches develop them further and apply them. Only rarely, Schmalensee writes, do erratic changes occur when seemingly unsolvable anomalies or other problems are overcome by "scientific revolutions". Such revolutions are accompanied by a development that Thomas Kuhn described as a "paradigm shift"—fundamental changes in the worldview that radically converted the entire discipline and its research agenda [57].

In the history of economics, such paradigm shifts have occurred frequently. Examples of these shifts are the methodological triumph of mathematical analysis or the neoclassical subjective theory of values, which radically changed the objective view. In today's world, economists such as Schmalensee lament that a large portion of today's economic research is merely concerned with the reworking and improving of concepts, such as those of rational behavior and competitive markets, which were already known by Marshall and even Smith [57].

The analogy with Newtonian mechanics by classical economics and the further integration of the general prin-

---

[23]This paper is not the appropriate context in which to comment on all of the details of Poincaré's results. Therefore, interested readers are referred to [50].

[24]Poincaré, cited according to [51].

[25]Chiarella states that most of the early authors who wrote about the dynamical, time-dependent cycle theory were not aware of Poincaré's work [52].

[26]For more information, cp., for example, [53].

[27]In addition to Lorenz, other scientists, such as Kolmogorow *et al.* and Smale, should be mentioned because these scientists also successfully researched the field of non-linear dynamics in the 1960s or perhaps as early as the 1950s. Interested readers are referred to, for example, [54] or [55].

ciples of mechanics by neoclassical economics have influenced many fields of economic science in a sustainable manner. Furthermore, this analogy reflected in the static, statically comparative or linear-dynamic model analyses rather than merely in neoclassical economics. Thus, this analogy also provides the foundation for economic approaches that contrast with neoclassical economics. For example, the Keynesian, mechanistic overall model suggests that the state can (e.g., by means of countercyclical fiscal policy and global regulation) affect the economic process of an entire national economy in a sustainable, positive manner. However, the stagflation problems in the 1970s demonstrated that these mechanistic concepts do not work or they only work for a short time. The failure of the mechanistic regulation approach in the former Eastern bloc countries, whose centrally controlled economic systems collapsed in the 1990s, proved to be significantly more serious. Thus, the theoretically justified breakdown of Laplace's worldview and the empirical findings in economics call the mathematical-mechanistic way of thinking as well as economic sciences in general into question.

When a shift in perspective proceeds rapidly, economic development proceeds more rapidly in highly industrialized states, and permanent change begins. Static theories, which are based on linear systems, are a good approximation for an economy with an unchanging structure. However, these theories do not help to explain evolutionary, nonlinear dynamical phenomena [25]. Therefore, some economists have abandoned mathematics in economics[28]. However, this complete abandonment is unnecessary. The poet Hölderlin writes that in situations in which there is danger, a rescuing element also grows [58]; thus, in particular, the mathematically influenced "theory of complex systems" initiates a rethinking in economic science[29].

The first indications of a paradigm shift have arisen because numerous recent publications have deliberately transitioned from the traditional economic models to a "theory of complex systems". For Instance, deterministic, market-oriented growth models to explain irregular business developments are developed in business economics. In the theory of business development, there are, for example, non-mechanistic explanatory approaches to determining why many processes are not predictable in the long term. The new concepts can be found in the organizational and process structures of businesses, human

resource development, marketing, knowledge management and strategic management, especially in "change management"[30].

Especially in the fields of human resource development and career research, the most recent works have abandoned the traditional linear-mechanistic approach with the emergence of numerous new empirical findings resulting from the use of innovative empirical methods beyond the traditional statistical methods [64].

Interesting research, which is not centered on general principles of mechanics, can be found in economics, for example, in the field of business cycles and growth models, particularly in the area of endogenous growth theory, consumption choice models and overlapping generation models. Additional economic topics that indicate a paradigm shift include research and model formation in subject areas that address exchange rate fluctuations, the development of share prices, the development of the gross national product and related time series analyses[31].

In the following discussion, the basic characteristics of the new approach are explained.

4.2. Simulation of a Complex System Using the Example of a Supply and Demand Model

Scientists from non-natural scientific disciplines are increasingly acknowledging that even experiences from everyday life are opposed to the beloved image of a well-regulated, clearly arranged and predictable world [66]. The "butterfly effect" can be found in many fields in which feedback affects and intensify irregularities. Any small change in the cause can result in an enormous change in the effects.

For the purposes of describing irregularities through the use of linear equations, a system must be "disturbed" exogenously (i.e., from the outside). None of the known patterns of dynamic-linear systems are able to create such behaviors by themselves[32]. If linear models are considered, then there are only three possibilities in terms of how a system can develop.

A linear dynamic system can engage in any of the following actions:

- converge to a fixed point
- feature a cyclical movement, i.e., "circle" around a fixed point in constant distance (thus, it has two accumulation points)
- diverge, i.e., remove itself from a fixed point[33]

---

[28]For instance, von Hayek developed a theory of complex phenomena without any recourse to mathematical concepts [1].

[29]As a supply and demand schema, static modeling can be traced back to Marshall. This schema shows that there is a tendency toward equilibrium in the case of functioning competition. For example, when examining it through the use of statically comparative analyses, a change of demand or supply would be illustrated by a shift in the curves in the graphical representation.

[30]With regard to organizational and process structures, see, e.g., [59]; with regard to marketing, see [60]; with regard to knowledge management, see, e.g., [61,62]; and with regard to change management, see, e.g., [63].

[31]Recently, numerous interesting publications addressing chaos theory and economics have been published. For example, the following monographs are cited: [15,16,19,65].

[32]For this, cp. the explanation by [66].

[33]Cp. in more detail [21].

Thus, in principle, nothing unpredictable, new or surprising is possible in linear systems. Considered from a historical point of view, economic events remain timeless. Röpke explicitly mentions this fact when he states that the closed models of equilibrium economics cannot—even if they are "dynamized"—have explanatory relevance beyond the processes that occur in a determinate-mechanical manner [32].

As previously mentioned, only three types of courses of movements can be simulated through the use of linear, discrete and dynamic recurrence relations. However, if non-linear equations are considered, then those courses of movement become simulatable, which thus far might be integrated into the system only as exogenous disturbance variables.

The following supply and demand model, whose equations result in a non-linear price function and which has been implemented using object-oriented simulation software [67], is intended to demonstrate that even simple non-linear equations can exhibit irregular behavior.

For this, the following price function will be considered:

$$P(t+1) = \lambda \cdot P(t) - \lambda \cdot P(t)^2 \tag{1}$$

The function is then formulated differently:

$$P(t+1) = \lambda \cdot P(t) \cdot (1 - P(t)) \tag{2}$$

This function is also referred to as a logistic function and is a fundamental discrete function in the theory of complex systems.

This mapping is a recursive function (*i.e.*, the respective price is dependent on the previous price). In this context, this dependency is quadratic and thus non-linear. In the simulation, the calculations of the market are conducted by means of iterations (*i.e.*, in which the calculated value is reinserted into the same equation as the initial value). This process can be repeated as frequently as necessary. For the considered market model, a number of basic conditions apply. There are many demanders and suppliers, who rationally behave as price takers and who can enter and leave the market without restrictions. Thus, none of the people involved is so important that he or she might influence the price individually. Furthermore, there are no transaction costs or taxes, and there is only one homogeneous good. In situations with a high degree of market transparency[34], this economic model largely corresponds to the model of "pure competition." It is assumed that the good that is traded on the market is the low-priced ballpoint pen, "Chaoswriter" (but, neverthe-

less, it is regarded as a trendsetter). At a price of 0.00, no supplier would be willing to offer only a single ballpoint pen. At a price of 1.00 or higher, no one would demand the good (prohibitive price); thus, the market price must be between 0.00 and 1.00.

In this model, the value λ reflects the market transparency. Here, a value of 1 denotes a very high degree of market transparency, and a value of 5 denotes a very low degree of market transparency[35].

The first simulation begins with a rather high degree of market transparency, $\lambda = 2.75$. With an arbitrary initial price, we obtain a converging development of the systems with one fixed point.

Price "P", which, in the initial situation, has been arbitrarily set very low relatively, is initially still comparatively far away from the actually higher equilibrium price. Already in the fifth period, the price reaches a peak value, and numerous suppliers are willing to offer many "Chaoswriters" at that high price. Due to high expectations of profits, new suppliers enter the market. However, the price has risen so high that, henceforth, the demanders react reluctantly, and the demand decreases. Consequently, the price decreases because the suppliers are apparently unable to sell the desired quantity of ballpoint pens when the price is excessively high. The price decreases but does not become as low as it was in the fourth period because this price was apparently too low. However, because of the fallen price, the demand for "Chaoswriters" increases. The increasing demand results in increasing prices because the suppliers are unable to immediately meet the increased demand. A smaller supply is associated with a higher price. This time, however, the suppliers raise the prices more cautiously to ensure that they do not frighten the demanders as they had when they previously raised the prices.

Nevertheless, demanders again withdraw after the price increase. The decline of demand with unchanging supply results in falling prices. Thus, the price amplitudes become smaller each time, and the price relatively quickly settles into an equilibrium, as shown in **Figure 2**. This cycle corresponds to the traditional pork cycle or a cobweb model.

If the market transparency is reduced (by setting the value at, for example, $\lambda = 3.2$), the system initially seems to diverge because of the insufficient market knowledge of all persons involved, but after some time, it stabilizes. As in the first situation, an equilibrium price is not achieved. At least two fixed points (or rather, accumulation points) are obtained, as shown in **Figure 3**.

In this case, the price fluctuates between two points.

[34]Market transparency indicates that suppliers and demanders know all of the development factors that are important to them. Examples of this transparency are knowledge regarding a particular good and its characteristics and the offered and demanded amount of goods and their prices.

[35]Lower values indicate that demanders and suppliers have more information regarding the market. Thus, the values mirror evaluation figures in the known grading system (Germany): 1 = excellent (sehr gut),..., 5 = inadequate (mangelhaft).

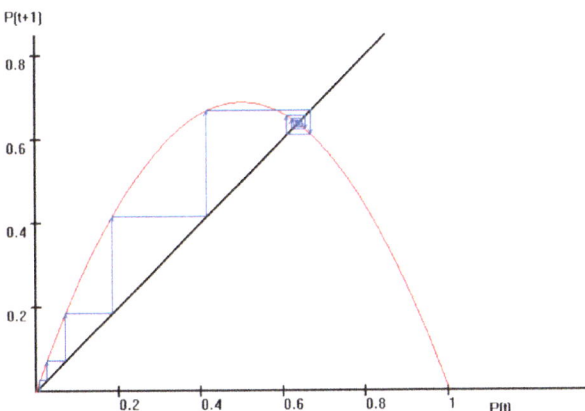

Figure 2. Fixed point attractor in the price system for the function $P(t+1) = \lambda \cdot P(t) \cdot (1 - P(t))$**, with** $\lambda = 2.75$ **and the initial value** $P(0) = 0.01$ **and 2000 iterations [67].**

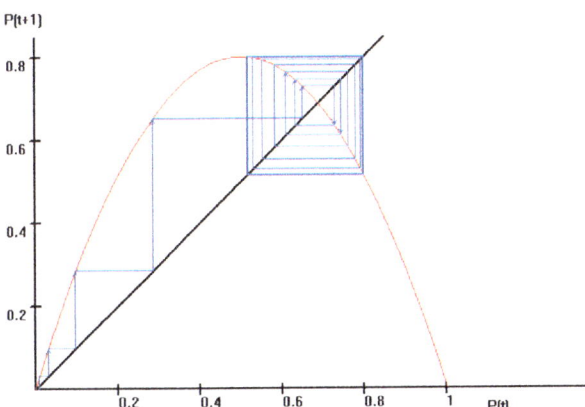

Figure 3. Double cycle attractor in the price system for the function $P(t+1) = \lambda \cdot P(t) \cdot (1 - P(t))$**, with** $\lambda = 3.2$ **and the initial value** $P(0) = 0.01$ **and 2000 iterations [67].**

At a higher price, the suppliers will be inclined to offer more products. However, many demanders consider the price to be excessively high; thus, they are unwilling to buy all of the goods offered for purchase. The price then decreases. However, when the price decreases, the demand increases again. Because the suppliers cannot entirely meet the increased demand, the prices increase.

Because there is a lack of market transparency, the businessmen ultimately set a price that is so high that the demand and consequently the price again decrease. Thus, the price ultimately fluctuates due to the low level of market transparency and does not achieve an equilibrium value.

If the system is modified in such a way that, for example, $\lambda = 4.0$, (whereby the market transparency worsens again), an unexpected result occurs: suddenly, the system is literally "thrown off joint" because suppliers and demanders no longer possess knowledge regarding the market. Irregular fluctuations occur.

Prices that are too high result in decreased demand and increased supply, whereas decreasing prices cause increased demand and decreased supply. Due to the lack of market transparency, the prices do not develop toward an equilibrium point or a cycle.

The values seem to jump completely randomly. In short, the system reacts chaotically. As a consequence, an extremely complex structure develops, as shown in **Figure 4**.

Remarkably, the irregular price developments are neither caused by exogenous shocks—and thus can be explained endogenously by the system itself—nor a stochastic process. The apparently arbitrary price trends are not random; rather, they are deterministic.

The price development over the course of time changes fundamentally in the system as soon as it is apparently calculated more accurately.

Figure 5 demonstrates what occurs if the accuracy of the result is increased (at a given (low) market transparency of $\lambda = 4.0$) by one decimal place at a time after 2000 iterations of the price function.

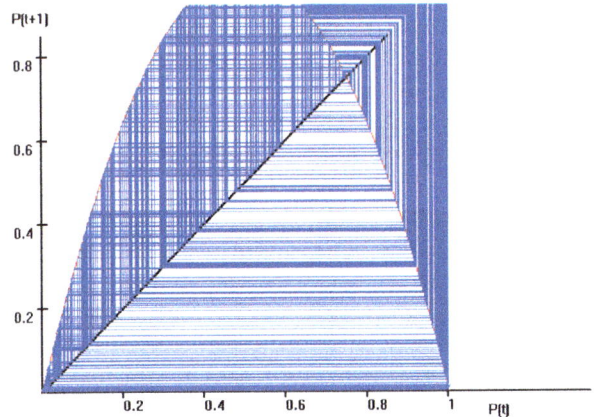

Figure 4. Chaos in the price system system for the function $P(t+1) = \lambda \cdot P(t) \cdot (1 - P(t))$**, with** $\lambda = 4.0$ **and the initial value** $P(0) = 0.01$ **and 2000 iterations [67].**

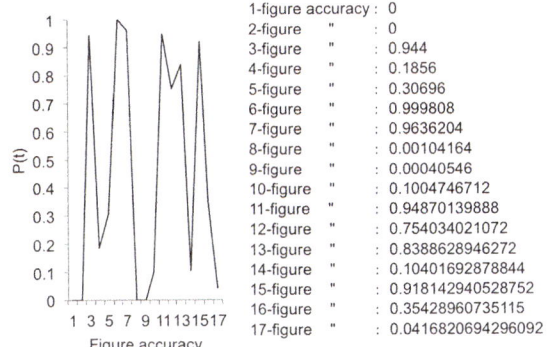

1-figure accuracy :		0
2-figure "	:	0
3-figure "	:	0.944
4-figure "	:	0.1856
5-figure "	:	0.30696
6-figure "	:	0.999808
7-figure "	:	0.9636204
8-figure "	:	0.00104164
9-figure "	:	0.00040546
10-figure "	:	0.1004746712
11-figure "	:	0.94870139888
12-figure "	:	0.754034021072
13-figure "	:	0.8388628946272
14-figure "	:	0.10401692878844
15-figure "	:	0.918142940528752
16-figure "	:	0.35428960735115
17-figure "	:	0.0416820694296092

Figure 5. Butterfly effect in a price system. [67] $P(t)$ **after 2000 iterations of the function** $P(t+1) = \lambda \cdot P(t) \cdot (1 - P(t))$**, with** $\lambda = 4.0$ **and the initial value** $P(0) = 0.01$**.**

As can be observed, the result does not "improve" as might be expected; each time, the calculated price is fundamentally different than the previous instance of increasing the accuracy of the decimal places. In the case of three-figure accuracy, the price is almost 0.94; in the case of five-figure accuracy, it is approximately 0.31; at six-figure accuracy, it is almost 1.00; in the case of fifteen-figure accuracy, we obtain a price of almost 0.92; and in the case of, for example, seventeen-figure accuracy, the price of the "Chaoswriter" is nearly 0.04[36].

Thus, any small change in the initial conditions (here, the increase of the exactness of the decimal places when calculating the price) leads to fundamentally different results. What is the correct result? This question cannot be answered because the results seem to be stochastically independent from one another. One might have a maximal amount of information regarding a complex system but will never successfully obtain an exact calculation or prediction of the system behavior. The reason can be observed in the complexity of the system and not in the lack of information. This idea is the butterfly effect that was described above.

If the state were to regulate this seemingly chaotic market (e.g., by means of a direct intervention by establishing minimum or maximum prices[37]), then this attempt would not be very successful because such efforts would result in a disruption of the price mechanism. Thus, the signal function of the prices (on the basis of which a market can function), which is so important for the market, would be further reduced. The only reasonable possibility of an intervention by the state would be to establish the general framework for the functioning of the market (in the sense of periodical price cycles); in our model, it must be initially discovered how high the market transparency must be to enable the chaos of the price development to evolve into a cyclical price development. Subsequently, the market transparency has to be supported according to this. To determine how high the market transparency must be to ensure that market prices stabilize, one would traditionally utilize a breakdown or reduction of the system to analyze it. However, due to

the butterfly effect, a reductive breakdown for the purpose of comprehension does not assist any further. Many systems, including economic systems, fall into this category and cannot be simplified or broken down without considerable problems. In particular, complex systems cannot be disassembled and reassembled as a mechanical clock can. Continuing with the clock analogy, it can be stated that, in particular, economic processes rather function like a quartz clock, whose connections between the single parts are not mechanical and which is irrevocably - and thus irreversibly-destructed when it is disassembled. Consequently, one must agree with Wesson, who states that the world of simplicity exists only in the imagination. According to Wesson, the world is a nirvana, in which science is treated in the same manner as a wish [68]. Thus, methods that differ from the traditional methods are necessary to research complex systems[38].

One possibility would be the execution of a bifurcation analysis[39]. For the purpose of this model, the market price is entered in a diagram after, for example, 2500 iterations of the model in the face of a gradual increase in market transparency. A bifurcation diagram is produced, and this diagram illustrates how the structure of the system changes at certain parameter values, under which the conditions (e.g., regular price fluctuations) become chaotic. **Figure 6** represents the bifurcation diagram.

At a market transparency of $\lambda < 3.68$, regular price fluctuations occur, whereas at $\lambda = 3.68$, the first aperiodic, chaotic price cycles appear.

Even at a lower level of market transparency, phases of regular price developments are possible. For example, at a value of $\lambda = 3.83$, a three-period price cycle occurs. Such "islands" in the chaos are also referred to as intermittence, and they are visible in the illustration as white, vertical stripes in the midst of the black area of chaos.

After all, the complexity can only have developed due to the feedback of the system as a result of the iteration.

---

[36]According to Voltaire, "Donnez-moi un ordinateur, et je vais faire une monde", as if the butterfly effect were computer-induced. This assessment is far from the truth. The world with its butterfly effect, which is illustrated here, does not correspond to its representation by a computer. Thus, it does not relate to inexact computer calculations, which are possible and occur absolutely algebraically. For a detailed explanatory statement and mathematical proof, cp [21].

[37]Even if the market featured a convergent cyclical movement and the state concluded that the equilibrium price was, for example, too high, intervention by means of an agreement regarding maximum prices would be rather problematic from an economic point of view. To have an effect, the maximum price would have to be considerably below the equilibrium price. However, the result of this price would be that the supply would decrease and ultimately be considerably lower than the demand, which would then increase due to the low maximum price. This maximum price-induced excess demand would be the consequence of the intervention by the state.

[38]Unfortunately, there is insufficient space in which to present such methods for the analysis of complex systems exhaustively. In addition to the method of bifurcation analysis, the calculation of Lyapunov exponents, the Li/Yorke theorem or the calculation of dimensions (e.g., box-counting dimension, Hausdorff dimension) are among the simplest methods of chaos theory. A detailed illustration, explanation and application can be found, for example, in [21]. Especially in the context of empirical studies, it has always been difficult to prove chaos on the sole basis of, for example, the calculation of Lyapunov exponents. It can be assumed that, in particular, the noise in the data, caused by incidental influences and exogenous shocks, complicates the proof cited by [21]. However, other methods, which to some extent must be considered in combination with one another, provide the opportunity to compensate for this deficit. Examples include methods that can be circumscribed with the keywords grammar complexity, recurrence plots, Kolmogorov-Sinai entropy or permutation entropy. Cp., e.g., [61,62,69].

[39]This term has been borrowed from Latin. In this language, the word "furca" refers to a fork with two tines. It is referred to as a bifurcation if in the case of the continuous alteration of the parameters of a system, an abrupt structural change occurs (for example, when a convergent behavior to a point attractor abruptly "turns into" a double cycle from a certain parameter value).

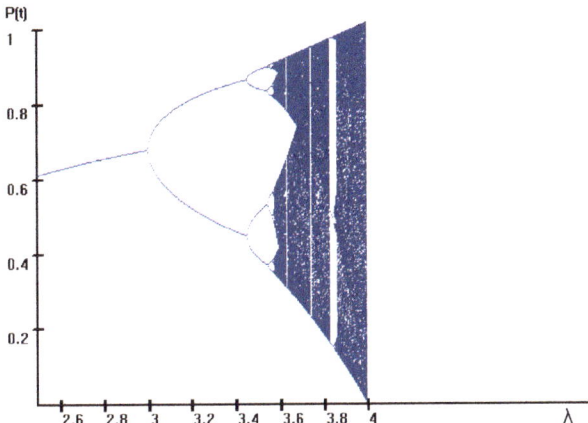

Figure 6. Bifurcation Diagram for the function
$$P(t+1) = \lambda \cdot P(t) \cdot (1 - P(t)) \quad [67].$$

However, if complex systems develop due to the feedback and iteration of the dynamics, then they are not reducible to single elements because these elements do not create complexity until there is a permanent feedback effect on them—recursion. The whole is greater and different than the sum of its parts.

The model described above demonstrates that by means of a mathematically simple, non-linear, recursive function, a much wider spectrum of possible system developments can be illustrated, as is the case for linear functions. Due to the non-linear feedback of the system, the irreversibility of the system becomes apparent. Here, in contrast with an unobstructed oscillating movement, it is important to consider whether time goes backward or forward. This irreversibility is the precondition for self-organization. With regard to this irreversibility, Ebeling states that self-organization can be viewed as the counterpart to the generally observed tendency of a spontaneous "drifting apart of sand dunes". However, in any case, this process is an irreversible process.

Because the irreversibility is a consequence of the "creative character" of mechanical movements (namely, its tendency for drifting apart, for divergence, and for diversity), self-organization establishes a new form of the creative potencies of matter [70].

The principle of self-organization states that order patterns do not develop as a result of determination from "outside"; rather, these patterns develop from the system itself[40]. This development process results in self-reproducing dynamic structures. Thus, self-organization is considered to be a process whose beginning is far from equilibrium and that causes complex order patterns by means of forces that are inherent to a system [70]. Therefore, self-organization is an attribute of systems—more precisely, an attribute of non-linear complex systems—that

produce effects under certain conditions. However, it is both a "surplus" of these systems and an inseparable characteristic. Self-organization is one component, or as Ebeling indicates, perhaps even the crucial component of the evolution of complexity [70].

Thus, irreversibility and self-organization are two further important characteristics of complex systems in addition to non-linearity and the recursive connection of the system elements.

5. Conclusions—A Short Closing Argument for a (Free) Market Economy

Rosser remarks that there are 45 definitions of complexity and this complexity is undoubtedly "a serious problem" [7, p. 170]. However, upon consideration of our former suggestions, it can be stated that complex systems reveal principles that cannot be derived from a high number of simple components or, perhaps, a high number of connections. Complex systems can also be composed of subsystems, but the type of connection, which becomes visible as a result of the dynamization of the system, seems to be decisive. Thus, the complexity of a system is not entirely determined by the number of elements of a system alone and the number of connections among these elements; this complexity is also determined by the following:

- the recursive type of connection
- the non-linear dynamics of the system

Recursion and non-linearity dynamics are generated in a self-organizing and irreversible manner. If complexity develops in the manner that has been described in the above explanations, then a new type of view is necessary to obtain a better understanding; in this view, the complex and simple elements are closely linked to one another, and by means of simple iterations, the complexity (which is hidden in seemingly simple things) is revealed and—as stated by Briggs and Peat—an approach to creative potential [46] is created. Therefore, the equations and parameters of a model do not represent the construction plan; rather, they represent only the initial point for the evolution of a figure, which, as a type of "creatio ex nihilo", gradually emerges [46] as a result of the feedback of the equations.

Even without knowledge of the theoretical approaches that have been presented in this essay (because of the increased use of computers, the mathematical findings did not become possible until the 1990s), von Hayek, in this context, appropriately discusses the pretension of knowledge[41] [1] when writing his work of the same title.

Baumol and Benhabib indicated that chaos theory has the power to provide "caveats" for economic analysts

---

[40]For more information, cp. the comments by [71].

[41]The included essay on the theory of complex phenomena was first published in 1967.

and policy designers:

The chaos theory "warns us that apparently random behavior may not be random at all. It demonstrates dramatically the dangers of extrapolation and the difficulties that can beset economic forecasting generally. It shows that negotiation processes may elicit erratic behavior patterns which no one intends and which can occur even if the positions taken by both parties are inherently simple and straightforward" [20].

The initial findings from the "theory of complex systems", which have been presented in this essay, need not result in—as may be assumed—an irreconcilability of "social justice" and "freedom" with regard to the market system. Nevertheless, these results can assist us in considering the profitable use of the self-organizing forces of freedom, which are inherent to the concept of a free market economy, but which, as a result of excessive interventions by the state, are decreased to the disadvantage of everyone.

However, the analysis of "complex systems" is far from complete. On the contrary, in this essay it was possible only to offer an introduction to this topic. A significant amount of research has yet to be conducted to better understand and evaluate complex systems and to identify options for action.

REFERENCES

[1] F. A. V. Hayek, "Die Anmaßung von Wissen," Mohr Siebeck Verlag, Thübingen, 1996.

[2] F. A. V. Hayek, "Kinds of Order in Society," In: R. Raico, Ed., *New Individualist Review*, Liberty Fund, Indianapolis, 1961, pp. 495-504.

[3] G. Niemeyer, "Kybernetische System-Und Modelltheorie," Vahlen, München, 1977.

[4] P. Nijkamp, A. Reggiani, "Nonlinear Evolution of Spatial Economic Systems," Springer-Verlag, Berlin, 1993.

[5] M. Faggini and A. Parziale, "The Failure of Economic Theory. Lessons from Chaos Theory," *Modern Economy*, Vol. 3, No. 1, 2012, pp. 1-10.

[6] G. Strunk and G. Schiepek, "Systemische Psychologie: Eine Einführung in die Komplexen Grundlagen Menschlichen Verhaltens," Spektrum-Akademischer-Verlag, München, 2006.

[7] B. J. Rosser, "On the Complexities of Complex Economic Dynamics," *Journal of Economic Perspectives*, Vol. 13, No. 4, 1999, pp. 169-192.

[8] F. Bestenreiner, "Der Phantastische Spiegel: Quanten, Quarks, Chaos-Oder vom Trost, der aus der Formel kommt," Fischer-Taschenbuch-Verlag, Frankfurt am Main, 1991.

[9] P. Brügge, "Mythos aus dem Computer. Über Ausbreitung und Mißbrauch der Chaostheorie," *SPIEGEL*, No. 39, 1993, pp. 156-164.

[10] P. Brügge, "Mythos aus dem Computer. Über Ausbrei-

tung und Mißbrauch der Chaostheorie," *SPIEGEL*, Vol. 47, No. 40, 1993, pp. 232-241.

[11] P. Brügge, "Mythos aus dem Computer. Über Ausbreitung und Mißbrauch der Chaostheorie," *SPIEGEL*, Vol. 47, No. 41, 1993, pp. 240-252.

[12] A. Liening, "Ökonomische Chaostheorie," In: H. May, Ed., *Lexikon der ökonomischen Bildung*, Oldenbourg Wissenschaftsverlag, München, 2007.

[13] M. Faggini and C. P. Vinci, "Decision Theory and Choices: A Complexity Approach," Springer-Verlag, Berlin, 2010.

[14] J. S. Metcalfe and J. Foster, "Evolution and Economic Complexity," Edward Elgar Publishers, Northampton, 2007.

[15] F. Trosky, "Heterogene Erwartungen auf dem Geldmarkt," Duncker & Humblot, Berlin, 2006.

[16] B. B. Mandelbrot and R. L. Hudson, "The Behavior of Markets: A Fractal View of Risk, Ruin and Reward," Basic Books, New York, 2004.

[17] W. A. Barnett, C. Deissenberg and G. Feichtinger, "Economic Complexity: Non-linear Dynamics, Multi-Agents Economies, and Learning," Emerald Group Publishing, Bingley, 2004.

[18] G. Zehetner, "Anwendungen der Chaostheorie in der Betriebswirtschaftslehre," Facultas Verlag, Wien, 2003.

[19] T. Puu, "Attractors, Bifurcations and Chaos: Nonlinear Phenomena in Economics," Springer-Verlag, Berlin, 2003.

[20] W. J. Baumol and J. Benhabib, "Chaos: Significance, Mechanism and Economic Applications," *Journal of Economic Perspectives*, Vol. 3, No. 1, 1989, pp. 77-105.

[21] A. Liening, "Komplexe Systeme Zwischen Ordnung und Chaos," Lit Verlag, Münster, 1999.

[22] H. Denis, "Geschichte der Wirtschaftstheorien. 1. Von Platon bis Marx," Schäuble, Rheinfelden, 1985.

[23] K. Mainzer, "Zeit-Von der Uhrzeit zur Computerzeit," Verlag C. H. Beck, München, 1995.

[24] G. Stavenhagen, "Geschichte der Wirtschaftstheorie," Vandenhoeck & Ruprecht, Göttingen, 1969.

[25] W. Lentz, "Neuere Entwicklungen der Theorie Dynamischer Systeme und Ihre Bedeutung für Die Agrarökonomie," Duncker & Humblot, Berlin, 1993.

[26] K.-H. Schmidt, "Merkantilismus, Kameralismus, Physiokratie," In: O. Issing, Ed., *Geschichte der Nationalökonomie*, Vahlen, München, 1994, pp. 43-45.

[27] H. Frank, "Geschichte der Wirtschaftspolitik," Oldenbourg Verlag, München, 1993.

[28] A. Smith, "Wealth of Nations: An Inquiry into the Nature and Causes of the Wealth of Nations," Modern Library, New York, 1994.

[29] A. Smith, "The Theory of Moral Sentiments," Liberty Fund, Indianapolis, 1976.

[30] K. J. Arrow and F. H. Hahn, "General Competitive Analysis," Holden-Day, Amsterdam, 1971.

[31] F. Söllner, "Neoklassik und Umweltökonomie," 1993.

[32] J. Röpke, "Die Strategie der Innovation: Eine System-Theoretische Untersuchung der Interaktion von Individuum, Organisation und Markt im Neuerungsprozess," Mohr Siebeck Verlag, Thybingen, 1977.

[33] B. F. Skinner and E. Ortmann, "Die Funktion der Verstärkung in der Verhaltenswissenschaft: Contigencies of Reinforcement," Kindler, München, 1974.

[34] J. B. Watson, "Behaviorismus," 1984.

[35] H. J. Schlösser, "Das Menschenbild in der Ökonomie," Wirtschaftsverlag Bachem, Köln, 1992.

[36] N. Luhmann, "Zweckbegriff und Systemrationalität," Mohr Siebeck Verlag, Tübingen, 1968.

[37] T. Burns and G. M. Stalker, "The Management of Innovation," Tavistock Publications, London, 1966.

[38] R.-D. Graß, "Vilfredo Pareto—Marx der Bourgeoisie," Schäffer-Poeschel Verlag, Stuttgart, 1994.

[39] S. Hawking, "Eine kurze Geschichte der Zeit," Rowohlt Verlag, Düsseldorf, 1988.

[40] I. Kant, "Immanuel Kant. Werke in Sechs Bänden," Wissenschaftliche Buchgemeinschaft, Darmstadt, 1983.

[41] U. Leonhardt, "Measuring the Quantum State of Light," Cambridge University Press, Cambridge, 1997.

[42] R. Worg, "Deterministisches Chaos—Wege in Die Nichtlineare Dynamik," BI Wissenschaftsverlag, Mannheim, 1993.

[43] P. S. Laplace, "Essai Philosophique sur les Probabilités," 1819.

[44] D. Ruelle, "Zufall und Chaos," Springer Verlag, Berlin, 1993.

[45] R. Descartes, "Discours de la Méthode," Meiner Verlag, Hamburg, 1990.

[46] J. Briggs and F. D. Peat, "Die Entdechung des Chaos. Eine Reise durch die Chaos-Theorie," Deutscher Taschenbuch Verlag, München, 1993.

[47] K. Dopfer, "Classical Mechanics with an Ethical Dimension: Professor Tinbergen's Economics," *Journal of Economic Issues*, Vol. 22, No. 3, 1988, pp. 675-706.

[48] A. Ryan, "The Philosophy of John Stuart Mill," Macmillan, London, 1987.

[49] K. Dopfer, "Evolutionsökonomie in der Zukunft: Programmatik und Theorieentwicklungen," In: H. R. Hanusch and C. Horst, Eds., *Ökonomische Wissenschaft in der Zukunft: Ansichten Führender Ökonomen*, Wirtschaft und Finanzen, Düsseldorf, 1992, pp. 1-28.

[50] H. Poincaré, "Les méthodes nouvelles de la mécanique céleste," Gauthier-Villars, Paris, 1899.

[51] J. P. Crutchfield, J. D. Farmer, N. H. Packard and R. S. Shaw, "Non-Linear Physics for Beginners: Fractals, Chaos, Pattern Formation, Solutions, Cellular Automata and Complex Systems," World Scientific, New Jersey, 1998.

[52] C. Chiarella, "Entwicklungen der Nichtlinearen, Dynamischen Ökonomischen Theorie: Vergangenheit, Gegenwart und Zukunft," In: H. R. Hanusch and C. Horst, Eds., *Ökonomische Wissenschaft in der Zukunft: Ansichten Führender Ökonomen*, Wirtschaft und Finanzen, Düssel-

dorf, 1992, pp. 74-91.

[53] A. Medio, "Chaotic Dynamics: Theory and Applications to Economics," Camebridge University Press, Cambridge, 1992.

[54] A. N. Kolmogorow, "Über die Entropie der Zeit. Eins als metrische Invariante von Automorphismen," *Dokladyi Akademii Nauk (UDSSR)*, Vol. 119, No. 5, 1958, pp. 861-864.

[55] S. Smale, "Differentiable Dynamical Systems," *Bulletin of the American Mathematical Society*, Vol. 73, No. 6, 1967, pp. 747-817.

[56] B. Schefold, "Wenn Du den Hals überschreitest : Gedanken zur Zukunft ökonomischer Wissenschaft," In: H. R. Hanusch and C. Horst, Eds., *Ökonomische Wissenschaft in der Zukunft: Ansichten Führender Ökonomen*, Wirtschaft und Finanzen, Düsseldorf, 1992, pp. 346-360.

[57] R. Schmalensee, "Kontinuität und Wandel in der Wirtschaftswissenschaft," In: H. R. Hanusch and C. Horst Eds., *Ökonomische Wissenschaft in der Zukunft: Ansichten Führender Ökonomen*, Wirtschaft und Finanzen, Düsseldorf, 1992, pp. 331-370.

[58] F. Hölderlin, "Sämtliche Gedichte und Hyperion," Insel Verlag, Leipzig, 2001.

[59] H. J. Warnecke, "Die Fraktale Fabrik: Revolution der Unternehmenskultur," Rowohlt, Reinbek, 1996.

[60] G. Gerken, "Die fraktale Marke," Econ Verlag, Wien, 1994.

[61] A. Liening and E. Mittelstädt, "Intellectual Capital Reporting in Schools: A Complexity-Scientific Approach to Educational Management," *The International Journal Learning*, Vol. 16, No. 7, 2009, p. 15.

[62] A. Liening and E. Mittelstädt, "Innovative Instrumente zur Anreizkompatiblen Selbstorganisation von Wissenschaft—Die Wissensbilanzierung," In: E. Brunner, Ed., *Selbstorganisation in der Wissenschaft*, Frege Centre for Structural Sciences, Jena, 2011.

[63] B. Glazinski, "Innovatives Change Management," Wileyvch, Weinheim, 2007.

[64] G. Strunk, "Die Komplexitätshypothese der Karriereforschung," Frankfurt am Main, Wien, 2009.

[65] M. Thiemann, "Chaostheorie auf Kapitalmärkten: Untersuchung des DAX, DOW und FTSE anhand modernerer Verfahren auf deterministisches Chaos," WiKu-Verlag, Stuttgart, 2004.

[66] O. Loistl and B. Iro, "Chaostheorie: Zur Theorie Nichtlinearer Dynamischer Systeme," Oldenbourg Wissenschaftsverlag, München, 1993.

[67] A. Liening, "Komplexe Systeme—Eine Software zur Simulation und Analyse," 2010.

[68] R. Wesson, "Chaos, Zufall und Auslese der Natur," Insel-Verlag, Leipzig, 1995.

[69] G. Strunk, *et al.*, "Lost in Transition? Complexity in Organisational Behaviour—The Contributions of Systems Theories," *Management Revue*, Vol. 15, No. 4, 2004, pp. 481-509.

[70] W. Ebeling, "Selbstorganisation und Entropie in Ökologischen und Ökonomischen Prozessen," In: F. B. A. H.

Diefenbacher, Ed., *Zwischen Entropie und Selbstorganisation—Perspektiven Einer Ökologischen Ökonomie*, Metropolis-Verlag, Marburg, 1994, pp. 29-45.

[71] M. Pasche, "Ansätze Einer Evolutorischen Umweltökonomik," In: F. B. A. H. Diefenbacher, Ed., *Zwischen Entropie und Selbstorganisation—Perspektiven einer ökologischen Ökonomie*, Metropolis-Verlag, Marburg, 1994, p. 75.

14

Irrelevance of Conjectural Variation in a Private Duopoly with Consistent Conjectures: The Relative Performance Approach and Network Effects[*]

Yasuhiko Nakamura
College of Economics, Nihon University, Tokyo, Japan

ABSTRACT

This paper explores the equilibrium market outcomes in the contexts of both quantity-setting and price-setting private duopolies with the consistent conjectures of two private firms, wherein they maximize the weighted sum of their own profits and their respective opponent firm's profit. Similar to the private duopoly without network effects wherein the two private firms maximize their genuine relative profits, in the private duopoly with network effects such that both firms maximize the weighted sum of their own profits and their respective opponent firm's profit, we show that the equilibrium outcomes in the quantity-setting competition with the consistent conjectures of both firms are equivalent to those in the price-setting competition with the consistent conjectures of both firms.

Keywords: Relative Profit Maximization; Conjectural Variation; Consistent Conjecture; Network Effects

1. Introduction

This paper tackles the problem of whether or not the consistent conjectures of two relative profit maximizing private firms yield the same equilibrium outcomes between a quantity-setting competition and a price-setting competition in the context of a private duopolistic market with differentiated and substitutable goods and with network effects. Conjectural variations in oligopolistic markets have been investigated for a long time. For example, Bresnahan [1], Perry [2], Boyer and Moreaux [3], Tanaka [4], and Tanaka [5] considered the effects of the conjectural variations of firms on equilibrium market outcomes in several economic contexts[1]. More recently, in private duopoly with the linear demand function and constant marginal cost functions composed of two symmetric private firms, Tanaka [6] showed that their equilibrium output and price levels in the Cournot equilibrium under their relative profit maximization are equal to those in the Bertrand equilibrium under their relative profit maximization[2].

As indicated in Matsumura et al. [8], the performances of firms' managers are often based on their relative performance and outperforming managers often obtain good positions in the management job markets. Taking the importance of the relative performance approaches into account, the relative profit approaches employed in this paper have been adopted in many modern theoretical oligopolistic works. In the context of evolutionary economics à la Schaffer [9], Vega-Redondo [10] found that each firm's adoption of its relative profit maximizing behavior yields the Walrasian equilibrium in the general equilibrium framework. Furthermore, Lundgren [11] presented a new economic method for preventing incentives for collusion by making managerial compensation which depends on relative profits rather than absolute profits. Kockesen et al. [12] derived the condition that the firm with interdependent preferences (i.e., the relative

---

[*]We are grateful for the financial support of KAKENHI (25870113). Any remaining errors are our own.

[1]In particular, Perry [2] showed that when the number of firms is fixed, their competitive behaviors are consistent in the case wherein their marginal costs are constant, but that when marginal costs are rising, the consistent conjectural variation will be between competitive and Cournot behavior. Furthermore, they found that when we allow free entry of firms, only their competitive behaviors will be consistent.

[2]In addition, Tanaka [7] found that in private duopoly with the linear demand and constant marginal cost functions, when the two symmetric private firms maximize their genuine relative profits, the choices of their strategic variables are irrelevant to the outcome of the game in the sense that the equilibrium outcomes are the same in all three types of market structures. Any combination of choices of the strategic variables by the private firms composes a subgame perfect equilibrium in the two stage game.

profit preference) obtains a strictly higher profit than the independent (*i.e.*, the absolute profit preference) firm in any equilibrium. Moreover, Matsumura and Matsushima [13] investigated the relationship between the degree of competition and the stability of collusive behavior by introducing the element of relative performance into the objective functions of the firms and showed that an increase in the degree of competition destabilizes collusion.

In this paper, we consider the equilibrium market outcomes between the quantity-setting competition and the price-setting competition in a private duopoly with network effects by adopting the maximization of the weighted sum of their own profit and the profit of their respective opponent firm including the case of their genuine relative profit maximization (the "extended" relative profit). The network effects that we consider in this paper were introduced in Katz and Shapiro [14] and applied in Hoernig [15], Nakamura [16], and Nakamura [17]. These effects reflected a simple mechanism where the surplus obtained by a firm's client increases directly with the number of other clients of this firm. Then, taking into account the network effects and the maximization of the extended relative profit of the private firms, in this paper, we confirm the robustness of the result on the coincidence of the equilibrium market outcomes in the contexts of both the quantity-setting competition and price-setting competition in the private duopoly.

Except for the question of whether or not there exists the presence of network effects à la Katz and Shapiro [14], the difference between the settings of Tanaka [6] and Tanaka [7] and this paper is whether or not to allow the private firm to maximize the weighted sum of its own profit and its opponent firm's profit. Tanaka [6] and Tanaka [7] considered the situation wherein the private firm maximizes the genuine relative profit, which is equal to the difference between its own profit and its opponent firm's profit. In this paper, we focus on the influence of the parameter of the degree of importance of each private firm's relative performance on the equilibrium market outcomes in the contexts of both the quantity-setting competition and price-setting competition[3]. In this paper, we show that even if we take into account both the network effects and the possibility of the weighted sum of each firm's profit and its opponent firm's profit, the equilibrium market outcomes in the quantity-setting competition are equivalent to those in the price-setting competition. Thus, the equivalence of Cournot and Bertrand equilibria in the private duopoly with differentiated

and substitutable goods still holds against the introduction of network effects à la Katz and Shapiro [14] and the possibility of maximization of the weighted sum of the profit of the private firm and its opponent firm's profit.

The remainder of this paper is organized as follows: in Section 2, we formulate the basis model employed in this paper. In Section 3, we derive the equilibrium outcomes in both the quantity-setting competition and price-setting competition with differentiated and substitutable goods in the private duopoly with network effects à la Katz and Shapiro [14] wherein the private firms maximize the weighted sum of their own profits and their respective opponent's profit. Section 4 concludes with several remarks.

2. Model

We formulate a private duopolistic model with differentiated and substitutable goods and consistent conjectures composed of two extended relative profit-maximizing private firms with an additional term that reflects the network effects introduced in Katz and Shapiro [14] and applied by Hoernig [15], Nakamura [16], and Nakamura [17]. Similar to Hoernig [15], Nakamura [16], and Nakamura [17], firm i faces a linear demand of the following form:

$$q_i = a + ny_i - p_i + bp_j, \text{ and } i = 0, 1; \ i \neq j \qquad (1)$$

where $a > 0$ and $b \in (0,1)$ are demand parameters[4]. $n \in [0,1)$ indicates the strength of network effects, and y_i is consumers' expectations of firm i's equilibrium market share. The ordinary demand function for the good of firm i is obtained from the inverse demand function given in Equation (1) as follows:

$$p_i = \frac{a(1+b) - q_i - bp_j + ny_i + bny_j}{1 - b^2} \qquad (2)$$
$$\text{and } i = 0, 1; i \neq j$$

As explained in Hoernig [15], Nakamura [16], and Nakamura [17], the above demand system can be derived from the following quasi-linear concave utility function of a representative consumer:

$$\begin{aligned} & U(q_0, q_1; y_0, y_1) \\ & = m + \frac{a(q_0 + q_1)}{1 - b} - \frac{q_0^2 + q_1^2}{2(1 - b^2)} - \frac{bq_0 q_1}{1 - b^2} \\ & \quad + n \frac{(y_0 + by_1)q_0 + (y_1 + by_0)q_1}{1 - b^2} + f(y_0, y_1) \end{aligned}$$

---

[3]A number of existing works have used relative performance approaches in the context of a mixed duopoly with one social welfare-maximizing public firm and one extended relative profit-maximizing private firm, Nakamura and Saito [18] investigated each firm's capacity choice in a quantity-setting competition, whereas Nakamura and Saito [19] considered each firm's capacity choice in a price-setting competition.

[4]The value of $b \in (0,1)$ indicates that the relation between the goods of firms 0 and 1 is substitutable. Moreover, the assumption that $a > (1 - b)c \geq 0$ is made to ensure the non-negativity of all equilibrium outcomes.

where m denotes the income of the representative consumer and $f(\cdot,\cdot)$ represents some symmetric function of expectations. In this paper, in the same manner as in Hoernig [15], Nakamura [16], and Nakamura [17], we suppose that

$$f(y_0, y_1) = -n\left(y_0^2/2 + by_0y_1 + y_1^2/2\right)\big/\left(1-b^2\right)^5.$$

We consider a private duopolistic market composed of two extended relative profit maximizing private firms (firms 0 and 1). We use q_i and p_i to represent firm i's output and price levels, respectively, $(i = 0,1)$. We adopt the constant marginal cost function, where c is a common marginal cost between firms 0 and 1, similar to Hoernig [15], Nakamura [16], and Nakamura [17][6]. The marginal cost of production of both firms 0 and 1 is commonly assumed to be c. The profit function of firm i is given by

$$\begin{cases} \pi_i(q_i, q_j) = \left[p_i(q_i, q_j) - c\right]q_i, \\ \left[\text{quantity-setting competition}\right], \\ \pi_i(p_i, p_j) = (p_i - c)q_i(p_i, p_j), \\ \left[\text{price-setting competition}\right], \\ \text{and} \quad i = 0,1; i \neq j, \end{cases}$$

where p_i is given in Equation (1) and q_i is given in Equation (2). Consumer surplus is expressed as the representative consumer's utility as follows:
$CS = U(q_0, q_1; y_0, y_1) - p_0q_0 - p_1q_1$, whereas producer surplus is given by the sum of the profits of both firms 0 and 1, $\pi_0 + \pi_1$. Finally, we suppose that social welfare is defined as the sum of consumer surplus and producer surplus. We consider the "rational expectations" subgame perfect Nash equilibrium by imposing the rational expectations condition that $y_0 = q_0$ and $y_1 = q_1$ à la Katz and Shapiro [14], Hoernig [15], Nakamura [16], and Nakamura [17].

3. Equilibrium Analysis

In this section, we derive the equilibrium market outcomes with firms 0 and 1 in the contexts of both the quantity-setting competition and price-setting competi-

tion with their consistent conjectures in the private duopoly with differentiated and substitutable goods wherein they maximize the extended relative profit.

3.1. Quantity-Setting Framework

In this subsection, we consider the situation wherein the strategic variables of firms 0 and 1 are their output levels. The objective functions of firms 0 and 1 are given as follows:

$$V_0^{qq}(q_0, q_1)$$
$$= \pi_0(q_0, q_1) - \alpha\pi_1(q_0, q_1)$$
$$= \left[\frac{a(1+b) - q_0 - bq_1 + ny_0 + bny_1}{1-b^2} - c\right]q_0$$
$$-\alpha\left[\frac{a(1+b) - bq_0 - q_1 + bny_0 + ny_1}{1-b^2} - c\right]q_1,$$

$$V_1^{qq}(q_0, q_1)$$
$$= \pi_1(q_0, q_1) - \alpha\pi_0(q_0, q_1)$$
$$= \left[\frac{a(1+b) - bq_0 - q_1 + bny_0 + ny_1}{1-b^2} - c\right]q_1$$
$$-\alpha\left[\frac{a(1+b) - q_0 - bq_1 + ny_0 + bny_1}{1-b^2} - c\right]q_0,$$

where $\alpha \in (-1,1)$[7].

Firm 0 decides its output level in order to maximize V_0^{qq} assuming that the reaction of the output level of firm 1 to the output level of firm 0 is given as follows:

$$\frac{\partial q_1}{\partial q_0} = \delta_0^{qq}.$$

On the other hand, firm 1 decides its output level in order to maximize V_1^{qq} assuming that the reaction of the output level of firm 0 to the output level of firm 1 is given as follows:

$$\frac{\partial q_0}{\partial q_1} = \delta_1^{qq}.$$

The first-order conditions of firms 0 and 1 in the quantity-setting market competition are given, and their real reaction functions of firms are obtained as follows[8]:

---

[5]This assumption in the form of $f(\cdot,\cdot)$ implies that the representative consumer's utility is highest with respect to the consumption vector of the goods produced by the two private firms, (q_0, q_1), when expectations are rational and correct.

[6]In their theoretical model, Tanaka [6], Tanaka [7], and Nakamura [20] adopted the genuine relative profit that is equal to the difference between each firm's absolute profit and its opponent firm's absolute profit.

[7]As indicated in Matsumura and Matsushima [13], parameter α is closely related to the "coefficient of effective sympathy" defined by Edgeworth [21] and the "coefficient of cooperation" defined by Cyert and de Groot [22].

[8]The second-order conditions of firms 0 and 1 are satisfied.

$$\frac{\partial V_0^{qq}}{\partial q_0}$$

$$=\frac{a(1+b)(1-\alpha\delta_0)-(1-b^2)c(1-\alpha\delta_0)-2q_0-bq_1+ny_0+bny_1+bq_1\alpha-bq_0\delta_0+bq_0\alpha\delta_0+2q_1\alpha\delta_0-bny_0\alpha\delta_0-ny_1\alpha\delta_0}{1-b^2}=0$$

$$\Leftrightarrow q_0(q_1)=\frac{a(1+b)(1-\alpha\delta_0)-(1-b^2)c(1-\alpha\delta_0)-bq_1+ny_0+bny_1+bq_1\alpha+2q_1\alpha\delta_0-bny_0\alpha\delta_0-ny_1\alpha\delta_0}{2+b(1-\alpha)\delta_0},$$

$$\frac{\partial V_1^{qq}}{\partial q_1}$$

$$=\frac{a(1+b)(1-\alpha\delta_1)-(1-b^2)c(1-\alpha\delta_1)-bq_0-2q_1+bny_0+ny_1+bq_0\alpha-bq_1\delta_1+2q_0\alpha\delta_1+bq_1\alpha\delta_1-ny_0\alpha\delta_1-bny_1\alpha\delta_1}{1-b^2}=0$$

$$\Leftrightarrow q_1(q_0)=\frac{a(1+b)(1-\alpha\delta_1)-(1-b^2)c(1-\alpha\delta_1)-bq_0+bny_0+ny_1+bq_0\alpha+2q_0\alpha\delta_1-ny_0\alpha\delta_1-bny_1\alpha\delta_1}{2+b(1-\alpha)\delta_1}.$$

From the real reaction function of the output level of firm i to the output level of firm j, we obtain the following result $(i,j=0,1;i\neq j)$:

$$\frac{\partial q_0}{\partial q_1}=-\frac{b-b\alpha-2\alpha\delta_0}{2+b(1-\alpha)\delta_0}$$

and $\dfrac{\partial q_1}{\partial q_0}=-\dfrac{b-b\alpha-2\alpha\delta_1}{2+b(1-\alpha)\delta_1}$,

respectively.

The conditions of the consistency of the conjectural variations of firms 0 and 1 are, respectively,

$$\begin{cases}-[b-b\alpha-2\alpha\delta_0]/[2+b(1-\alpha)\delta_0]=\delta_1,\\-[b-b\alpha-2\alpha\delta_1]/[2+b(1-\alpha)\delta_1]=\delta_0,\end{cases}$$

yielding

$$\delta_0^{qq}=\frac{-1+\sqrt{1-b^2}}{b},$$

$$\delta_1^{qq}=\frac{-1+\sqrt{1-b^2}}{b}.$$

From the symmetry of firms 0 and 1, we notice that $\delta_0^{qq}=\delta_1^{qq}$. The above values of firms 0 and 1 are the equilibrium consistent conjectures in the quantity-setting competition under the assumption that $\delta_0^{qq}\in(-1,1)$ and $\delta_1^{qq}\in(-1,1)$. Thus, by substituting the rational expectations assumption that $y_0=q_0$ and $y_1=q_1$, the equilibrium output levels and price levels of firms 0 and 1 under the assumption that $\delta_0=\delta_0^{qq}$ and $\delta_1=\delta_1^{qq}$ are obtained as follows:

$$q_0^{qq}=\frac{(1+b)[a-(1-b)c](b+\alpha-\sqrt{1-b^2}\alpha)}{(1-\sqrt{1-b^2})(2-n)\alpha+b^2(1-n-\alpha)+b\{1+\sqrt{1-b^2}+\alpha-\sqrt{1-b^2}\alpha-n[1+(1-\sqrt{1-b^2})\alpha]\}},$$

$$q_1^{qq}=\frac{(1+b)[a-(1-b)c](b+\alpha-\sqrt{1-b^2}\alpha)}{(1-\sqrt{1-b^2})(2-n)\alpha+b^2(1-n-\alpha)+b\{1+\sqrt{1-b^2}+\alpha-\sqrt{1-b^2}\alpha-n[1+(1-\sqrt{1-b^2})\alpha]\}},$$

and

$$p_0^{qq}=\frac{(1-b^2)c(1-n)(b+\alpha-\sqrt{1-b^2}\alpha)+a(b\sqrt{1-b^2}+\alpha-b^2\alpha-\sqrt{1-b^2}\alpha)}{(1-b)\{(1-\sqrt{1-b^2})(2-n)\alpha+b^2(1-n-\alpha)+b(1+\sqrt{1-b^2}+\alpha-\sqrt{1-b^2}\alpha-n[1+(1-\sqrt{1-b^2})\alpha]\}},$$

$$p_1^{qq}=\frac{(1-b^2)c(1-n)(b+\alpha-\sqrt{1-b^2}\alpha)+a(b\sqrt{1-b^2}+\alpha-b^2\alpha-\sqrt{1-b^2}\alpha)}{(1-b)\{(1-\sqrt{1-b^2})(2-n)\alpha+b^2(1-n-\alpha)+b(1+\sqrt{1-b^2}+\alpha-\sqrt{1-b^2}\alpha-n[1+(1-\sqrt{1-b^2})\alpha]\}}.$$

3.2. Price-Setting Framework

In this subsection, we consider the situation wherein the strategic variables of firms 0 and 1 are their price levels. The objective functions of firms 0 and 1 are given as follows:

$$V_0^{pp}(p_0, p_1) = \pi_0(p_0, p_1) - \alpha \pi_1(p_0, p_1)$$

$$= (p_0 - c)(a - p_0 + bp_1 + ny_0)$$

$$- \alpha(p_1 - c)(a + bp_0 - p_1 + ny_1),$$

$$V_1^{pp}(p_0, p_1) = \pi_1(p_0, p_1) - \alpha \pi_0(p_0, p_1)$$

$$= (p_1 - c)(a + bp_0 - p_1 + ny_1)$$

$$- \alpha(p_0 - c)(a - p_0 + bp_1 + ny_0).$$

Firm 0 decides its price level in order to maximize V_0^{pp} assuming that the reaction of the price level of firm 1 to the price level of firm 0 is given as follows:

$$\frac{\partial p_1}{\partial p_0} = \delta_0^{pp}.$$

On the other hand, firm 1 decides its price level in order to maximize V_1^{pp} assuming that the reaction of the price level of firm 0 to the price level of firm 1 is given as follows:

$$\frac{\partial p_0}{\partial p_1} = \delta_1^{pp}.$$

The first-order conditions of firms 0 and 1 in the price-setting competition are given, and the real reaction functions of firms are obtained as follows[9]:

$$\frac{\partial V_0^{pp}}{\partial p_0} = a - p_0 + bp_1 + ny_0 - (p_1 - c)\alpha(b - \delta_0) - (a + bp_0 - p_1 + ny_1)\alpha\delta_0 - (p_0 - c)(1 - b\delta_0) = 0$$

$$\Leftrightarrow p_0(p_1) = \frac{a + bp_1 + ny_0 - bp_1\alpha - a\alpha\delta_0 + 2p_1\alpha\delta_0 - ny_1\alpha\delta_0 + c(1 + b\alpha - b\delta_0 - \alpha\delta_0)}{2 - b(1 - \alpha)\delta_0},$$

$$\frac{\partial V_1^{pp}}{\partial p_1} = a + bp_0 - p_1 + ny_1 - (p_0 - c)\alpha(b - \delta_1) - (a - p_0 + bp_1 + ny_0)\alpha\delta_1 - (p_1 - c)(1 - b\delta_1) = 0$$

$$\Leftrightarrow p_1(p_0) = \frac{a + bp_0 + ny_1 - bp_0\alpha - a\alpha\delta_1 + 2p_0\alpha\delta_1 - ny_0\alpha\delta_1 + c(1 + b\alpha - b\delta_1 - \alpha\delta_1)}{2 - b(1 - \alpha)\delta_1}.$$

From the real reaction of the price level of firm i to the price level of firm j, we obtain the following result $(i, j = 0, 1; i \neq j)$:

$$\frac{\partial p_0}{\partial p_1} = \frac{b - b\alpha + 2\alpha\delta_0}{2 - b(1 - \alpha)\delta_0} \quad \text{and} \quad \frac{\partial p_1}{\partial p_0} = \frac{b - b\alpha + 2\alpha\delta_1}{2 - b(1 - \alpha)\delta_1},$$

respectively.

The conditions of the consistency of the conjectural variations of firms 0 and 1 are, respectively,

$$\begin{cases} (b - b\alpha + 2\alpha\delta_0)/[2 - b(1 - \alpha)\delta_0] = \delta_1, \\ (b - b\alpha + 2\alpha\delta_1)/[2 - b(1 + \alpha)\delta_1] = \delta_0, \end{cases}$$

yielding

$$\delta_0^{pp} = \frac{1 - \sqrt{1 - b^2}}{b}, \quad \delta_1^{pp} = \frac{1 - \sqrt{1 - b^2}}{b}.$$

The above values of firms 0 and 1 are the equilibrium consistent conjectures in the price-setting competition under the assumption that $\delta_0^{pp} \in (-1, 1)$ and $\delta_1^{pp} \in (-1, 1)$. Note that each firm's consistent conjectural variation in the price-setting competition is different from that in the quantity-setting competition[10]. Thus, by substituting the rational expectations assumption that $y_0 = q_0$ and $y_1 = q_1$, the equilibrium price level and output level under the assumption that $\delta_0 = \delta_0^{pp}$ and $\delta_1 = \delta_1^{pp}$ are obtained as follows:

$$p_0^{pp} = \frac{(1 - b^2)c(1 - n)(b + \alpha - \sqrt{1 - b^2}\alpha) + a(b\sqrt{1 - b^2} + \alpha - b^2\alpha - \sqrt{1 - b^2}\alpha)}{(1 - b)\{(1 - \sqrt{1 - b^2})(2 - n)\alpha + b^2(1 - n - \alpha) + b(1 + \sqrt{1 - b^2} + \alpha - \sqrt{1 - b^2}\alpha - n[1 + (1 - \sqrt{1 - b^2})\alpha])\}},$$

---

[9]The second-order conditions of firms 0 and 1 are satisfied.

[10]In Tanaka [23], in a private duopoly composed of two absolute profit maximizing firms, it is shown that their consistent conjectural variations in the quantity-setting competition are also different from those in the price-setting competition.

$$p_1^{pp} = \frac{(1-b^2)c(1-n)(b+\alpha-\sqrt{1-b^2}\alpha)+a(b\sqrt{1-b^2}+\alpha-b^2\alpha-\sqrt{1-b^2}\alpha)}{(1-b)\left\{(1-\sqrt{1-b^2})(2-n)\alpha+b^2(1-n-\alpha)+b(1+\sqrt{1-b^2}+\alpha-\sqrt{1-b^2}\alpha-n[1+(1-\sqrt{1-b^2})\alpha])\right\}},$$

and

$$q_0^{pp} = \frac{(1+b)[a-(1-b)c](b+\alpha-\sqrt{1-b^2}\alpha)}{(1-\sqrt{1-b^2})(2-n)\alpha+b^2(1-n-\alpha)+b\left\{1+\sqrt{1-b^2}+\alpha-\sqrt{1-b^2}\alpha-n[1+(1-\sqrt{1-b^2})\alpha]\right\}},$$

$$q_1^{pp} = \frac{(1+b)[a-(1-b)c](b+\alpha-\sqrt{1-b^2}\alpha)}{(1-\sqrt{1-b^2})(2-n)\alpha+b^2(1-n-\alpha)+b\left\{1+\sqrt{1-b^2}+\alpha-\sqrt{1-b^2}\alpha-n[1+(1-\sqrt{1-b^2})\alpha]\right\}}.$$

Thus, we have the result that $q_i^{qq} = q_i^{pp}$ and $p_i^{qq} = p_i^{pp}$, $(i=0,1)$. Summing up the rational expectations equilibrium market outcomes with consistent conjectures including the output and price levels of firms 0 and 1 between the quantity-setting competition and price-setting competition, we obtain the following proposition:

Proposition 1 *In the private duopoly with consistent conjectural variations composed of the two extended relative profit maximizing private firms, the rational expectations equilibrium outcomes including their output and price levels, profit, consumer surplus, and social welfare in the quantity-setting competition are equivalent to those in the price-setting competition.*

Note that the statement of Proposition 1 is relevant to the private duopoly composed of extended relative profit-maximizing private firms that is without network effects à la Katz and Shapiro [14] since it includes the case of $n=0$. On the other hand, the statement of Proposition 1 is relevant to the private duopoly with the network effects à la Katz and Shapiro [14] composed of the absolute profit-maximizing private firms since it includes the case of $\alpha=0$.

4. Concluding Remarks

In this paper, we considered the equilibrium market outcomes in a private duopoly with differentiated and substitutable goods and with an additional term that reflects network effects in the fashion of Katz and Shapiro [14], Hoernig [15], Nakamura [16], and Nakamura [17], wherein the private firms maximize the weighted sum of their own profits and their respective opponent firm's profit. Similar to the private duopoly without network effects composed of two absolute profit maximizing firms and of two relative profit maximizing firms investigated in Tanaka [6], we show that the equilibrium outcomes in the quantitysetting competition are equivalent to those in the price-setting competition even in the private duopoly with network effects à la Katz and Shapiro [14], wherein the two private firms maximize their ex-

tended relative profits, which are equal to the weighted sum of the firm's own profit and its opponent firm's profit. In this paper, we also showed that in the above private duopolistic market, the equilibrium market outcomes in the quantity-setting competition are the same as those in the price-setting competition. Thus, the above so-called irrelevance result that the equilibrium market outcomes are the same between the quantity-setting competition and price-setting competition is robust against the introduction of both network effects à la Katz and Shapiro [14] and the presence of the weighted relative profit-maximizing private firms.

Finally, we identify several topics to be addressed in our future research. In a symmetric private duopoly with differentiated and substitutable goods wherein two private firms maximize their genuine relative profits, Tanaka [7] showed that the choice of the strategic variables of the two firms is irrelevant to the outcome of the game in the sense that since their equilibrium output, price levels, and profits are the same in all situations, any combination of their strategy choices comprises a subgame perfect equilibrium in the game on the endogenous selections of their strategic variables. Then, as one of our future studies, we will consider the two-stage game on the endogenous selections of each firm's strategic variable in a private duopoly with differentiated and substitutable goods and with network effects wherein two private firms maximize the weighted sum of their own profits and their respective opponent firm's profit. Second, as indicated in Tanaka [6] and Tanaka [7], as one of our future studies, we should check the robustness of the results obtained in this paper against the general numbers of the existing private firms and the general demand function.

REFERENCES

[1] T. Bresnahan, "Duopoly Models with Consistent Conjectures," *American Economic Review*, Vol. 71, No. 5, 1981, pp. 934-945.

[2] M. Perry, "Oligopoly and Consistent Conjectural Varia-
     tions," *Bell Journal of Economics*, Vol. 13, No. 1, 1982,
     pp. 197-205.

[3] M. Boyer and M. Moreaux, "Consistent versus Non-
     Consistent Conjectures in Duopoly Theory: Some Exam-
     ples," *Journal of Industrial Economics*, Vol. 32, No. 1,
     1983, pp. 97-110.

[4] Y. Tanaka, "Consistent Conjectures in Free Entry Oli-
     gopoly," *Economics Letters*, Vol. 17, No. 1-2, 1985, pp.
     15-18.

[5] Y. Tanaka, "On Multiplicity of Consistent Conjectures in
     Free Entry Oligopoly," *Economics Letters*, Vol. 28, No. 2,
     1985, pp. 109-115.

[6] Y. Tanaka, "Equivalance of Cournot and Bertrand Equi-
     libria in Differentiated Duopoly under Relative Profit
     Maximization with Linear Demand," *Economics Bulletin*,
     Vol. 33, No. 2, 2013, pp. 1479-1486.

[7] Y. Tanaka, "Irrelevance of the Choice of Strategic Vari-
     ables in Duopoly under Relative Profit Maximization,"
     Economics and Business Letters, Vol. 2, No. 2, 2013, pp.
     75-83.

[8] T. Matsumura, N. Matsushima and S. Cato, "Competi-
     tiveness and R&D Competition Revisited," *Economic
     Modelling*, Vol. 31, 2013, pp. 541-547.

[9] M. E. Schaffer, "Are Profit Maximizers the Best Survi-
     vors?" *Journal of Economic Behavior and Organization*,
     12, 1, 1989, 29-45.

[10] F. Vega-Redondo, "The Evolution of Walrasian Behavior,"
     Econometrica, Vol. 65, No. 2, 1997, pp. 375-384.

[11] C. Lundgren, "Using Relative Profit Incentives to Prevent
     Collusion," *Review of Industrial Organization*, Vol. 11,
     No. 4, 1996, pp. 533-550.

[12] L. Kockesen, E. A. Ok and R. Sethi, "The Strategic Ad-
     vantage of Negatively Interdependent Preferences," *Jour-
     nal of Economic Theory*, Vol. 92, No. 2, 2000, pp. 274-
     299.

[13] T. Matsumura and N. Matsushima, "Competitiveness and
     Stability of Collusive Behavior," *Bulletin of Economic
     Research* 64, Supplement, Vol. 64, Suppl. 1, 2012, pp. 22-
     31.

[14] M. Katz and C. Shapiro, "Network Externalities, Compe-
     tition, and Compatibility," *American Economic Review*,
     Vol. 75, No. 3, 1985, pp. 424-440.

[15] S. Hoernig, "Strategic Delegation under Price Competi-
     tion and Network Effects," *Economics Letters*, Vol. 117,
     No. 2, 2012, 487-489.

[16] Y. Nakmaura, "Social Welfare under Quantity Competi-
     tion and Price Competition in a Mixed Duopoly with Net-
     work Effects: An Analysis," *Theoretical Economics Let-
     ters*, Vol. 3, No. 4, 2013, pp. 211-215.

[17] Y. Nakmaura, "Endogenous Timing in Price-Setting Pri-
     vate and Mixed Duopoly with Network Effects," 2013,
     Mimeo.

[18] Y. Nakamura and M. Saito, "Capacity Choice in a Mixed
     Duopoly: The Relative Performance Approach," *Theo-
     retical Economics Letters*, Vol. 3, No. 2, 2013, pp. 124-
     133.

[19] Y. Nakamura and M. Saito, "Capacity Choice in a Price-
     Setting Mixed Duopoly: The Relative Performance Ap-
     proach," *Modern Economy*, Vol. 4, No. 4, 2013, pp. 273-
     280.

[20] Y. Nakamura, "Price versus Quantity in a Mixed Duopoly:
     The Case of Relative Profit Maximization," 2013, Mimeo.

[21] F. Y. Edgeworth, "Mathematical Physics," P. Kegan,
     London, 1881.

[22] R. M. Cyert and M. H. de Groot, "An Analysis of Coop-
     eration and Learning in a Duopoly Context," *American
     Economic Review*, Vol. 63, No. 1, 1973, pp. 24-37.

[23] Y. Tanaka, "Irrelevance of Conjectural Variation in Du-
     opoly under Relative Profit Maximization and Consistent
     Conjectures," 2013, Mimeo.

15

Threshold Effects in the Foreign Aid-Economic Growth Relationship: The Role of Institutional Quality and Macroeconomic Policy Environment

Daniel Komlan Fiodendji[1]*, Kodjo Evlo[2]

[1]Departement of Economics, University of Ottawa, Ottawa, Canada
[2]Faculté des Sciences Economiques et de Gestion (FASEG), Université de Lomé, Lomé, Togo

ABSTRACT

Since the influential paper of [1], the issue relating to the conditions in recipient countries has become central in the foreign aid debate. Scholars and policymakers alike are interested in identifying the conditions which make foreign aid more effective. To contribute to this growing debate, this paper investigates the role of macroeconomic policy environment, institutional policy and a combination of these two previous variables in aid-growth relationship. The empirical analysis is based on a panel data set including 13 ECOWAS[1] countries during the period from 1984 to 2010. Using a modified panel threshold model, the evidence strongly supports the view that the relationship between aid and economic growth is nonlinear with a unique threshold. The paper finds that a stable macroeconomic environment and better institutional quality are sine qua non for the effective contribution of aid to sustainable growth in ECOWAS countries. Furthermore, we find that institutional quality is an important determinant condition which allows aid affects economic growth. One of main contributions of this paper is to successfully identify the conditions under which the aid has a positive impact on economic growth. It is desirable to keep the combination condition in States II and IV (the macroeconomic policy environment is below or above and institutional quality above their threshold respectively) because it may be helpful for the achievement of sustainable economic growth. The results seem to indicate that bad institutional quality may have detrimental effects on economic growth. This will be an important result for the policymakers and international financial institutions, which increasingly favour conditionality and selectivity in the allocation of aid resources. The major policy implication of our results is not a call for a reduction of foreign aid but rather a call for rethinking strategies for international assistance and redesigning existing aid programs.

Keywords: Foreign Aid; Economic Growth; Threshold Effects; Institutional Quality; Economic Policy

1. Introduction

The impact of foreign aid on economic growth in developing countries has been emphasized in the literature over the past few decades. The importance of this topic stems from its policy-relevance, given the focus African countries and their financial and technical partners put on poverty reduction in the conduct of development policy. Several studies have tried to capture the effectiveness of aid on economic growth and poverty reduction. Previous empirical studies on foreign aid and economic growth come to contradictory results. There are three possible results regarding the impact of foreign aid on growth: 1) foreign aid has no effect on economic growth; 2) foreign aid has a positive impact on growth, but with diminishing returns; and 3) foreign aid has a conditional relationship with economic growth, helping to accelerate growth only under certain circumstances.

The negative or, at best, insignificant growth effect of aid supported by the majority of studies lies in the central assumption that the relationship between aid and growth is uniform across countries. [2] did not find evidence on

---

*Corresponding author.
[1]Economic Community of West African States (Benin, Burkina Faso, Côte d'Ivoire, Gambia, Ghana, Guinea, Guinea Bissau, Mali, Niger, Nigeria, Senegal, Sierra Leone and Togo). 13 ECOWAS countries were selected in a panel regression due to data availability.

the relationship between aid and growth rate in developing countries. [3] finds that aid has no impact on growth or investment. However, [4,5] report a positive effect of aid on economic growth, although aid is shown to have diminishing returns. The recent literature has tried to establish that aid works under certain conditions. Various scholars have argued that aid is indeed effective in good policy environments (see [6,7]).

Since the influential paper of [1], the issue relating to the conditions in recipient countries has become central in the foreign aid debate. Scholars and policymakers alike are interested in identifying the conditions which make foreign aid more effective. Does aid effectiveness vary with the recipient country or with domestic regime type? Is foreign aid more effective at promoting growth in good macroeconomic environments or in settings where institutional quality is good?

Motivated by these questions, the crucial goal of this paper is to contribute to the inconclusive debate on aid and growth relationship. More specifically, this study empirically examines the link among aid and growth conditioned to the role of macroeconomic policy environment and institutional quality in ECOWAS countries.

Developing countries are in fact specified by the various economic problems these countries are often faced. For example, a low level of income, a high level of unemployment, a very low industrial capacity utilization, and a high poverty level. In addressing these problems, foreign aid has been suggested as a veritable option for augmenting the insufficient domestic resources. While some countries that have benefited from foreign assistance at one time or the other have grown such that they have become aid donors (South Korea, China etc.), majority of countries in Africa have remained backward. ECOWAS countries have continued to benefit from all sorts of foreign assistance and in fact still collect at least as much as the amount collected in the early 1980s, yet socio-economic development has remained dismal. Whilst there could be so many determinants explaining these unfavourable trends, the incessant socio-political crisis, policy inconsistencies, macroeconomic instability and bad institutional quality evident in many ECOWAS countries which are indeed indicators of poor policy framework, should give one a pause. On the contrary, however, [8] suggested that empirically, aid is effective everywhere, even in bad policy environments.

To address these issues, this paper applies an alternative modelling approach on which uses a threshold variable to investigate whether the relationship between aid and growth is different in each sample grouped on the basis of certain thresholds. Threshold models are simple yet efficient methods to capture nonlinearities in cross section and time series models. They split the sample into classes based on the value of observed variables according to threshold values. Indeed, there are various

ways to identify the presence of a threshold in an economic relationship, depending on the criteria used to determine how to split the sample. [9] applies the technique of exogenously imposed data splits as a straightforward technique to select sub-sample. In order to determine the existence of threshold effects between two variables is different from the traditional approach in which the threshold level is determined exogenously. However, under this approach both the number of regimes and the location of sample splits are arbitrarily selected and not based on prior economic guidance. Another limitation of this approach is that it is not possible to derive confidence intervals for the location of the threshold. The robustness of the results from the conventional approach is likely to be sensitive to the level of the threshold. The econometric estimator generated on the basis of exogenous sample splitting may also generate serious inferential problems (for further details, see [10,11]). Threshold models have some popularity in current applied econometric practice. The model splits the sample into classes based on the value of an observed variable-whether or not it exceeds some threshold. When the threshold is unknown (as is typical in practice) it needs to be estimated, and this increases the complexity of the econometric problem. A theory of estimation and inference is fairly well developed for linear models with exogenous regressors, including [10-13].

These papers explicitly exclude the presence of endogenous variables, and this has been an obstacle to empirical application, including panel models. Advantages of the endogenous threshold regression technique over the traditional approach are that: 1) it does not require any specified functional form of non-linearity, and the number and location of thresholds are endogenously determined by the data; and 2) asymptotic theory applies, which can be used to construct appropriate confidence intervals. A bootstrap method to assess the statistical significance of the threshold effect, in order to test the null hypothesis of a linear formulation against a threshold alternative, is also available. This approach is supposed to eliminate multicollinearity problems among some of the regressors, in order to be able to identify the partial effects of these variables on the dependent variable. For this purpose we used a sample of 13 ECOWAS countries covering the period 1984-2010.

For the purpose of presentation, the rest of this paper is structured as follows: Sections 2 describes the evolution of aid in ECOWAS countries, Section 3 provides econometrics methodology, Section 4 sets out our empirical analysis and interpretation of our results, and Section 5 provides concluding remarks.

2. Foreign Aid in ECOWAS Countries

Figure 1 depicts the evolution of the ratio of total foreign aid to GDP. For the whole ECOWAS countries, the

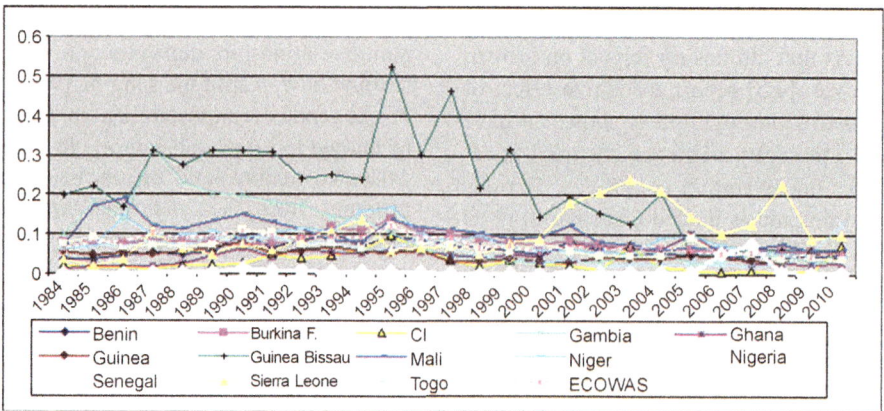

Figure 1. Trends in Aid to ECOWAS countries, 1984-2010.

average variations seem to stable around 10%.

In Guinea Bissau, aid has reached its highest levels in the 1990s, with a peak of 51% in 1996. Three countries have received relatively small amounts of aid. These countries are Côte d'Ivoire, Guinea and Nigeria. Furthermore in the latter country, the ratio of aid was around 1% during 1990s. After that, it became almost nil from 1995 to 2005 before rising slightly and making a jump to 8% in 2007. The trend is stable at our countries sample level. However, for Sierra Leone, there is a change sawtooth. For example, the ratio of aid is around 5% in 1990 except for 2003 (22%) and 2008 (21%). In general case, we have been observed some convergence of ratio of aid for most of ECOWAS countries from the 2000s. In fact the ratio of aid is between 1% and 10%.

3. Econometric Methodology

Threshold models are simple yet efficient methods to capture nonlinearities in cross section and time series models. The main purpose of this paper is to use a threshold variable to investigate whether the relationship between Aid and economic growth through the policy environment and institutional quality is different in each sample grouped on the basis of certain thresholds. The endogenous determination of threshold effects between variables is different from the traditional approach in which the threshold level is determined exogenously. If the threshold level is chosen arbitrarily, or is not determined within an empirical model, it is not possible to derive confidence intervals for the chosen threshold. The robustness of the results from the conventional approach is likely to be sensitive to the level of the threshold. The econometric estimator generated on the basis of exogenous sample splitting may also pose serious inferential problems (for further details, see [10,11]).

3.1. Econometric Framework: Panel Threshold Models

[10] developed the econometric techniques appropriate

for threshold regression with panel data. Allowing for fixed individual effects, the panel threshold model divides the observations into two or more regimes, depending on whether each observation is above or below the threshold level. The general specification threshold model takes the following form:

$$y_{it} = \mu_i + \sum_{k=0}^{K-1} \beta_{k+1} x_{it} I\left(\gamma_k < q_{it} \leq \gamma_{k+1}\right)$$
$$+ \beta_{K+1} x_{it} I\left(\gamma_K < q_{it} \leq \gamma_{K+1}\right) + \varepsilon_{it} \quad (1)$$

where subscripts i stands for the cross-sections with $(1 \leq i \leq N)$ and t indexes times $(1 \leq t \leq T)$. μ_i is the countries-specific fixed effect and the error term ε_{it} is independent and identically distributed (iid) with mean zero and finite variance σ_ε^2. $I(.)$ is the indicator function indicating the regime defined by the threshold variable q_{it} the threshold parameter γ. y_{it} is dependent variable and x_{it} the vector of explanatory variables. $\gamma_0 = -\infty$, $\gamma_{K+1} = +\infty$. Equation (1) allows for K threshold values and, thus, $(K+1)$ regimes. In each regime, the marginal effect of $x_{it} (\beta_k)$ on y_{it} may differ.

Following the modified version of [10] panel threshold model proposed by [14], we consider a discriminator constant which is not individual specific but captures a common effect for all cross-sections. According to these authors, ignoring regime dependent intercepts (δ_k) can lead to biased estimates of both the thresholds and the corresponding marginal impacts.

$$y_{it} = \mu_i + \sum_{k=0}^{K-1} \left(\beta_{k+1} + \delta_{k+1}\right) x_{it} I\left(\gamma_k < q_{it} \leq \gamma_{k+1}\right)$$
$$+ \beta_{K+1} x_{it} I\left(\gamma_K < q_{it} \leq \gamma_{K+1}\right) + \varepsilon_{it} \quad (2)$$

This formulation assumes that the difference in the regime intercepts, represented by (δ_k), is not individual specific but the same for all cross-sections. According to [14], omission of any variable correlated with at least one regressor and the dependent variable causes biased estimates, but regime intercepts are a particularly interesting

Threshold Effects in the Foreign Aid-Economic Growth Relationship: The Role of Institutional Quality and Macroeconomic Policy Environment

177

case. First, the bias can be clearly interpreted. Second, availability of regime intercepts as regressors is not an issue since they are as easily constructed as the regime-dependent exogenous regressors for a given threshold.

3.2. Estimation and Test Strategy

3.2.1. Estimation Method

Estimation of the panel threshold model involves several stages. First, estimation of the parameters model requires eliminating the individual effects μ_i by removing individual-specific means and then applying the least squares sequential procedure (see [10] for more details). Indeed, the individual specific effects are eliminated using the standard fixed-effects transformation implying for the identification of β_k and β_{k+1} that the elements of x_{it} are neither time-invariant nor adding up to a vector of ones. This case applies to regime intercepts which are usually included in each regime in threshold models in pure cross-sectional or time-series contexts. For example, in the case of two regimes, even in the presence of fixed effects it is possible to control for differences in the regime intercepts by including them in all but one regime as in the extension of the following equation[2]:

$$y_{it} = \mu_i + \left(\delta_1 + \beta_1\right)x_{it}I\left(q_{it} \leq \gamma\right) + \beta_2 x_{it}I\left(q_{it} > \gamma\right) + \varepsilon_{it} \quad (3)$$

The seminal contribution of [11] allows us to estimate and make valid statistical inferences on the threshold. There are three statistical issues that need to be addressed in a threshold model: 1) how to jointly estimate the threshold value γ and the slope parameters; 2) how to test the hypothesis that a threshold exists and; 3) how to construct confidence intervals for γ and β. We briefly discuss each in turn. [11] recommends obtaining the least squares estimate $\hat{\gamma}$ as the value that minimizes the concentrated sum of squared errors, $S_1(\gamma)$. The sum of the squared error function depends on γ only through the indicator function. Hence, the minimization problem is a step procedure where each step occurs at distinct values of the observed threshold variable $\left(q_{it}\right)$. After the threshold value γ is estimated, it is important to determine whether the threshold effect is statistically significant. In order to test the statistical significance of a threshold effect typically we would want to test the null hypothesis of no threshold effect, $H_0 : \beta_1 = \beta_2$. However, since γ is only identified under the alternative $\left(H_1 : \beta_1 \neq \beta_2\right)$, the distribution of classical test statistics, such as the Wald and Likelihood ratio tests, are not asymptotically Chi-squared. In essence this is because the likelihood surface is flat with respect to γ, consequently the information matrix becomes singular and standard

asymptotic arguments no longer apply. There are methods for handling hypothesis testing within these contexts. In some instances, we are able to bind the asymptotic distribution of likelihood ratio statistics ([15,16]); alternatively their asymptotic distribution must be derived by bootstrap methods (see [11]). The appropriate test statistic is $F_1 = \dfrac{S_0 - S_1\left(\hat{\gamma}\right)}{\hat{\sigma}^2}$ where S_0 and S_1 are, respectively, the residual sum of squares under the null hypothesis H_0 and the alternative H_1 with $\hat{\sigma}^2$ the residual variance under the alternative hypothesis. Once the threshold effect exists, the next question is whether or not the threshold value can be known. The null hypothesis of the threshold value is $H_0 : \gamma = \gamma_0$, and the likelyhood ratio statistics is $LR_1\left(\gamma\right) = \dfrac{S_1\left(\gamma\right) - S_1\left(\hat{\gamma}\right)}{\hat{\sigma}^2}$ where $S_1\left(\gamma\right)$ and $S_1\left(\hat{\gamma}\right)$ are the residual sum of squares from Equation (3) given the true and estimated value, respectively. The null hypothesis is rejected for large value of LR_1. The asymptotic distribution of $LR_1\left(\gamma_0\right)$ can be used to form valid asymptotic confidence interval about the estimated threshold values. The statistics of $LR_1\left(\gamma_0\right)$ are not normally distributed and [11] computed their no-rejection region, $c\left(\alpha\right)$ with α the given asymptotic level. He proves that the distribution function has the inverse $c\left(\alpha\right) = -2\ln\left(1 - \sqrt{1-\alpha}\right)$ from which it is easy to compute the critical values. The test rejects the null hypothesis at the asymptotic level α if $LR_1\left(\gamma_0\right)$ exceeds $c\left(\alpha\right)$. The asymptotic $\left(1-\alpha\right)$ confidence interval for γ is set of values of γ such that $LR_1\left(\gamma_0\right) \leq c\left(\alpha\right)$.

3.2.2. Regime Intercepts

The role of regime intercepts will be discussed in the context of a single threshold model, though it is straightforward to introduce them in a model with multiple thresholds. The elimination of the individual specific effect in Equation (3) with the standard fixed-effects transformation implies for the identification of slope coefficients β_1 and β_2 that the elements of x_{it} are neither time-invariant nor adding up to a vector of ones. This latter case applies to regime intercepts which are usually included in each regime in threshold models in pure cross-sectional or time-series contexts. Even in the presence of fixed-effects it is possible to control for differences in the regime intercepts by including them in all but one regime as in the following extension of Equation (3):

$$y_{it} = \mu_i + \beta_1 x_{it}I\left(q_{it} \leq \gamma\right) + \delta_1 I\left(q_{it} \leq \gamma\right) + \beta_2 x_{it}I\left(q_{it} > \gamma\right)$$

$$(4)$$

This formulation assumes that the difference in the regime intercepts, represented by δ_1, is not individual

---

[2]There is no reason to limit our analysis to just two regimes. Hence, the estimation approach proposed by [10] and extended by [14] allows a more general specification with K thresholds (*i.e.* $K + 1$ regimes).

specific but the same for all cross-sections. Since Equation (4) has neither been considered by [10] nor any of the numerous studies, e.g. [17,18] or [19], applying his methodology, it seems worthwhile to briefly discuss the role of regime intercepts for the estimation results in the [10] framework.

In case a regime intercept is included, as in specification (4), the slope estimates for each regime are identical to those from a regression using only observations from the respective regime which reflects the orthogonality of the regressors $I(x_i \leq x_m)$ and $x_i I(x_i > x_m)$. Omission of any variable correlated with at least one regressor and the dependent variable causes biased estimates, but regime intercepts are a particularly interesting case. First, the bias can be clearly interpreted. Estimating Equation (3) in the presence of a regime intercept in the data generating process results in a bias proportional to $\hat{\delta}_1$ because the orthogonality of the regressors is not preserved anymore. Second, availability of regime intercepts as regressors is not an issue since they are as easily constructed as the regime-dependent exogenous regressors for a given threshold.

Biased estimates of the regression slopes have further consequences in the panel threshold model because the threshold estimates are also obtained by least squares. Only by coincidence, these estimates will be the same for specifications (3) and (4) if a regime intercept is present in the data generating process. Moreover, unbiased estimates of β_1 and β_2 are crucial for the test of the significance of a threshold which is based on the null hypothesis of equality of the two coefficients.

Eventually, the setup in [10] has to be extended to allow for regime intercepts as in Equation (4). First, the null hypothesis to test for the significance of the threshold has to be extended by $\delta_1 = 0$. Second, the derivation of the asymptotic distribution of the threshold estimate now relies on the additional technical assumption that $\delta_1 \to 0$ as $N \to \infty$. It means that the difference in the intercepts between the two regimes is 'small' relative to sample size which is completely analogous to the assumption regarding the slope coefficients. Third, the proof in the appendix in [10] now relies on the following two expressions taking the regime intercept as an additional regressor into account: $\theta' = \left((\beta_2 - \beta_1)' - \delta_1 \right)$ and $z_{it} = (x_{it}' 1) C$.

4. Empirical Analysis

4.1. The Variables

The set of explanatory variables that constitute the vector x_{it} include; foreign aid as a percentage of GDP, policy index, the institutional quality index, investment as a percentage of GDP and human capital as a measured of secondary enrollment schools and initial income.

The policy variables are openness, inflation and fiscal policy. Openness, a measure of international trade, is believed to affect growth through several channels, such as access to technology from abroad, greater access to a variety of inputs for production and access to broader markets that raise the efficiency of domestic production through increased specialization. There are various measures of openness but in this paper, we use ratio of total trade to GDP. As suggested by [1], budget surplus as a percentage of GDP is included as a measure of fiscal policy. The budget surplus is believed to be an indicator of the stabilizing role of government. In line with [20] inflation is taken as a measure of monetary policy.

$$\text{Policy}_{it} = w_0 + w_1 \text{fispolicy}_{it} + w_2 \text{opens}_{it} - w_3 \inf_{it} + \varepsilon_{it} \quad (5)$$

where w_0 the constant term is the country's predicted growth rate for given values of budget surplus (fishpolicy), trade openness (opens) and the inflation rate (inf) assuming that it had the mean values of all other characteristics. The weights w_1, w_2 and w_3 are obtained from OLS regression of these variables on growth. The intuition is that the policy index should weight the policies according to their impact on growth.

The policy index is a measure of the quality of economic policy; the higher the index the higher the quality of economic policy. Obviously, countries with good economic policies tend to grow faster than countries with bad economic policy.

The institutional quality index (ircg) is not a weighted average of the institutional variables[3], but is obtained from OLS regression of corruption, ethnic tension, socioeconomic conditions, law and order, profile investment and government stability.

$$\begin{aligned} \text{icrg}_{it} = {} & k_0 + k_1 \text{corr}_{it} + k_2 \text{ethnics}_{it} + k_3 \text{socioec}_{it} + k_4 \text{law}_{it} \\ & + k_5 \text{proinv}_{it} + k_6 \text{govstab}_{it} + v_{it} \end{aligned} \quad (6)$$

The institutional settings within which economic policies are formulated are of crucial importance, because the quality of these institutions can be a primary source of the differences in economic growth among nations. Countries with good institutions such as lower level of confiscation of private properties, lower level of governmental corruption, lower ethnic tensions, and efficient profile investment are expected to grow faster than countries with bad institutions. Poor institutions interfere with economic growth by inducing economic agents to engage in redistributive politics rather economic activity with lower economic returns. The coefficient of institutional quality is expected to be positive.

Another control variable included in equation is investment and human capital. The level of investment is also included as a control variable. The investment/GDP ratio (invest) is used as a proxy for the growth rate of

---

[3]See Ali *et al.* (2009) for more details.

Threshold Effects in the Foreign Aid-Economic Growth Relationship: The Role of Institutional Quality and Macroeconomic Policy Environment

179

the capital stock. Since the investment/GDP ratio is not reported for the majority of the ECOWAS countries, gross fixed capital formation as a share of GDP is used to represent investment/GDP ratio. The higher the investment is, the higher the growth rate is. Therefore, we expect a positive sign for the coefficient of investment. Human capital (human) is Secondary School Enrollment Rate measures the percentage of school age population that was enrolled in secondary schools. Thus, the GDP growth rate is a positive function of education. We expect a positive sign for the coefficient of this variable.

The key independent variable and the variable of interest is (aid) which is foreign aid expressed as percentage of GDP. The aid variable used is the Effective Development Assistance (EDA), which measures official aid flows as the sum of grants and the grant equivalent of official loans. The grant equivalent of a financial inflow is the amount that, at the time of its commitment, is not expected to be repaid, *i.e.*, the amount subsidized through below-market terms at the time of commitment.

The initial income level (*initial*) measured as GDP per capita is included to verify the convergence hypothesis. The convergence hypothesis and the steady-state theory predicted in the neoclassical growth theory rests on the premise that countries are similar except for their starting GDP level. Therefore, poor countries are predicted to grow faster than rich countries. If this is true, we expect a negative sign for the coefficient of this variable.

4.2. Data and Preliminary Analysis

In this paper, we consider annual data from the ECOWAS countries which are collected from various sources and covered the period 1984 to 2010. Data are collected from the Penn World Table 6.1 and 6.2, World Development Indicators (WDI), the IMF's International

Financial Statistics and the International Country Risk Guide (ICRG).

We are able to identify the regime of the economy with respect to the macroeconomic policy environment and institutional quality which depend on the estimate of the policy index and institutional quality thresholds. Thus we can also investigate all combinations of those regimes. So we can distinguish between four different states as shown in **Figure 2**.

Figure 2 displays the four states the donors can face when deciding about the aid in recipient countries.

We have to use the threshold estimated γ_{policy} and $\gamma_{\text{institutions}}$ to determine the regime. We are able to distinguish with this approach between a situation where the macroeconomic policy environment and institutional quality are below $\gamma_{\text{policy}}/\gamma_{\text{institutions}}$ (**State I**), the macroeconomic policy environment is below and institutional quality above $\gamma_{\text{policy}}/\gamma_{\text{institutions}}$ and vice versa (**States II and III**), and a situation where both are above $\gamma_{\text{policy}}/\gamma_{\text{institutions}}$ (**State IV**). We can therefore estimate for each case the aid impact on economic growth and compare those to each other.

However, some differences are of special economic growth. Since when comparing States I and II it becomes obvious that only the sign of the institutional quality has changed while the macroeconomic policy environment remains negative (below the threshold value γ_{policy}) in both cases. The same holds for the States III and IV where again only the macroeconomic policy environment remains positive (above the threshold value γ_{policy}). The same argumentation applies when comparing States I and III with respect the negative sign of institutional quality (below the threshold value $\gamma_{\text{institutions}}$) or positive (above the threshold value $\gamma_{\text{institutions}}$). According to our analysis, we expect that the aid negatively affects growth in States I and III and has positive impact in States II and IV.

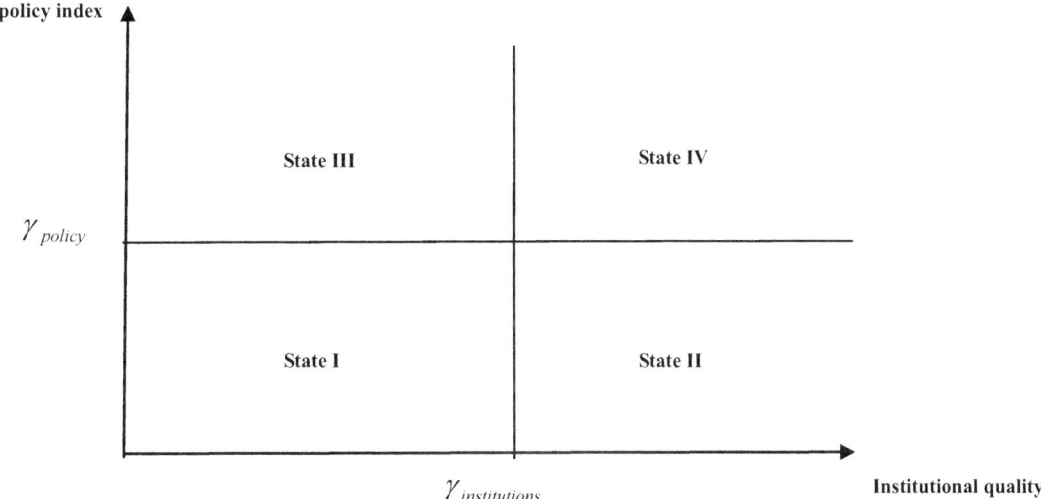

Figure 2. The four states of the economy.

Having constructed the data we can now separate them into the four states by simply introducing the threshold measures explained in **Figure 2**.

The summary statistics of the different states together with those for each threshold and linear relationship between aid and growth are given in **Table 1**. Several interesting insights can be drawn from **Table 1**. First, following [10], each regime contains at least 5% of all observations. So we have enough data points for each regime in order to get consistent estimates. Furthermore, for their combination given by the four states the same conclusion can be drawn. Second, the descriptive statistics show that the aid is lower if the policy environment

and institutional quality are above their threshold values. This suggests that a stable macroeconomic policy environment and better institutional quality allow a little aid to improve economic grow. However, the aid is higher when the policy environment and institutional quality are below their threshold values. This implies that even they have more quantitative aid; its impact on growth is unclear. Following, the four states, our statistics show that economic is highly efficient if the institutional quality achieves optimal value.

Before conducting the regression investigation as proposed in the recent panel data econometric literature, we tested for possible unit roots in the panels. [10] panel

Table 1. Descriptive statistics.

	Linear	Aid		Policy index		Institutional quality	
		<0.087	>=0.087	<1.880	>=1.880	<0.571	>=0.571
$\overline{grow}$	0.007	0.005	0.010	0.007	0.004	0.000	0.017
σ_{grow}	0.044	0.037	0.059	0.046	0.035	0.048	0.035
$grow_{max}$	0.226	0.122	0.226	0.226	0.080	0.122	0.226
$grow_{min}$	−0.296	−0.191	−0.296	−0.296	−0.170	−0.296	−0.067
$\overline{policy}$	1.794	1.811	1.750	1.758	1.934	1.768	1.839
σ_{policy}	0.898	0.658	1.294	0.862	0.264	1.039	0.466
$policy_{max}$	2.056	2.004	2.056	1.880	2.056	2.007	2.056
$policy_{min}$	0.040	0.858	0.040	0.040	1.882	0.040	1.363
$\overline{institutions}$	0.539	0.550	0.511	0.536	0.554	0.496	0.615
$\sigma_{institutions}$	0.074	0.072	0.074	0.076	0.066	0.054	0.032
$institutions_{max}$	0.712	0.712	0.673	0.698	0.712	0.570	0.712
$institutions_{min}$	0.325	0.325	0.353	0.325	0.395	0.325	0.571
$\overline{aid}$	0.079	0.048	0.157	0.083	0.063	0.087	0.065
σ_{aid}	0.068	0.024	0.080	0.069	0.061	0.077	0.045
aid_{max}	0.525	0.086	0.525	0.525	0.319	0.525	0.241
aid_{min}	0.001	0.001	0.087	0.001	0.001	0.001	0.001
$\overline{invest}$	0.178	0.173	0.190	0.179	0.172	0.171	0.190
σ_{invest}	0.062	0.052	0.081	0.064	0.049	0.065	0.054
$invest_{max}$	0.484	0.310	0.848	0.484	0.310	0.484	0.310
$invest_{min}$	0.035	0.035	0.067	0.035	0.087	0.035	0.067
$\overline{income}$	5.898	6.023	5.579	5.840	6.139	5.809	6.053
σ_{income}	0.492	0.479	0.364	0.476	0.484	0.496	0.444
$income_{max}$	7.222	7.222	6.648	7.157	7.222	7.222	7.157
$income_{min}$	4.878	4.878	4.935	4.878	5.352	4.878	5.217
$\overline{human}$	0.220	0.247	0.149	0.207	0.271	0.188	0.275
σ_{human}	0.119	0.121	0.082	0.118	0.109	0.099	0.132
$human_{max}$	0.590	0.590	0.560	0.590	0.560	0.440	0.590
$human_{min}$	0.030	0.030	0.050	0.030	0.040	0.030	0.060
N	351	252	99	283	68	223	128

Continued

	State 1	State II	State III	State IV
$\overline{grow}$	−0.003	0.021	0.004	0.004
σ_{grow}	0.049	0.037	0.043	0.019
$grow_{max}$	0.122	0.226	0.080	0.038
$grow_{min}$	−0.296	−0.067	−0.170	−0.036
$\overline{policy}$	1.726	1.813	1.940	1.924
σ_{policy}	0.990	0.377	0.234	0.293
$policy_{max}$	1.876	1.880	2.007	2.056
$policy_{min}$	0.040	1.363	1.882	1.885
$\overline{institutions}$	0.493	0.614	0.508	0.620
$\sigma_{institutions}$	0.057	0.030	0.035	0.038
$institutions_{max}$	0.570	0.698	0.571	0.712
$institutions_{min}$	0.325	0.571	0.395	0.579
$\overline{aid}$	0.091	0.068	0.068	0.054
σ_{aid}	0.078	0.045	0.070	0.046
aid_{max}	0.525	0.241	0.319	0.179
aid_{min}	0.001	0.001	0.001	0.015
$\overline{invest.}$	0.171	0.193	0.168	0.179
$\sigma_{invest.}$	0.069	0.053	0.046	0.053
$invest._{max}$	0.848	0.309	0.282	0.310
$invest._{min}$	0.035	0.067	0.087	0.096
$\overline{income}$	5.731	6.041	6.168	6.097
σ_{income}	0.443	0.472	0.572	0.326
$income_{max}$	7.109	7.157	7.222	6.734
$income_{min}$	4.878	5.217	5.352	5.601
$\overline{human}$	0.179	0.259	0.230	0.330
σ_{human}	0.102	0.130	0.071	0.127
$human_{max}$	0.440	0.590	0.390	0.560
$human_{min}$	0.030	0.060	0.040	0.180
N	183	100	40	28

Notes: $\overline{x}$ stands for the mean of the respective variable, x_{max} and x_{min} for the maximum and minimum realization, while σ_x is the standard deviation, N = number of observations.

threshold regression model is an extension of the traditional least squared estimation method, in fact. It requires that variables considered in the model need to be stationary in order to avoid the so-called spurious regression[4]. Since the stationarity properties of the variables are studied, *i.e.* the examination of whether or not the variables appear to contain panel unit roots. Non-stationary panels have become extremely popular and have attracted much attention in both theoretical and empirical research over

the last decade. A number of panel unit root tests have been proposed in the literature, in this research, we use [21-24] all based on a null hypothesis that a unit root exists in the panels. Indeed, the [21,22] panel unit root tests assume a homogeneous autoregressive unit root under the alternative hypothesis whereas [23] allows for a heterogeneous autoregressive unit root under the alternative hypothesis. Fundamentally, the [23] test averages the individual augmented Dickey-Fuller (ADF) test statistics. Both the [21,23] tests suffer from a dramatic loss of power when individual specific trends are included, which is due to the bias correction. However, the [22]

[4]Spurious regression is argued in Granger and Newbold (1974) that the estimation of the relationship among non-stationary series is easily getting higher R^2 and t statistics.

panel unit root test does not rely on bias correction factors. Monte Carlo experiments showed that the [22] test yields substantially higher power and smallest size distortions compared to [21,23]. [24,25] suggest comparable unit root tests to be performed using the non-parametric Fisher statistic.

Table 2 displays the results of panel unit root tests in levels for all the variables. All tests reject the null hypothesis of a unit root in the examined series. As regards to institutional quality and investment, the tests failed to reject the null hypothesis of unit root. According to [26], this result may be due to the fact that the tests have a low power against nonlinear stationary process. From the nonlinear unit root test, we can conclude that all the variables in the paper are stationarity. It was deemed safe to continue with the panel data estimates of the above econometric specification.

Suspecting strong collinearity between some regressors, **Table 3** reports the pairwise correlation coefficients between all the candidate variables of the models. As can be seen, our results suggest that the inclusion of all these variables in the same model pose none problem of multicollinearity. Indeed, coefficients of correlation appear quite low on the whole.

Table 2. Panel unit root test results.

	Aid	Policy	Institutions	Investment	Initial income	Human capital
Intercept						
Levin, Lin and Chin	-2.928^a	-2.242^b	-1.244	1.714	-4.851^a	-2.247^b
	(0.002)	(0.013)	(0.101)	(0.957)	(0.000)	(0.012)
Breitung	-2.543^a	-1.761^b	0.559	-0.379	-3.711^a	-3.913^a
	(0.006)	(0.039)	(0.712)	(0.352)	(0.000)	(0.000)
Im, Pesaran and Shin	-2.779^a	-1.745^b	-0.497	0.668	-4.251^a	-2.554^a
	(0.003)	(0.041)	(0.310)	(0.748)	(0.000)	(0.005)
Fisher-ADF	49.383^a	41.953^b	30.353	24.192	68.092^a	69.023^a
	(0.004)	(0.025)	(0.253)	(0.565)	(0.000)	(0.000)
Fisher-PP	72.120^a	76.062^a	35.575^c	37.930^c	174.617^a	148.824^a
	(0.000)	(0.000)	(0.090)	(0.062)	(0.000)	(0.000)
Intercept + trend						
Levin, Lin and Chin	-3.499^a	-3.265^a	1.282	1.278	-8.500^a	-5.813^a
	(0.000)	(0.000)	(0.900)	(0.899)	(0.000)	(0.000)
Breitung	-2.562^a	-0.450	-2.185^b	3.096	-7.400^a	-4.259^a
	(0.005)	(0.326)	(0.014)	(0.999)	(0.000)	(0.000)
Im, Pesaran and Shin	-2.678^a	-1.879^b	1.237	1.087	-6.352^a	-6.011^a
	(0.004)	(0.029)	(0.897)	(0.861)	(0.000)	(0.000)
Fisher-ADF	48.013^a	46.674^a	18.472	21.340	92.614^a	94.777^a
	(0.005)	(0.008)	(0.858)	(0.724)	(0.000)	(0.000)
Fisher-PP	67.405^a	86.773^a	20.553	40.996^b	151.377^a	166.730^a
	(0.000)	(0.000)	(0.765)	(0.031)	(0.000)	(0.000)

Notes: Figures in square brackets are probability values. a, b, and c represent significance at 1%, 5%, and 10% respectively. The maximum number of lags is set to be four. MAIC is used to select the lag length. The bandwidth is selected using the Newey-West method. Barlett is used as the spectral estimation method.

Table 3. Correlation matrix of the variables include in the model.

	Aid	Growth	Policy	Institutions	Investment	Initial income	Human capital
Aid	1.000						
Growth	0.055	1.000					
Policy	−0.311	0.018	1.000				
Institutions	−0.224	0.170	0.381	1.000			
Investment	0.321	0.188	0.018	0.249	1.000		
Initial income	−0.419	0.066	0.387	0.360	0.058	1.000	
Human capital	−0.369	0.112	0.174	0.300	0.201	0.429	1.000

In fact, several reasons might explain the low correlation between aid and economic growth outcomes. One of them is the phenomenon of aid fungibility, *i.e.* aid could be redirected by the recipient country toward sectors other than those originally provided in the commitments.

In order to test the presence of non-linear effect with respect to aid, institutional quality and the policy index we apply the Hansen's test described above, with 1000 bootstrap replication to compute the p-value of the F-test statistic.

The estimated threshold and the p-value of the F-test for the null of no threshold are reported in **Table 4**. The results show that the linearity hypothesis is strongly rejected in favour of threshold regression for both three variables. This confirms the presence of nonlinearities in aid–growth relationship. Once the presence of threshold effect is confirmed the next step is to estimate the threshold regression following the procedure as discussed in the methodology section.

4.3. Aid Thresholds and Economic Performance

Let us now apply the modified panel threshold model to the analysis of the impact of aid on economic growth in ECOWAS countries. To that aim, consider the following threshold model of the aid-growth relationship:

$$\text{grow}_{it} = \mu_i + \beta_1 \text{Aid}_{it} I\left(\text{Aid}_{it} < \gamma\right) + \delta_1 I\left(\text{Aid}_{it} < \gamma\right)$$
$$+ \beta_2 \text{Aid}_{it} I\left(\text{Aid}_{it} \geq \gamma\right) + \theta_1 \text{invest}_{it} + \theta_2 \text{initial}_{it} \quad (7)$$
$$+ \theta_3 \text{human}_{it} + \theta_4 \text{policy}_{it} + \theta_5 \text{ircg}_{it} + \varepsilon_{it}$$

where $I\left(\text{Aid}_{it} < \gamma\right)$ and $I\left(\text{Aid}_{it} \geq \gamma\right)$ are indicator functions which take the value of one if the term between parentheses is true, and are zero otherwise. This model specifies the effects of Aid with two coefficients: of β_1 and β_2. β_1 denotes the effect of Aid below the threshold level γ, and β_2 denotes the effect of Aid exceeding the threshold level γ.

Table 5 presents the estimation results obtained of Equation (7) and includes two parts. The first part of the table displays the regime-dependent coefficients of aid on growth. Specifically, $\hat{\beta}_1 \left(\hat{\beta}_2\right)$ denotes the marginal

effect of aid on growth in the low (high) aid regime, *i.e.* when aid is below (above) the estimated threshold value. The coefficients of the control variables are presented in the second part of the table. Our results reveal that the coefficients of aid have different signs and significances across the low and high aid regimes. When aid is above the threshold value $\left(\hat{\gamma} \geq 0.087\right)$, our results indicate that foreign aid have positive but insignificant impact on economic growth. However, when aid is below the threshold value, there are negative relationship between aid and growth and aid marginal effect is significant. This negative impact can be explained by the simple fact that a permanent rise in aid reduces long term capital accumulation and labour supply and by extension reduces the rate of economic growth [27]. These findings suggest that foreign aid perpetuates poor economic policies and postpone reform; limited absorptive capacity in the recipient country reduces the effectiveness of aid and aid reduces both domestic private and public saving (see [28,29]). Moreover, our results have shown how development assistance leads to distortion and disruption in the domestic economy.

Regarding the control variables, we notice that investment and institutional quality and human capital have positive impact on growth, while the initial income is negatively and significantly correlated with economic growth. This result confirms the conditional convergence hypothesis of [30-32].

Table 4. F-test of null of no threshold $\left(H_0 : \beta_1 = \beta_2\right)$.

	Aid	Policy index	Institutional quality
Estimated threshold	0.087	1.880	0.571
Confidence Interval	[0.004 0.210]	[1.432 1.952]	[0.545 0.632]
LM-test	25.435	17.952	37.930
p-value	0.015	0.037	0.008
critical values			
10%	16.370	13.946	20.790
5%	20.617	16.747	24.724
1%	26.674	21.648	34.230

Table 5. Aid-growth threshold regressions using Aid as a threshold.

Regime-dependent coefficients		Regime-independent coefficients					
β_1	β_2	initial income	invest.	Human capital	Policy index	Institutional quality	$\hat{\delta}_1$
−0.186[a]	0.017	−0.010[a]	0.097[a]	0.014[c]	−0.002	0.099[a]	0.014[b]
(0.059)	(0.039)	(0.002)	(0.025)	(0.008)	(0.002)	(0.015)	(0.007)
R2 = 0.344							
F-stat = 24.748							
p-value = 0.000							

Notes: Standard errors are given in parentheses. a, b and c indicate significance at the 1%, 5% and 10% level.

4.4. Aid Impact Conditional to Policy Environment

Following [33] argument that aid positively influences long term growth in countries with good policy environment, we use panel threshold model to investigate impact of aid conditional to stable macroeconomic policy environment. With regard to aid, variable that holds the interest of this research, it is expected that the relationship is positive growth in normal regime, $i.e.$, when policy index is greater or equal to an endogenous threshold value (good policy environment). We assume that the aid impact on economic growth depends on a level of policy index. Thus our nonlinear model specification is as follows:

$$\text{grow}_{it} = \mu_i + \beta_1 \text{Aid}_{it} I\left(\text{Policy}_{it} < \gamma\right) + \delta_1 I\left(\text{Policy}_{it} < \gamma\right)$$
$$+ \beta_2 \text{Aid}_{it} I\left(\text{Policy}_{it} \geq \gamma\right) + \theta_1 \text{invest}_{it} + \theta_2 \text{initial}_{it}$$
$$+ \theta_3 \text{human}_{it} + \theta_4 \text{ircg}_{it} + \varepsilon_{it}$$
$$(8)$$

where $I\left(\text{Policy}_{it} < \gamma\right)$ and $I\left(\text{Policy}_{it} \geq \gamma\right)$ are indicator functions which take the value of one if the term between parentheses is true, and are zero otherwise. This model specifies the effects of Aid with two coefficients: of β_1 and β_2. β_1 denotes the effect of Aid below the threshold level γ, and β_2 denotes the effect of Aid exceeding the threshold level γ.

To examine the affect of aid on growth in the presence of good policy environment, we estimate the Equation 8 the results are reported in **Table 6**. Our investigation shows that, on unstable macroeconomic policy environment (low policy regime) foreign aid has a positive effect on the economic growth rate; however, this positive relationship is not statistically significant. This result is consistent with [7,8,34-36] analysis which states that macroeconomic environment has no significant influence on the link between aid and economic growth. On the other side, in high policy regime, the marginal impact of aid on economic performance is positive and statistically significant. These findings indicate that foreign aid does have some positive impact on economic performance, conditional on stable macroeconomic policy environment

(when policy index is above 1.880). The result is similar to that found by [33]. It shows that the effectiveness of aid in the growth process depends on the level and quality of economic policies. In addition, when country size is included the growth model, the impact of aid is positive, larger and significant (see [33,1,37]). These results imply aid effectiveness depends upon macroeconomic policies. There are two possible justifications for the positive effect of aid on growth in the presence of good policy. Stable macroeconomic indicators are more attractive for the investor. High inflation and high budget deficit may cause the macroeconomic instability which discourages the investment. High non developing expenditures cause the high budget deficit. In case of high budget deficit, foreign aid may be used for government consumption instead of investment purpose. All of the control variables (the regime independent regressors) have expected sign and are statistically significant.

Our finding suggests that sound economic management policy in terms of low inflation, trade openness and low budget deficit is crucial for aid effectiveness. There is need to implement appropriate policy measure, in order to achieve the positive impact of foreign aid on economic growth through minimizing budgetary deficits, lower the inflation rate and to achieve trade openness.

4.5. Aid Impact Conditional to Institutional Quality

Let us now use the panel threshold model specification to the investigation of the effect of aid on economic growth conditional to institutional quality in ECOWAS countries. To that aim, consider the following threshold model of the Aid-growth nexus:

$$\text{grow}_{it} = \mu_i + \beta_1 \text{Aid}_{it} I\left(\text{ircg}_{it} < \tau\right) + \delta_1 I\left(\text{ircg}_{it} < \tau\right)$$
$$+ \beta_2 \text{Aid}_{it} I\left(\text{ircg}_{it} \geq \tau\right) + \theta_1 \text{invest}_{it}$$
$$+ \theta_2 \text{initial}_{it} + \theta_3 \text{human}_{it} + \theta_4 \text{Policy}_{it} + \varepsilon_{it}$$
$$(9)$$

where $I\left(\text{ircg}_{it} < \tau\right)$ and $I\left(\text{ircg}_{it} \geq \tau\right)$ are indicator functions which take the value of one if the term between parentheses is true, and are zero otherwise.

Table 6. Aid-growth threshold regressions using a conditional variable (policy index) as a threshold.

Regime-dependent coefficients		Regime-independent coefficients				
β_1	β_2	Initial income	invest.	Human capital	Institutional quality	$\hat{\delta}_1$
0.027	0.125[a]	−0.006[b]	0.073[a]	0.025[a]	0.103[a]	−0.007[c]
(0.036)	(0.037)	(0.003)	(0.026)	(0.009)	(0.016)	(0.004)
R2 = 0.362						
F-stat = 26.726						
p-value = 0.000						

Notes: Standard errors are given in parentheses. a, b and c indicate significance at the 1%, 5% and 10% level.

Table 7 indicates the results obtained with respect to the institutional quality conditioned in aid-growth nexus. Our findings suggest that for the low-institutional quality regime (in which the institutional quality is below 0.571), the marginal impact of aid on economic growth is negative and strongly significant. In the better institutions regime, our results show a positive impact of aid on growth and this impact is statistically significant. Strongly positive and significant coefficient of aid in aid-growth relationship implies that impact of aid on growth is function of institutional quality. An interesting finding is that the marginal impacts of aid on growth when we take institutional quality as condition variable are more important than to consider macroeconomic policy environment as condition variable. Therefore, controlling low institutional quality regime should be the main goal for policymakers in ECOWAS zone since in this regime more aid is detrimental to economic growth.

From the previous results, it is clear that in the midst of current efforts to achieve the Millennium Development Goals (MDGs) in ECOWAS zone, the need for foreign assistance is inevitable. However, no amount of foreign assistance will promote sustainable growth and development in ECOWAS countries if the problem of unstable macroeconomic environment and bad institutional quality persists. It is, therefore, crucial for governments in the ECOWAS area to improve institutional quality and to pursue economic policies that are conducive to, among others, low inflation, productive budgetary balance and a competitive environment, and that attend to the incessant corruption and political instability.

4.6. Aid Impact Conditional to Combination of Two Indexes

From this econometric approach, we identify four states of the economy consistent with the results of the growth framework. Using these four states, we are able to estimate the relation between aid and economic growth in nonlinear fashion in each state based on the deviation from macroeconomic policy environment and the institutional quality. Our model specification is:

$$
\begin{aligned}
\text{grow}_{it} = {}& \mu_i + \beta_1 \text{Aid}_{it} I\left(\text{Policy}_{it} < \gamma; \text{ircg}_{it} < \tau\right) + \delta_1 I\left(\text{Policy}_{it} < \gamma; \text{ircg}_{it} < \tau\right) \\
& + \beta_2 \text{Aid}_{it} I\left(\text{Policy}_{it} < \gamma; \text{ircg}_{it} \geq \tau\right) + \beta_3 \text{Aid}_{it} I\left(\text{Policy}_{it} \geq \gamma; \text{ircg}_{it} < \tau\right) \\
& + \beta_4 I\left(\text{Policy}_{it} \geq \gamma; \text{ircg}_{it} \geq \tau\right) + \theta_1 \text{invest}_{it} + \theta_2 \text{initial}_{it} + \theta_3 \text{human}_{it} + \varepsilon_{it}
\end{aligned}
\tag{10}
$$

where $\left(\text{Policy}_{it} < \gamma; \text{ircg}_{it} < \tau\right)$ indicates state 1, $\left(\text{Policy}_{it} < \gamma; \text{ircg}_{it} \geq \tau\right)$ state 2, $\left(\text{Policy}_{it} \geq \gamma; \text{ircg}_{it} < \tau\right)$ state 3 and $\left(\text{Policy}_{it} \geq \gamma; \text{ircg}_{it} \geq \tau\right)$ represents state 4. This model specifies the effects of Aid with four coefficients: of β_1, β_2, β_3 and β_4. β_j denotes the effect of Aid in state j ($j = 1, 2, 3, 4$).

The estimation results of Equation 10 are presented in Table 8. Using the combination terms which signal the state of the economy, we find that the impact of aid on growth is negative in the States I and III (situation where institutional quality is below its threshold value and macroeconomic policy environment is above or below its threshold value). The marginal impact of aid is statistically insignificant in state I but strongly significant in state III. This negative relationship between aid and economic growth strength the idea that resources transfer from donors to ECOWAS countries are oriented towards their own economic and strategic interest instead of needs of the recipient countries. The negative effect of aid on growth in these countries can be justified on the following arguments. First, aid may be used to invest either in less productive sector or to increase government consumption. This is consistent with finding of [27] that aid leakage (outflow) into non-productive expenditures in the public sector may be the cause of negative relationship between aid and economic growth. In fact, in a recent book, [38,39] argues that not only billions of dollars of aid spent have not significantly improved the well-being of Africans, but rather they have worsened the situation. Second, unstable aid volatile macroeconomic environment and bad institutional quality have spoiled the favorable effect of aid on economic growth. Third, aid into ECOWAS countries is used to substitute government's inability to tax its own citizens because of political pressure from elite groups.

In contrast to States I and III, our results show the positive and statistically significant relationship between aid and growth in States II and IV. However, the marginal effect of aid on growth is more consistent in terms of magnitude in state II $\left(\beta_2 = 0.206\right)$ against $\left(\beta_4 = 0.120\right)$ in state IV. Our results suggest that foreign aid accelerates economic growth by supplementing domestic capital formation.

Researcher highlights some key issues which may undermine the impact of foreign aid on economic growth. These include donors conditionality attached to aid inflow, stable macroeconomic environment in aid recipient country, institutional quality, governance issues; donors tide the some portion of aid and donors strategic motives for the allocation of aid. Among these two reasons are highly concerned in the management of aid inflow into ECOWAS countries and its contribution for ECOWAS economy. These reasons are institutional quality in

Table 7. Aid-growth threshold regressions using a conditional variable (institutional quality) as a threshold.

Regime-dependent coefficients		Regime-independent coefficients				
β_1	β_2	initial income	invest.	Human capital	Policy index	$\hat{\delta}_1$
-0.096^a	0.201^a	-0.006^b	0.139^a	0.018^c	-0.001	0.008^b
(0.033)	(0.064)	(0.003)	(0.023)	(0.010)	(0.002)	(0.004)
R2 = 0.350						
F-stat = 21.701						
p-value = 0.000						

Notes: Standard errors are given in parentheses. a, b and c indicate significance at the 1%, 5% and 10% level.

Table 8. Estimation results of Aid-growth threshold depending on the state of the economy.

Regime-dependent coefficients				Regime-independent coefficients			
β_1	β_2	β_3	β_4	initial income	invest.	Human capital	$\hat{\delta}_1$
-0.022	0.206^a	-0.096^a	0.120^b	-0.007^b	0.098^a	0.023^b	-0.014^a
(0.033)	(0.048)	(0.033)	(0.054)	(0.003)	(0.022)	(0.009)	(0.003)
R2 = 0.429				Wald-test			
F-stat = 30.855				F-stat = 18.011			
p-value = 0.000				p-value = 0.000			

Notes: Standard errors are given in parentheses. a, b and c indicate significance at the 1%, 5% and 10% level.

ECOWAS zone and macroeconomic policy instability in this area.

The major point emerging from this study is that foreign aid has positive impact on economic growth of ECOWAS countries conditional on sound macroeconomic policies and better institutional quality. Based on the empirical results we find that foreign aid and growth has negative relationship in States I and III while this relation has positive and significant in States II and IV. The interesting results emerge in state II, *i.e.* if macroeconomic policy environment is below its threshold value and institutional quality is above its threshold value. Our finding suggests that better institutional quality in terms of lower risk of contract repudiation, lower level of governmental corruption, efficient government stability and lower ethnic tensions is crucial for aid effectiveness. Therefore, it is desirable for ECOWAS policymakers to target state II and good institutional quality regime should be the main goal for these countries.

5. Conclusions

The belief that foreign aid helps to promote sustainable economic growth and improves the welfare in developing countries is debatable issue since its start. A large body of literature now is available on aid effectiveness but the issue regarding its contribution for growth and welfare remains controversy. The aim of our paper is to investigate whether aid effectiveness depends on the macroeconomic policy environment and institutional quality in ECOWAS countries. For this purpose, we have estimated the impact of foreign aid on economic growth by considering the macroeconomic policy environment, institutional quality and the combination of two latter indexes. Therefore, we use [14] the approach based on the panel of 13 ECOWAS countries covering the period from 1984 to 2010. According to our econometric results, the null hypothesis of linearity against the alternative of a nonlinear specification is rejected by the data. Hence, the relationship between aid and growth can be better modeled as a nonlinear model. The paper finds that aid into ECOWAS area will be effectively conditional on a stable macroeconomic policy environment and better institutional quality. In other words, the increasing flows of aid into ECOWAS countries have not promoted meaningful development due to the unstable macroeconomic environment and bad institutional quality. Most countries are characterized by policy inconsistencies, the poor institutional framework, the high level of corruption, incessant political crises and ethnic tension. This will be an important result for the policymakers and international financial institutions, which increasingly favour conditionality and selectivity in the allocation of aid resources. The major policy implication of our results is not a call for a reduction of foreign aid but rather a call for rethinking strategies for international assistance and redesigning existing aid programs.

From a policy perspective, the present research offers three interesting insights. First, increasing transfer without any conditions may not only be ineffective but may strongly hurt economic performance of ECOWAS countries. According to our investigation, no amount of foreign assistance will promote sustainable growth and development in ECOWAS countries if the problem of unstable macroeconomic environment and bad institutional quality persists. The second insight is that institutional quality is a sine qua non condition for aid to promote economic performance. Hence, States II and IV are identified as determinant regimes for the effective contribution of aid to sustainable growth and improve the welfare in ECOWAS countries. Finally, from the two conditional indexes, institutional quality is more important condition through which aid positively affects economic growth. Making access to better institutional quality may be a way to spur economic growth even in a bad macroeconomic policy environment. It is, therefore, crucial for governments in the ECOWAS area to improve institutional quality and to pursue economic policies that are conducive to, among others, low inflation, productive budgetary balance and a competitive environment, and that attend to the incessant corruption and political instability. Unless such measures are taken, the problem of slow growth will remain unabated. Our results also advocate the development of alternative mechanisms for aid, as aid flows are shown to have an uncertain effect on the growth performance of the recipients. Therefore, it is worth investigating how the two instruments, foreign aid and institutional quality, work together.

REFERENCES

[1] C. Burnside and D. Dollar, "Aid, Policies, and Growth: Revisiting the Evidence," Policy Research Working Paper No. 3251, The World Bank, Washington DC, 2004.

[2] P. Mosley, J. Hudson and S. Horrell, "Aid, the Public Sector and the Market in Less Developed Countries," *Economic Journal*, Vol. 97, No. 387, 1987, pp. 616-641.

[3] P. Boone, "Politics and the Effectiveness of Foreign Aid," *European Economic Review*, Vol. 40, No. 2, 1996, pp. 289-329.

[4] H. Hansen and F. Tarp, "Aid and Growth Regressions," *Journal of Development Economics*, Vol. 64, No. 2, 2001, pp. 547-570.

[5] G. F. Papanek, "The Effect of Aid and Other Resource Transfers on Savings and Growth in Less Developed Countries," *Economic Journal*, Vol. 82, No. 327, 1972, pp. 934-950.

[6] M. Islam, "Regime Changes, Economic Policies and the Effect of Aid on Growth," *Journal of Development Studies*, Vol. 41, No. 8, 2005, pp. 1467-1492.

[7] C. Dalgaard, H. Hansen and F. Tarp, "On the Empirics of Foreign Aid a01Vol. 32, No. 3, 1993, pp. 485-511.

[8] A. Levin, C. F. Lin and C. Chu, "Unit Root Tests in Panel Data: Asymptotic and Finite-Sample Properties," *Journal of Econometrics*, Vol. 108, No. 1, 2002, pp. 1-24.

[9] J. Breitung, "The Local Power of Some Unit Root Tests for Panel Data," *Advances in Econometrics*, Vol. 15, 2001, pp. 161-177.

[10] K. S. Im, M. H. Pesaran and Y. Shin, "Testing for Unit Roots in Heterogeneous Panels," *Journal of Econometrics*, Vol. 115, No. 1, 2003. pp. 53-74.

[11] G. S. Maddala and S. Wu, "A Comparative Study of Unit Root Tests with Panel Data and a New Simple Test," *Oxford Bulletin of Economics and Statistics*, Special Issue, 1999, pp. 631-652.

[12] I. Choi, "Unit Root Tests for Panel Data," *Journal of International Money and Finance*, Vol. 20, No. 2, 2001, pp. 249-272.

[13] T. Omay and E. O. Kan, "Re-Examining the Threshold Effects in the Inflation-Growth Nexus with Cross-Sectionally Dependent Non-Linear Panel: Evidence from Six Industrialized Economies," *Economic Modelling*, Vol. 27, No. 5, 2010, pp. 998-1005.

[14] L. Gong and H.-F. Zou, "Foreign Aid Reduces Labour Supply and Capital Accumulation," *Review of Development Economics*, Vol. 5, No. 1, 2001, pp. 105-118.

[15] P. Boone, "The Impact of Foreign Aid on Savings and Growth," Centre for Economic Performance, Working Paper No. 677, 1994.

[16] R. Rajan and A. Subramanian, "Aid and Growth, What Does the Cross Country Evidence Really Show?" IMF Working Paper No. 05/127, 2005.

[17] R. J. Barro, "Economic Growth in A Cross-Section of Countries," *Quarterly Journal of Economics*, Vol. 106, No. 2, 1991, pp. 407-443.

[18] R. J. Barro and X. Sala-i-Martin, "Economic Growth," 2nd Edition, MIT Press, Cambridge, 2004.

[19] R. J. Barro and X. Sala-i-Martin, "Convergence," *Journal of Political Economy*, Vol. 100, No. 2, 1992, pp. 223-251.

[20] C. Burnside and D. Dollar, "Aid, Policies and Growth," *American Economic Review*, Vol. 90, No. 4, 2000, pp. 847-868.

[21] W. Easterly, R. Levine and D. Roodman, "Aid, Policies, and Growth: Comment," *American Economic Review*, Vol. 94, No. 3, 2004, pp. 774-780.

[22] W. Easterly, R. Levine and D. Roodman, "New Data, New Doubts: A Comment on Burnside and Dollar's 'Aid, Policies, and Growth' (2000)," *American Economic Review*, Vol. 94, No. 3, 2003, pp. 774-780.

[23] R. G. Murphy and N. G. Tresp, "Government Policy and the Effectiveness of Foreign Aid," Department of Economics, Boston College, Chestnut Hill, 2006.

[24] E. Alvi, D. Mukherjee and E. K. Shukralla, "Foreign Aid, Growth, Policy and Reform," *Economics Bulletin*, Vol.

15, No. 6, 2006, pp. 1-9.

[25] D. Moyo, "Dead Aid: Why Aid Is Not Working and How There Is a Better Way for Africa," Farrar, Straus and Giroux, New York, 2009.

[26] Y. M. Batana, "Aid and Poverty in Africa: Do Well-Being Measures Understate the Progress?" *African Development Review*, Vol. 22, No. 3, 2010, pp. 452-469.

16

Manufacturer-Dealer Relationships: The Influence of Trust and Commitment to Technological Interface Adoption

José R. Concha
Universidad Icesi, Cali, Colombia

ABSTRACT

The steep increase in the number and variety of exchange relations, the increased complexity and uncertainty of the business environment cannot be managed without the presence of interpersonal and/or interorganizational trust and relationship commitment. Manufacturer firms have to pay close attention to developing and maintaining relationship commitment and dealers' trust. The value of such efforts is the most apparent when high levels of competition threaten market shares and the stability of the dealers' network. This empirical study shows that trust and relationship commitment are important assets for the technological interface adoption and bring significant savings for the manufacturer and dealer.

Keywords: Trust; Marketing Relationship; Technological Interface; Commitment

1. Introduction

Understanding relationship marketing requires distinguishing between a discrete transaction, with a distinct beginning, short duration, and sharp ending by performance, and relational exchange, which relies on previous agreements and is longer in duration, reflecting an ongoing process [1]. Categorized with reference to a dealer and its relational exchange with the manufacturer, there are two forms of relationship marketing: one is the relational exchange to obtain the goods on time, and the other is the strategic alliance between the dealer and the manufacturer obtaining a "total quality management." This second form builds a stronger relationship as a way to earn the position of preferred supplier by developing trust in the dealers over a period of time.

Antecedents of Trust

In the manufacturer-dealer context, the supplier firm provides elements to encourage trust in the dealer through its policies, actions, and personnel [2]. The major characteristics of the firm to influence trust development in the dealer are: 1) supplier reputation; 2) manufacturer size; 3) manufacturer's willingness to customize for buyer; 4) manufacturer confidential information sharing; and 5) length of the relationship with manufacturer.

2. Model

This study analyzes (**Figure 1**) how the dealer's trust and relationship commitment influences the adoption of technological interface. For the study, trust is considered the willingness to rely on an exchange partner in whom one has confidence. This definition highlights the importance of confidence. The literature on trust suggests that confidence that the trustee is reliable and has high integrity is associated with such qualities as consistency, competence, honesty, fairness, responsibility, and benevolence [3].

The other initial variable in the model is relationship commitment, which is defined as an exchange partner believing that an ongoing relationship with another is so important as to warrant maximum efforts at maintaining it [4].

Included in the model for the empirical study is also the adoption of technological interface, which is affected by the influence of relationship commitment and trust, as well as by four external observed variables which are: operational benefits, financial benefits, accessibility, and relational benefits.

FULL MODEL

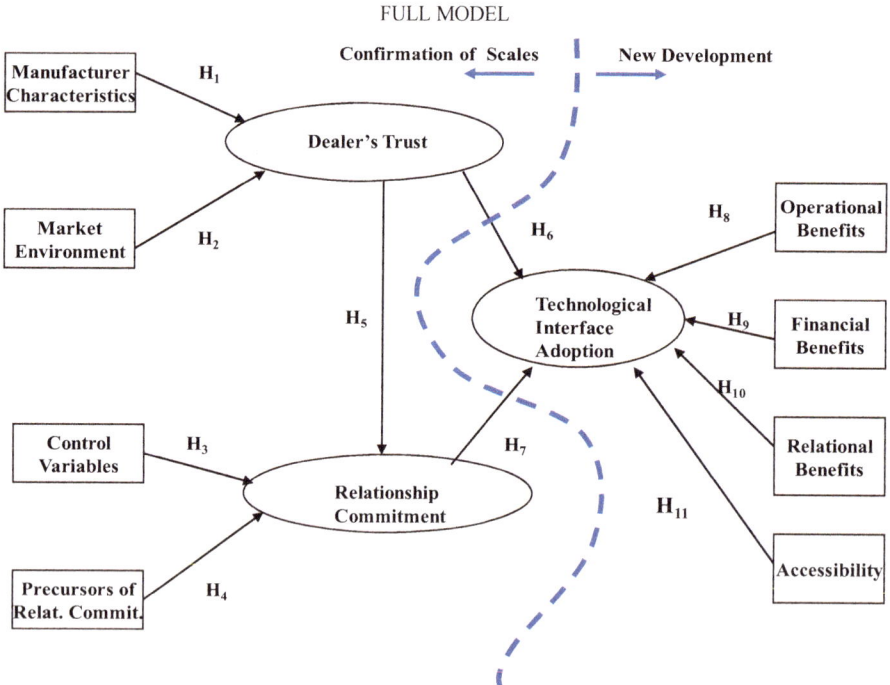

Figure 1. The influence of relationship commitment and dealer's trust in adopting technological interface.

2.1. Characteristics of the Manufacturer

Characteristics of the manufacturer play an important role in relations with the dealers and in building a long-term oriented partnership. To better understand these relationships, I will explain the main factors necessary for an overall perspective and definition of a manufacturer firm and their effect on the trust-building in the relationship.

H_1: A dealer's trust is directly related to manufacturer characteristics.

The market environment has a significant effect on decision-making uncertainty in making channel relations [5]. Because different facets of uncertainty have opposite effects on channel structure and channel member behavior [6], five dimensions of market environment predictability, accuracy, certainty, complexity, and stability, were examined by Ganesan [7] who found that they have strong effects on the trust of organizations. These dimensions will be evaluated again in the present study. The previous analysis supports our next hypothesis and states that.

H_2: A dealer's trust is directly related to market environment.

2.2. Manufacturer Performance

Considerable empirical and anecdotal evidence suggests that the primary criteria for current manufacturer selection decisions and future purchase intentions involve manufacturer performance which is named by Doney and

Canon [2] as control variables. Reviewing the organizational buying literature revealed three aspects of manufacturer performance that consistently emerged as central to the dealer's evaluation of a manufacturer's product offering: 1) delivery performance; 2) relative price/cost; and 3) product/service performance [8].

H_3: A dealer's relationship commitment is directly related to manufacturer performance.

2.3. Relationship Commitment

The major precursors of relationship commitment were identified in Chapter I as: relationship termination costs, communications, and opportunistic behavior. Morgan and Hunt [4] and studied the effects of these factors, concluding that they positively affect relationship commitment.

In this research, I am measuring the same factors, using their questionnaire designed for automobile tire retailers in the United States of America. Then the conclusions obtained in this study can be used also as a cross-cultural evaluation of the hypothesis:

H_4: There is a positive relationship between precursor's factors and relationship commitment.

2.4. Dealer's Trust

As a variable that reduces risk, trust supports close relations and cooperation. However, when a party believes that a partner engages in opportunistic behavior, such behavior most of the time results in a decrease of relationship commitment because partners believe that they can no longer trust one another. Thus, when talking about commitment and cooperation, I posit that firms that receive benefits from their relationship will be committed to its development in the future as well [9].

I propose that trust is a major determinant of relationship commitment, as does Achrol [10]; hence, we hypothesized that:

H5: Relationship commitment is directly related to a dealer's trust.

2.5. Technological Interface Adoption

Technology has significantly influenced the ways in which people communicate and exchange information both within and among organizations. The development and growing use of technology in all areas of life have brought about a need to take into account this variable into business relationships [11]. While in the past, suppliers were mainly dependent on the work and feedback of the manufacturers and dealers, now they are discovering the advantages of technological interface. However, one common thread in the electronic communication literature is that messages sent via e-mail are, in their current text-based format, lacking when it comes to conveying certain types of information [12]. From these facts we can conclude that:

H6: There is a positive relationship between technological interface adoption and relationship commitment.

H7: There is a positive relationship between technological interface adoption and dealer's trust.

2.6. Technological Interface Antecedents

The decision to adopt new technologies is difficult because of the associated uncertainties: switching costs in equipment and training, the necessity to develop new skills with the personnel, the possibility that the technology will become obsolete quickly, accessibility problems that interface technology has in developing countries, difficulties evaluating the real incomes that the new technology adoption will have for the dealer's business in terms of financial and managerial benefits, and the responsibility in terms of the relationship with the manufacturer [13].

For that reason, a company decision to adopt new technologies is linked to its business strategy, because it will be affected by the level of the relationship and the dealer's trust in the manufacturer.

2.7. Operational Benefits

Operational benefits are defined as the adopter beliefs of the likelihood that the technological interface adoption can improve the quality, security, opportunity, and reliability of the information. Benefits may come from qual-

ity improvement, timely information to his/her customers, new market development, improvement in job performance and the associated intrinsic and extrinsic rewards. Hence, it is hypothesized that

H8: A dealer's technological interface adoption is directly related to operational benefits.

2.8. Financial Benefits

I consider that the prospective adopter's subjective probability that applying the new technology from the manufacturer will be economical beneficial to his personal and/or the adopting company's well-being. To the adopting organization, utility means economic or financial benefits resulting from adopting new technology. These benefits may consist in reduces inventory, increases profitability, increases sales, reduces delivery costs, improves delivery times, and makes delivery more accurate.

H9: A dealer's technological interface adoption is directly related to financial benefits.

2.9. Relational Benefits

The adoption of new technology carries a high risk, then the level of perceived commitment from the manufacturer can help reduce this risk though the transmission of adequate information from the manufacturer to the dealer. The relational benefits perceived by the dealer are very critical and affect the dealer's interest to absorb the technology. The more extensive the relational benefits, the more positive are the interest to adopt the new form of technology. Thus, we hypothesized that:

H10: A dealer's technological interface adoption is directly related to relational benefits.

2.10. Accessibility

I defined accessibility as the degree to which the perceived application of new technological interface is free of efforts. The lower the difficulty to use the new technology, the lower is the level of perceived risk and the higher is the probability of a successful adoption. Measures of this construct reflect the potential difficulty for the adopting firm to use the technology, as well as the satisfaction degree that the user has with its adoption. Therefore, the following hypothesis is:

H11: A dealer's technological interface adoption is directly related to accessibility.

3. Method

For the study, we use the data from a sample of Goodyear tire dealers in Colombia. All the Colombian tire dealers are independent and, thus, are able to make free choices and decisions about the manufacturers of the products they sell. Most of the dealers are family-run businesses or assigned distributors that cooperate with the big automobile tire manufacturers and sell their products to the customers.

3.1. Sample

To construct the sample of dealers, we asked Goodyear to assist and supply us with lists of their 128 retailers in the Colombian territory that represent the total population of the Goodyear dealers. This list was the sample for the research.

3.2. Measure Development

To be in agreement with previous studies made by other researchers, preexisting scales will be identified where possible and will be adapted to this study. Then, trust in manufacturer characteristics was measured by adapting Doney and Cannon's [2] questionnaire. Market environment was measured using the questionnaire adapted from Ganesan [7]. Relationship commitment was measured by adapting the questionnaire from Morgan and Hunt [4]. For the measure of control variables, we use the scales developed by Ganesan [7]. Because a scale for one key construct in my research, technological interface, was not available, we developed a scale then applied an appropriate refinement procedure [14]. **Table 1** show the different variables included in our survey.

Table 1. Description of variables.

Latent Exogenous	Latent Endogenous	Observable
Dealer's trust	Manufacturer Characteristics Doney and Cannon (1997)	Manufacturer Reputation
		Manufacturer Size
		Mfr. Willingness to Customize
		Mfr. Confidential Inf. Sharing
		Length of Relationship
	Market Environment Ganesan (1994)	Predictability
		Accuracy
		Certainty
		Complexity
Relationship Commitment	Relationship Commitment Morgan & Hunt (1994)	Relationship Termination Costs
		Communications
		Opportunistic Behavior
	Control Variables Doney & Canon (1994)	Delivery Performance
		Relative Price/Cost
		Product/Service
Technological Interface	Usage Characteristics	Operational Benefits
		Financial Benefits
		Relational Benefits
		Accessibility

ent variables included in our survey.

4. Results

All measures were analyzed for validity and reliability following the guidelines supplied by Jöreskog and Sörbom [15]. The full model measured through a confirmatory factor analysis using LISREL 8.52 shows a good fit with $\chi^2_{(101)}$ =117.04 (p = 0.131) which is not significant at 0.05; suggesting that the proposed model is consistent with the observed data. Below I discuss in detail each of the partial models and the origins of the measures used.

4.1. Influence of Manufacturer Characteristics on Dealer's Trust

The five observed variables used in this study were manufacturer firm reputation, manufacturer firm size, and manufacturer firm willingness to customize for the dealer, manufacturer confidential information sharing, and length of relationship with the dealer. These measures of dealer's trust on the manufacturer were obtained from Doney and Canon's [2] study. The observed variables exhibit a good reliability, with lower values for size ($\alpha = 0.53$) and reputation ($\alpha = 0.58$), but we obtain Cronbach alpha over 0.70 for the other variables.

For assessing discriminant validity, we conducted exploratory factor analysis to ensure high loadings on hypothesized factors and low cross-loadings. The test provided evidence of discriminant validity among all the observed variables in the set, but different to the Doney and Canon [2] decision, who removed reputation construct from the set for further analysis because the construct shows high cross loadings, we included it because this variable did not show high cross loadings and, for the market studied in this research, manufacturer reputation is a very big asset for the dealers.

We used two methods for assessing convergent validity; one was the LISREL estimates of paths from individual items to latent factors that were all statistically significant (p < 0.01), and the other was the results of the exploratory factor analysis showed no high cross loadings.

We evaluated the properties of all the observed variables by conducting a confirmatory factor analysis on the covariance matrices using LISREL 8.52. The reliability analysis for the five observed variables considered shows a relatively good Cronbach alpha value of $\alpha = 0.60$. The chi-squared statistic was statistically non significant ($\chi^2_{(5)}$ = 5.7; p = 0.33), which is very good. The absolute goodness of fit indexes RMSEA = 0.04, GFI = 0.97, and AGFI = 0.91 suggests that these data provide a good fit with the hypothesized measurement model, the H_1 is accepted.

4.2. Influence of Market Environment on Dealer's Trust

We used measures of market environment influence on dealer's trust from Ganesan [7] that was adapted for this research. All the five items considered were included in six questions of the survey, evaluating: accuracy, predictability, certainty, complexity, and stability. However the reliability analysis (see Appendix I) shows a very low Cronbach alpha value (0.31), the Kaiser-Meyer-Olkin measure of sampling adequacy is only 0.66, and the exploratory factor analysis shows high cross-loadings between the measures.

Taking in account the previous statistical results, it is important to consider the market environment in the context of this research: Colombia, as an undeveloped country, does not have a stability situation in the long-term, then the small and medium enterprises in this country does not consider the stability as an important factor when they evaluate the market environment, because they are living for decades under unstable circumstances handling their business. Therefore, I made the decision to remove the stability construct for further analysis.

With the remaining four constructs accuracy, predictability, certainty and complexity, the reliability Cronbach alpha value is 0.66, which is relatively good. Also the group shows a Kaiser-Meyer-Olkin measure of 0.72, and the cross-loadings were reduced in the factor analysis.

The evaluation of the properties of the four observed variables was made conducting a confirmatory factor analysis on the covariance matrices using LISREL 8.52. The reliability analysis for the four observed variables, considered as the constructs, shows a good Cronbach alpha value of $\alpha = 0.66$. The chi-squared statistic was statistically non significant ($\chi^2_{(26)} = 35.77$; p = 0.10), which is very good. The absolute goodness of fit indexes RMSEA = 0.08, GFI = 0.90, and AGFI = 0.83, and the standardized residuals were generally small and non significant. These results confirm the H_1 hypothesis.

4.3. Influence of Manufacturer Performance on Relationship Commitment

To measure the influence of manufacturer performance on relationship commitment, we used the scale proposed by Doney and Canon [2], which includes three groups of constructs: supplier performance, purchase experience with the vendor, and purchase choice. In the present research, our sample is uni-brand tire dealers, because they do not have purchase choice and the purchase experience is unique with Goodyear, I used the scale with the supplier performance that include three aspects of manufacturer: 1) delivery; 2) relative price/cost; and 3) product/service performance.

Reliability (coefficient alpha) for the groups ranges from 0.62 for delivery performance, 0.66 for relative price/cost, and 82 for product/service performance. We used exploratory factor analysis to confirm high loadings on hypothesized factors and low cross-loadings. The test provided evidence of discriminant validity among all the observed variables in the set.

To assess convergent validity, we took into consideration the paths from individual items to latent factors, obtained using LISREL 8.52, that was all statistically significant (p < 0.01). The reliability analysis for the group of three observed variables considered to measure relationship commitment shows a relatively good Cronbach alpha value of $\alpha = 0.70$. The model using LISREL shows that is saturated, which means it has as many parameters as there are non-redundant elements in the covariance matrix, and then the model fit perfectly, and the H_3 is confirmed.

4.4. Influence of Precursors of Relationship Commitment

The items used to confirm this hypothesis came from the scale developed by Morgan and Hunt [4] and were adapted in the dealers' questionnaire. The analysis of the variables in the group shows a good reliability Chronbach alpha index, with $\alpha = 0.87$ for relationship termination cost, $\alpha = 0.87$ for communication, and $\alpha = 0.84$ for opportunistic behavior. The global scale reliability for this group of antecedents all shows a good level of $\alpha = 0.67$.

Examining assessed convergent validity of the facet scales and the global scale whether each indicator's pattern coefficient from the measurement model was significant. This is what Bagozzi [16] calls "convergence in measurement," because the t-value of each item is greater than 2 in all three paths of the measurement model. In this case, we obtained through LISREL a saturated model that fits perfectly and the H_4 is also confirmed positively.

4.5. Influence of Observed Variables on Technological Interface Adoption

As the questionnaire used in this group was developed based on the initial survey, initially we conducted an exploratory factor analysis to evaluate ensuring high loadings on hypothesized factors and low cross-loadings. The test provided evidence of four important factors to build the scale: operational benefits, managerial benefits, relational benefits, and accessibility. The data obtained for the reliability test were: $\alpha = 0.92$ for operational benefits, $\alpha = 0.90$ for managerial benefits, $\alpha = 0.79$ for relational benefits, and $\alpha = 0.69$ for accessibility.

Cronbach alpha for the technological interface adoption is good ($\alpha = 0.82$). The descriptive statistics indicate that the dealers in our sample rated themselves as rather more prone to adopt technological interface because the mean score of 132.62 (range 25 to 175) and a standard deviation of 24.94. Our model for the antecedents of technological interface adoption yields non-significant with $\chi^2_{(2)}$ = 0.30; p = 0.86, which is very good. The fit indexes were for root mean square residual, RMR = 0.01, for root mean square error of approximation, RMSEA = 0.00, for goodness of fit index, GFI = 1.00, and for adjusted goodness of fit index, AGFI = 0.99.

4.6. Full Model: Influence of Trust and Relationship Commitment on Technology Interface Adoption

To evaluate the full model we created a more detailed procedure evaluating the assessment individually:

4.6.1. Assessment of Reliability

To assess reliability, I used Cronbach's alpha index for each of the observed variables in the model, and for the global scales; the individual reliabilities for the variables were reported in the previous results, and the global scale exhibits high reliability with α = 0.88 [17].

4.6.2. Assessment of Convergent Validity

Convergent validity was evaluated by examining whether each indicator pattern coefficient from the measurement model was significant. The t values for each parameter were supplied by the LISREL program, showing that all of them have a value greater than +2 or less than –2; then the parameters are referred to as significant and can be considered distinct from 0 in the population [18].

4.6.3. Assessment of Discriminant Validity

To establish discriminant validity between the facets, we used the final model as the base model. Constraining the phi value for a pair of variables to unity and then estimating the resulting measurement model assessed discriminant validity. Because the base model gave a significantly better fit than the constrained model, it indicates that the traits are not perfectly correlated, and discriminant validity was achieved.

4.7. The Final Model

The resulting measurement full model (see **Table 2**) through a confirmatory factor analysis using LISREL 8.52 shows a good fit with $\chi^2_{(101)}$ =117.04 (p = 0.131), which is not significant at 0.05. I remember that this way of looking at statistical inference in structural equation modeling may appear to be reverse at the one used in the framework of traditional hypothesis testing [18]. The model fit is as follows: RMR = 0.09, RMSEA = 0.05, GFI = 0.76, AGFI = 0.68, NFI = 0.83, NNFI = 0.93 and

Table 2. Full model. Factor loadings and errors.

Observed Variable	Latent Variable	λ	e
Manufacturer Reputation		0.79	3.36
Manufacturer Size		1.18	5.16
Manufacturer Willingness	Dealer's Trust	4.94	1.34
Manufacturer Confidential Information Sharing		1.67	3.51
Length of Relationship		.43	3.71
Market Environment		1.21	25.70
Delivery Performance		1.23	2.27
Service Performance		1.34	6.73
Relationship Termination Costs	Relationship Commitment	5.88	28.74
Communications		3.73	11.44
Opportunistic Behavior		3.02	13.88
Operational Benefits for Dealer		8.98	46.98
Financial Benefits for Dealer	Technological Interface Adoption	7.54	19.97
Relation. Benefits for Dealer		2.06	9.30
Accessibility		5.63	6.96

CFI = 0.94. In summary, the full model for technological interface adoption shows an acceptable fit.

The size of the factor loadings (λ) in the **Table 2**, indicates how much they contribute to predicting or to measuring the latent variable. Based on the final model obtained, we can establish the importance that the factors have for the different latent variables:

Manufacturer willingness to customize for dealer has an important influence developing dealer's trust (λ = 4.94).

Relationship termination cost is the observed variable affecting considerably the relationship commitment of the dealer (λ = 5.88).

The adoption of technological interface has three most important observed variables with high loading factors; operational benefits (λ = 8.98), financial benefits (λ = 7.54), and accessibility (λ = 5.63).

4.8. Total Effects

The structural equation model permits obtaining both the direct and indirect effects of the various variables included in the model. Direct effects are the effects that go directly from one variable to a second variable and were evaluated previously. Indirect effects are the effects between two variables that are mediated by one or more intervening variables, often referred to as a mediating variable. The combination of direct and indirect effects makes up the total effect of the explanatory variable on a dependent variable. For this research the mediating variable is the technological interface adoption. The total effects of the observed variables on trust and relationship commitment are in **Table 3**.

5. Conclusions

In the business-to-business markets, relationship commitment nowadays is one of the "order qualifiers", where the firms are more oriented to achieving future goals with long-term outcomes. This study shows that the adoption of technology interface is possible if the manufacturer has developed relationship commitment and trust in its dealers. The paths from trust and relationship commitment to technological interface in the full model show a positive sign for the regression coefficient between relationship commitment and technological interface adoption and a negative value for the factor loading between trust and technological interface adoption. This result reflects the following findings: high levels of relationship commitment are expected to cause high levels of technological interface adoption; in contrast, high levels of dealer's trust are expected to generate low levels of technological interface adoption.

Furthermore, I confirm that the operational benefits, financial benefits, relational benefits, and accessibility influence the adoption of new forms of technology that facilitate the communication and operations between the manufacturer and the dealers. The effects of each of the paths showing these influences determine the importance that they have in the adoption of new forms of technology. Moreover, the total effects on relationship commitment and trust are very important findings to be taken into account for the manufacturers.

In Colombia, under different cultural influences, we were able to confirm the findings made by other researchers. Both dealers focus on the characteristics of the firm [2] and on the market environment [7] to develop trust. However, in Colombia unlike in the US, the manufacturer characteristic of reputation must be taken into account. In the survey study developed by Doney and Canon [2] with a sample from members of the National Association of Purchasing Management, this reputation construct was removed.

In reference to the market environment influence to develop trust, dissimilar to Ganesan [7] survey, I find that the stability construct is not an important element for the Colombian Goodyear dealers in the trust-building process.

Table 3. Total effects on latent variables.

	Trust	Relationship Commitment
Operational benefits	−5.02	13.73
Financial benefits	−4.22	11.53
Relational benefits	−1.15	3.15
Accessibility	−3.15	8.61

We also used the scales developed by Morgan and Hunt [4] to determine the precursors of relationship commitment. The samples in both studies were independent automobile tire retailers, and then the findings showed a cross-cultural evaluation of the process. Finally, in this study, we confirmed that the control variables were antecedents of relationship commitment, according with the scales developed by Doney and Canon [2].

The manufacturers should promote strongly the adoption of technological interface by the dealers. The development of this kind of communication represents an investment with a long-term payoff. Therefore, when the manufacturer considers the costs and benefits of investing in developing a technological interface, it must consider that relationship commitment and dealer's trust are factors that influence positively the adoption process. The fact is that trust and relationship commitment developed in a dealer brings about bigger benefits than cooperation alone.

Manufacturer firms have to pay close attention to developing and maintaining relationship commitment and dealers' trust [19]. The value of such efforts is the most apparent when high levels of competition threaten market share and the stability of the dealers' network. With this study I showed that trust and relationship commitment were important assets for the technological interface adoption and bring significant savings for the manufacturer and dealer.

In summary, in all demand situations, the adoption of technology interface requires the consideration of external and internal variables. For the manufacturers, it is advisable to "market" the technology on its operational and financial benefits and accessibility but also considering the relationship commitment and trust building with their dealers.

REFERENCES

[1] F. R. Dwyer, P. H. Schurr and S. Oh, "Developing Buyer-Seller Relationships," *Journal of Marketing*, Vol. 51, No. 2, 1987, pp. 11-27.

[2] P. M. Doney and J. P. Cannon, "An Examination of the Nature on Trust in Buyer-Seller Relationships," *Journal of Marketing*, Vol. 61, No. 2, 1997, pp. 35-51.

[3] I. Altman and D. A. Taylor, "Social Penetration: The Development of Interpersonal Relationships," Holt, Rinehart, and Winston, New York, 1973.

[4] R. M. Morgan and S. D. Hunt, "The Commitment-Trust Theory of Relationship Marketing," *Journal of Marketing*, Vol. 58, No. 3, 1994, pp. 20-38.

[5] R. S. Achrol, L. K. Scheer and L. W. Stern, "Designing Successful Transorganizational Marketing Alliances," Marketing Science Institute, Working Paper No. 90-118, Marketing Science Institute, Cambridge, 1990.

[6]   S. Balakrishnan and B. Wernerfelt, "Technical Change, Competition and Vertical Integration," *Strategic Management Journal*, Vol. 7, No. 4, 1986, pp. 347-359.

[7]   S. Ganesan, "Determinants of Long-Term Orientation in Buyer-Seller Relationships," *Journal of Marketing*, Vol. 58, No. 2, 1994, pp. 1-19.

[8]   E. J. Wilson, "The Relative Importance of Supplier Selection Criteria: A Review and Update," *International Journal of Purchase and Materials Management*, Vol. 30, No. 2, 1994, pp. 35-41.

[9]   A. Wong and A. Sohal, "An Examination of the Relationship between Trust, Commitment and Relationship Quality," *International Journal of Retail & Distribution Management*, Vol. 30, No. 1, 2002, pp. 34-50.

[10] R. Achrol, "Evolution of the Marketing Organization: New forms for Turbulent Environments," *Journal of Marketing*, Vol. 55, No. 4, 1991, pp. 77-93.

[11] O. Turel, Y. Yuan and C. E. Connelly, "In Justice We Trust: Predicting User Acceptance of e-Customer Services," *Journal of Management Information Systems*, Vol. 24, No. 4, 2008, pp. 123-151.

[12] N. F. Awad and A. Ragowsky, "Establishing Trust in Electronic Commerce through Online Word of Mouth: An Examination across Genders," *Journal of Management Information Systems*, Vol. 24, No. 4, 2008, pp. 101-121.

[13] D. J. Kim, D. L. Ferrin and H. R. Rao, "A Trust-Based Consumer Decision-Making Model in Electronic Commerce: The role of Trust, Perceived Risk, and Their Antecedents," *Decision Support Systems*, Vol. 44, No. 2, 2008, pp. 544-564.

[14] G. A. Churchill, "A paradigm for Developing Better Measures of Marketing Constructs," *Journal of Marketing Research*, Vol. 16, No. 1, 1979, pp. 64-73.

[15] K. G. Jöreskog and D. Sörbom, "User's Reference Guide," Scientific Software, Mooresville, 2000.

[16] R. P. Bagozzi, "Evaluating Structural Equation Models with Unobservable Variables and Measurement Error: A Comment," *Journal of Marketing Research*, Vol. 18, No. 3, 1981, pp. 375-381.

[17] J. C. Nunally, "Psychometric Theory," 2nd Edition. McGraw Hill Book, New York, 1978.

[18] T. Raykov and G. Marcoulides, "A First Course in Structural Equation Modeling," Lawrence Erlbaum Associates, Publishers, Mahwah, 2000.

[19] D. Peppers andM. Rogers, "Customer Loyalty: A Matter of Trust," *Sales & Marketing Management*, Vol. 158, No. 5, 2006, p. 22.

Limitations of Kuwait's Economy: An Absorptive Capacity Perspective[*]

Mohammad Ramadhan[1], Abdulhameed Hussain[2], Reem Al-Hajji[3]

[1]Techno Economic Division, Kuwait Institute for Scientific Research, Kuwait City, Kuwait
[2]Supreme Council for Privatization, Council of Ministers, Kuwait
[3]Techno Economic Division, Kuwait Institute for Scientific Research, Kuwait City, Kuwait

ABSTRACT

This paper aims to examine the absorptive capacity of Kuwait's economy over the period (1970-2010). The paper will expand on the analytical framework to estimate the absorptive capacity of the Kuwaiti economy developed previously by the main author. The absorptive capacity of the Kuwaiti economy has been increasing steadily over the years. Domestic absorption depicted a slow growth pattern during the period 1970-2000. However, it has accelerated significantly over the last decade rising by almost three fold from $29.1 bil in 2001 to $82.2 bil in 2010. However, the constant positive resource balance and the excess of foreign exchange earnings indicate the limitations of the economy absorptive capacity. The paper highlights the main constraints that limit the ability of the Kuwaiti economy to absorb resources and provide few policy recommendations that should help in increasing the absorptive capacity in long run.

Keywords: Absorptive Capacity; Kuwait's Economy; Resource Balance

1. Introduction

The State of Kuwait is characterized as a small rich open economy with abundance in crude oil that is entirely owned by the state. The economy depends heavily on oil exports, and specifically, oil revenues accounts for 50% of GDP, 95% of exports, and 90% of government income (GDP in 2010 was around 125 bil US$). The other two important economic activities with sizable contribution to GDP were financial and personal services (35% of GDP), and the trade and logistics activities (12% of GDP). The remaining economic activities had minimal contribution toward the GDP. More importantly, the huge oil revenues over the last decade allowed the government to enjoy constant surpluses in the public budget. For example, in 2010 oil income was around 65.2 bil US$, representing around 92.0% of total government income (70.9 bil US$). Fiscal expenditures were around 53.4 bil US$, hence the government was able to realize a budget surplus of 17.5 bil US$. While constant budget surpluses emphasize strong fiscal position, it also points out the weakness of the government in spending within the domestic economy, particularly in initiating developmental projects and upgrading the current deteriorating infrastructure.

It should be emphasized that the economy generated high rates of savings, mostly through the public sector, while investing surprisingly little in the domestic economy. Most of Kuwait's high savings are invested abroad, both in the form of FDI and as portfolio investment. These large capital outflows largely serve to balance the country's international accounts, offsetting the large visible trade surplus (mostly a consequence of high oil exports). During the oil boom period (1976-1982), Kuwait enjoyed huge surpluses in its public budget and balance of payments. Yet, most of the financial surpluses were not channeled back to be invested in the economy. In fact, large part of the financial surpluses fled out of the country for investment in income-producing assets abroad, which took a huge hit after the 2008 global financial crisis. The constant capital outflow supported the widely held view that Kuwait has a limited absorptive capacity, since it was unable to utilize these surpluses internally in productive investment projects.

The fiscal situation had changed radically following the downturn in oil prices in late 1982, leading to real budget deficits over the period (1983-1989). The Iraqi invasion in August 1990 reinforced this trend, which

[*]This project was partially funded by Kuwait Foundation for the Advancement of Sciences under Project Code: 2010-1103-02.

resulted in both internal and external deficits. Presently, the Kuwaiti economy is going through a critical stage. After the liberation of Iraq in 2003, the private sector has benefited from government spending on developmental projects and the opportunity of increased business activities due to the rebuilding of Iraq. Unfortunately, this recent growth in economic activities has resulted in unprecedented levels of inflation, mainly due to the lack of absorptive capacity, and the inability to absorb the large amounts of liquidity generated from these surpluses. In comparison, the average level of inflation during the periods 2006-2008, and 2003-2008 were 7.34% and 4.77%, respectively. However, this business environment was halted by the sever hit of the financial crisis in the late 2008.

Based on the aforementioned, this paper aims to analytically address the concept of absorptive capacity in Kuwait's economy over the last four decades. The paper will expand on the analytical framework to estimate the absorptive capacity of the Kuwaiti economy developed by the main author [1]. The paper consists of the following sections: Section two explains the concept of absorptive capacity. Section three presents the theoretical background for the absorptive capacity mathematical model. Section four analyzes the results of Kuwait's absorptive capacity model. The main constraints that limit the ability of the Kuwaiti economy to absorb resources are highlighted in section five. Finally, conclusions and policy recommendations are summarized in section six.

2. The Concept of Absorptive Capacity

One of the earlier definitions for the concept of "absorptive capacity" was affirmed by Stevens, who stated that the absorptive capacity of a country is the ability of the domestic economy to absorb resources at an acceptable rate of return within a given period [2]. However there was no consensus among economists in regard to the nature of resources and the component that lead to and define an acceptable rate of return. Within the context of oil producers such as the GCC, economists interpret absorptive capacity in terms of the ability to utilize foreign exchange effectively [3]. Put differently, to the extent that oil revenues are received by the governments in these countries and financial surpluses are accumulated over the years, the concept of absorptive capacity becomes the ability of the government to spend the oil revenues within a given productivity criterion.

Another predicament with the broad definition of absorptive capacity is how to derive the notion of an acceptable rate of return. It is recognized that the relevant rate which must be considered by policy makers is the "social rate of return". However, societies differ in the way they assign weights to social values. In the case of Kuwait, the social well being of nationals must depend

on how successful the policy makers are in investing the oil revenues and surpluses (funds) in ventures, which would not only pay for themselves, but also generate sufficient returns for future development. Moreover, the public sector which constitutes 70% of the GDP must be efficient in its public expenditures by minimizing unnecessary spending and promoting productivity. Hence, a more productive way to expand the absorptive capacity of the Kuwaiti economy is to expand the marginal efficiency of investment of most projects by systematically improving the quality of input factors of production.

Within the broad context of the relation between investments and economic growth that leads to more absorption of resources, the connections between investment and GDP growth are not as precise as one might expect, and are often less direct than the growth models implied [4]. This is for several reasons:

- Growth models tend to assume that investment will be in productively relevant "objects", that good investment projects will be selected and that they will be efficiently implemented; if this is not the case in practice, then a given volume of investment will deliver less growth than a simple model would suggest. Hence, absorption capacity will not be enhanced.

- The sectoral composition of investment may differ from that assumed in a given model, and since some sectors are inherently far more capital intensive than others, the link between investment and growth naturally becomes less predictable.

- Investment may be less effective than it should be due to regulatory and bureaucratic barriers that cause delays and higher costs. This is a well known constraint within the GCC countries, particularly in Kuwait.

3. Production Expenditure Identities

The concept of the absorptive capacity model for the State of Kuwait was stated previously by El-Mallakh and Atta through a simple system of national income and production accounts [5]. The absorptive capacity mathematical model was elaborated by the main author to allow for detailed analysis of constraints and challenges.

The production expenditure identities that explain the conceptual issues can be structured within the production-consumption framework.

$$Y = C + I + G + X - M \qquad (1)$$

where $(X - M)$ is net exports.

The national income identity indicates that income can be either consumed or saved (private and government), and can be stated as:

$$Y = C + G + S \qquad (2)$$

where, $\quad C$ = Private consumption;

G = Government consumption;
I = Total domestic investment;
M = Total imports;
S = Total saving;
X = Total exports;
Y = Gross domestic product.

Identities (1) and (2) specify the uses to which the resources may be allocated. By equating the production and income identities the following equation is obtained:

$$I = S + M - X \qquad (3)$$

Therefore, investment is financed through saving and net capital inflow (M-X). Since the Kuwaiti economy has, in most years, a balance of payments surplus, the expression which more appropriately describes its situation can be derived from rearranging Equation (3) as follows:

$$S - I = X - M \qquad (4)$$

The excess of domestic savings over investment is equal to the net capital outflow. More specifically, Equation (4) indicates that when domestic absorptive capacity is limited, the economy seeks outside channels to invest its surplus savings.

4. The Absorptive Capacity Model

The Kuwaiti absorptive capacity can be measured according to the following mathematical relationship:

$$AC = C + I + G \qquad (5)$$

where, AC = Absorptive capacity;
C = Private consumption;
I = Total domestic investment;
G = Government expenditure.

The economy is said to have a limited absorptive, when it persistently has a positive resource balance; $i.e.$

$$X - M > 0 \qquad (6)$$

Applying the conditions specified in (5) and (6) to the Kuwaiti economy over the period (1970-2010), we obtain the data in **Tables 1** and **2**. Specifically, the components (variables) of Kuwait's domestic absorptive capacity and resource balance are identified and presented in **Table 1**. Moreover, **Table 2** shows the share of these components in the GDP in order to demonstrate the significance of each variable within the domestic absorption concept. Estimating the absorptive capacity model reveals the following important facts:

Table 1. Indicators of Kuwait absorptive capacity (billions US dollars at current prices).

Years	Gross Domestic Product	Household Cos.	Govt. Exp.	Gross Fixed Capital Formation	Domestic Absorption	Total Exports	Total Imports	Resource Balance	Net National Saving	Gross Domestic Savings
	GDP	C	G	I	C + G + I	X	M	X-M	Sn	Sd
1970	2.87	1.11	0.39	0.35	1.85	1.72	0.69	1.02	--	1.37
1973	5.41	1.48	0.72	0.49	2.69	3.89	1.2	2.69	--	3.21
1977	14.14	4.76	2.04	2.84	9.65	10.18	6.14	4.04	7.4	7.34
1981	25.25	9.43	3.56	3.85	16.84	17.41	9.33	8.09	16.9	11.94
1985	21.45	10.25	4.8	4.25	19.3	11.51	9.17	2.34	7.85	6.39
1989	24.31	12.47	6.17	2.5	21.13	12.74	10.06	2.68	10.26	5.67
1992	19.87	7.62	11.04	3.45	22.11	8.04	10.77	-2.73	3.23	1.71
1993	23.96	10.41	8.59	3.62	22.63	11.44	10.61	0.83	5.58	4.95
1994	24.86	10.2	8.43	3.31	21.95	12.64	10.44	2.21	5.65	6.13
1995	26.55	10.96	8.76	3.69	23.4	14.23	11.41	2.82	7.87	6.84
1996	31.49	14.02	8.59	4.4	27.01	16.47	12.34	4.12	10.33	8.88
1997	30.35	14.11	8.08	4.09	26.28	16.04	12.02	4.03	10.63	8.17
1998	25.95	15.12	7.91	4.75	27.79	11.38	13.26	-1.88	4.48	2.91
1999	30.12	15.69	8.09	4.27	28.05	13.84	11.88	1.96	7.43	6.34
2000	37.72	15.66	8.1	3.95	27.72	21.3	11.37	9.93	15.92	13.95
2001	34.89	16.15	8.24	4.77	29.16	17.9	12.4	5.5	9.97	10.49
2002	38.14	18.91	9.64	6.1	34.65	17.01	13.96	3.05	6.57	9.59
2003	47.87	20.46	11.01	7.8	39.27	24.94	16.5	8.44	12.75	16.40
2004	59.44	22.24	11.8	8.9	42.95	33.83	19.25	14.58	23.7	25.40
2005	80.8	25.98	12.7	11.82	50.49	51.69	22.84	28.85	40.4	42.13
2006	101.56	29.01	14.11	16.24	59.36	66.57	24.54	42.02	59.78	58.43
2007	114.64	34.9	16.05	20.43	71.38	72.7	32.46	40.23	58.63	63.73
2008	147.38	41.47	19.74	27.24	88.45	98.39	38.21	60.18	78.72	87.59
2009	105.9	35.43	19.58	18.99	74.01	62.98	31.13	31.85	--	--
2010	124.33	37.84	20.75	23.68	82.27	74.69	32.68	42.01	--	--
Average	**47.97**	**17.43**	**9.56**	**7.83**	**34.82**	**28.14**	**15.39**	**12.76**	**19.24**	**17.81**

Source: [6] and [8].

Table 2. Share of absorptive capacity indicators in total GDP.

Years	Gross Domestic Product (GDP)	Household Consumption	Govt. consumption	Gross fixed capital formation (I)	Domestic Absorption (C + G + I)	Total Exports (X)	Total Imports (M)	Resource Balance (X-M)
	GDP	C	G	I	C+G+I	X	M	X-M
1970	100	38.6	13.5	12.3	64.4	59.8	24.2	35.7
1973	100	27.3	13.4	9.1	49.8	72.0	22.2	49.8
1977	100	33.6	14.5	20.1	68.2	72.0	43.4	28.6
1981	100	37.4	14.1	15.2	66.7	69.0	37.0	32.0
1985	100	47.8	22.4	19.8	90.0	53.7	42.7	10.9
1989	100	51.3	25.4	10.3	86.9	52.4	41.4	11.0
1992	100	38.3	55.5	17.4	111.3	40.5	54.2	-13.7
1993	100	43.5	35.9	15.1	94.5	47.8	44.3	3.5
1994	100	41.0	33.9	13.3	88.3	50.9	42.0	8.9
1995	100	41.3	33.0	13.9	88.1	53.6	43.0	10.6
1996	100	44.5	27.3	14.0	85.8	52.3	39.2	13.1
1997	100	46.5	26.6	13.5	86.6	52.9	39.6	13.3
1998	100	58.3	30.5	18.3	107.1	43.9	51.1	-7.2
1999	100	52.1	26.9	14.2	93.1	45.9	39.4	6.5
2000	100	41.5	21.5	10.5	73.5	56.5	30.1	26.3
2001	100	46.3	23.6	13.7	83.6	51.3	35.5	15.8
2002	100	49.6	25.3	16.0	90.9	44.6	36.6	8.0
2003	100	42.7	23.0	16.3	82.0	52.1	34.5	17.6
2004	100	37.4	19.9	15.0	72.3	56.9	32.4	24.5
2005	100	32.2	15.7	14.6	62.5	64.0	28.3	35.7
2006	100	28.6	13.9	16.0	58.5	65.5	24.2	41.4
2007	100	30.4	14.0	17.8	62.3	63.4	28.3	35.1
2008	100	28.1	13.4	18.5	60.0	66.8	25.9	40.8
2009	100	33.5	18.5	17.9	69.9	59.5	29.4	30.1
2010	100	30.4	16.7	19.0	66.2	60.1	26.3	33.8
Average	100	40.1	23.1	15.3	78.5	56.3	35.8	20.5

Source: [6] and [8].

1) The absorptive capacity of the Kuwaiti economy has been increasing steadily over the years. The capacity is measured by domestic absorption ability (consumption, gross fixed capital formation, government expenditure). The average domestic absorption for the period was estimated at $34.8 bil (around 78.5% of average GDP). While the growth of domestic absorption depicted a slow pattern during the period 1970-2000, the size of domestic absorption has accelerated significantly over the last decade rising by almost three fold from $29.1 bil in 2001 to $82.2 bil in 2010.

2) On average, consumption constituted the largest component of domestic absorption around 50%, followed by government consumption at 27% and then gross fixed capital formation at 23%. However, a close look at the data reveals that GFCF has passed government consumption in total values over the period (2006-2010), except for 2009. This has to do with increased oil revenues that facilitated more developmental projects.

3) Kuwaiti enjoyed a positive resource balance over the last four decades, except for 1992 and 1998. The persistence of a positive resource balance is a significant indicator of absorptive capacity limitations. The average resource balance over the period was estimated at $12.7 bil (around 20.5% of average GDP). While resource balance has fluctuated below the average for most of the period, it has increased significantly since 2004 reaching the highest in 2008 at $60. 2 bil. The resource balance has declined sharply after the global financial crisis in 2008.

4) The continual positive resource balance (due to net exports) suggests that Kuwaiti foreign exchange earnings exceeded its currencies requirements for imports of goods and services (plus workers' remittances). A country is said to have a limited absorptive capacity if its foreign exchange earnings persistently exceed its foreign exchange requirements. The fact that Kuwaiti economy has a persistent foreign exchange surpluses is another

clear indication of its limited absorptive capacity.

5) Domestic saving exceeded gross domestic investment in each year during the last four decades. The excess saving is almost equal to the resource balance. In other words, the economy tends to save more than its ability to invest, which is another indicator of absorptive capacity limitations. Again the accumulation of positive resources (financial revenues) over the years in terms of foreign currencies from oil exports verify the fact that oil surpluses did not find the proper opportunities to be channeled back into the economy.

6) Gross national saving has been much greater than gross domestic saving. The excess of domestic savings over investment is equal to the net capital outflow. The accumulated savings is another indicator of absorptive capacity. When domestic absorptive capacity is limited, the economy seeks outside outlets for its surplus savings.

7) The share of government consumption in Kuwaiti absorptive capacity has been increasing at a much faster rate than other types of domestic spending. This government spending represents merely spending on education, health and social welfare. Some might argue that human development through spending on education and health is vital for economic growth. However, irrational and inefficient spending on social welfare, particularly hikes in wages/salaries and subsidies can have a diverse affect on growth and development in the long run.

The above findings indicate that Kuwait's average domestic absorption for the period represented around 78.5% of average GDP. It should be noted that in comparison with three selected developed economies (Japan, United Kingdome, USA), the average domestic absorption for these economies during the period (1970-2010), constituted around 98.1%, 99.9%, and 101.5% of average GDP, respectively [6]. In other words, the above developed economies have the ability to absorb resources effectively, even though their resource balances vary to a large degree (surpluses in the case of Japan and deficits in the case of UK and USA). The gap between Kuwait's domestic absorption and GDP entails the introduction of economic initiatives to enhance the economic ability to absorb resources. Moreover, determining the size of the absorptive capacity signifies the importance of the private sector bridging the gap between current and potential domestic absorptive capacity.

5. Absorptive Capacity Constraints

The ability of Kuwait to undertake investments at a desirable rate of (social) return, or to absorb foreign exchange through increased imports has been limited by a number of constraints and limitations that can be identified in the following:

- **Market limitations**: The small and limited market size is probably the most influential factor in con-

straining Kuwait's absorptive capacity. By the end of 2010, total labor force in Kuwait reached 2,158,210 (365,585 Kuwaiti and 1,792,625 Non-Kuwaiti). The purchasing power of the two types of population differs significantly. The main source of income of the non-Kuwaiti labor force is the compensation of employees of foreign labor in the private sector. The fact that the private sector role in economic activities is very limited (around 30% of GDP in 2010), it tends to employ unskilled and inefficient foreign labor at low wages. On the other hand, over 93% of the Kuwaiti labor force is employed in the public sector with lucrative wage and compensation structure. Thus, the domestic market of the Kuwaiti economy is limited by the relatively low income of the majority of the labor force which is expatriates. This fact has some serious implications for large-scale industries and highly priced products which must be produced in large quantities for efficient operation.

- **Compensation of labor**: The private sector is reluctant to pay high wages to Kuwaiti nationals despite the fact that the producers sell their goods and services at prices comparable to international prices. The private sector has unlimited supply of unskilled and inefficient foreign labor at low wages. As a result of selling at international prices while paying low wage rates; the operating surplus in the Kuwaiti private industries is extremely high relative to the compensation of employees [7]. Moreover, the private sector would not accept to offer Kuwaiti nationals similar lucrative conditions of employment as the public sector. This dichotomy in compensation between the public and private sectors will reinforce the structural imbalances with the domestic economy. The end results are the unwillingness of the national labor force to move to the private sector, and the inability of the private sector to increase its role in economic activities.

- **Development of pro ductive sectors**: The market limitations and unavailability of factors inputs have put real constraints on the development of various non-oil productive sectors. The government efforts to expand the productive capacity of the economy are still below expectations. This is an important factor for seeking outside outlets for the excess foreign exchange. The industrial sector which can be a good source for huge investments in large industrial projects constitute only 5.80% of GDP in 2010. Many factors inhibit the development of the industrial sector including; smallness of domestic market, inadequate business environment, lack of foreign direct investment and technology, and dependence on unskilled and inefficient expatriate labor.

- **Dominance of service-based activities**: The large services sector comprises the following activities: wholesale and retail trade, restaurants and hotels; transport, storage and communication, finance, insurance, real estate and business services and community social and personal services. This sector employed over 70 per cent of total labor force and contributed 48.1 per cent of GDP in 2010. As to the absorptive capacity of this sector, we notice that the services provided by the government (education, health and economical services) have consumed a large volume of resources over the years. With the aid of increased oil revenues, Kuwait has created one of the most comprehensive welfare systems in the world. Government spending on education and health has contributed to the development of human capital, which raised the productive capacity of the economy. Investments in education and health services takes time to yield dividends and will contribute indirectly in future growth and development. However, the real question is whether this type of spending results in an "acceptable rate of social return". Allocating a large share of oil revenues for the expansion in public goods will result in bias towards service-based activities and national labor force compensation over output-based activities. This will distort income diversification efforts of stimulating the non-oil activities and increasing absorptive capacity.

6. Conclusions and Policy Recommendations

The above analysis indicates clearly that Kuwait has a limited absorptive capacity over the last four decades. This is evident from the fact that the economy persistently has a positive resource balance. Moreover, the foreign exchange earnings of Kuwait exceeded its foreign exchange requirements. The analysis suggests that the limitations on the absorptive capacity of Kuwait are likely to continue unless some fundamental measures are adopted to create new investment opportunities in the economy. New measures and initiatives include: in order to overcome the problem of market limitations, Kuwait must look outward toward regional markets, particularly

within the GCC. This entails among others energizing the role of the private sector in the manufacturing sector and in trade and logistics activities. Kuwait must adopt sound measures to attract FDI and bring the multinational corporations into the local market (Kuwait currently attracts hardly any incoming FDI). This approach is the most appropriate and efficient way to transfer technology and managerial know-how. The FDI can significantly increase the absorptive capacity of Kuwait by easing its bottlenecks in the areas of entrepreneurial and managerial capabilities, international marketing, innovative business development, new export opportunities, availability of financial resources, and lastly state-of-the-art technology. Finally, Kuwait must work hard in achieving its strategic vision of becoming a regional Trade and Financial Center. This should promote the private sector in providing services in the trade and financial activities. This vision will open the economy to new frontiers in trade and finance and sets Kuwait in its along waited proper place in the region.

REFERENCES

[1] M. Ramadhan, "The Absorptive Capacity of Kuwaiti Economy: Analysis of Size and Determinants," *Journal of the Gulf & Arabian Peninsula Studies*, Vol. 31, No. 116, 2005, pp. 11-29.

[2] W. J. Stevens, "Capital Absorptive Capacity in Developing Countries," A.W. Sijthoff, Leiden, 1971.

[3] D. Soliman, "The Kuwait Fund and the Political Economy of Arab Regional Development," Praeger, New York, 1976.

[4] M. M. Shirley and P. Walsh, "Public versus Private Ownership: The Current State of the Debate," World Bank Working Paper 2420, The World Bank, Washington DC, 2001.

[5] R. El-Mallakh and J. K. Atta, "The Absorptive Capacity of Kuwait," Lexington Books, Toronto, 1981.

[6] United Nations Conference of Trade and Development, UNCTAD Handbook of Statistics, 2012.

[7] M. Metwally, "Causes and Consequences of Wage Differentials in the GCC Countries: A Case Study," *The Middle East Business and Economic Review*, Vol. 9, No. 2, 1997, pp. 22-32.

[8] World Bank, World Development Report, 2001.

Permissions

The contributors of this book come from diverse backgrounds, making this book a truly international effort. This book will bring forth new frontiers with its revolutionizing research information and detailed analysis of the nascent developments around the world.

We would like to thank all the contributing authors for lending their expertise to make the book truly unique. They have played a crucial role in the development of this book. Without their invaluable contributions this book wouldn't have been possible. They have made vital efforts to compile up to date information on the varied aspects of this subject to make this book a valuable addition to the collection of many professionals and students.

This book was conceptualized with the vision of imparting up-to-date information and advanced data in this field. To ensure the same, a matchless editorial board was set up. Every individual on the board went through rigorous rounds of assessment to prove their worth. After which they invested a large part of their time researching and compiling the most relevant data for our readers. Conferences and sessions were held from time to time between the editorial board and the contributing authors to present the data in the most comprehensible form. The editorial team has worked tirelessly to provide valuable and valid information to help people across the globe.

Every chapter published in this book has been scrutinized by our experts. Their significance has been extensively debated. The topics covered herein carry significant findings which will fuel the growth of the discipline. They may even be implemented as practical applications or may be referred to as a beginning point for another development. Chapters in this book were first published by Scientific Research Publishing Inc.; hereby published with permission under the Creative Commons Attribution License or equivalent.

The editorial board has been involved in producing this book since its inception. They have spent rigorous hours researching and exploring the diverse topics which have resulted in the successful publishing of this book. They have passed on their knowledge of decades through this book. To expedite this challenging task, the publisher supported the team at every step. A small team of assistant editors was also appointed to further simplify the editing procedure and attain best results for the readers.

Our editorial team has been hand-picked from every corner of the world. Their multi-ethnicity adds dynamic inputs to the discussions which result in innovative outcomes. These outcomes are then further discussed with the researchers and contributors who give their valuable feedback and opinion regarding the same. The feedback is then collaborated with the researches and they are edited in a comprehensive manner to aid the understanding of the subject.

Apart from the editorial board, the designing team has also invested a significant amount of their time in understanding the subject and creating the most relevant covers. They scrutinized every image to scout for the most suitable representation of the subject and create an appropriate cover for the book.

The publishing team has been involved in this book since its early stages. They were actively engaged in every process, be it collecting the data, connecting with the contributors or procuring relevant information. The team has been an ardent support to the editorial, designing and production team. Their endless efforts to recruit the best for this project, has resulted in the accomplishment of this book. They are a veteran in the field of academics and their pool of knowledge is as vast as their experience in printing. Their expertise and guidance has proved useful at every step. Their uncompromising quality standards have made this book an exceptional effort. Their encouragement from time to time has been an inspiration for everyone.

The publisher and the editorial board hope that this book will prove to be a valuable piece of knowledge for researchers, students, practitioners and scholars across the globe.

List of Contributors

Ignacio Ortuño-Ortin
Department of Economics, University Carlos III, Madrid, Spain

Andrés Romeu
Department of Economic Analysis, University of Murcia, Murcia, Spain

Mario Arturo Ruiz Estrada
Faculty of Economics and Administration, University of Malaya, Kuala Lumpur, Malaysia

Georgios L. Vousinas
Department of Economics, Athens University, Athens, Greece

Rufus Adebayo Ajisafe and Anthony Enisan Akinlo
Department of Economics, Obafemi Awolowo University, Ile-Ife, Nigeria

Francesca Gastaldi
Department of Economics and Law, Sapienza Università di Roma, Rome, Italy

Paolo Liberati
Department of Economics, Università Roma Tre, Rome, Italy

Antonio Scialà
Department of Law, Università Roma Tre, Rome, Italy

Philippe Gilles, Marie-Sophie Gauvin, Nicolas Huchet
Université de Toulon, LEAD, Toulon, France

Hsiang-Hsi Liu and Tser-Yieth Chen
Graduate Institute of International Business, National Taipei University, New Taipei City, Taiwan

Yung-Ho Chiu
Department of economics, Soochow University, Taipei City, Taiwan

Fu-Hsiang Kuo
Department of Information Management, Chaoyang University of Technology, Taichung City, Taiwan

John Ulimwengu
International Food Policy Research Institute, Washington DC, USA

Prabuddha Sanyal
Sandia National Laboratory, Albuquerque, USA

Chibamba Mwansakilwa
Research Fellow, Palm Associates Limited, Lusaka, Zambia

Gelson Tembo
Department of Agricultural Economics and Extension, University of Zambia, Lusaka, Zambia

Johnny Mugisha
Department of Agribusiness and Natural Resource Economics, Makerere University, Kampala, Uganda

Renata Turola Takamatsu and Luiz Paulo Lopes Fávero
School of Economics, Business and Accountancy University of São Paulo, São Paulo, Brazil

Sami Alpanda
Canadian Economic Analysis Department, Bank of Canada, Ottawa, Canada

Adam Honig and Geoffrey Woglom
Department of Economics, Amherst College, Amherst, USA

Andreas Liening
Faculty of Economics, Business Administration and Social Sciences, University of Dortmund, Dortmund, Germany

Yasuhiko Nakamura
College of Economics, Nihon University, Tokyo, Japan

Daniel Komlan Fiodendji
Departement of Economics, University of Ottawa, Ottawa, Canada

Kodjo Evlo
Faculté des Sciences Economiques et de Gestion (FASEG), Université de Lomé, Lomé, Togo

José R. Concha
Universidad Icesi, Cali, Colombia

Mohammad Ramadhan
Techno Economic Division, Kuwait Institute for Scientific Research, Kuwait City, Kuwait

Abdulhameed Hussain
Supreme Council for Privatization, Council of Ministers, Kuwait

Reem Al-Hajji
Techno Economic Division, Kuwait Institute for Scientific Research, Kuwait City, Kuwait

CPSIA information can be obtained
at www.ICGtesting.com
Printed in the USA
BVOW07*0632130617

486758BV00007B/2134/P

9 781632 403650